AutoCAD Releas

Dennis S. Balagtas

Michael E. Beall

Jim Fitzgerald

New Riders Publishing, Indianapolis, IN

AutoCAD Release 13 for Beginners

By Dennis S. Balagtas, Michael E. Beall, and Jim Fitzgerald

Published by:
New Riders Publishing
201 West 103rd Street
Indianapolis, IN 46290 USA

Printed in the United States of America 1 2 3 4 5 6 7 8 9 0

```
Balagtas, Dennis S., 1970-
    AutoCAD 13 for Windows for Beginners / Dennis S. Balagts,
Michael E. Beall, Jim Fitzgerald
        p.   cm.
    Includes index.
    ISBN 1-56205-243-8
    1. Computer graphics.  2. AutoCAD for Windows.   I.Beall,
Michael E., 1953-   II. Fitzgerald, Jim, 1964-     .
  III. Title
  T385.B349    1995
  620'.0042'02855369--dc20
```

Warning and Disclaimer

Publisher	*Don Fowley*
Associate Publisher	*Tim Huddleston*
Product Development Manager	*Rob Tidrow*
Marketing Manager	*Ray Robinson*
Managing Editor	*Tad Ringo*

Product Director
Jim Fitzgerald

Acquisitions Editor
Alicia Buckley

Senior Editor
Lisa Wilson

Copy Editors
Amy Bezek
Laura Frey
John Sleeva

Technical Editor
Alex Lepeska

Marketing Copywriter
Tamara Apple

Acquisitions Coordinator
Tracey Turgeson

Publisher's Assistant
Karen Opal

Cover Designer
Dan Armstrong

Book Designer
Kim Scott

Production Team Supervisor
Katy Bodenmiller

Graphics Image Specialists
Dennis Sheehan
Clint Lahnen

Production Analysts
Dennis Clay Hager
Angela Bannan

Production Team
Georgiana Briggs
Mona Brown
Michael Brumitt
Elaine Brush
Jama Carter
Mary Ann Cosby
Terrie Deemer
Judy Everly
Donna Harbin
Mike Henry
Louisa Klucznik
Ayanna Lacey
Kevin Laseau
Shawn MacDonald
Donna Martin
Cheryl Moore
Brian-Kent Proffitt
Erich J. Richter
SA Springer
Suzanne Tully
Mark Walche
Jeff Weissenberger
Dennis Wesner
Michelle Worthington

Indexer
Chris Cleveland

About the Authors

Dennis S. Balagtas is a student at Oregon Institute of Technology working toward a Bachelors degree in Surveying. He has worked as a Student Supervisor at the Oregon State University computer labs. Born in the Philippines, Mr. Balagtas grew up in Guam and taught himself and others how to get the most from computers. He owes much of his talents to his father, Prudencio.

Michael E. Beall is the owner of Computer Aided Management and Planning near Louisville, KY. Mr. Beall offers contract services and training exclusively on AutoCAD, 3D Studio, and the leading furniture specification and facility management software for AutoCAD. He has been presenting CAD training seminars to architects and engineers since 1982. He also has presented professional training programs on AutoCAD, CADVANCE, VersaCAD, and Microstation. As owner of the former Computer Training Services in San Jose, CA, Mr. Beall developed a highly successful six month Architecture and Facility Planning program for reentry adults at a local ATC. He received a Bachelor of Architecture degree from the University of Cincinnati and is a member of IFMA.

Jim Fitzgerald is a CAD Product Development Specialist for New Riders Publishing in Gresham, OR. Prior to joining New Riders, he was the Director of Training for a CAD training and consulting organization in Philadelphia. He has been working with AutoCAD since 1988 and studied mathematics and education at Linfield College in McMinnville, OR.

Trademark Acknowledgments

All terms mentioned in this book that are known to be trademarks or service marks have been appropriately capitalized. New Riders Publishing cannot attest to the accuracy of this information. Use of a term in this book should not be regarded as affecting the validity of any trademark or service mark. AutoCAD is a registered trademark of Autodesk.

Acknowledgments

Michael Beall would like to thank a loving God for the strength it took to complete this task with a sense of humor still intact. Providing additional love, encouragement, and endless understanding are wife, Donna, and son, Joshua. A special thank you to both Alicia Buckley and Jim Fitzgerald, whose nurturing and support of a new author was deeply appreciated and whose friendship and professional insight were of great value. Thanks also go to Margaret Berson for her diligence and to all the editors, especially Lisa, John, and Amy for their unflagging efforts in putting it all together. Finally, an acknowledgement to the on-going support, suggestions, and interest of the dozens of design professionals across the country with whom it is a sincere pleasure to work.

Contents at a Glance

Table of Contents

Part IV: Annotation and Plotting

14 Dimensioning   395

15 Adding Style to Dimensions   423

16 Composing and Plotting a Drawing   453

Part V: Appendices

Introduction

AutoCAD *Release 13 for Beginners* introduces you to the world of computer-aided design. If you are reading this book, you want to learn how to use AutoCAD Release 13. Perhaps you are a student who wants to learn AutoCAD to get that dream job, or maybe you are a drafting veteran with a new computer on your desk with AutoCAD Release 13 installed. Whatever your background, this book can help ease your transition into AutoCAD. You will learn how to use AutoCAD both as a design tool and as a communications tools.

The use of visual images to convey ideas has been around far longer than written language. Symbols, first written on clay tablets, later evolved into words. Early engineers designed and directed the building of ancient structures with the use of drawings. One of the most effective ways to communicate is through a drawing.

This is true even today. Drawings are still used to effectively communicate ideas, only the tools used to create drawings have changed. One of these new tools is *CAD*, which stands for *computer-aided design*. As computers have become more advanced, CAD has evolved as well, becoming easier to use and to obtain.

Using CAD To Help You Work More Efficiently

Early in the computer revolution, the word processor radically altered the communications industry. Before the advent of the computer, people used typewriters to make documents and to correspond with each other. One problem with the typewriter was the difficulty of making changes to the documents. If changes were needed, one had to retype the whole document. If the new document had errors, again one needed to retype it. The introduction of the word processor improved things considerably. The word processor enabled users to edit their documents without having to retype them. They could keep their documents in the computer and make changes only to the needed portions. This dynamic, or constantly changing, capability within word processors enabled users to work with the same document repeatedly.

CAD provides that same dynamic capability to your drawings. CAD lets you store your design electronically, in a form you can access again and again. If your drawing needs to change, you can open the drawing, make the changes, and replot the drawing. All of the objects in a CAD drawing can be organized like words in a word processing document. You can click on a circle and move it to a different location. You can change a line's color. You don't need to draw an assembly part again and again. You can copy the original and reuse it.

Introducing AutoCAD Release 13 for Windows

CAD was first developed in the 1960s. There were not many CAD users during the early days as the CAD programs were expensive and difficult to use. The computers that ran the CAD programs were large, bulky, expensive machines that filled entire rooms. As computers evolved, CAD became easier to use and more accessible to the mainstream computer user.

AutoCAD was first introduced in 1982. It could be run on IBM XT systems with 540 KB of RAM and DOS. The early versions were simple tools for generating basic 2D drawings. They were extremely slow and incorporated only the basics of drafting. AutoCAD, however, was a success because it provided an inexpensive way to get into CAD. Other CAD programs required a six-digit investment in the computer system. Because of the ease of obtaining a personal computer, anyone could use CAD as a way to communicate ideas. AutoCAD became a tool that everyone could get and everyone could use.

AutoCAD Release 13 is the latest step in the evolution of AutoCAD. Release 13 is by far the biggest and most complex version of AutoCAD to date, but don't be intimidated by its size and complexity. *AutoCAD Release 13 for Beginners* will guide you through the basics of AutoCAD and help you build a solid foundation of AutoCAD skills.

Who Should Read this Book

This book is structured toward beginners. All the exercises, concepts, and commands are explained with a minimum of high-brow terminology and fuss. This book takes more time to make things simpler and concentrates on key concepts to understand. After you are done with the exercises, you can use this book as a reference guide to help you remember the concepts and commands you learned.

What You Need To Use this Book

To use *AutoCAD Release 13 for Beginners*, you need, at least, the following software and hardware. This book assumes the following:

- You have a computer with both DOS and Windows 3.1 or later and AutoCAD Release 13 for Windows or Windows NT installed and configured. Appendix A provides more specific information and recommendations on system requirements, and on installing, configuring, and maximizing the performance of AutoCAD.

- You have at least 5 MB of free hard disk space left after you have installed and configured Windows and AutoCAD.

- You are familiar with Windows and PC DOS/MS-DOS and can use the basic Windows features and DOS commands and utilities. (For help in learning Windows features, in the Windows Program Manager, choose **H**elp, then **W**indows Tutorial.)

If you use the Windows NT version of Release 13, note that this book was developed with AutoCAD Release 13 for Windows, prior to the official release of AutoCAD Release 13 for Windows NT. While the final Windows NT version should have the same interface and functionality as the Windows version, you might find minor differences. Those differences, however, should not affect the book's exercises or other content.

Finding Your Way around this Book

AutoCAD Release 13 for Beginners is designed as a tutorial to help new users learn how to use AutoCAD Release 13. Concepts and exercises are organized to build your knowledge and understanding gradually. To achieve this goal, this book is organized into four parts. In Part One, you will learn the fundamental commands and concepts. Part Two introduces you to the commands that control and organize your drawing and working environment. Part Three explores the advanced tools and techniques to create your design efficiently. In Part Four, you will learn how to add annotation to your drawing and to plot your drawing. This book also has appendices and an index as references.

Part One—Getting Started

Part One has three chapters that introduce you to AutoCAD Release 13—the elements of the program, how to tell it what to do, and how it interacts with you and your computer. You will learn the fundamental concepts of CAD while exploring how to create and edit drawing entities.

Chapter 1, "Setting Up," shows you how to set up AutoCAD Release 13 to use this book. You learn how to create a working directory for the drawing files that you create, and how to back up your AutoCAD configuration files.

Chapter 2, "Getting to Know AutoCAD," introduces you to AutoCAD Release 13's graphic user interface. You will explore the various ways of communicating with AutoCAD and the ways in which AutoCAD communicates with you. This chapter also includes information on how to find out more about AutoCAD Release 13 from the online help.

Chapter 3, "A Quick Drawing," will walk you through a typical AutoCAD drawing session. This will give you an introduction to some of the concepts presented in the book and give you a taste of what working in AutoCAD is like.

After you have completed Part One, you will have learned the basic methods of controlling the AutoCAD environment and should start to feel comfortable working with AutoCAD. In Part Two, you begin to develop some basic skills.

Part Two—Developing Basic AutoCAD Drawing Skills

Part Two introduces you to the tools and concepts that help you make your work efficient. You will explore the controls that set up your drawing and the commands that help you draw, view, and edit your design. The exercises will show how you can draw accurately and organize the data in your drawing.

Chapter 4, "Preparing Your Drawing," shows you how set up your drawing to fit the way you work. This chapter also shows you how to use layers to organize your drawing. You learn the key practices involved in planning and setting up your work space. You will learn how the concept of scale is used in the design of your drawing. You will learn how to make changes to your environment and then how to save those settings in a prototype file.

Chapter 5, "The Basic Drawing Commands," discusses the core drawing commands—the basic commands that are used most often during the course of a drawing. You will learn the various techniques and options for drawing lines, circles, arcs, rectangles, and polygons.

Chapter 6, "Controlling What You See," is a discussion of how to move around in AutoCAD Release 13's drawing environment. This chapter shows how you can control the display to see exactly what you want to see. The exercises illustrate how you can change the view of your design as well as how to work with model space and paper space.

Chapter 7, "Drawing Accurately," addresses the issue of drawing accuracy and precision. By using CAD, you can make calculations and measurements from your design. You will learn how to make this possible by using object snaps, point filters, and the drawing aids to create an accurate design.

Chapter 8, "Editing with Grips," introduces you to the basics of editing using grips. By using grips, you have immediate access to the edit commands, which makes editing objects easier and more efficient.

After completing Part Two, you will have learned the basics of creating your design. You will be ready for Part Three, which introduces the techniques for efficient drawing.

Part Three—Advanced Drawing and Editing

Part Three is a collection of topics that illustrate the value of using CAD. You will learn how to use some of AutoCAD's advanced drawing and editing tools as well as how to use blocks and external references. You will explore how to add text to your drawing and how to gradually build a design by using construction techniques.

Chapter 9, "More Drawing Commands," introduces you to some of the more complex objects in AutoCAD. You will learn the nature and use of polylines, ellipses, and multilines.

Chapter 10, "Selecting and Editing Objects," further explores the selecting and editing tools. This chapter will introduce you to various object selection techniques that will make editing easier. You also will learn more about the editing commands and their available options.

Chapter 11, "Text," shows how to add annotation to your drawing with text. You will learn the basics of controlling the look and placement of text, as well as the special characters and options used to format text. This chapter includes the commands used to edit your text.

Chapter 12, "Constructive Editing," introduces you to some of the most powerful editing features of AutoCAD. Not all designs can be created by using simple lines, circles, and arcs. You will learn how to use construction lines to create parts of your drawing and how to reuse parts of your design over and over.

Chapter 13, "Blocks and Overlays," shows you how to create symbols (called blocks) and how to view and reference external drawings. You will learn how blocks can add functionality and detail to your drawing. For collaborative projects, you will learn how to pull seemingly separate projects together into one using external references. The exercises will show you how these tools can help you work with other tools in AutoCAD.

After finishing Part Three, you will have a solid understanding of the tools and techniques used to create a drawing. Part Four will show you how to add the finishing touches to your design and get it ready to plot.

Part Four—Annotation and Plotting

Part Four explores how to measure elements of your design and finalize your drawing to plot. You will learn the dimensioning commands and how to set up dimension styles.

Chapter 14, "Dimensioning," continues the idea of drawing accurately in CAD by showing you how to add dimensions to your drawing. The dimensioning commands can help convey more information about what is in your drawing and also enable you to check the accuracy of your design. You will learn how to place and edit basic dimensions.

Chapter 15, "Adding Style to Dimensions," explores dimensioning further by showing you how to control the look of dimensions through the use of dimension styles. Like layers, dimension styles are an efficient way to manage changes within your drawing. You will learn how to update and edit dimensions.

Chapter 16, "Composing and Plotting a Drawing," details the process of putting your drawing on paper. You will learn how to set up and lay out plot sheets using paper space and floating viewports, as well as how to set up and send the drawing to an output device.

Part Five—Appendices

The appendices provide reference material and information to make working with AutoCAD easier.

Appendix A, "Installation and Configuration," guides you through the process of installing and setting up AutoCAD Release 13. Included in this appendix are tips to make installing easier and relatively error-free.

Appendix B, "Troubleshooting," discusses some of the typical problems encountered when using AutoCAD, and how to deal with problems when they appear.

Appendix C, "Optimizing AutoCAD for Windows Performance," shows you how to optimize AutoCAD to perform faster and more efficiently in the Windows environment.

Appendix D, "AutoCAD Command Equivalency Table," is a table of AutoCAD commands and where to locate them.

Appendix E, "AutoCAD System Variables Table," is a table of the AutoCAD system variables and the effect they have on AutoCAD.

Appendix F, "Menu Maps and Toolbars," provides a visual key to all the maps and toolbars in Release 13.

Last but not least, inside the front cover of the book, you will find an annotated illustration of the AutoCAD Release 13 for Windows interface.

Learning from this Book

The information in this book is presented in stages. The concepts of CAD are presented gradually, giving you time to absorb them. After an explanation of the concepts, an exercise will demonstrate the concepts in use. To ensure you get the most from this book, read on to find out how instructions and concepts are explained to you.

How Exercises are Shown

A sample exercise is shown below. Exercises consist of the exercise instructions and one or more illustrations of what your computer screen looks like. The exercise instructions are arranged in two columns. The left column shows you the direct instructions. The right column explains the direct instructions. The following exercise draws two lines and a circle as shown in figure I.1.

Figure I.1

A sample exercise illustration.

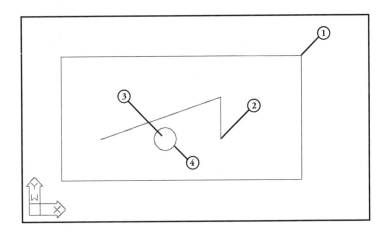

A Quick Sample Exercise

Begin a new drawing called INTRO using the default ACAD.DWG prototype drawing.

Command: *Choose Line (Draw, Line)*	Issues the LINE command
_line From point: *Type* **4,4** (Enter)	Specifies the starting coordinate of the line
To point: *Pick the point at* ① (*see fig. I.1*)	Draws the line
To point: *Press F8*	Turns on ortho mode
To point: *Pick the point at* ②	Draws the second line
To point: (Enter)	Ends the LINE command

The LINE command draws multiple line segments using the endpoint of the previous segment as the start point of the next segment. Next, you will add a circle to the drawing.

Command: *Choose Circle Center Radius (Draw, Circle)*	Issues the CIRCLE command
_circle 3P/2P/TTR/<Center point>: *Pick the point at* ③	Specifies location of circle's center
Diameter/<Radius>: *Pick the point at* ④	Sets the circle's size with its radius
Command: *Choose Save (Standard Toolbar)*	Saves your drawing

Using the Windows Pointing Device

You will be using your Windows pointing device (referred to throughout this book as a mouse) for much of your input in AutoCAD. You should become familiar with the following terms, which are used to describe mouse actions:

- **Click.** To press and release the pick button.
- **Click on, click in.** To position the cursor on the appropriate user interface object (icon, input box, menu item, and so on) and click the pick button.
- **Double-click.** To press and release the pick button twice in rapid succession.

- **Pick.** To position the cursor on the appropriate object or point and click the pick button.

- **Select.** To highlight an object in the AutoCAD drawing area by picking it or by using other object selection methods. Also, to highlight an item, word, or character in a drop-down or dialog box list or text input field by clicking on it.

- **Choose.** To select an item in a menu or dialog box by either clicking on it or typing its hot-key letter.

- **Drag.** To move the mouse and cursor, causing lines or objects on the screen to move with the cursor.

- **Press and drag.** To press and hold down a mouse button, drag something on screen, and then release the mouse button.

Pull-Down Menu Selections

When you see instructions such as *Choose* Item in an exercise, this means to move the pointer to Item on the menu bar and click the left mouse button. You also can use a hot key—a key combination consisting of the Alt key and the letter underlined in the menu bar item—to display the menu. If you are instructed to Choose File, New, for example, you could either click on the File pull-down menu, then click on New, or press Alt+F and then N.

Toolbars Selection

New to Release 13 are the many command toolbars. On some toolbars, choosing a tool will cause another set of tools to pop-up either to the right or below the tool. These are known as *flyouts*. Tools are referred to by their name and the name of their corresponding toolbar (and flyout). If you were instructed to *Choose Dtext (Draw, Text)*, for example, you would choose the Dtext tool, which is located in the Draw toolbar in the Text flyout.

Keyboard Entry

In some instructions, you will see *Press Enter*. Your computer will have a key labeled Enter, Return, or (Enter). *Press Enter* means to press this key. You will also see the symbol (Enter) in the exercises. This symbol means the same thing as *Press Enter*.

Some commands cannot be accessed through menus. Point coordinates, distances, and option keywords must be typed. The exercise will indicate when typed input is required by showing it in bold text following a prompt, such as Command: **LIMITS** (Enter) or To point: **5,26** (Enter). You should type the input as it appears, and then press Enter.

This book will present commands and their prompts in their entirety early on. As you read through the book, later exercises will omit familiar prompts that have become routine.

The exercises sometimes finish with an instruction to end or save the drawing. Build the habit of saving your drawing at the end of each exercise. Some chapters can be finished in one or two sittings. Or, if you prefer, you can proceed at a more leisurely pace. You can take a break and continue your drawing later. Just save your drawing and reload it later.

Exercises and the Graphics Display

This book's illustrations were created by capturing the screen displays during the process of performing the exercise. All screen displays were captured from systems using a resolution of 800×600-pixels, 256-color mode under Windows. If your display is set to a higher or lower resolution, your screen display might not match the illustrations. Menus and screen elements can appear larger or smaller than they do in the illustrations and you might want to zoom in or out farther than the instructions indicate. You should adjust your display according to the current task and the resources available. You might find that if you use colors that are different from those specified in the exercises, the entities are easier to see, especially if you are working with a white background rather than a black background.

Notes, Tips, Warnings, and Command Sidebars

AutoCAD Release 13 for Beginners features special sidebars, which are shown apart from the normal text by icons. This book includes four types of sidebars: notes, tips, warnings, and command sidebars. These sidebars provide you extra help and information to supplement the general discussion.

A note gives you extra information that is not critical to the subject at hand, but can be useful. A note can tell you how to avoid problems with your computer. Notes can describe situations that can occur under certain circumstances and might tell you what steps to take.

A tip can tell you how to get the most from your AutoCAD system as you follow a discussion of a topic. A tip might show how to make your system run a little faster, how to speed up a procedure, or how to perform one of the time-saving and system-enhancing techniques.

A warning alerts you to when a procedure might be dangerous—when you run the risk of losing data, locking your system, or even damaging your hardware. Warnings can tell you how to avoid these situations, or they describe the steps you can take to remedy these situations.

Each command in AutoCAD will be introduced in a command sidebar. The command sidebars describe the function of the command and also list the various means of accessing the command. The command sidebars look like the following:

LINE. The LINE command draws one or more straight line segments.
Toolbar: *Choose Line (Draw, Line)*
Screen: *Choose* Draw1, Line
Alias: **L**

Command Option Lists

Some commands in Release 13 have several options available. The following are examples of the LINE command options:

- **From point.** At the From point: prompt, you specify the first point of the first line.

- **continue.** Press Enter at the From point: prompt to start the line from the endpoint of the most recently drawn line or arc.

- **To point.** At the To point: prompt, you specify the point to which a line is drawn from the previous point.

- **Undo.** At the To point: prompt, you enter **u** (Undo) to undo the last line segment, stepping back to the previous point.

- **Close.** At the To point: prompt, you enter **c** (Close) to close a series of two or more line segments.

Handling Problems

As you work through the exercises in *AutoCAD Release 13 for Beginners*, you might experience some problems. These problems can occur for any number of reasons, from input errors to hardware failures. If you have trouble performing any step described in this book, take the following actions:

- Try again. Double-check the steps you performed in the previous exercise(s), as well as earlier steps in the current exercise.

- Check the settings of any AutoCAD system variables or dialog boxes modified in any previous exercise sequences. (See the system variables table in Appendix E for a listing of all system variables.)

- See the troubleshooting section of Appendix B.

- Check the AutoCAD Release 13 documentation or online help that came with your copy of AutoCAD.

If none of the above suggestions help, call New Riders Publishing (503-661-5745) *only* if the problem relates to a specific exercise, instruction, or error in the book. Otherwise, try the following for further help:

- Call your AutoCAD dealer.

- Log in to the ACAD forum on CompuServe, and ask or search for help.

Other AutoCAD Titles from New Riders Publishing

New Riders Publishing offers the widest selection of books on AutoCAD available anywhere. New Riders also offers an extensive selection of books on Windows, DOS, and other operating systems, on NetWare and other networking operating systems, and on communications, including the Internet and CompuServe. See the back of the book for information on selected New Riders' titles or call New Riders at 1-800-653-6156 to request a catalog or information. You can order any New Riders title by calling 1-800-653-6156 for customer service.

Contacting New Riders Publishing

The staff of New Riders Publishing is committed to bringing you the very best in computer reference material. Each New Riders book is the result of months of work by authors and staff who research and refine the information contained within its covers.

As part of this commitment to you, the NRP reader, New Riders invites your input. Please let us know if you enjoy this book, if you have trouble with the information and examples presented, or if you have a suggestion for the next edition.

Please note, though: New Riders staff cannot serve as a technical resource for *AutoCAD Release 13 for Beginners* or for questions about software- or hardware-related problems. Please refer to the documentation that accompanies AutoCAD or to the application's Help systems.

If you have a question or comment about any New Riders book, there are several ways to contact New Riders Publishing. We will respond to as many readers as we can. Your name, address, or phone number will never become part of a mailing list or be used for any purpose other than to help us continue to bring you the best books possible. You can write us at the following address:

New Riders Publishing
Attn: Associate Publisher
201 W. 103rd Street
Indianapolis, IN 46290

If you prefer, you can fax New Riders Publishing at (317) 581-4670.

You can send electronic mail to New Riders from a variety of sources. NRP maintains several mailboxes organized by topic area. Mail in these mailboxes will be forwarded to the staff member who is best able to address your concerns. Substitute the appropriate mailbox name from the list below when addressing your e-mail. The mailboxes are as follows:

ADMIN	Comments and complaints for NRP's Publisher
APPS	Word, Excel, WordPerfect, and other office applications
ACQ	Book proposals and inquiries by potential authors
CAD	AutoCAD, 3D Studio, AutoSketch, and CAD products
DATABASE	Access, dBASE, Paradox, and other database products
GRAPHICS	CorelDRAW!, Photoshop, and other graphics products
INTERNET	Internet
NETWORK	NetWare, LANtastic, and other network-related topics
OS	MS-DOS, OS/2, and all other operating systems except Unix and Windows
UNIX	Unix
WINDOWS	Microsoft Windows (all versions)
OTHER	Anything that doesn't fit into the preceding categories

If you use an MHS e-mail system that routes through CompuServe, send your messages to the following:

mailbox @ NEWRIDER

To send NRP mail from CompuServe, use the following address:

MHS: *mailbox* @ NEWRIDER

To send mail from the Internet, use the following address format:

mailbox@newrider.mhs.compuserve.com

NRP is an imprint of Macmillan Computer Publishing. To obtain a catalog of information, or to purchase any Macmillan Computer Publishing book, call (800) 428-5331.

Thank you for selecting *AutoCAD Release 13 for Beginners*!

Taking the First Step

You're now ready to start learning how to use AutoCAD Release 13. This might look like a daunting task, but it's not. The most difficult obstacle is to sit down and get started. Once you start, this book will present the concepts gradually. You will find that the more you use this book, the easier AutoCAD gets.

So, let's take that first step!

PART I

Getting Started

Chapter Snapshot

This chapter shows you how to set up your computer to use the exercises in this book. Even experienced CAD users should set up their system according to this chapter. In its discussion, this chapter includes the following topics:

- Creating a working directory

- Copying AutoCAD configuration files

- Creating a program group and startup icon

- Starting AutoCAD

Setting Up

Setting Up AutoCAD for Exercises

Setting up your system for *AutoCAD Release 13 for Beginners* requires you to set aside space on your hard disk for a directory called \AB. This ensures that any AutoCAD drawings created in the exercises in this book do not interfere with any other AutoCAD projects that you or your coworkers might be working on. Also, you can easily remove all practice files after you are through with the book's exercises.

The following exercises will lead you through the process of creating the \AB directory and copying AutoCAD configuration files into it. You then will create a program group and a startup icon to use when you want to use AutoCAD to perform the exercises in this book.

The following installation instructions assume that you are using the DOS operating system with Microsoft Windows 3.1, that AutoCAD is installed in the C:\ACADR13 directory, and that AutoCAD runs and is configured properly.

Your hard drive letter or directory names might differ from those shown in this chapter. If they do, substitute your hard drive letter and directory names wherever you encounter drive letters (such as the C in C:) or the directory names (such as \ACADR13 or \AB) throughout this book.

Creating the AB Directory

The book assumes that you will be working in the \AB directory. You need to create the \AB directory and then place copies of the AutoCAD configuration files in the \AB directory. This creates a self-contained AutoCAD environment that enables you to complete the exercises in the book without interfering with any other AutoCAD projects on which you may be working.

To begin, you will first switch to the DOS prompt before creating the AB directory.

If you are familiar with the Windows File Manager, you might want to use it to create the \AB directory. After creating the \AB directory, you can use the File Manager to copy the ACAD.CFG and ACAD.INI configuration files from the \ACADR13\WIN directory to the \AB directory.

Creating the AB Directory

Open the Windows Program Manager and in the Main program group, double-click on the MS-DOS Prompt icon. This takes you to the following DOS prompt.

C:\WINDOWS> **CD** (Enter)	Sets the root directory current
C:\> **MD AB** (Enter)	Creates the AB directory
C:\> **DIR *.** (Enter)	Displays a list of directory names, as shown in the following list

```
Directory of C:\

AB          <DIR>      09-30-94   11:41a
ACADR13     <DIR>      09-28-94    8:22A
DOS         <DIR>      06-07-94    3:27P
WINDOWS     <DIR>      06-07-94    4:45P
```

Your disk may contain other directories as well.

Copying Configuration Files

AutoCAD Release 13 for Windows requires two configuration files:
ACAD.CFG and ACAD.INI. The ACAD.CFG file specifies which hardware
devices (such as video display cards, pointing devices, and plotters) you
are using with AutoCAD. The ACAD.INI files contain information about
how AutoCAD will interact with the operating system (such as where to
find support files and how the toolbars are displayed). These files are
created the first time you start AutoCAD.

If AutoCAD has not yet been configured, see Appendix A of this book or
the *AutoCAD Installation, Interface, and Performance Guide* for more
information on installing and configuring AutoCAD.

> The following exercise assumes that you have AutoCAD installed on
> the C:\ drive and that the configuration files are located in the
> \ACADR13\WIN directory. If you installed AutoCAD on a drive
> other than C:\, or your files reside in a directory other than
> \ACADR13\WIN, substitute the correct drive and directory names
> for C:\ACADR13\WIN in the following exercise.

Copying the Configuration Files

Continue from the previous exercise.

`C:\> CD\ACADR13\WIN` (Enter)	Makes the \ACADR13\WIN directory current
`C:\ACADR13\WIN> COPY ACAD.CFG .\AB` (Enter) `1 File(s) copied`	Copies the ACAD.CFG file to the AB directory

continues

continued

`C:\ACADR13\WIN> `**`COPY ACAD.INI \AB`**` `(Enter) `1 File(s) copied`	Copies the ACAD.INI file to the AB directory
`C:\ACADR13\WIN> `**`EXIT`**` `(Enter)	Returns you to the Windows Program Manager

Creating a Program Group and the AB Icon

The AutoCAD for Beginners program group is where the AB icon will be located. Creating a separate icon allows you to start AutoCAD using the configuration files located in the AB directory. This ensures that changes you make to AutoCAD while using the book will not interfere with your working version of AutoCAD. Feel free to try new things and experiment with AutoCAD knowing that any changes you make will not affect other AutoCAD projects on which you may be working.

In the following exercises you will create the AutoCAD for Beginners program group and the AB icon.

Creating the AutoCAD for Beginners Program Group

Continue from the Windows Program Manager.

Choose **F**ile, *then* **N**ew	Opens the New Program Object dialog box
Choose Program **G**roup, *then* OK	Opens the Program Group Properties dialog box (see fig. 1.1)
In the **D**escription *box type* **AutoCAD for Beginners**, *then choose* OK	Creates the AutoCAD for Beginners program group (see fig. 1.2)

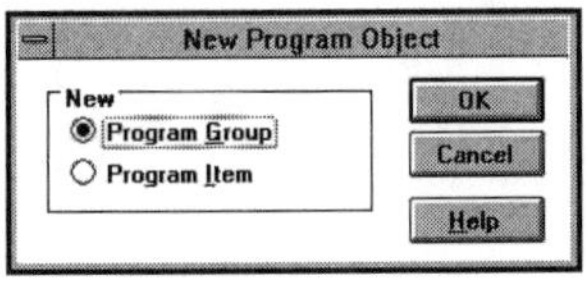

Figure 1.1

The Program Group Properties dialog box.

New Program Object

New
◉ Program Group
○ Program Item

OK
Cancel
Help

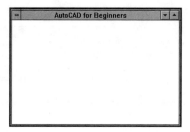

Figure 1.2

The AutoCAD for Beginners program group.

TIP

You can change the size of the AutoCAD for Beginners program group by moving your cursor to the border of the program group, holding down the pick button, and dragging the edge of the window. You can move the program group by moving your cursor to the title bar of the program group, holding down the pick button, and dragging the program group to a new location.

Now that you have created the AutoCAD for Beginners program group, you can create the AB icon.

Creating the AB Icon

Continue from the previous exercise.

Choose **F**ile, *then* **N**ew	Opens the New Program Object dialog box
Choose Program **I**tem, *then* OK	Opens the Program Item Properties dialog box (see fig. 1.3)
Click in the **D**escription *box and type* **AB**	Specifies the name of the icon
Click in the **C**ommand Line *box and type* **C:\ACADR13\WIN\ACAD.EXE /C C:\AB**	Specifies ACAD.EXE as the program to run upon selecting the icon and \AB as the location of the configuration files
Click in the **W**orking Directory *box and type* **C:\AB**	Specifies the default directory for saving drawing files
Choose OK	Creates the AB icon (see fig. 1.4)

Figure 1.3

*The Program Item
Properties dialog
box.*

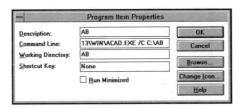

Figure 1.4

The AB icon.

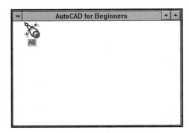

TIP

You can change the appearance of the icon by clicking once on the
icon and choosing **F**ile, **P**roperties, Change **I**con. You will see a
number of icons from which to choose. Select the icon you want to use
and choose OK, then OK again to make the change.

Starting AutoCAD for this Book

Now that the AB icon has been defined and the proper files copied to the
\AB directory, you can start AutoCAD by double-clicking on the AB icon
you just created. After double-clicking on the AB icon, AutoCAD should
start, and after a few moments, you should see the AutoCAD application
window as shown in figure 1.5.

If AutoCAD does not start properly, return to the Program Manager and
check the following:

- Make sure AutoCAD is installed and properly configured by starting
  AutoCAD using the default AutoCAD Release 13 icon that was
  created when you installed AutoCAD.

- Verify that the ACAD.INI and ACAD.CFG files were correctly copied
  from the \ACADR13\WIN directory to the \AB directory.

● Double-check the AB icon properties by clicking once on the AB icon
  and choosing **F**ile, **P**roperties from the Program Manager pull-down
  menu.

> Always use the AB icon to start AutoCAD for use with this book.
> Otherwise, you might have trouble locating the book's files.

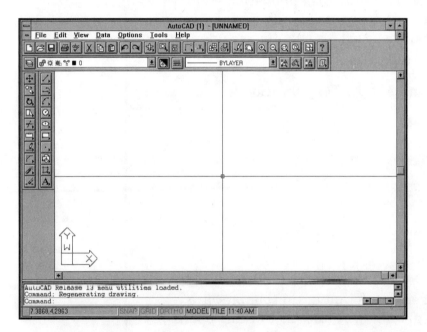

Figure 1.5

*The AutoCAD
application
window.*

> To open another software application without ending your AutoCAD
> for Windows session, you can click on the down-arrow button in the
> upper right corner of the AutoCAD window. This step reduces the
> AutoCAD window to an icon located at the bottom of your screen.
> When you want to switch back to AutoCAD, double-click on the icon
> to open the window again.

After successfully starting AutoCAD, you will see the AutoCAD Release
13 application window. The next chapter will give you a guided tour of
this window.

Chapter Snapshot

Now that you have successfully loaded AutoCAD, take a moment to examine the AutoCAD application window. This chapter will give you a guided tour of the various parts of the AutoCAD application window and show you how to modify and control it to suit your needs. This chapter includes the following topics:

- The AutoCAD application window

- The status and menu bars

- The command line area

- Toolbars

- The drawing window

- The screen menu

The exercises found in this chapter are based upon how AutoCAD initially opens—the *default configuration*. There are several ways by which you can alter the look of the AutoCAD application window, but as a point of reference, the exercises and discussions will be based on the default values and conditions, and will equip you with a better understanding of how to get around in AutoCAD Release 13 for Windows.

Getting to Know AutoCAD

I t's probably a safe bet that most of you have either rented a car or driven one that was less familiar than your own. As you get inside the car, there are a lot of things you should become familiar with before you even pull out onto the road—the lights, the wipers, the seatbelt, the seat position, radio, defroster, and shifting configuration—each one having a different set of controls.

Working with AutoCAD for the first time might prove to be a similar experience. As you first enter the AutoCAD drawing environment you might ask: What do those buttons mean, where are the commands, what do I look at first, what if I make a mistake, how do I backup, where is my cursor, and so on. This chapter will help you "get on the road" with AutoCAD by answering those questions along with some others you might have about the AutoCAD for Windows drawing environment.

The AutoCAD Application Window

The AutoCAD application window appears after you double-click on the AutoCAD icon to begin AutoCAD. Figure 2.1 shows how the AutoCAD application window will look.

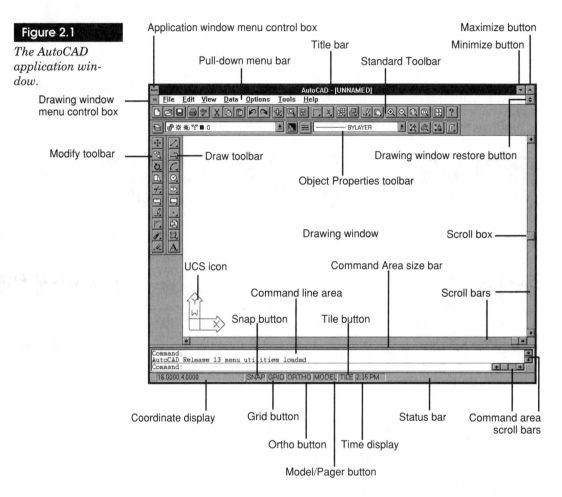

Figure 2.1

The AutoCAD application window.

Application window menu control box

Maximize button

Minimize button

Title bar

Pull-down menu bar

Standard Toolbar

Drawing window menu control box

Modify toolbar

Draw toolbar

Drawing window restore button

Object Properties toolbar

Drawing window

Scroll box

UCS icon

Command Area size bar

Command line area

Scroll bars

Snap button

Tile button

Coordinate display

Grid button

Status bar

Command area scroll bars

Ortho button

Time display

Model/Pager button

Your application window might look slightly different, but in the following sections, you will learn how to adjust and control the various parts of the application window. To take the car analogy further, this is where you learn how to adjust your window visibility, windshield wipers, visor, power windows, rearview mirror, outside mirror—the stuff around the edges.

The Application Window Controls

AutoCAD Release 13 for Windows is a standard Windows application. Therefore, like other Windows programs, it can be maximized, minimized, resized, and moved around the screen.

In the following exercise, you will get a feel for the application window controls. You'll restore the window to its un-maximized size and move the application window.

Manipulating the AutoCAD Application Window

From the Windows Program Manager, start AutoCAD by double-clicking on the AutoCAD for Beginners icon.

Click on the Restore *button (the up / down arrow in the upper right corner)*	Restores the application window to its un-maximized size
Click anywhere on the title bar *and hold the mouse button down*	Activates the mobility of the application window
Move the window and release the mouse button	Relocates the application window

Click anywhere on the title bar again and return the application window to its original location.

Place your pointer on the thin horizontal line just above the AutoCAD title bar	Changes cursor to an up/down arrow
Hold the mouse button down and move the mouse down about 1 inch and release the mouse button	Makes the application window shorter

Now use the same technique to return the application window to its original size.

Mobility of the application window is important especially when you begin using other Windows applications such as word processors or spread sheets. By using the techniques demonstrated in the previous exercise, you can move or resize the AutoCAD application window so that you can address other tasks, such as writing a letter or report, and still have AutoCAD ready when you return.

Manipulation of application windows is one of the basic concepts of working in the Windows environment. For a more complete explanation of how to manipulate the application windows, refer to the Windows Tutorial (from the Program Manager, choose **H**elp, **W**indows Tutorial).

The Pull-Down Menu Bar

The pull-down menu bar (see fig. 2.1) contains a number of the commands you will use when working with AutoCAD. The following list is a brief overview of the AutoCAD pull-down menus:

- **File.** The **F**ile menu contains commands for opening, saving, and printing drawings as well as commands for importing and exporting drawing data. The last four drawing files on which you worked are also listed here.

- **Edit.** The **E**dit menu contains Windows editing functions such as cutting and pasting from the drawing window to the Clipboard. Object linking and embedding commands are also located here.

- **View.** The **V**iew menu contains commands for controlling the display of the drawing window. Zoom and pan controls are located here as well as commands for saving and restoring views.

- **Data.** The **D**ata menu contains commands that enable you to control how objects are created in AutoCAD. Settings for layers, text styles, dimension styles, and multiline styles can all be accessed from this pull-down menu.

- **Options.** The **O**ptions menu contains settings that control the way AutoCAD looks and acts. Settings for grid, snap, objects snap, and grips can all be controlled from this pull-down menu. You also can reconfigure AutoCAD and control the appearance of the application window from this menu.

- **Tools.** The **T**ools menu gives you access to various productivity tools within AutoCAD. Features like toolbars, Aerial View, Spell Check, and the Calculator are all accessed from the **T**ools menu.

- **Help.** The **H**elp menu gives you access to the various forms of online help available in AutoCAD.

For a complete list of the contents of the menu bar see the menu maps located in Appendix F.

When you choose a pull-down menu, some of the items in the menu are followed by ... (three dots). Any item followed by these three dots displays a dialog box that provides additional options. Other menu items have an arrow pointing to the right. Choosing a menu item with an arrow after it results in a submenu of additional options. Figure 2.2 displays the Options menu, which contains items with both the dots and the arrows.

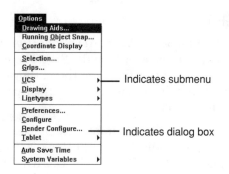

Figure 2.2

The Options menu.

Indicates submenu

Indicates dialog box

2

The following exercise will walk you through a couple of menu bar choices to demonstrate these features.

Choosing a Pull-Down Menu Bar Item

Command: *Choose* **O**ptions	Displays the Options menu
Choose **P**references *from the list*	Displays the Preferences dialog box (see fig. 2.3)
Choose the **M**isc *tab*	Displays the Misc page of preferences
Click on the X *next to* Maximize **A**pplication on Startup	Clears the X and turns off the option
Choose OK	Closes the Preferences dialog box
Command: *Choose* **T**ools	Displays the Tools menu
Choose **T**oolbars *from the menu*	Displays the Toolbar submenu
Choose **O**bject Snap *from the submenu*	Displays the Object Snap toolbar
Click on the control bar in the upper left corner of the toolbar	Closes the Object Snap toolbar

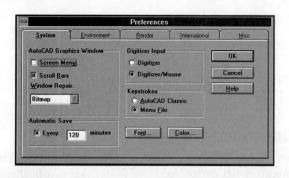

Figure 2.3

The Preferences dialog box.

The Status Bar

Located at the bottom of the AutoCAD application window are the status bar and the command line area (see fig. 2.1). They are a lot like the dashboard of that rental car. Between them, they contain information about the current drawing environment, cursor position, the current time, and your current command.

The status bar displays current information about the AutoCAD environment. There are seven indicators (or buttons) on the status bar: the coordinate display, SNAP, GRID, ORTHO, MODEL, TILE, and the current time. Of these seven buttons, five of them, SNAP, GRID, ORTHO, TILE, and the coordinate display, can be turned on or off by double-clicking on the button. If the item is on, the characters are black. If the item is off, the letters are grayed out.

The MODEL button switches between model space and paper space (see Chapter 6, "Controlling What You See," and Chapter 16, "Composing and Plotting a Drawing," for more on model space and paper space). The time button does nothing but display the current time.

In the following exercise you experiment with turning on a few of the status bar buttons.

Turning On and Off Items from the Status Bar

Begin by moving your cursor around the drawing area. Notice that the coordinate display changes as you move the cursor around.

Command: *Double-click on the coordinate display*   Turns off the coordinate display

Notice that now as you move the cursor around, the coordinate display doesn't change.

Command: *Double-click on the coordinate display*   Turns on the coordinate display

Command: *Double-click on* GRID   Turns on the grid

Turning on the grid displays a regular pattern of dots on the screen that can be used as a visual reference.

Command: *Double-click on* GRID   Turns off the grid

The AutoCAD Command Line Area

The command line area is an important area to keep an eye on. This is where you communicate with AutoCAD, and AutoCAD communicates with you. When you type a command from the keyboard, it is displayed on the command line. When you choose a menu item or tool from a toolbar, AutoCAD typically displays the command on the command line. When AutoCAD needs information from you, it will usually ask for it at the command line. When there is no active command, the command line simply reads, Command: (hence its name).

The command line area is located by default at the bottom of the AutoCAD application window, just above the status bar. There are three lines displayed in the command line area. By default, the top line is what happened two commands ago, the middle command line is what happened last, and the bottom command line is the current command. The current command line is separated from the others by a horizontal line.

The command line area actually maintains a command history of more than just the last two commands. It keeps track of everything that has happened in the current AutoCAD session. Using the scroll bars on the right and bottom of the command line area, you can look back at everything that has happened since you started AutoCAD. You also can resize and detach the command line area so that it becomes a separate window.

The following exercise demonstrates some of the command line area controls.

Controlling the Command Line Area

Continue from the previous exercise.

Command: *Position the cursor on the thin horizontal border of the drawing window just below the horizontal scroll bar*	Displays a vertical window-sizing indicator for adjacent windows
Command: *Pick and drag the horizontal bar up to just below the Modify toolbar, then release the button*	Changes the height of the command line window
Command: *Place your cursor on the thin horizontal border of the command line area just below the position you picked to size the window*	Displays a cursor pointer
Command: *Pick the horizontal border with the pointer and drag the command line area to the position shown in figure 2.4*	Undocks the command line area and automatically reduces the size and displays three lines

continues

continued

At this point, the command line window can be maximized, minimized, and resized using the typical window sizing control features covered earlier in this chapter. In the following steps, you dock the window to the original location.

Command: *Pick in the title bar of the command line window and drag the window to the bottom of the application window where the status bar normally appears*	Docks the command line window and resizes the window
Command: *Pick and drag the vertical sizing arrow of the command line window / graphics window down to display only three command lines*	Reduces the command line window to the default height

Figure 2.4

The floating command line window.

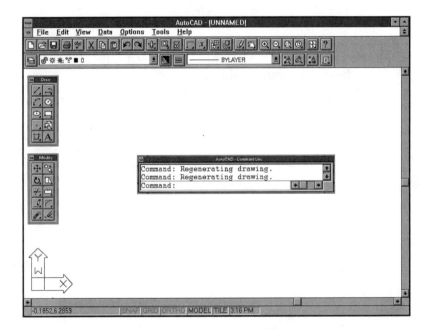

The AutoCAD Text Window

In addition to the command line area, AutoCAD also has a separate text window. Press the F2 key to display the AutoCAD Text Window which, like the command line area, displays a history of everything that has happened since you started the current AutoCAD session (see fig. 2.5).

When you press F2 again, the text window is closed and you are returned to the AutoCAD application window.

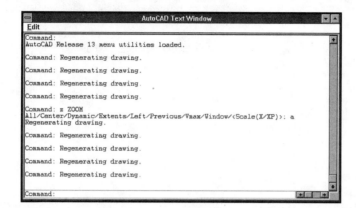

Figure 2.5

The AutoCAD text window.

2

When using the scroll bars in the command line area or the AutoCAD text window, the bottom command line does not change. It always maintains the separation between the current command and the commands listed above it.

Toolbars

The toolbars like the buttons, levers, and knobs found on the console of the car—radio buttons, tape deck/CD player buttons, heater sliders and dials, and anything else that can be pushed or turned.

The AutoCAD toolbars provide access to nearly every AutoCAD command. Intended for ease of use, toolbars enable you to execute a command more quickly than typing or choosing a command from a pull-down menu. Unlike the pull-down menu, you can control the location, size, and orientation of toolbars. This allows you to place a toolbar anywhere on the screen that is convenient for you.

Toolbars can be either floating or docked. A *docked toolbar* is a toolbar that is attached to either the top, bottom, left, or right of the application window. A *floating toolbar* has a title bar and can be positioned freely anywhere in the graphics area. The Standard Toolbar and Object Properties toolbars are docked at the top of the application window by default. The Draw and Modify toolbars are floating by default (see fig. 2.6).

Figure 2.6

*The floating Draw
and Modify
toolbars.*

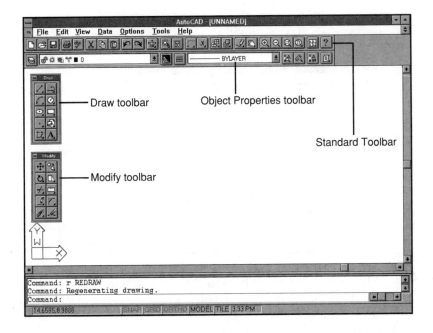

Draw toolbar

Object Properties toolbar

Standard Toolbar

Modify toolbar

TIP

If you choose the control button in the upper left corner of a floating
toolbar, the toolbar will close. To open the toolbar again, choose
Tools, **T**oolbars, then choose the toolbar you want to open from the
list.

In the following exercise you will dock the Modify and Draw toolbars.

Docking the Toolbars

Docking the toolbars is similar in process to that of docking the command line window in
the previous exercise.

Command: *Pick and drag the title bar of the
Modify toolbar to a position between the
Draw toolbar and the left edge of the
drawing window*

Displays a dynamic, vertical rectangle

Command: *Position the top of the dynamic
rectangle slightly over the Object
Properties toolbar, then release the button*

Docks the toolbar vertically along the left
side of the graphics window, adjacent to
the Object Properties toolbar

Command: *Pick and drag the title bar of the Draw toolbar to a position that displays a vertical rectangle to the right of the Modify toolbar*	Displays a dynamic, vertical rectangle
Command: *When the top of the dynamic vertical rectangle is slightly over the Object Properties toolbar, release the button*	Docks the toolbar vertically to the right of the Modify toolbar, adjacent to the Object Properties toolbar (see fig. 2.7)

2

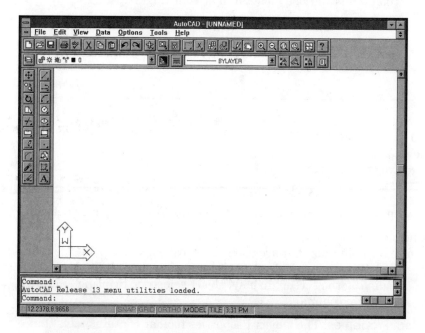

Figure 2.7

The docked Draw and Modify toolbars.

AutoCAD for Windows includes a nice feature called *tool tips* that give descriptions of the tools. Tool tips are activated by resting the cursor on a tool without clicking on it. If you rest your cursor on the first tool at the beginning of the Standard Toolbar, for example, you will see the tool tip *New* (see fig. 2.8). This is the tool you use to begin a new drawing.

Figure 2.8

The New tool tip.

Some tools have a small black arrow in the lower right corner, similar to the menu bar. If you press one of these tools and hold down the mouse button, several other tools will appear. These are called *flyouts* because several other tools flyout from the original. To select a tool from a flyout, hold down your mouse button, drag your cursor over the desired tool, and release the mouse button. Figure 2.9 shows the Line flyout from the Draw toolbar. When you select a tool from a flyout, that tool becomes the default tool for that flyout. In this way, AutoCAD adapts to the way you work, leaving the commands you use most often at your fingertips.

Figure 2.9

The Line toolbar flyout.

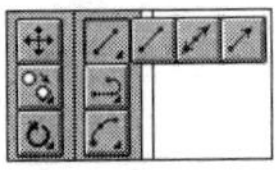

TIP

Toolbars can also be customized. See Appendix C, "Optimizing AutoCAD for Windows Performance," for information on how to create new toolbars and customize the look of any existing toolbar with your favorite commands.

The following list explains the four toolbars AutoCAD displays by default:

- **Standard Toolbar.** The tools on the Standard Toolbar issue common AutoCAD commands that are used in almost every AutoCAD session. These include commands dealing with opening and saving drawing files, modifying the screen display, object selection, printing, and the AutoCAD Help command.

- **Object Properties.** The Object Properties toolbar contains tools that enable you to control the way objects are created, stored, and displayed in AutoCAD.

- **Draw.** The Draw toolbar contains the majority of the tools for drawing objects.

- **Modify.** Similar in format to the Draw toolbar, the Modify toolbar contains the most frequently used editing tools.

The next exercise goes through the process of drawing and editing using the toolbars. As you continue through this book, you will have many · opportunities to use the tools found in the toolbars.

Drawing and Editing with Tools

Command: *Choose Layers (Object Properties)*	Displays the Layer Control dialog box
Type **SHAPES** *in the edit box and choose* **N**ew	Adds the new layer SHAPES to the layer list
Click on SHAPES *in the list box*	Highlights the SHAPES layer, and enables several dialog box buttons
Choose the **C**urrent *button*	Sets the layer SHAPES current
Choose OK	Closes the Layer Control dialog box, the layer SHAPES appears in the layer list box on the toolbar
Command: *Choose Rectangle (Draw, Polygon)*	Issues the RECTANG command
_rectang First corner: *Pick the point at* ① *(see fig. 2.10)*	Places the first corner of the rectangle
Other corner: *Pick the point at* ②	Draws a rectangle and ends the command
Command: *Choose Copy Object (Modify, Copy)*	Issues the COPY command
_copy Select objects: *Select the edge of the rectangle at* ③	Selects the rectangle as the object to copy
Select objects: **(Enter)**	Ends the object selection process
\<Base point or displacement>/ Multiple: *Pick the point at* ④	Establishes a basepoint for the COPY command
Second point of displacement: *Pick at* ⑤	Places a copy of the selected object and ends the COPY command
Command: *Choose Erase (Modify)*	Issues the ERASE command
_erase Select objects: *Select the rectangle at* ⑥	Selects the rectangle as the object to erase
Select objects: **(Enter)**	Erases the selected object and ends the ERASE command

The previous two exercises covered the docking and floating of toolbars and using some tools from the Draw and Modify toolbars to give you a general feel for the tools available. Sort of like figuring out which button on the radio switches from AM to FM and checking out the station presets left by the last person who rented that car.

Figure 2.10

Drawing and copying the rect-angle.

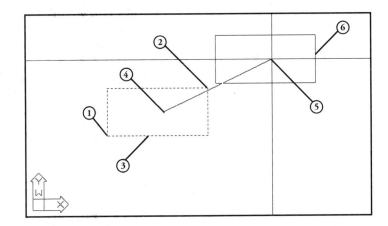

The Drawing Window

The drawing window is the area of the application window where all of the drawing or graphics are created (refer to fig. 2.1). The drawing window actually is a window within the application window that is maximized by default. Like most windows, it can be moved, resized, or minimized. AutoCAD Release 13, however, will only display one drawing window at a time, so it's typically left maximized.

The vertical bar along the right edge of the drawing window and the horizontal bar along the bottom are scroll bars that allow you to scroll the contents of the drawing. By clicking on the up or down arrow on the vertical scroll bar or the right or left arrow on the horizontal scroll bar, you can control the area of your drawing that appears in the drawing window.

The following exercise demonstrates the use of the scroll bars.

Scrolling the Drawing Window

Continue from the previous exercise.

Command: *Click on the down arrow of the vertical scroll bar*

Scrolls the rectangle up

Command: *Click on the right arrow of the horizontal scroll bar*

Scrolls the rectangle to the left

Command: *Press and drag the vertical scroll box to the top of the scroll bar*

Scrolls the rectangle to the bottom of the drawing window

| Command: *Press and drag the horizontal scroll box to the left of the scroll bar* | Scrolls to the rectangle to the right side of the drawing window |
| Command: *Choose Zoom All (Standard Toolbar, Zoom)* | Displays the entire drawing |

2

> If you scroll into oblivion, choose Undo (Standard Toolbar) to undo the scroll. You may use this tool as often as you need to return to a comfortable display.

The scroll bars for the graphics window take a little bit of time to get used to. Think of the directional arrows as pointing in the direction you move your eyes. If you turn your head to the left to look out the driver's side window, the road you're driving on now is to your right. If you pick the left arrow on the scroll bar, the objects appear to move to the right. Although, you have not actually used the MOVE command to move them, you have simply modified your display in the drawing window.

Another way of looking at it, so to speak, is to pick the direction of the new center of the screen. Chapter 6, "Controlling What You See," goes into more detail on scrolling, panning, and zooming your drawing window as well as using the Aerial View window.

The AutoCAD Screen Menu

The AutoCAD screen menu (see fig. 2.11) has had an interesting past and has served its purpose, but with the penetration Windows is making in the marketplace with the Graphical User Interface (GUI), it's rather out-moded. It's like finding an 8-track tape player in your rental car. Now with the numerous toolbars and GUIs found throughout AutoCAD for Windows, a screen menu is unnecessary, although perfectly functional.

Initializing the Screen Menu

| Command: *Choose* **O**ptions, **P**references | Displays the Preferences dialog box |
| *Click in the box beside* Screen Men**u** | Enables the screen menu |

continues

continued

Choose OK	Closes the Preferences dialog box and displays the screen menu (see fig. 2.11)
Command: *Choose* AutoCAD *at the top of the screen menu*	Returns to the main menu
Command: *Choose* DRAW1	Opens the primary DRAW menu
Command: *Choose* Rectang	Issues the RECTANG command
_rectang	
First corner: *Pick the point at* ① *(see fig. 2.12)*	Specifies the first corner of the rectangle
Other corner: *Pick the point at* ②	Specifies the second corner and draws the rectangle
Command: *Choose* **O**ptions, **P**references	Displays the Preferences dialog box
Click in the box beside Screen Men**u**	Disables the screen menu
Choose OK	Closes the Preferences dialog box

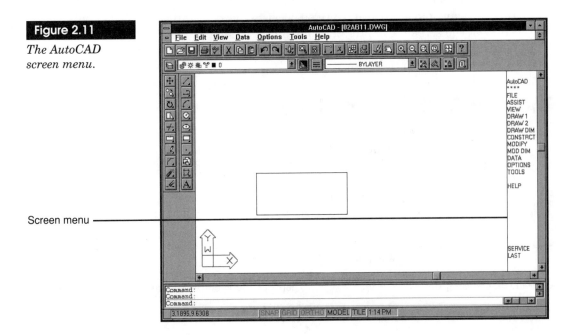

Figure 2.11

The AutoCAD screen menu.

Screen menu

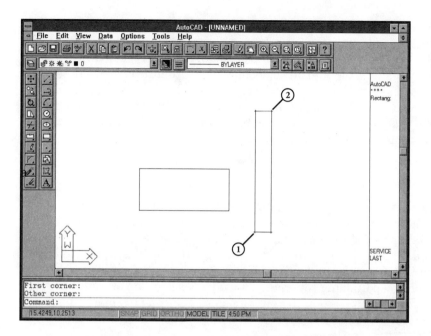

Figure 2.12

Drawing with the screen menu.

The AutoCAD screen menu is a useful method by which to create and edit your drawing, but given that AutoCAD Release 13 for Windows has so many tools available that automate the command selection process, using the screen menu for command selection might not be the best approach.

Correcting Mistakes

We're all human and are thus prone to making mistakes. AutoCAD recognizes this and provides a number of ways to undo and correct mistakes.

Canceling a Command

One common error is to start a command accidentally, or change your mind after starting a command. You can stop any command by pressing the Esc key. Keep in mind that some of the commands, tools, and menu selections actually do more than one thing. So you might need to press Esc a number of times before AutoCAD returns you to the Command: prompt.

Another common mistake is to pick within the drawing area accidentally. If you pick in a blank area of the drawing, AutoCAD may prompt you for the Other corner:. If you happen to pick on an object in the drawing, the object may highlight and little boxes may appear on the object. Those boxes, called *grips*, allow you to edit objects. In either case, press Esc a few times, then choose Redraw (Standard Toolbar) to refresh the drawing area. See Chapter 3, "A Quick Drawing," and Chapter 8, "Editing with Grips," for more information on editing using grips.

Undoing Errors

The Esc key will usually stop mistakes before they happen, but what if you actually do something you wish you hadn't? The Undo and Redo tools in the Standard Toolbar (see fig. 2.13) enable you to backup and retry any command. The Undo tool will simply undo the results of the previous command. You can choose Undo as many times as you want, AutoCAD will simply keep undoing commands until you either stop or undo everything in the current session! If you happen to undo one too many times, the Redo tool will undo the undo.

Figure 2.13

The Undo and Redo tools.

Undo ————— ◨◨◨ ————— Redo

Although you can undo as many commands as you want, the Redo tool will only take back the last undo. AutoCAD cannot redo two times in a row so use the Undo tool cautiously.

Getting Help When You Need It

Virtually all computer programs have help of some type or another, like the model specific owners manual that comes with your car. AutoCAD Release 13 for Windows, however, has provided you with an impressive array of fingertip information. Help can be accessed in several ways, depending upon where you are in the product at the time you request it. Figure 2.14 shows the AutoCAD Help window.

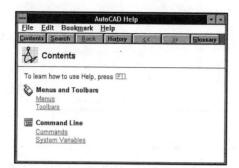

Figure 2.14

The AutoCAD Help window.

Accessing Help

You can access Help by using any of these methods:

- Choosing **H**elp from the Pull-down menu bar
- Choosing Help (Standard Toolbar)
- Choosing the Help button in most dialog boxes
- Typing HELP at the command line
- Typing ? at the command line
- Pressing F1

If you click on the Help button in a dialog box or press F1 while using a command, AutoCAD will respond with context sensitive help.

Context-Sensitive Help

Context-sensitive help simply means that help will be provided with respect to the current command or dialog box. When F1 is pressed while using a command, help will appear that is command specific.

Using F1 To Get Help with a Command

Command: *Choose Line (Draw, Line)*	Issues the LINE command
From point: *Pick a beginning point for the line*	Begins the line
Press F1	Opens the Help window that is specific to the LINE command

continues

continued

*In the Help window, choose **F**ile, E**x**it to close the Help window*	Returns to the application window and the current command
To point: *Pick another point*	Draws a line
To point: *Press Enter*	Ends the LINE command

TIP

You also can close an application window by typing Alt+F4 as an alternative to File, Exit, or Close from the control bar. This holds true for virtually all Windows applications.

The HELP Button

The HELP button is in nearly every dialog box of AutoCAD. Because a command is active when a dialog box is on the screen, the HELP button also results in context sensitive help. In the following exercise, you use the Help feature available from the Layer Control dialog box, which will illustrate the context sensitive nature of Help.

Using the HELP Button in a Dialog Box

Command: *Choose Layers (Object Properties)*	Opens the Layer Control dialog box
*Click on the **H**elp button*	Opens the Help window for Layer Control
*Choose **F**ile, then E**x**it*	Closes the Help window and returns to the Layer Control dialog box
Choose OK	Closes the Layer Control dialog box

Searching HELP

While in the context sensitive help, there also is a button for **S**earch below the AutoCAD HELP menu bar, which provides an alphabetical, topical list to search for Help. The **B**ack button will go back to the previous Help Window display and the **<<** and **>>** buttons will go backward or forward through the alphabetical Help listings. The **G**lossary provides an alphabetical glossary of the Help items from which you can choose with the pointer.

All in all, the various help routines amount to a very comprehensive and informative tool.

The Online Tutorials

AutoCAD Release 13 provides two very nice introductions of the product to both the new user and the veteran through Quick Tour and What's New in AutoCAD Release 13. Accessed through Help on the menu bar or from the AutoCAD Release 13 Program Group from the Windows Program Manager, these items provide self-paced information on AutoCAD.

The Quick Tour

The Release 13 Quick Tour provides a dynamic graphical user interface for exploring many of the features found in AutoCAD. The six sections include Using Quick Tour, AutoCAD Basics, Two-dimensional Drawing, Three-dimensional Drawing and Viewing, Plotting and Printing, and Rendering. Within each of the six sections are several topics that review that section using forward and backward arrows as well as a Show button for additional graphics.

What's New in AutoCAD Release 13

The What's New portion of Help contains four sections with topics for each. Through the course of the What's New program, the user is given graphical and textual descriptions of the new features found in Release 13 by way of button selections, scroll bars, and the Show button for dynamic graphic demonstrations.

Online Documentation

As if there isn't enough information at your keyboard fingertips, Release 13 for Windows also provides a document viewer containing documentation for AutoCAD Release 13 for Windows. For more information on loading and using the document viewer, refer to the AutoCAD installation guide.

Summary

By now, you should feel pretty comfortable with the AutoCAD Release 13 application window; positioning and sizing of windows, docking and floating toolbars, choosing items from menus and dialog boxes—almost makes you feel like you could drive AutoCAD for awhile, doesn't it? And best of all, you know how to get help in AutoCAD when you're in a bind, which is much better than asking the rental car people where the latch is for the fuel tank. In the next chapter, you create a TV remote control using rectangles, circles and text as well as learning about some basic editing commands like COPY and MOVE.

Related Topics

- Using grips—Chapter 3, "A Quick Drawing," and Chapter 8, "Editing with Grips"

- Layers—Chapter 4, "Preparing Your Drawing"

- Paper space and model space—Chapter 6, "Controlling What You See," and Chapter 16, "Composing and Plotting a Drawing"

- Zoom and pan features—Chapter 6, "Controlling What You See"

Chapter Snapshot

This chapter introduces you to some of the basic concepts of AutoCAD by walking you through the creation of a simple drawing. Throughout the chapter are a number of exercises that include the following:

- Drawing preparation

- Basic drawing tools

- Display features such as Zoom and Pan

- Basic editing tools

- Plotting your drawing

This chapter should whet your appetite for discovering the additional tools presented in this book. References to other chapters tell where you can find additional information about commands.

A Quick Drawing

T his chapter jumps right into using the AutoCAD drawing and editing tools and introduces you to some of the basic concepts and techniques involved in working with AutoCAD Release 13. Through a series of exercises, you can create a simple drawing of a TV remote control—something you've probably had an opportunity to use and perhaps wondered who designed it. Well, now it's your turn!

Before You Start

The exercises in this chapter walk you through the process of setting up, creating, and plotting a drawing. Detailed explanations of the commands used in this chapter are covered more extensively in the remaining chapters of the book. For now, though, just follow the exercises then refer to the chapters noted for more detailed information.

If you get lost or make any mistakes, use the Undo and Redo tools in the Standard Toolbar to return to a known point in the exercise. Press Esc to cancel a command and return to the Command: prompt.

Before you begin drawing, keep these concepts in mind as you look at your drawing:

- Everything in AutoCAD is drawn full scale, 1:1. The plot scale (1:2, 1:10, 1/8"=1') isn't assigned until the drawing is plotted. See Chapter 16, "Composing and Plotting a Drawing" for more on assigning plot scales.

- By default, the AutoCAD drawing window displays an area of approximately 16"×9". This can be modified using ZOOM and PAN commands as well as the scroll bars. It's just the default display that is 16"×9". The AutoCAD drawing area is virtually limitless.

Among other things, Chapter 2 introduced you to the status bar at the bottom of the AutoCAD application window. The ever-changing numbers at the left of the status bar are called *coordinates*. The coordinate display shows you the position of your cursor as an X,Y coordinate. If you move your cursor to the lower-left corner of the drawing window, the coordinate display should read very close to 0,0.

At times during the course of the exercises, you might be asked to pick a point at a specific coordinate such as 4.000,6.000. At that time, simply move your cursor so that the coordinate display matches the coordinates given in the exercise and click your mouse button.

Setting Up the Drawing

The first step in the process of creating a drawing is to set up the drawing environment. This involves setting up a work area (known as the *drawing limits*), setting the type of units you are going to use, and setting up a reference grid and cursor snap. See Chapter 4, "Preparing Your Drawing," for more on these settings and how to automate the setup process through the use of prototype drawings.

Setting Up the Drawing

Start by creating a new drawing using the default AutoCAD prototype drawing.

Command: *Choose New (Standard Toolbar)*	Issues the NEW command and displays the Create New Drawing dialog box
Type **TVREMOTE** *in the* New **D**rawing Name *edit box, then choose* OK	Creates a new drawing named TVREMOTE.DWG and places it in the current directory (\AB)
Command: *Choose* **D**ata, Un**i**ts	Issues the DDUNITS command and displays the Units control dialog box

In the Units *area, choose* 0.00 *from the* **P**recision *drop-down list, and then choose* OK	Sets the units precision to two decimal places
Command: *Choose* **D**ata, Dr**a**wing Limits	Issues the LIMITS command

`LIMITS`
`Reset Model space limits: ON/OFF/`
`<Lower left corner> <0.00,0.00>:` (Enter)
	Accepts the default lower left coordinate for the drawing limits

`Upper right corner` `<12.00,9.00>:` (Enter)	Accepts the upper right coordinate of the drawing limits to create a 12"x9" work area
Command: *Double-click on the* GRID *button in the status bar*	The grid dots appear and GRID on the status bar is black

Move your cursor around and notice that the crosshairs don't stop on the grid dots. In the next steps, you turn on the snap setting allowing you to control the cursor movement.

Command: `<Grid on>` *Double-click on the* SNAP *button in the status bar*	The snap turns on and the cursor snaps to the grid dots
Command: *Choose* **O**ptions, *then* **D**rawing Aids	Issues the DDRMODES command and displays the Drawing Aids dialog box
Double click in the **X** Spacing *edit box under* **S**nap, *then type* **.1** (Enter)	Sets the X and Y Spacing for snap to .1
Double click in the **X** Spacing *edit box under* **G**rid, *then type* **.5** (Enter)	Sets the X and Y Spacing for the grid to .5
Choose OK	Closes the Drawing Aids dialog box

Now that the environment is set up, you can create some drawing layers. In the following steps, you create three new layers and set one of them to be current.

Command: *Choose Layers (Object Properties)*	Issues the DDLMODES command and displays the Layer Control dialog box
Type **REMOTE,BUTTONS,TEXT** *in the edit box and choose* Ne**w**	Creates three new layers called REMOTE, BUTTONS, and TEXT, and displays them in the La**y**er Name list box
Select the layer TEXT *in the* La**y**er Name *list box, then choose* **S**et Color	Highlights the TEXT layer and displays the Select Color dialog box
Choose the color red from the Standard Colors *area and choose* OK	Assigns the color red to the TEXT layer

continues

continued

Select the layers REMOTE *and* TEXT *in the* La**y**er Name *list box*	Highlights the REMOTE layer and removes the highlight from the TEXT layer
Choose **C**urrent, *then choose* OK	Sets the REMOTE layer current and closes the dialog box
Command: *Choose Save (Standard Toolbar)*	Saves the drawing

Your drawing now displays a .5"×.5" grid spacing and a snap spacing of .1". When both grid and snap are turned on, the status bar displays the words SNAP and GRID in black. As you work in a drawing, you might find it convenient to turn on or off the snap and grid to accommodate object selection and editing.

TIP

> Pressing the F7 function key turns on and off the GRID, and the F9 function key turns on and off the SNAP.

At the beginning of the previous exercise you set the distance between grid dots to be .5 units. For this drawing, 1 unit equals 1 inch. One unit, however, could just as easily represent 1 foot, 1 mile, 1 mm, and so on.

NOTE

> Notice that when you pressed (Enter) after typing the X Spacing value that the Y Spacing value was automatically set to equal the X Spacing. Also, the Grid X and Y spacing are automatically set to the same values as the Snap spacing, although it is not initially reflected in the dialog box.

Drawing the Remote Control

Now that the drawing environment is set up, you are ready to draw. This section introduces some basic drawing and editing commands. Typically, several options exist for accomplishing any one task. The flexibility of AutoCAD enables you to select a method that works for you.

Command Selection Options

The exercises in this section introduce you to the various means of issuing commands in AutoCAD, by either typing the command or choosing the command from one of the menus or toolbars.

The basic TV remote is rectangular with a wide assortment of buttons in all types of shapes and textures. In the following exercise, you create the basic outline of the remote.

Creating the TVREMOTE

Continue from the previous exercise.

Command: **RECTANG**	Starts the RECTANG command
First corner: **4,1** (Enter)	Places the first corner of the rectangle at ① (see fig. 3.1)
Other corner: **7.5,8.5** (Enter)	Places the second corner of the rectangle at ② and ends the command
Command: *Choose Rectangle (Draw, Polygon)*	Issues the RECTANG command
RECTANG First corner: **4.2,8.3** (Enter)	Places the first corner of the rectangle at ③
Other corner: **7.3,7** (Enter)	Places the second corner of the rectangle at ④ and ends the command
Command: (Enter)	Repeats the RECTANG command
RECTANG First corner: **4.2,2.5** (Enter)	Places the first corner of the rectangle at ⑤
Other corner: **7.3,6.8** (Enter)	Places the second corner of the rectangle at ⑥ and ends the command
Command: *Choose Save (Standard Toolbar)*	Saves the drawing

The previous exercise introduced the concept of pressing (Enter) to execute the previous command. You drew the first rectangle, so to begin the RECTANG command again, you pressed Enter. This doesn't mean, of course, that every time you press Enter you get the RECTANG command. You get whatever command was used last, and if you don't remember what command you were in, you always can press F2 to Flip to the Text Window.

Figure 3.1

The basic outline of the TVREMOTE.

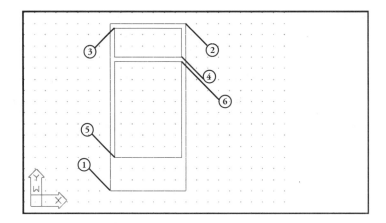

TIP

In AutoCAD, you can issue an (Enter) by either pressing the Enter key, pressing the spacebar, or right-clicking your mouse.

Command Aliases: AutoCAD's Quick Keys

In the previous exercise, you saw how you can type a command at the Command: prompt. This may seem cumbersome, but AutoCAD provides a shortcut to typing commands—command aliases. An *alias* is a one- or two-key shortcut you can enter to begin a command. For example, typing **c** and pressing Enter at the Command: prompt begins the CIRCLE command. For a complete listing of the default command aliases for Release 13, see Appendix D.

Aliases are extremely handy because, most of the time, one hand is probably resting near the keyboard, and it may be easier to type the alias than it would be to click on the tool that executes the command.

Command aliases are customizable, as well. *Inside AutoCAD Release 13 for Windows and Windows NT* explains the relatively simple way in which the keyboard can serve as the only place you really need to execute your most frequently used commands.

In addition to using aliases, the next exercise also introduces the ORTHO mode. You turn on the ORTHO mode when you want to draw or edit something vertically or horizontally, such as a line that is orthogonal in orientation. Chapter 4, "Preparing your Drawing," goes into more detail about using the ORTHO mode.

The power button on your basic TV remote is not always obvious to the touch. In the following exercise, you make a big round one at the top of the remote for "ease of use."

Adding the Power Button

Continue from the previous exercise.

Command: *From the Layer Control (Object Properties) drop-down list, choose* BUTTONS	Set the current layer to BUTTONS
Command: **C** (Enter)	Starts the CIRCLE command
CIRCLE 3P/2P/TTR/<Center point>: *Pick the point 5.7,7.6*	Places the center of the circle at ① (see fig. 3.2)
Diameter/<Radius> <0.0000>: **.4** (Enter)	Specifies the radius and draws the circle
Command: **L** (Enter)	Starts the LINE command
LINE From point: *Pick the point 4.2,4.0*	Places the start of the line at ②
To point: *Double-click on* ORTHO *in the status bar, then pick* ③	Turns on ORTHO mode then places the endpoint of the line
To point: (Enter)	Ends the LINE command
Command: **R** (Enter)	Issues the REDRAW command
Command: *Choose Save (Standard Toolbar)*	Saves the drawing

Your drawing should now resemble figure 3.2.

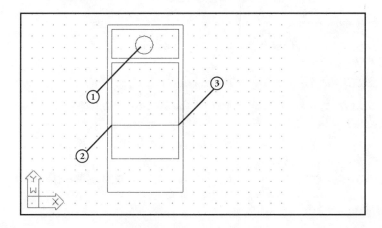

Figure 3.2

The power button.

TIP

In addition to the F7 (Grid) and F9 (Snap) keys, the function key F8 turns on and off ortho mode.

Adding Text to the Drawing

Lines and circles are nice, but you need some text to know which button is which on your TV remote. The next exercise uses DTEXT, or Dyanamic Text, to place text on the drawing. As you go through this exercise, you can see the characters appear on the drawing as they are typed. That's what makes dynamic text dynamic.

So far, commands have been executed through the toolbars or the command alias. Some toolbars, as you discovered in Chapter 2, have *flyouts* of additional related tools. These flyouts are found with tools that have the little black triangle in the lower right corner. The DTEXT command is located on the Text flyout of the Draw toolbar.

TIP

If you mistakenly press and drag on a tool that has flyouts, drag your cursor to any location in the graphics window and release. This keeps AutoCAD from executing one of the flyout commands when you release the mouse button.

Entering Dynamic Text

Continue from the previous exercise.

Command: *From the Layer Control (Object Properties) drop-down list, choose* TEXT

Set the current layer to TEXT

Command: *Choose Dtext (Draw, Text)*

Begins the DTEXT command

Command:_dtext Justify/Style/ <Start point>: **J** (Enter)

Selects the Justify option

Align/Fit/Center/Middle/Right /TL/TC/TR/ML/MC/MR/BL/BC/BR: **M** (Enter)

Specifies a Middle text justification

Middle point: *Pick the point 5.7,8.1*

Establishes the middle point of the text at ① (*see fig. 3.3*)

`Height <0.2000>: .125` (Enter)	Assigns a text height of .125
`Rotation angle <0>:` (Enter)	Retains the default of 0 degrees
`Text:` **POWER** (Enter)	Enters the text
`Text:` *Press Enter*	Ends the DTEXT command
`Command:` *Choose Save (Standard Toolbar)*	Saves the drawing

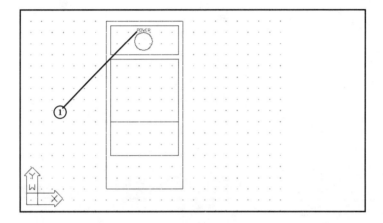

Figure 3.3

*The power button
and its label.*

Don't be too concerned about the exact placement of the text for now. As long as you have a drawing that looks "remotely" like figure 3.3, you're doing fine.

Changing the Screen Display

Sometimes you need to get closer to a specific area of the drawing. Chapter 6 goes into more detail on the various display options, but now would be a good time to look into some quick and easy ways to change your screen display.

The primary commands for changing your screen display are ZOOM and PAN. The ZOOM command is the most extensive in scope, and the PAN command is complemented by the scroll bars on the right side and bottom of the drawing area. The next few exercises, which use these two commands, will continue to be referenced through the rest of the chapter.

ZOOM...as in Camera Lens

The ZOOM command is analogous to the zoom lens of a camera. Just as a zoom lens will move the viewer closer to or farther from a scene, the ZOOM command also moves your drawing closer to or farther from you.

In the following exercise, use the Zoom Window tool to get a closer look at the remote.

Using ZOOM To Change the Display

Continue from the previous exercise.

Command: *Choose Zoom Window (Standard Toolbar)*	Issues the ZOOM command with the Window option
Command: `'_zoom` `All/Center/Dynamic/Extents/Left/` `Previous/Vmax/Window/<Scale(X/XP)>:` `_w`	
First corner: *Pick* ① *(see fig. 3.4)*	Places the first corner of the zoom window
Other corner: *Pick* ②	Places the other corner and update the display to show the windowed area
Command: *From the Layer Control (Object Properties) drop-down list, choose* BUTTONS	Sets the current layer to BUTTONS
Command: *Choose Rectangle (Draw, Polygon)*	Issues the RECTANG command
First corner: *Pick the point* **4.4,6.3**	Places the first corner of the rectangle at ① (see fig. 3.5)
Other corner: *Pick the point* **4.8,6.5**	Places the other corner of the rectangle at ②
Command: *Choose Save (Standard Toolbar)*	Saves the drawing

The ZOOM command and its various options are extremely useful in moving about your drawing. The ability to change your display to a more workable area is very important as you develop your skills with AutoCAD.

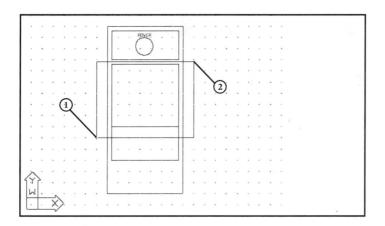

Figure 3.4

Zooming into the drawing.

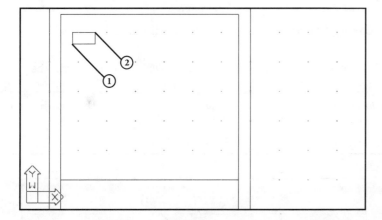

Figure 3.5

Adding another button.

3

Panning the Drawing to a New Position

One method of panning the drawing was covered briefly in Chapter 2 during the exercise of using the scroll bars located along the edge of the graphics window. Another method used frequently to modify the display is the PAN command.

In the following exercise, you use the ZOOM and PAN commands in some simple display routines commonly used when working on a drawing.

Zooming and Panning the Display

Continue from the previous exercise.

Command: *Choose Zoom Previous (Standard Toolbar, Zoom)*

Returns the display to previous view of the current drawing

Command: *Choose Zoom Out (Standard Toolbar)*

Reduces the size of the display by half

Command: *Turn off the ORTHO button*

Turns off ORTHO

Command: *Choose Pan (Standard Toolbar)*

Executes the PAN command

'pan Displacement: *Pick ①*

Places the first point for PAN as shown in fig. 3.6

Second point: *Pick ②*

Updates the display and ends the PAN command

Command: *Choose Zoom All (Standard Toolbar)*

Returns the display to the drawing Limits

Command: *Choose Zoom Window (Standard Toolbar)*

Issues the ZOOM command with the Window option

Command: *Pick ①, then ② (see fig. 3.7)*

Places a window around the drawing and updates the display

Command: *Choose Save (Standard Toolbar)*

Saves the drawing

Figure 3.6

Pick points for the PAN command.

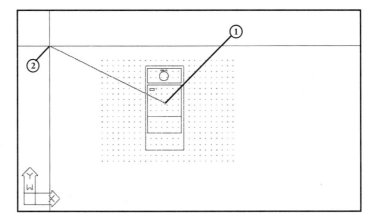

The PAN command takes some getting used to at first, but once you have mastered it, your ability to move about the drawing is greatly improved.

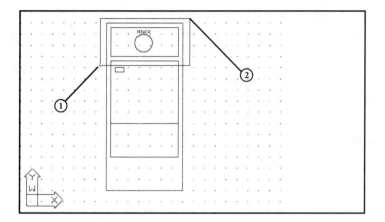

Figure 3.7

Pick points for the zoom window.

3

By way of illustration, you can think of the panning process this way. If you come up to a wooden fence taller than you, and you would like to see over it, you would grab the top of the fence (your hands would be the first PAN pick point) and pull yourself up (the position of your hands is now the second PAN pick point). In other words, you push the fence down, essentially pushing yourself up. The fence doesn't really move, just like the objects in the drawing don't really move, you're just moving the position of your eyeball by picking one point as the hold spot and picking another point for where you want the new focus to be. I want this part of the drawing (first pick point) ...over here (second pick point). Try it!

Basic Editing Tools

The exercises in this section introduce you to the use of grips. Grips are a feature that enables you to stretch, move, copy, rotate, scale, or mirror an object by simply picking a grip position and cycling through the editing options. Chapter 8 covers grips more extensively, but in this chapter you can get the feel for some basic grip sequences.

When You Get a Grip, What Do You Do?

You might have encountered grips accidentally by picking an object when no command was active. By default, grips appear as blue boxes on the endpoints of lines, arcs, and rectangles, the quarter points (quadrants) of circles, and the centers of circles and arcs. If you activate the grips by accident, simply press the Esc key twice to remove them.

These are called grips because when you place your crosshairs close enough to a grip box, the crosshairs are "gripped" by the grip box, similar to how a magnet works. The radial magnetic field around a magnet immediately grips metal objects when they fall within that field. The same concept applies to grips. Once a grip is picked, it turns red and is referred to as a *hot grip*.

When a grip is hot, there are five editing options available with which you can edit the gripped object: Stretch, Move, Rotate, Scale, and Mirror. By pressing Enter, you can cycle to the next editing option. Chapter 8 covers grips extensively, but you get an idea about their operation in the next exercise.

In this next exercise, you use grips to complete the TV remote control. You have the basic shapes you need for all the buttons, now it's just a matter of some edits that can easily be done with grips.

Moving and Sizing and Object Using Grips

Continue from the previous exercise.

Command: *Select the circle*

Displays the grips for the circle and highlights the circle

Command: *Pick the center grip of the circle*

Begins the grip options sequence starting with Stretch

`** STRETCH **`
`<Stretch to point>/Base point/`
`Copy/Undo/eXit:` (Enter)

Cycles to the Move option

`** MOVE **`
`<Move to point>/Base point/Copy`
`Undo/eXit:` *Pick the point 4.7,7.5*

Moves the circle to ① (see fig. 3.8)

Command: Select the grip on the left quadrant of the circle

Makes the left quadrant grip hot and starts the grip editing modes

`** STRETCH **`
`<Stretch to point>/Base point/`
`Copy/Undo/eXit:` *Move the cursor to the right by one snap unit*

Reduces the radius by .1 then ends the grip editing modes

Command: *Select the center grip on the circle*

Makes the center grip hot and starts the grip editing modes

`** STRETCH **`
`<Stretch to point>/Base point/`
`Copy/Undo/eXit:` (Enter)
	Cycles to the Move option

`** MOVE **`
`<Move to point>/Base point/Copy`
`Undo/eXit:` **C** (Enter)
	Enables the Copy option

`** MOVE (multiple) **`
`<Move to point>/Base point/Copy`
`Undo/eXit:` **@2.1<0** (Enter)
	Copies the circle 2.1" to the right

`** MOVE (multiple) **`
`<Move to point>/Base point/Copy`
`Undo/eXit:` *Press Esc*
	Ends the grip editing

`Command:` *Press Esc*	Deselects the circle, the grips remain visible
`Command:` *Press Esc*	Turns off the grips
`Command:` *Choose Redraw* *(Standard Toolbar)*	Refreshes the screen

Your drawing should now resemble figure 3.9.

`Command:` *Choose Save (Standard Toolbar)*	Saves the drawing

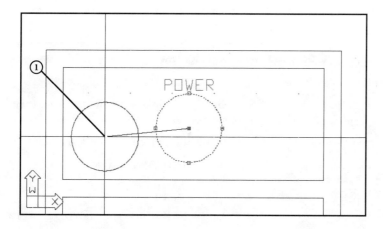

Figure 3.8

New position when moving the circle with the grip.

Grips are fairly easy to work with once you get a feel for the process. As you saw in the exercise, pressing (Enter) cycles to the next grip option.

*New position for
POWER text.*

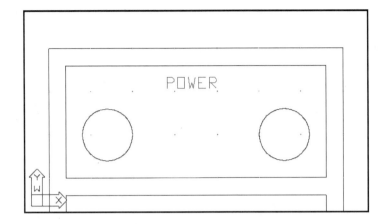

In the next series of steps, you use the grip options to copy the text
"POWER" to the middle of the two buttons and then edit the text to read
"TV" and "VCR."

Even though the first grip option is for STRETCH, when selecting
the center of a circle or text, the object doesn't stretch but is edited in
a fashion identical to the MOVE option.

Copying and Editing Text

Continue from the previous exercise.

Command: *Select the text and the two circles*	Highlights the objects and turns on their grips
Command: *Select the middle text grip*	Begins the grip editing for the text
** STRETCH ** \<Stretch to point>/Base point/ Copy/Undo/eXit: **C** (Enter)	Specifies the Copy option
** STRETCH (multiple) ** \<Stretch to point>/Base point/Copy/ Undo/eXit: *Pick the center grip of each circle*	Copies the text to ① and ② (see fig. 3.10)
Command: *Press ESC three times*	Ends the grip editing, deselects the objects, and turns off the grips

Command: *Choose DDEDIT (Modify, Special Edit)*	Issues the DDEDIT command
`<Select a TEXT or ATTDEF object>/Undo:` *Select the left "POWER" text*	Displays the Edit Text dialog box
In the edit box, type **TV** *and choose* OK	Changes the text to TV, returns to the DDEDIT command
`<Select a TEXT or ATTDEF object>/Undo:` *Select the right "POWER" text*	Displays the Edit Text dialog box
In the edit box, type **VCR** *and choose* OK	Changes the text to VCR, returns to the DDEDIT command
`<Select a TEXT or ATTDEF object>/` `Undo:` (Enter)	Ends the DDEDIT command
Command: *Choose Save (Standard Toolbar)*	Saves the drawing

Your drawing now should look like figure 3.11.

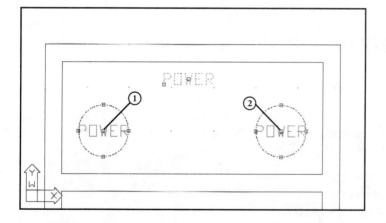

Figure 3.10
Copy points for text.

As you learned in the previous two exercises, grip options can be cycled through by pressing (Enter) after a grip has been selected. If you pass the option you wish to use, just keep pressing (Enter) until the desired option comes back.

While grips are an easy way to edit objects, AutoCAD has many other editing commands available. The following exercise uses the ARRAY command, which allows you to create multiple copies of objects in either a rectangular or circular pattern. See Chapter 10, "Selecting and Editing Objects," for more on using the ARRAY command.

Figure 3.11

The TV Remote text.

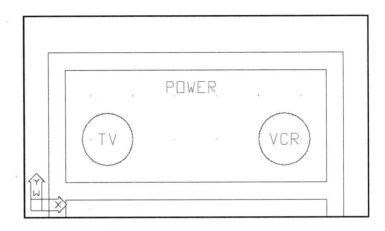

Completing the TV Remote

Continue from the previous exercise.

Command: *Pick once in the middle of the vertical scroll bar*	Pans the screen down
Command: *Select the small rectangle*	Highlights the rectangle, turns on the grips
Command: *Choose Rectangular Array (Modify, Copy)*	Issues the ARRAY command with the Rectangular option
`Rectangular or Polar` `array (R/P) <R>: r` `Number of rows (---) <1>:` **3** `(Enter)`	Specifies the number of rows in the array
`Number of columns (¦¦¦) <1>:` **4** `(Enter)`	Specifies the number of columns
`Unit cell or distance` `between rows (---):` **-.76** `(Enter)`	Specifies the distance between the rows
`Distance between columns (¦¦¦):` **.76** `(Enter)`	Specifies the distance between the columns and creates the array of buttons

The −.76 indicates to copy the buttons down .76", while the +.76 indicates to copy to the buttons .76" to the right.

Command: *Choose Zoom All (Standard Toolbar)*	Updates the display with the drawing limits
Command: *Double-click on the* GRID *button in the status bar*	Turns off the grid

Command: *Choose Save (Standard Toolbar)*   Saves the drawing

Your drawing should look like figure 3.12.

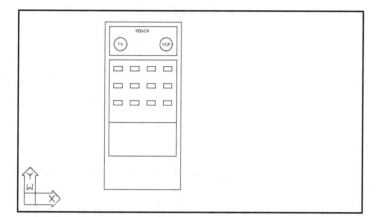

Figure 3.12

The completed remote.

3

Setting Up a Plot Sheet

The remote control is now fairly complete. Using the methods demonstrated in the previous exercises, you could add numbers to the buttons and add additional buttons for other remote control features. But now that you have a real drawing, how do you get it from the computer onto paper? Start by setting up a plot sheet with a title block.

Model Space and Paper Space

AutoCAD actually has two drawing environments. The default drawing environment, called *model space*, is where you have been working so far. The other environment, called *paper space*, enables you to create and compose the drawing layout.

In the following exercise you set up the paper space drawing environment. When you first enter paper space, you will notice that your model disappears from the screen. Don't panic, it's still there, you just won't see it until a viewport is created through which you will once again be able to see the drawing in model space. To do this, you will use the MVSETUP command to create an A-size (11"×8.5") title block.

Setting Up Paper Space

Continue from the previous exercise.

Command: *Double-click on the* TILE *button in the status bar* — Switches to paper space, the remote control disappears

Command: *Choose Layers (Object Properties)* — Issues the DDLMODES command and displays the Layer Control dialog box

Type **TITLE,VPORTS** *in the edit box and choose* Ne**w** — Creates two new layers called TITLE and PORTS, and displays them in the Layer Name list box

Select the layer TITLE *in the* La**y**er Name *list box, then choose* **S**et Color — Highlights the TITLE layer and displays the Select Color dialog box

Choose the color blue from the Standard Colors *area and choose* OK — Assigns the color blue to the TITLE layer

Choose **C**urrent, *then choose* OK — Sets the TITLE layer current and closes the dialog box

Command: *Choose* **D**ata, Dr**a**wing Limits — Issues the LIMITS command

```
LIMITS
Reset Model space limits: ON/OFF/
<Lower left corner>
<0.00,0.00>: (Enter)
```
Accepts the default lower left coordinate for the drawing limits

```
Upper right corner
<12.00,9.00>: 11,8.5
```
Sets the upper right corner at 11,8.5 to create a 11"x8.5" work area

Command: *Choose* **V**iew, Floating Viewports, MV **S**etup — Issues the MVSETUP command

```
Command: _mvsetup
Initializing...
Align/Create/Scale viewports
/Options/Title block/Undo: T
```
Specifies the Title block option

```
Delete objects/Origin/Undo/
<Insert title block>: (Enter)
```
Accepts the default option to insert a title block

You will see the AutoCAD Text window appear with a list of available title blocks. You will be using the ANSI-A Size(in) title block.

```
Add/Delete/Redisplay/
<Number of entry to load>: 7 (Enter)
```
Specifies option 7 (ANSI-A Size) and creates the title block

```
Create a drawing named
ansi-a.dwg? <Y>: N (Enter)
```
Specifies No so that a new drawing is not created

`Align/Create/Scale viewports` `/Options/Title block/Undo:` (Enter)	Ends the MVSETUP command
Command: *Choose Save (Standard Toolbar)*	Saves the drawing

Your drawing should now look like figure 3.13.

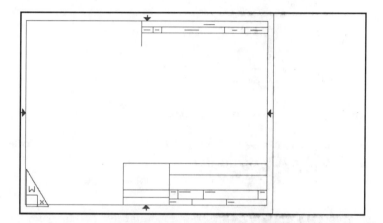

The A-size title block.

3

Creating Multiple Views of the Remote

Now that you have the paper space environment set up, you can create viewports through which to view the remote control (which is still in model space). The views are created with the MVIEW command. In the following exercise, you create a couple of floating viewports and compose the viewport display in the title block.

Creating Model Viewports

Continue from the previous exercise.

Command: *From the Layer Control (Object Properties) drop-down list, choose* **VPORTS**	Sets the current layer to VPORTS
Command: *Choose* **V**iew, Floating Viewports, **1** Viewport	Issues the MVIEW command
Command: `_mview` `ON/OFF/Hideplot/Fit/2/3/4/Restore/` `<First Point>:` *Pick* ① *(see fig. 3.14)*	Specifies the first corner of the viewport

continues

continued

`Other corner:` *Pick* ②	Creates the viewport
`Command:` *Choose* **V**iew, Floating Viewports, **1** Viewport	Issues the MVIEW command

`Command: _mview`
`ON/OFF/Hideplot/Fit/2/3/4/`
`Restore/<First Point>:` *Pick* ③
	Specifies the first corner of the viewport

`Other corner:` *Pick* ④	Creates the viewport
`Command:` *Double-click on* PAPER *in the status bar*	Switches you to floating model space

When you move your cursor, you should see the crosshairs appear inside the right viewport. This is known as floating model space, which enables you to work on the model space drawing while paper space is active. In the next steps, you adjust the scale of the viewports using the ZOOM command.

`Command:` *Choose Zoom Center (Standard Toolbar, Zoom)*	Issues the ZOOM command with the Center option

`All/Center/Dynamic/Extents/Left/`
`Previous /Vmax/Window/<Scale(X/XP)>: c`
`Center point:` *Pick point* ⑤
	Specifies the center point of the zoom

`Magnification or Height` `  <25.84190>:` **1xp** (Enter)	Sets the display to full scale
`Command:` *Pick anywhere in the left viewport*	Sets the left viewport current
`Command:` *Choose Zoom Center (Standard Toolbar, Zoom)*	Issues the ZOOM command with the Center option

`All/Center/Dynamic/Extents/Left/`
`Previous /Vmax/Window/<Scale(X/XP)>: c`
`Center point:` *Pick point* ⑥
	Specifies the center point of the zoom

`Magnification or Height` `  <25.84190>:` **.5xp** (Enter)	Sets the display to half scale
`Command:` *Double-click on* MODEL *in the status bar*	Switches you to paper space
`Command:` *Choose Layer Control (Object Properties) and from the drop-down list select layer* 0	Set the current layer to 0

Command: *Choose Layer Control (Object Properties) and from the drop-down list click on the sun icon next to the VPORTS layer, then press Enter*   Freezes the layer VPORTS so the viewport edges are no longer visible

Command: *Choose Save (Standard Toolbar)*   Saves the drawing

Your drawing now should resemble figure 3.15.

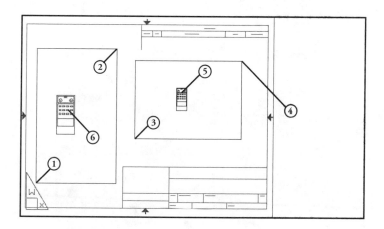

Figure 3.14

The floating model space viewports.

3

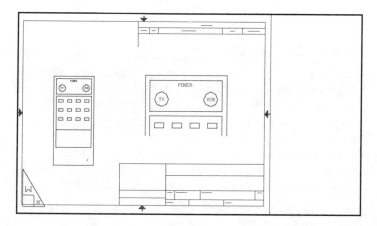

Figure 3.15

The scaled model space viewports.

The views now are scaled so that when the title block is plotted full size, the right viewport plots at a scale of 1:1 and the left viewport plots at a scale of 1:2.

Running a Check Plot

Sending a drawing to the printer is frequently referred to as a creating a check plot. It might not be the final sheet size, but it gives you something tangible to run past the boss or the customer for approval before the final plot. In AutoCAD, printing and plotting are created with the PLOT command. The PLOT command displays the Plot Configuration dialog box (see fig. 13.16), which enables you to control virtually every aspect of the plot.

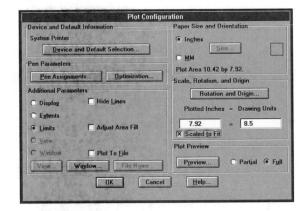

Selecting the Output Device

During the installation process of AutoCAD, you were prompted for an output device. If you elected to configure AutoCAD for a printer, at the completion of this section, you will have a check plot of the TV remote drawing. If you have yet to install a printer, you can still benefit from this section because the Plot Preview capability shows you exactly what you would get if you were actually to send it to the printer. Refer to Appendix A, "Installation and Configuration," or the *AutoCAD Installation Guide* for more information on installing and configuring your output device.

If you have more than one output device, such as a PaintJet and a LaserJet, the Device and Default Selection dialog box enables you to assign which device is to be used for the output.

Establishing What's To Be Plotted

AutoCAD has several choices for what is to be plotted: the display, a view, a window, limits, and extents. These enable you to plot all or selected areas of the drawing to plot.

Choosing the Paper Size and Rotation

The Paper Size and Orientation dialog box is where a sheet size is selected for those plotters with varying ranges from A to E in both English and Metric. Chapter 16, "Composing and Plotting a Drawing," reviews the options more fully for plotting a drawing.

The Rotation and Origin button gives the user the opportunity to set the output rotation to 0, 90, 180, or 270 degrees by way of the Plot Rotation and Origin dialog box. This typically is used when the drawing would fit more efficiently in a different orientation. The X Origin and Y Origin fields provide the means by which the user can reposition the drawing on the sheet.

Setting the Plot Scale

In Chapter 2, "Getting to Know AutoCAD," there was a brief explanation regarding AutoCAD drawing everything in real inches (1:1) in the graphics window, then assigning a plot scale when it was time to plot. It's time to plot.

Usually a check plot is output to fit the available sheet size so that a plot scale at this point is not overly important. When plotting a finished plot from paper space, you typically plot at a scale of 1:1. If you are plotting from model space, the plot scale must be set so that the model fits on the paper (for example 1/8"=1' or 1":50').

Taking a Practice Shot with Plot Preview

The Preview feature in the Plot Configuration dialog box is a real time saver. There are two modes for the Preview: Partial and Full. The Partial mode shows a rectangle for the sheet size and a rectangle on the sheet representing the requested plot area, in our case, the plot window. A little page icon is shown in the lower left corner of the plot area.

The Full preview mode shows the plotted page exactly as it will appear when plotted. Obviously, this is a very timely feature for large plots when you need to confirm the content and positioning of the final plot.

In the following exercise, you create a check plot of the remote control drawing.

Creating a Check Plot

Continue from the previous exercise.

Command: *Choose Print (Standard Toolbar)*	Opens the Plot Configuration dialog box
Click on **D**evice and Default Selection	Opens Device and Default Selection dialog box
Select the printer you want to print to, then choose OK	Assigns your printer as the output device and returns to the Plot Configuration dialog box
In the Additional Parameters area choose **L**imits	Assigns Limits as the area to plot
If your printer supports multiple sheet sizes, choose **S**ize, *select the sheet size you want to use, then choose* OK	Opens Paper Size dialog box and selects the paper size
In the Scale, Rotation, and Origin *area, choose* Rotation and Ori**g**in, **0**, *then choose* OK	Opens the Plot Rotation and Origin dialog box
In the Scale, Rotation, and Origin *area, put a check in the* Scaled **t**o Fit *box*	Sets plot scale to Fit the plot area of the selected sheet size
In the Plot Preview *area, choose* F**u**ll, *then choose* P**r**eview	Displays a graphic plot preview, opens the Plot Preview dialog box

If the Plot Preview dialog box is on top of your drawing, you can move it by dragging the dialog box title bar. Examine the plot preview to make sure the plot fits on the page and is rotated properly.

Choose **E**nd Preview	Closes the dialog box and returns to Plot Configuration dialog box
In the Scale, Rotation, and Origin *area, choose* Rotation and Ori**g**in	Opens the Plot Rotation and Origin dialog box
If the plot was not rotated properly on the sheet, choose **9**0, *then choose* OK	Sets the plot rotation to 90 degrees

In the Plot Preview *area, choose* **Fu**ll, *then choose* P**r**eview	Displays a graphic plot preview, opens the Plot Preview dialog box
Choose **E**nd Preview	Closes the dialog box and returns to Plot Configuration dialog box
Choose OK	Closes the Plot Configuration dialog box and returns to the drawing

You might see a prompt asking you to press return when the printer is ready. If so, check that the printer is on and ready to print, then press Enter. After a few moments, your drawing should plot.

Command: *Choose Save (Standard Toolbar)*   Saves the drawing

Congratulations! You have just finished your first AutoCAD drawing session. If you experienced any problems in plotting, check the printer connections and refer to Appendix A, "Installation and Configuration," or Appendix B, "Troubleshooting," for help.

Summary

This chapter gave you an introduction to some of the major commands and concepts involved in using AutoCAD. You now should have a pretty good feel for how AutoCAD works. In the next chapter, you will learn more about setting up and controlling the AutoCAD environment and how to automate some of the setup work.

Related Topics

- Using grips—Chapter 3, "A Quick Drawing," and Chapter 8, "Editing with Grips"

- Layers—Chapter 4, "Preparing Your Drawing"

- Paper space and model space—Chapter 6, "Controlling What You See," and Chapter 16, "Composing and Plotting a Drawing"

- Zoom and pan features—Chapter 6, "Controlling What You See"

PART II

Developing Basic AutoCAD Drawing Skills

Before you can start drawing your design, you must prepare your drawing, which means you must make AutoCAD Release 13 aware of how you work and what you need. One of the advantages of AutoCAD Release 13 is how flexible it can be to your needs.

This chapter will do the following:

- Show you how to work with the plot scale factor

- Introduce you to paper space and model space

- Show you how to set the working units

- Introduce layers and how to use them

- Show you how to automate drawing setup with prototype drawings

4

Preparing Your Drawing

In manual drafting, you start a new project by collecting all your drawing tools, reorganizing your workplace, and getting your paper ready. You then examine your project and decide how it will look on paper. You prepare your AutoCAD drawing in much the same way. You examine the project, decide on the type of units to use (inches, feet, mm, meters, and so forth), choose the size of paper on which to plot, and calculate the plot scale.

Another aspect of preparing your AutoCAD drawing involves organizing your work. During the course of a project, you will edit, revise, and expand your design many times before it is finalized. Editing a large, complex drawing can be difficult. The more drawing objects you work with, the more difficult your editing process is. With some advance planning, your editing process can be streamlined by the use of layers. You can place objects in separate layers and deal only with the objects you need.

AutoCAD takes this drawing preparation further by automating your setup process. By saving your settings in a prototype drawing, you then can create new drawings with your settings already in place.

This chapter explores two areas of planning your work in AutoCAD Release 13. First, you are introduced to the commands that shape the AutoCAD environment. You setup AutoCAD to fit the needs of your drawing. Second, this chapter shows you how to organize your drawing with layers. This enables you to view and work on various parts of your drawing instead of the whole drawing, which can make editing your drawing easier and faster.

The following Quick Tour exercise introduces you to some of the concepts presented in this chapter. In the exercise, you create a prototype mechanical drawing by setting the drawing's units and limits, create some mechanical layers, and save the drawing for use as a prototype drawing.

The Quick Tour

The first step is to set up a new drawing and set up its units.

Command: *Choose New (Standard Toolbar)*	Issues the NEW command
In the New **D**rawing Name *edit box, type* **MET-PRO**, *then choose the* OK *button*	Creates a new drawing named MET-PRO
Command: *Choose* **D**ata, *then* Un**i**ts	Issues the DDUNITS command
In the Units *area, select* 0.00 *from the* **P**recision *drop-down list, then choose* OK	Sets the drawing to display units to the second decimal place

The following instructions show you how to set up your drawing limits and drawing aids.

Command: *Choose* **D**ata, *then* Dr**a**wing Limits	Issues LIMITS command for model space
Reset Model space limits: ON/OFF/ <Lower left corner> <0.00,0.00>: (Enter)	Accepts the default lower left limit at coordinates 0,0
Upper right corner <12.00,9.00>: **72,48** (Enter)	Sets the upper right limit at coordinates 72,48 in model space
Command: *Double-click on the* TILE *button (in the status bar)*	Issues the TILEMODE command and switches to paper space
Command: *Choose* **D**ata, *then* Dr**a**wing Limits	Issues LIMITS command for paper space
Reset Paper space limits: ON/OFF/ <Lower left corner> <0.00,0.00>: (Enter)	Accepts the default lower left limit at coordinates 0,0

Upper right corner <12.00,9.00>: **36,24** (Enter)	Sets the upper right limit at coordinates 36,24 in paper space
Command: *Double-click on the* TILE *button (in the status bar)*	Returns to model space
Command: *Choose* **O**ptions, *then* **D**rawing Aids	Issues the DDRMODES command and displays the Drawing Aids dialog box
In the **G**rid *area, put an* X *inside the* On *check box and in the* X S**p**acing *text box, type* **2**	Turns the grid on and sets the grid spacing to 2"
In the Snap *area, put an* X *inside the* On *check box and in the* **X** Spacing *text box type* **0.25**	Turns the snap on and sets the snap spacing to 0.25"
In the Modes *area, put an* X *in the* **O**rtho *check box, and then choose the* OK *button*	Turns ortho on and exits the Drawing Aids dialog box

The next instructions show you how to set up the layers in the drawing.

Command: *Choose Layers (Standard Toolbar)*	Issues the DDLMODES command and displays the Layer Control dialog box
In the edit box, type **DIMS,OBJECT, HIDDEN,CENTER,TITLE,VPORTS,NOTES**, *and then choose the* Ne**w** *button*	Creates the new layers DIMS, OBJECT, HIDDEN, CENTER, TITLE, VPORTS, and NOTES
In the Layer Names *list box, click on the layer* DIMS	Highlights the layer DIMS
Choose the **S**et Color *button, click on the color blue, and then choose* OK	Assigns the color blue to the layer DIMS and returns to the Layer Control dialog box
Click on the layer DIMS	Deselects the layer DIMS
Click on the layer HIDDEN, *choose the* **S**et Color *button, select the color green, and then choose* OK	Highlights the layer HIDDEN and assigns the color green to the layer
Click on the Set **L**type *button*	Displays the Select Linetype dialog box
Choose L**o**ad	Displays the Load or Reload Linetype dialog box
From the Available Linetypes *list box, choose* CENTER *and* HIDDEN, *then choose* OK	Loads the CENTER and HIDDEN linetypes and returns to the Select Linetype dialog box

continues

continued

Select the linetype HIDDEN, *then* *choose* OK	Assigns the linetype HIDDEN to the layer HIDDEN
Click on the layer HIDDEN	Deselects the layer HIDDEN
Click on the layers CENTER *and* VPORTS, *choose the* **S**et Color *button, click on the color yellow, and then choose* OK	Highlights the layers CENTER and VPORTS and assigns the color yellow to the layers
Click on the layer VPORTS	Deselects the layer VPORTS but leaves the layer CENTER highlighted
Click on the Set **L**type *button, select the linetype* CENTER, *then choose* OK	Assigns the linetype center to the layer CENTER
Click on the layer CENTER	Deselects the layer CENTER
Click on the layer TITLE, *choose the* **S**et Color *button, click on the color red, and then choose* OK	Highlights the layer TITLE and assigns the color red to the layer
Choose the OK *button*	Exits the Layer Control dialog box
Command: *Choose Layer Control (Object Properties)*	Displays all the layers in a drop-down list
Click on the layer OBJECT	Sets the layer OBJECT as the current layer
Command: *Choose Zoom All (Standard Toolbar)*	Zooms to the drawing limits
Command: *Choose Save (Standard Toolbar)*	Saves the drawing MET-PRO

Now your prototype drawing is ready and should resemble figure 4.1. The following instructs you how to create a new drawing using the drawing MET-PRO as the prototype drawing.

Command: *Choose New (Standard Toolbar)*	Issues the NEW command
Choose the **P**rototype *button, change to the* \AB *directory, select the drawing* MET-PRO, *and choose* OK	Changes the prototype drawing to the MET-PRO drawing
In the New **D**rawing Name *text box, type* CHAP4, *and choose* OK	Enters a name for the new drawing based on the MET-PRO prototype drawing

A new drawing CHAP4 with the same settings as MET-PRO is now created.

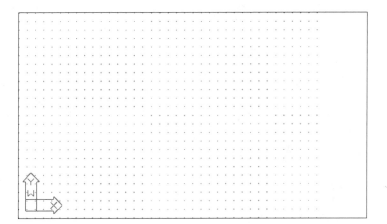

Figure 4.1

The MECH-PRO prototype drawing.

The AutoCAD Environment

AutoCAD Release 13's drawing environment is a powerful tool for drawing your designs. Part of that power comes from the drawing environment's capability to be flexible. The drawing environment is an infinitely large space that enables you to draw extremely large designs as well as extremely small designs, and you can display and use measurements and angles of several types.

The AutoCAD Coordinate System

AutoCAD's drawing environment uses a three-dimensional Cartesian coordinate system. This coordinate system is referred to as the *World Coordinate System* (WCS). This system has three perpendicular axes: the X, Y, and Z axes. By default, the X axis is horizontal and the Y axis is vertical on your display. The Z axis is perpendicular to the X and Y axes, extending into and out of the display. Figure 4.2 shows the orientation of the axes relative to your screen display. The UCS icon at the lower left corner of the drawing area shows the orientation of the axes.

The X, Y, and Z axes intersect at a point called the *origin*. When you specify a point, AutoCAD reads the point as a set of numbers in the form X,Y,Z. These numbers (called *coordinates*) represent the distance from the origin along the X, Y, and Z axes. The origin has the coordinate value of (0,0). For 2D drawings, the Z value typically is ignored and AutoCAD automatically assigns it a value of 0.

Figure 4.2

The orientation of the X, Y, and Z axes relative to the screen.

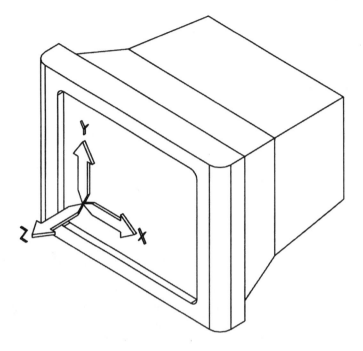

The X coordinate values increase as you move to the right of the origin and decrease as you move to the left. The Y coordinate values increase as you move up from the origin and decrease as you move down. If a point is located at (6,4), for example, the point is 6 units from the origin in the positive X axis direction and 4 units from the origin in the positive Y axis direction (see fig. 4.3).

The coordinate display in the status bar shows you the current X,Y coordinate location of your cursor. By default, the origin is located in the lower left corner of the drawing area. If you move the cursor to the lower left corner of the drawing area, you can see the coordinates get closer to 0,0.

Most objects in AutoCAD are defined by their coordinates. A line is defined by two coordinates, for example, its starting point and its ending point.

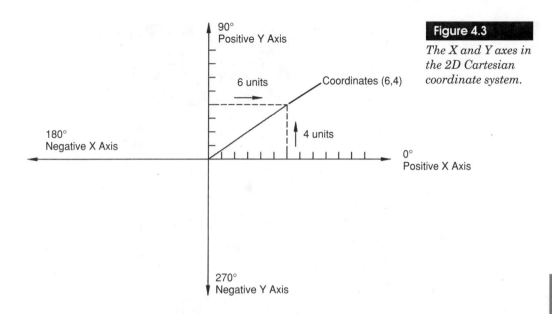

Figure 4.3

The X and Y axes in the 2D Cartesian coordinate system.

Setting the Working Units

By default, AutoCAD displays distances and angles in a decimal format. You can, however, control how these values are displayed. You might want to display distances in feet and inches, for example, or perhaps you want to show angles in radians. You can change these settings with the DDUNITS command.

'DDUNITS. The DDUNITS command enables you to control how distances and angles are displayed. You also can control the precision of how these values are displayed.

Pull-down: *Choose **D**ata, Uni**t**s*
Screen: *Choose DATA, Units:*

The Units Control dialog box (see fig. 4.4) enables you to choose how AutoCAD displays distances and angles. You can choose the format of the values and how precise you want values to be shown. The Units Control dialog box is divided into two areas: Units and Angles.

Figure 4.4

The Units Control dialog box.

Linear Units

The Units area controls how linear units such as coordinates and distances are displayed. The following options are available:

- **Scientific.** Displays values in terms of 1×10^n. The values 15.50 and .0025, for example, are displayed as 1.5500E1 and 2.500E-03, respectively.

- **Decimal.** This is the default option. Values are shown in the form 15.5000 and .0025.

- **Engineering.** Units are displayed in feet and decimal inches. The values 15.5 and .0025, for example, are displayed as 1'–3.5000" and 0'–0.0025".

- **Architectural.** Displays feet and fractional inches. The distance 15.50 feet, for example, is displayed as 1'–3 1/2".

- **Fractional.** Similar to the Decimal option, but displays fractions. The value 15.50 is displayed as 15–1/2.

The **P**recision drop-down list enables you to control the precision of the values displayed. With units set to decimal and the precision set to two decimal places, for example, the number 1.3125 is displayed as 1.31.

The units precision only controls the way the number is displayed, *not* the way it is stored. AutoCAD stores values in a decimal format to more than 10 places of accuracy, but displays values according to the units and precision settings.

Angular Measurements

Angles also can be displayed in different formats. The Angles area of the Units Control dialog box enables you to control how angles are displayed. The following options are available:

- **Decimal Degrees.** This option displays angles as decimal degrees. 360 degrees comprise an entire circle. Decimal degrees, for example, have the form 33.6647° or 22.9788°.

- **Deg/Min/Sec.** This option displays angles as degrees, minutes, and seconds. Parts of a degree are divided into minutes and seconds. Sixty seconds equal one minute, and 60 minutes equal one degree. Angles are displayed in the form 38°43'50" and 58°24'40".

- **Grads.** This option displays angles as grads. Four hundred grads comprise an entire circle. Angles in grads have the form 332.889.

- **Radians.** This option displays angles in the form of radians. One hundred and eighty degrees equal pi (3.14159265359) radians.

- **Surveyor.** This option displays angles in surveyor angles. Angles are measured from the north-south line. The North, South, East, and West directions represent the 90–, 270–, 0–, and 180– angles. To specify angles in this format, a line with a direction of 37°26'23" is shown as N37°26'23"E. This stands for north 37 degrees, 26 minutes, 23 seconds east.

By default, 0° is to the right, along the same direction as the X axis (see fig. 4.5). Positive angles are measured in the counter-clockwise direction. The **D**irection button enables you to change the direction for 0° as well as the direction in which angles are measured.

The following exercise walks you through the process of setting the drawing's units. In the following exercise, you begin to set up an architectural drawing by setting the units to display feet and inches.

4

How angles are measured in AutoCAD.

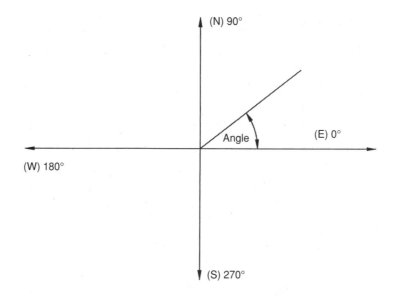

Setting Up Your Drawing To Use Feet and Inches

To begin this exercise, you create a new drawing called ARCH-PRO.

Command: *Choose New (Standard Toolbar)*	Issues the NEW command
In the New Drawing Name *edit box, type* **ARCH-PRO** *and choose* OK	Creates a new drawing named ARCH-PRO
Command: *Choose* **D**ata, *then* Un**i**ts	Issues the DDUNITS command
In the Units *area click on the* **A**rchitectural *radio button*	Sets up the drawing to use Architectural units
In the Angles *area, choose* 0.0 *from the* **P**recision *drop-down list*	Sets the drawing precision to display angles rounded to one decimal place
Choose OK	Closes dialog box and returns you to the drawing editor with the new settings

Move your cursor and look at the coordinate display in the status bar. Notice that the coordinates are displayed as feet-inches rounded to the nearest 1/16".

Command: *Choose Save (Standard Toolbar)*	Saves the drawing

Drawing Full Scale

With a paper drawing, you begin with a fixed size of paper and draw at a particular scale factor so that the drawing fits on the paper. This involves either shrinking or enlarging every dimension on the drawing. A 24' wall drawn at 1/4"=1', for example, actually is 6" long on the paper.

Because the AutoCAD drawing environment is unlimited in size, you can draw your designs at their actual (full) size. A 24' wall is drawn 24' long. You can control the size of the drawing on the screen by either zooming in (moving closer) or zooming out (moving farther away) from the model. Chapter 6, "Controlling What You See," covers the details of displaying your drawing on the screen. The time most likely will come, however, when you need to get your drawing out of the computer and onto a sheet of paper.

Model Space and Paper Space

AutoCAD actually has two drawing environments, model space and paper space. Model space is where you draw your design in its real world size. You create your 2D or 3D model in model space. So far, you have been working in model space.

Paper space is where you lay out views of your model to be plotted. Paper space can be thought of as a piece of paper on which you place your title block, add any general notes, and arrange the various views of your model. Each view can be assigned a scale at which it will be plotted.

You can switch between model space and paper space by double-clicking on the TILE button in the status bar. You can tell you are in paper space by looking at the UCS icon in the lower left part of the drawing area. The UCS icon resembles the corner of a sheet of paper. Figure 4.6 shows both the model space and paper space UCS icons.

4

Model Space

Paper Space

Figure 4.6

The model space and paper space UCS icons.

System variables are settings that control various aspects of the AutoCAD environment. For a complete list of the AutoCAD system Variables, see the AutoCAD System Variable table in Appendix E, "AutoCAD Systems Variables Table."

Using both model space and paper space has many advantages. For starters, it gives you the ability to draw most things full size. You don't have to scale objects as you draw them. Second, it gives you the ability to create multiple views of your drawings without duplicating your original model. This can be a great time saver because when you make changes to your model, all of the views of that model update automatically. Figures 4.7 and 4.8 show you a model created in model space and that same model plotted in paper space.

Figure 4.7

A plot sheet using only model space.

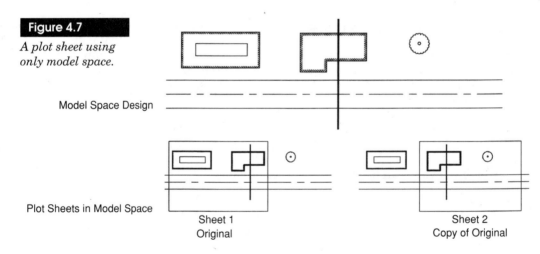

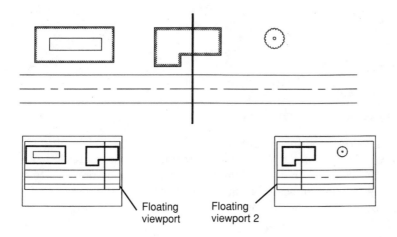

Figure 4.8

A plot sheet using both model space and paper space.

Floating
viewport

Floating
viewport 2

Determining the Plot Scale Factor

In manual drafting, not all of the objects in the drawing were drawn to scale. Things such as text, dimensions, and symbols all are drawn full size. If you want your text to be 1/8" tall, you draw it that tall.

In AutoCAD, this process is reversed. Because your model is drawn full scale, objects such as text, dimensions, and symbols must be scaled so that they appear correctly on the plotted paper. This is known as the *plot scale factor*.

The plot scale factor is found the same way in AutoCAD as it is in manual drafting. AutoCAD just uses the scale factor differently. You convert the scale factor used in manual drafting to the plot scale factor used in AutoCAD. The plot scale factor can be found by converting the drawing scale to a ratio of 1:n, where n is your plot scale factor.

You start work on the floor plan of a building, for example, and you want to plot it at the scale 1/4"=1'. The scale of 1/4"=1'-0" converts into a plot scale factor of 48. The math looks like this:

1/4":1-0' converts to 1/4":12".

Multiply both sides by 4 to convert it to 1":48" or 1:48.

The plot scale factor is 48.

After you determine the plot scale factor for a drawing, you can use it to calculate the size of various objects in the drawing. The following is a list of some of the settings that the plot scale factor affects in AutoCAD:

4

- Text height
- Symbol sizes
- Linetype scale
- Dimension scale
- Display scale in floating viewports

The plot scale is referred to throughout the rest of the book. Chapter 11, "Text," shows you how to use the plot scale factor to calculate text size. Chapter 13, "Blocks and Overlays," deals with finding the appropriate size for symbols using the plot scale factor. In Chapter 16, "Composing and Plotting a Drawing," you learn how to set the plot scale in a floating viewport to plot in paper space.

Using Drawing Limits

Although the size of the model space and paper space environments is unlimited, setting limits on the areas in which you are going to draw helps you better manage your drawing. You can set the drawing limits with the LIMITS command.

LIMITS. The LIMITS command defines the drawing area by specifying its lower left and upper right coordinates.
Pull-down: *Choose* **D**ata, Dr**a**wing Limits
Screen: *Choose* Data, Limits

The LIMITS command has four options. The following list shows these options and what they affect:

- **ON.** This option turns on limits checking. If you draw outside your limits, AutoCAD notifies you.

- **OFF.** This option turns off limits checking. AutoCAD does not tell you when you draw outside your limits.

- **Lower left corner.** This option sets the lower left coordinate of your limits. (The default is 0,0.)

- **Upper right corner.** This option sets the upper right coordinate of your limits. (The default is 12,9.)

Because model space and paper space are two separate environments, they have separate limits. In paper space, your drawing limits are the size of the paper on which you are plotting. If you are plotting to a 24"×36" sheet of paper, you would set the lower left corner to 0,0 and the upper right corner to 36,24. This would create a 36"×24" drawing area.

In model space, your drawing limits should be set so that the drawing area is larger than the overall size of your model. An easy way to determine the model space limits is to multiply your paper size by the plot scale factor. For the 100'×75' floor plan, for example, you have the following information:

Floor plan dimensions:	100'×75'
Scale:	1/4"=12"
Plot scale factor:	48
Paper size:	36"×24"

To determine the model space limits, multiply the paper size by the plot scale factor:

36"×48 = 1,728" or 144'

24"×48 = 1,152" or 96'

Setting your model space limits to 0,0 and 144'×96' would ensure your model would fit inside the drawing limits.

Fortunately, AutoCAD automates the setting of model space limits with the MVSETUP command.

4

MVSETUP. The MVSETUP command automates the process of setting the drawing units and the model space limits. When run in paper space, it includes options for creating title blocks, creating and aligning floating viewports, and assigning a plot scale to floating viewports. The pull-down menu option only can be selected while in paper space. In model space, you must type the command.
Pull-down: *Choose* **V**iew, Floatin**g** Viewports, MV **S**etup

---

When you first start MVSETUP, AutoCAD gives you the prompt Enable paper space? (No/<Yes>):. If you answer No, AutoCAD prompts you for the type of units you want to use, the plot scale, and the length and width of your paper. AutoCAD then computes and sets the model space limits, and sets the specified units.

If you answer Yes to the prompt, AutoCAD switches to paper space and presents you with a number of options to help you prepare your drawing for plotting. See Chapter 16, "Composing and Plotting a Drawing," for more information on using MVSETUP in paper space.

The following exercise sets the model space and paper space limits for an architectural floor plan to be plotted at a scale of 1/8"=1'-0" on a 36"×24" sheet of paper.

Setting Limits for an Architectural Drawing Sheet

Continue from the previous exercise.

Command: **MVSETUP** (Enter)	Starts MVSETUP command
Enable paper space? (No/<Yes>): **N** (Enter)	Lets you set up model space
Units type (Scientific/Decimal/ Engineering/Architectural/Metric): **A** (Enter)	Selects the Architectural units

```
Architectural Scales
====================
 (480)  1/40"=1'
 (240)  1/20"=1'
 (192)  1/16"=1'
  (96)  1/8"=1'
  (48)  1/4"=1'
  (24)  1/2"=1'
  (16)  3/4"=1'
  (12)  1"=1'
   (4)  3"=1'
   (2)  6"=1'
   (1)  FULL
```

Enter the scale factor: **96** (Enter)	Selects the scale 1/8"=1, which is a plot scale factor of 96
Enter the paper width: **36** (Enter)	Sets the paper width to 36"
Enter the paper height: **24** (Enter)	Sets the paper height to 24"
Command: *Double-click on the* TILE *button*	Switches to paper space

```
New value for TILEMODE <1>: 0
Entering Paper space. Use MVIEW to
insert Model space viewports.
Regenerating drawing.
```

Command: *Choose* **D**ata, Dr**a**wing Limits	Issues LIMITS command

```
Reset Paper space limits: ON/OFF/
<Lower left corner> <0'-0",0'-0">:
```
(Enter)

Keeps the default lower right limit at coordinates 0,0.

```
Upper right corner <1'-0",0'-9">:
```
36,24 (Enter)

Sets the upper left corner at coordinates 36,24 for the paper size 24×36

Command: *Choose Zoom All (Standard Toolbar)* — Zooms to the drawing limits.

```
All/Center/Dynamic/Extents/Left/Previous/
Vmax/Window/<Scale(X/XP)>: _all
Regenerating drawing.
```

Command: *Double-click the* TILE *button* — Returns to model space

```
New value for TILEMODE <0>: 1
Regenerating drawing.
```

Command: *Choose Save (Standard Toolbar)* — Saves the drawing

4

Using Snap, Grid, and Ortho

In Chapter 3, "A Quick Drawing," you gave AutoCAD the coordinates of a line's endpoints by entering the coordinate values. You also can locate points accurately by using the pointing device. AutoCAD provides a number of drawing aids to help you locate and select points. Among these drawing aids are the snap, grid, and ortho settings.

You can control these drawing aids with the DDRMODES command.

'DDRMODES. The DDRMODES command displays the Drawing Aids dialog box. This dialog box controls the snap, grid and ortho settings as well as a number of other drawing aids.
Pull-down: *Choose* **O**ptions, **D**rawing Aids
Screen: *Choose* OPTIONS, DDrmodes

The DDRMODES command displays the Drawing Aids dialog box, as shown in figure 4.9.

Figure 4.9

The Drawing Aids dialog box.

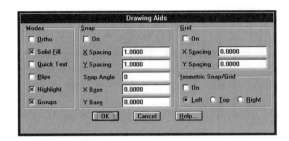

Setting Up Snap Points

You already have seen that the coordinate display on the status bar shows you the location of your cursor in the drawing area. While this is useful, it is not very accurate. It's difficult to get the cursor to stop on a specific coordinate. Also, depending on the units' precision, AutoCAD rounds the coordinate display values so that the point displayed in the coordinate display is not the exact location of the cursor.

The Snap area of the Drawing Aids dialog box enables you to control the cursor by restricting its movement to the snap increments. If you set the snap spacing to .25, for example, your cursor only rests on coordinates that are multiples of .25.

TIP

You can press Ctrl+B or F9, or double-click the SNAP button on the status bar to turn the snap on or off. These are transparent commands and can be done in the middle of another command.

When you use a snap spacing, the pointing device moves in a jerky motion. This is because the pointing device jumps from one snap point to another. In the following exercise, you set up your snap spacing to make it easy to choose points.

Using Snap Points To Draw Objects

Continue from the previous exercise. Move the cursor around and watch the coordinate display. Notice that the cursor moves smoothly around the drawing and that the coordinates display is rounded to the nearest 1/16".

Command: *Choose* **O***ptions, then* **D***rawing Aids*	Displays the Drawing Aids dialog box
In the **S***nap area, place an* X *in the* On *check box*	Turns the snap on
Press Tab, then type `1'` *in the* **X** Spacing *text box*	Sets snap X spacing to 1'
Click in **Y** Spacing *text box*	The Y Spacing is automatically set to equal the X spacing
Click on the OK *button*	Returns you to the drawing editor with the snap on

Notice that when you move the cursor, the cursor is more jerky. Look at the status bar's coordinate display. When you move the cursor around, only coordinates to the nearest 1' are shown. Using the cursor and snap, you can pick points accurately.

Command: *Choose Line (Draw, Line)*	Issues LINE command
`_line From point:` *Using the pointing device, pick the point* `8'-0", 8'-0"`	Starts a line at coordinates 8'–0",8'–0"
`To point:` *Pick the point* `280'-0",8'-0"`	Draws a line to coordinates 136'–0",8'–0"
`To point:` *Pick the point* `280'-0",184'-0"`	Draws a line to coordinates 136'–0",80'–0"
`To point:` *Pick the point* `184'-0",8'-0"`	Draws a line to coordinates 80'–0",8'–0"
`To point:` *Pick the point* `8'-0",8'-0"`	Draws a line back to the starting point
`To point:` (Enter)	Exits the LINE command
Command: *On the status bar, double-click on the* SNAP *button*	Turns off the snap spacing; this button is useful for turning on and off the snap spacing quickly
Command: *On the status bar, double-click on the* SNAP *button*	Turns on the snap spacing back
Command: *Choose Save (Standard Toolbar)*	Saves the drawing

Your drawing now should resemble figure 4.10.

4

Figure 4.10

Drawing with snap.

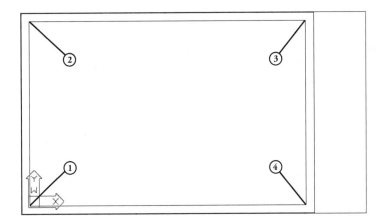

Using GRID

While you can use the coordinate display and snap to locate points on the screen, a grid often is more useful because it provides a visual reference on the drawing. The grid is a rectangular array of dots on the screen, similar to the horizontal and vertical lines on graph paper. It provides a visual indicator of distance and coordinates in your drawing. The Grid area of the Drawing Aids dialog box enables you to turn the grid on and off, as well as enabling you to set the grid spacing along the X and Y axes.

TIP

> You can press Ctrl+G or F7, or double-click the GRID button on the status bar to turn the grid on or off. These are transparent commands and can be done in the middle of another command.

In the following exercise, you will specify a grid spacing to set up the grid.

Setting Up and Using the Grid

Continue from the previous exercise.

Command: *Choose* **O**ptions, *then* **D**rawing Aids	Displays the Drawing Aids dialog box
In the **G**rid *area, place an* X *in the* On *check box*	Turns on the grid

Press Tab, then type **5'** *in the* X Sp**a**cing *box* ⏎(Enter)	Sets the grid's X spacing to 5', the Y spacing is updated automatically
Choose OK	Returns you to the drawing editor with the grid on
Command: *On the status bar, double-click on* GRID *button*	Turns off the GRID; this button is useful for turning on and off the GRID quickly
Command: *On the status bar, double-click on the* GRID *button*	Turns on the GRID again
Command: *Choose Save (Standard Toolbar)*	Saves the drawing

Your drawing now should resemble figure 4.11.

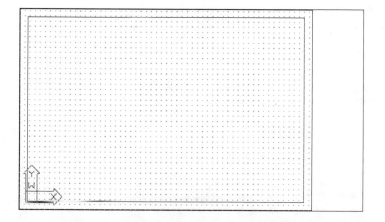

Figure 4.11

The AutoCAD grid.

4

Drawing Straight Lines with Ortho

The Ortho setting (which stands for "orthogonal") in the Drawing Aids dialog box limits the cursor to horizontal or vertical movement when drawing or editing objects. When ortho is turned on, for example, any lines you draw are parallel to either the X or Y axis.

> You can press Ctrl+L or F8, or double-click the ORTHO button on the status bar to turn ortho mode on or off. These are transparent commands and can be done in the middle of another command.

The following exercise shows you how to turn ortho on and how to draw lines with ortho.

Using Ortho To Draw Objects

Continue from the previous exercise.

`Command:` *Choose Line (Draw, Line)*	Issues the LINE command.
`From point:` **130',120'** (Enter)	Starts a line from ① (see fig. 4.12)
On the status bar, double-click on the ORTHO *button*	Turns on ortho

Move the cursor around and notice how the cursor can only move in a horizontal or vertical direction.

`To point:` *Press Esc*	Cancels the LINE command

Figure 4.12

Drawing with ortho.

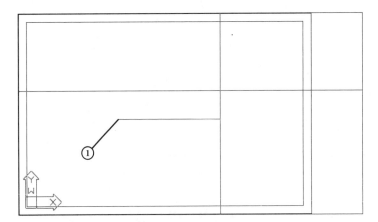

Layers, Colors, and Linetypes

Every object in a drawing has three object properties: layer, color, and linetype. In previous chapters, you used the default object properties— black on a white background (or white on a dark background), continuous linetype, and layer 0. In this section, you learn how to use layers, colors, and linetypes to enhance your drawings, make them more readable, and make it easier for you to locate information.

Using Drawing Layers

You might have used a manual drafting technique called *overlay drafting*, in which you use multiple sheets to draw different parts of a drawing and *overlay* the sheets for reference or to print a composite drawing.

AutoCAD's layers are somewhat similar in concept, as illustrated in figure 4.13. They enable you to separate different parts of the drawing. A layer in an AutoCAD drawing is not a physical thing—it is a property that is assigned to each entity in your drawing. AutoCAD uses this property to sort entities for various purposes.

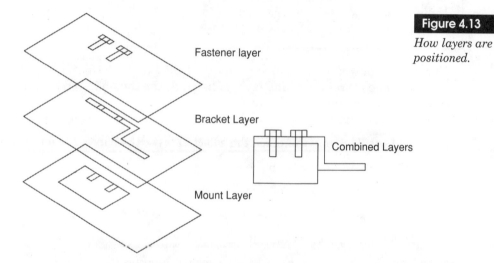

Fastener layer

Bracket Layer

Combined Layers

Mount Layer

Figure 4.13

How layers are positioned.

4

What benefit do you derive from using layers? Many objects you draw easily can be organized into layers; printed circuit boards have different layers of conductive patterns, and other objects can be broken up in a similar fashion. Architectural drawings for buildings might have different drawings for different floors or trades (electrical, plumbing, and so on). Layers give you a way to separate some data from other data on the same drawing. You can, for example, place a site plan on one layer, a floor plan on another, services on another, the roof plan on another, and so on. Layers also are used to differentiate and group entities by visibility, linetype, and color. Colors can be mapped to plotter pens, which enable you to control line weights in a plot.

AutoCAD automatically creates a single layer when you begin a new drawing. The layer is given the name 0. Layer 0 uses the CONTINUOUS linetype and the color white by default (more about color and linetype shortly). You can create as many additional layers as you need, assigning each one a unique name as you create it. Anything you draw is assigned to the current, or active, layer.

'DDLMODES. The DDLMODES (Dynamic Dialogue Layer modes) command displays the Layer Control dialog box, which enables you to create new layers, rename layers, and modify layer properties (linetype and color), visibility (on/off and freeze/thaw), and status.
Toolbar: *Choose Layers (Object Properties)*
Pull-down: *Choose **D**ata, **L**ayers*
Screen: *Choose **D**ata, DDlmode*

The Layer Control dialog box contains all of the layer information in the drawing. The current drawing layer is listed at the top, followed by a list of the layers currently defined in the drawing and their current status (see fig. 4.14). The Layer Control dialog box has the following options:

- **Current.** This option makes the selected layer the current layer.

- **On.** This option turns on the selected layer(s).

- **Off.** This option turns off the selected layers(s).

- **Freeze.** This option freezes the selected layer(s).

- **Thaw.** This option thaws the selected layer(s).

- **Unlock.** This option unlocks the selected layer(s).

- **Lock.** This option turns on the selected layer(s).

- **Cur VP Thw.** Use Cur VP Thw to thaw the selected layer(s) in the current mview viewport.

- **Cur VP Frz.** This option freezes the selected layer(s) in the current mview viewport.

- **New VP Thw.** This option thaws the selected layer(s) for all new viewport entities.

- **New VP Frz.** This option freezes the selected layer(s) for all new viewport entities.

- **Set Color...** This option opens a Select Color dialog box to assign a color to the selected layer(s).

- **Set Ltype...** This option opens a Select Linetype dialog box to assign a linetype to the selected layer(s). You can select a previously loaded linetype or load a linetype from a linetype definition file.

- **Filters Set...** This option displays the Set Layer Filters dialog box.

- **Filters On.** This option turns on layer name list filters.

- **Rename.** Use this option to rename the selected layer. The selected layer is assigned the name in edit box.

- **New.** Use New to make AutoCAD accept a typed layer name as a new layer. You can create multiple layers by typing their name followed by a comma (,). Typing **OBJECTS,CENTER,HIDDEN** and then choosing New, for example, would create three new layers.

- **Select All.** This option selects all layers for applying attributes.

- **Clear All.** This option deselects all layers.

Figure 4.14

The Layer Control dialog box.

4

In the following exercise, you will create a set of layers for your drawing and set one layer as the current layer.

Creating New Layers and Selecting the Current Layer

Continue from the previous exercise.

Command: *Choose Layers (Object Properties)*	Issues DDLMODES command and displays Layer Control dialog box
Type **DIMS,DOOR,FURN,WALL,NOTE,SHBD GRID**, *and then choose the* New *button*	Creates the new layers DIMS, DOOR, FURN, WALL, NOTE, SHBD, and GRID all at once
Click on the layer WALL	Highlights the layer WALL

continues

continued

Choose the **C**urrent *button*	Sets the layer WALL as the current layer
Click on the layer WALL	Deselects the layer WALL

You now have a new set of layers to work with in your drawing.

Setting the Layer's Color

When you create, or define, a new layer, AutoCAD assigns it the color White and the linetype CONTINUOUS. You can change layer colors and linetypes at any time with the COLOR button in the Layer Control dialog box, as shown in figure 4.15. Assigning different colors makes it easier to keep track of entity layer assignments while you are drawing, and it enables you to either plot in color or plot with pens of different widths.

Figure 4.15

The Select Color dialog box.

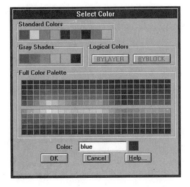

AutoCAD has (depending on your video display) 256 colors available to it. The first seven colors are known as the basic colors and can be specified by their color number or name. The colors after these seven do not have names and are referred to only by their numbers.

Table 4.1 shows the basic colors that AutoCAD Release 13 provides.

Table 4.1
The Basic Colors

Color	Name
1	Red
2	Yellow

Color	Name
3	Green
4	Cyan
5	Blue
6	Magenta
7	White

Before you use color in your drawing, you should think about how you want the various layers to be plotted. When plotting, AutoCAD can map pen numbers and line weights to object colors. The color red, for example, can be assigned a pen with a .35mm line weight. See Chapter 16, "Composing and Plotting a Drawing," for more on plotting.

Setting the Layer's Linetype

In the previous exercises, the layers you created used the linetype CONTINUOUS by default. In drafting, various linetypes have different meanings in a drawing. A center linetype, for example, can be used to represent the centerline of a road. The hidden linetype is used for objects in drawings that are hidden from view.

AutoCAD gives you the ability to create and assign linetypes to a layer. Any objects drawn on that layer are shown with that linetype. Choosing the Set **L**type button in the Layer Control dialog box displays the Select Linetype dialog box (see fig. 4.16), from which you can assign linetypes to the selected layer(s).

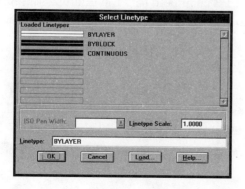

Figure 4.16

The Select Linetype dialog box.

AutoCAD comes with a number of predefined linetypes, which are stored in the ACAD.LIN file. Linetypes are loaded into the drawing as they are needed, using the **L**oad button in the Select Linetype dialog box. The L**o**ad button displays the Load or Reload Linetypes dialog box as shown in figure 4.17. Select the linetypes you wish to load and choose OK.

Controlling Linetype Spacing

Linetypes other than CONTINUOUS are defined by the dash/dot spacing. You can control this spacing somewhat by choosing the *name2* or the *nameX2* linetype variations. The linetype HIDDEN2, for example, has dashes that are half as large as the HIDDEN linetype. When plotting at a scale smaller than .5 or greater than 2, however, the linetype spacing does not look right.

Just as you scale symbols and text, you need to scale linetypes. You do this with the LTSCALE command.

> **'LTSCALE.** The LTSCALE command sets the linetype scaling factor for dash/dot linetypes. The LTSCALE typically is set to 1/3 to 1/2 the plot scale.
> Pull-down: *Choose* **O**ptions, **L**inetypes, **G**lobal Linetype Scale

Typically, the LTSCALE is set to roughly 1/2 the plot scale. If you were plotting a drawing at a scale of 1:50, for example, setting the LTSCALE variable to roughly 25 produces linetypes of adequate spacing.

In the following exercise, you will assign colors and linetypes to the layers you created.

Assigning Colors and Linetypes to Layers

Continue from the previous exercise. The Layer Control dialog box should still be displayed on the computer screen.

Click on the DIMS *and* NOTE *layers*	Selects the layers DIMS and NOTE
Choose the **S**et Color *button*	Displays the Select Color dialog box
Click on the color green, then choose the OK *button*	Assigns the color green to the layers DIMS and NOTE
Choose Clea**r** All	Deselects the layers DIMS and NOTE
Click on the DOOR *and* GRID *layers*	Selects the layers DOOR and GRID
Choose the **S**et Color *button*	Displays the Select Color dialog box
Click on the color blue, then choose the OK *button*	Assigns the color blue to the selected layers
Choose Clea**r** All	Deselects the layers
Click on the SHBD *and* WALL *layers*	Highlights the layers SHBD and WALL
Choose the **S**et Color *button*	Displays the Select Color dialog box
Click on the color red, then choose the OK *button*	Assigns the color red to the layers SHBD and WALL
Choose Clea**r** All	Deselects the layers
Click on the FURN *layer*	Highlights the FURN layer
Click on the **S**et Color *button*	Displays the Select Color dialog box
Click on the color magenta, then choose the OK *button*	Assigns the color magenta to the layer FURN
Choose Clea**r** All	Deselects the layer

Now your layer colors are all set up. The next steps show you how to assign a linetype to a layer.

Click on the GRID *layer*	Highlights the layer GRID
Choose the Set **L**type *button*	Displays the Select Linetype dialog box
Choose the L**o**ad *button*	Displays the Load or Reload Linetypes dialog box
In the Available linetypes *area, select the linetype* CENTER *and choose the* OK *button*	Loads the linetype CENTER into the drawing

continues

continued

In the Select Linetype *dialog box, select the* CENTER *linetype and choose the* OK *button*	Assigns the linetype CENTER to the layer GRID
Choose the OK *button*	Exits the Layer Control dialog box and returns to the drawing editor

Now draw a rectangle on the current layer WALL.

Command: *Choose Rectangle (Draw, Polygon)*	Issues the RECTANG command
First corner: **20',20'** (Enter)	Sets the lower left corner of rectangle at ①
Other corner: **120',95'** (Enter)	Sets the upper right corner of rectangle at ②
Command: *Choose Layer Control (Object Properties)*	Displays Layer Control drop list
Click on the GRID *layer*	Sets the GRID layer as the current layer
Command: *Choose Line (Draw, Line)*	Issues LINE command
_line From point: **5',40'** (Enter)	Sets a starting point for the line at ③
To point: **125',40'** (Enter)	Sets an ending point for the line at ④
To point: (Enter)	Exits the LINE command
Command: (Enter)	Repeats the LINE command
LINE From point: **5',70'** (Enter)	Sets a starting point for the line at ⑤
To point: **125',70'** (Enter)	Sets an ending point for the line at ⑥
To point: (Enter)	Exits the LINE command
Command: (Enter)	Repeats the LINE command
From point: **45',15'** (Enter)	Sets a starting point for the line at ⑦
To point: **45',100'** (Enter)	Sets an ending point for the line at ⑧
To point: (Enter)	Exits the LINE command
Command: (Enter)	Repeats the LINE command
From point: **65',15'** (Enter)	Sets a starting point for the line at ⑨
To point: **65',100'** (Enter)	Sets an ending point for the line at ⑩

To point: (Enter)	Exits the LINE command
Command: *Choose* **O**ptions, **L**inetypes, **G**lobal Linetype Scale	Issues the LTSCALE command
New scale factor <1.0000>: **48** (Enter)	Sets the linetype scale to 48 and regenerates the drawing.
Command: *Choose Save (Standard Toolbar)*	Saves the drawing

Your drawing now should resemble figure 4.18.

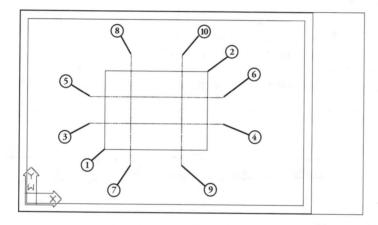

The building shell.

Your layers now are set up and ready to be used. You can select the layer you want to draw on by using the **C**urrent button in the Layer Control dialog box, or by selecting the layer from the Layer Control drop-down list in the Object Properties toolbar. The Layer Control drop-down list lists all of the layers defined in the drawing as well as their current state. You can change the state of the layer by double-clicking on the icon.

Controlling Layer Visibility

Because drawings can be quite complex, sometimes you will want to work on an aspect of your design instead of the whole design. If parts of your design reside on separate layers, you can use layers to hide what you are not working on. When you are done, you can make those layers visible again.

Layers can be suppressed in two ways; they can be *frozen* or turned *off*. You can use the Freeze/Thaw and the On/Off buttons in the Layer Control dialog box, or the On/Off (open/closed eyes) and Freeze/Thaw (snowflake/ sun) icons in the Layer Control drop-down list to control layer visibility. Freezing a layer and turning off a layer both cause the objects on the layers disappear from view, and both options suppress redrawing and replotting. AutoCAD does, however, regenerate layers that are turned off, but not those that are frozen. In general, you should freeze layers you do not need to display so you can speed up display times.

Locking Layers

The Lo**ck** button in the Layer Control dialog box sets a specified layer as a *locked* layer. The objects on the layer cannot be edited or changed, but the layer still is visible. If you try to select an object on a locked layer, AutoCAD ignores the object. You also can lock and unlock layers in the Layer Control drop-down list by double-clicking on the Lock/Unlock icon.

In the following exercise, you experiment with freezing, thawing, and locking layers.

Setting a Layer's Visibility

Continue from the previous exercise.

Command: *Choose Layer Control (Object Properties)*	Displays Layer drop list
Click on the DOOR layer	Sets the DOOR layer as the current layer
Command: *Choose Layer Control (Object Properties)*	Displays Layer drop list
On the GRID layer, choose the Freeze / Thaw icon	Freezes the GRID layer
On the WALL layer, choose the Lock / Unlock icon and press (Enter)	Locks the WALL layer
Command: *Choose Erase (Modify, Erase)*	Issues ERASE command
Select objects: *Pick* ① *(see fig. 4.19)*	Selects the rectangle on WALL layer to erase
1 was on a locked layer. Select objects: (Enter)	Rectangle could not be erased; exits the ERASE command

Command: *Choose Layer Control (Object Properties)*	Displays Layer drop list
On the WALL layer, choose the Lock / Unlock icon and press (Enter)	Unlocks the WALL layer
Command: *Choose Save (Standard Toolbar)*	Saves the drawing

The layer GRID is left as frozen, so the grid lines you drew are no longer visible, as shown in figure 4.19.

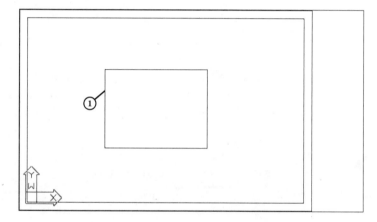

Figure 4.19

Freezing layer GRID.

Exploring Object Properties

When you draw an object, AutoCAD assigns it three properties: layer, color, and linetype. These properties are part of the objects definition. The property assignments are determined by the current layer, color, and linetype settings.

Using Color and Linetype

The color and linetype settings are set to BYLAYER by default. BYLAYER means that an objects assumes the color and linetype of its assigned layer. In the previous exercise, for example, you drew a line on layer GRID and it appeared yellow and had a CENTER linetype. Yellow and CENTER are the color and linetype of layer GRID. You can override the layer color and linetype settings by assigning an *explicit* object color and linetype. This is done with the DDEMODES command.

> **'DDEMODES.** The DDEMODES command displays the Object
> Creation Modes dialog box, which enables you to set the current
> object properties such as layer, color, linetype, text style, and
> linetype scale.
> Toolbar: *Choose Object Creation (Object Properties)*
> Pull-down: *Choose **D**ata, **O**bject Creation*
> Screen: *Choose Data, DDemode*

The DDEMODES command displays the Object Creation Modes dialog
box, as shown in figure 4.20. The DDEMODES command has the following
options:

- **Color.** This option sets the default color for all new objects. Any new
  objects will appear with the specified color.

- **Layer.** This option sets the default layer for all new objects. All new
  objects will be drawn on the specified layer.

- **Linetype.** This option sets the default linetype for all new objects.
  Any new object will appear with the specified linetype.

- **Text Style.** For text objects, this option specifies which text style to
  use.

- **Linetype Scale.** This option sets the default linetype scale. Any new
  object with a linetype other than CONTINUOUS will be shown at
  the specified linetype scale.

- **Elevation.** This option specifies the default Z coordinates for new
  objects.

- **Thickness.** This option sets the 3D thickness of objects. This enables
  you to create the effect of 3D thickness on 2D objects.

Figure 4.20

*The DDEMODES
dialog box.*

There might be times when you need to explicitly assign a color or linetype to an object. Using the BYLAYER color and linetype, however, gives you greater flexibility in managing your drawing objects. By using the BYLAYER color and linetype, you globally can change the color and linetype of objects by changing the layer definition.

Renaming Layers

Setting up layers is a matter of standard practice and style. Layers are used to organize different types of objects in your drawing. Anticipating what type of objects a layer will contain is important. The naming of layers helps identify the type of objects on layers.

Having too many objects in your drawing can make editing difficult; the same can be said for layers. Too many layers can make getting around AutoCAD time-consuming. For most uses, 10 to 20 layers is more than enough. AutoCAD can accommodate layer names up to 31 characters, but the layer display only shows the first eight. All layer names are converted to uppercase. You can use letters, numbers, dollar signs ($), hyphens (-), and underscore (_).

The DDRENAME command enables you to change the name of existing objects, such as layer names or block names. While the Rename button in the Layer Control dialog box only enables you to rename a single layer at a time, the DDRENAME command enables you to change the names of multiple objects by using the * and ? wildcard.

DDRENAME. The DDRENAME command displays the RENAME dialog box, which enables you to change the names of existing drawing objects such as layers, blocks, text styles, and dimension styles. You can use the * and ? wildcards to globally change object names.

Pull-down: *Choose* **D**ata, **R**ename
Screen: *Choose* Data, Rename

The DDRENAME command displays the Rename dialog box, as shown in figure 4.21.

Figure 4.21

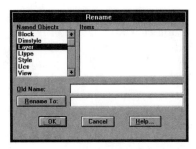

The DDRENAME dialog box.

The following exercise renames the layers you created in earlier exercises to conform to a layer naming scheme. In the exercise, you will add an A- to the front of the architectural layers and an S- to the front of structural layers.

Renaming Your Layers

Continue from the previous exercise.

Command: *Choose* **D**ata, **R**ename	Issues the RENAME command
In the Named Objects *list, click on* Layer	Displays a list of layers that you can rename
In the Items *list, click on* GRID	Selects the layer GRID to rename
In the Rename to *text box, type* **S-GRID** *and click the* Rename to *button*	Renames the layer GRID to S-GRID
In the Items *list, click on* DIMS, DOOR, FURN, NOTE, SHBD, *and* WALL	Highlights the other layers to rename
In the Rename to *text box, type* **A-*** *and click the* Rename to *button*	Renames all the highlighted layers to add the prefix A-
Choose the OK *button*	Exits the DDRENAME command
`7 Layers renamed.`	
Command: *Choose Save (Standard Toolbar)*	Saves the drawing

Saving Settings to a Prototype Drawing

In the previous exercises, you set the drawing units and limits, created a set of layers, and changed their colors and linetypes. This can be a tedious procedure if you have to do this every time you create a new drawing. You can use a prototype drawing to automate this task.

A *prototype* drawing is a drawing containing all of the settings and layers that you use most often. When you create a new drawing, you can specify the name of a prototype drawing to use. AutoCAD then makes a copy of the prototype drawing for you to start with.

You can have a set of prototype drawings, each addressing particular situations. One prototype drawing, for example, can contain settings for a scale of 1"=40' and a paper size of 24×36. Another prototype drawing can contain settings for a scale of 1/4":1'-0" and a paper size of 18×24.

In the following exercise, you will save the ARCH-PRO drawing as a prototype drawing, saving this particular setup. You will create a new drawing OFFICE, based on the ARCH-PRO prototype drawing.

4

Saving Your Settings in a Prototype Drawing

Command: *Choose Erase (Modify)*	Issues the ERASE command
_erase Select objects: **ALL** (Enter)	Selects all of the drawing's objects
Select objects: (Enter)	Erases all drawing objects
Command: *Choose Save (Standard Toolbar)*	Saves the drawing
Command: *Choose New (Standard Toolbar)*	Issues the NEW command
Choose **P***rototype and select the drawing* ARCH-PRO, *which is located in the \AB directory, and choose* OK	Lets you choose another prototype file instead of the default.
In **N***ew Drawing Name box, type* **OFFICE** *then choose* OK	Creates a new drawing called OFFICE, based on the prototype file ARCH-PRO

Notice that the new drawing has all of the settings of the prototype.

Summary

This chapter showed you how to prepare your drawing for input. You set up your units to enter data the way you want to enter it. You learned how to set up the drawing environment to create an atmosphere ready for drawing. You learned how to choose a plot scale factor for your drawing and use the plot scale factor to set your limits. You were introduced to layers and how they can be used to streamline your editing process. The final preparation had you create a prototype file in which to save your settings. This chapter helped illustrate how you can set up AutoCAD Release 13 to work for you.

Now that your drawing is ready to be used, Chapter 5, "The Basic Drawing Commands," introduces you to the basic drawing commands. You will learn more about the drawing commands that were just touched upon here. You also learn how to draw new types of objects.

Related Topics

- Drawing lines and circles—Chapter 5, "The Basic Drawing Commands"
- Changing the view and using floating viewports—Chapter 6, "Controlling What You See"
- Drawing with pinpoint accuracy—Chapter 7, "Drawing Accurately"
- More about grid, snap, and ortho—Chapter 7, "Drawing Accurately"
- Freezing layers within viewports—Chapter 16, "Composing and Plotting a Drawing"

Chapter Snapshot

In its most basic form, a drawing is just a collection of lines, arcs, and circles. You arrange these objects in a drawing to represent your design. This chapter shows you how to use some of AutoCAD's tools to draw lines, arcs, circles, rectangles, and polygons. You will explore each drawing command's options and learn how the drawing commands are used.

In this chapter, you will learn the following:

- How to draw lines, arcs, and circles

- How to create rectangles and polygons

- How to use these objects to create the needed geometry in a particular drawing

The Basic Drawing Commands

In Chapter 4, "Preparing Your Drawing," you learned how to prepare your drawing space to receive information. The next step is to start the drawing process. In paper drawings, you use pencils to draw lines, circles, and arcs to represent your design. With CAD, the process is similar. You use the LINE command to draw straight lines, CIRCLE to draw circles, and ARC to draw arc circles.

You used the LINE command in the previous chapters. In this chapter, you will explore the LINE, CIRCLE, ARC, RECTANG, and POLYGON commands. The exercises in this chapter give you a more detailed explanation of each drawing command's options and some tips on using them effectively.

The following Quick Tour exercise gives you an overview of the drawing commands covered in the chapter. In the exercise, you set up a metric prototype drawing and use it to create a toolplate.

The Quick Tour

You start by creating a metric prototype drawing that will be used for the exercises in this chapter.

Command: *Choose New (Standard Toolbar)*	Issues the NEW command and displays the Create New Drawing dialog box
In the New **D**rawing Name edit box *type* **MET-PRO**, *and then choose* OK	Creates the new drawing MET-PRO
Command: *Choose* **D**ata, *then* Dr**a**wing Limits	Issues the LIMITS command
`Reset Model space limits ON/OFF/` `<Lower left corner> <0.0000,0.0000>:` (Enter)	Sets the lower left limit
`Upper right corner <12.0000, 9.0000>:` **200,100** (Enter)	Sets the upper right limit to 200,100
Command: *Choose Layers (Object Properties)*	Issues the DDLMODES command and displays the Layer Control dialog box
Type **OBJECTS**, *then choose* Ne**w**	Creates the new layer OBJECTS
In the Layer Name *list, select layer* OBJECTS, *then choose* **C**urrent, *then OK*	Changes the current layer to OBJECTS and exits the dialog box
Command: *Choose Zoom All (Standard Toolbar, Zoom)*	Zooms out to the drawing limits
Command: *Choose Save (Standard Toolbar)*	Saves the drawing

In the following steps, you will use this drawing as a prototype for the toolplate.

Command: *Choose New (Standard Toolbar)*	Issues the NEW command and displays the Create New Drawing dialog box
Choose Prototype, *and select the file* \AB\MET-PRO.DWG, *then choose* OK	Selects the drawing MET-PRO.DWG as the prototype drawing
In the New Drawing Name *edit box type* **TOOLPLT**, *then choose* OK	Creates the new drawing TOOLPLT.DWG
Command: *Choose Rectangle (Draw, Polygon)*	Issues the RECTANG command
`First corner:` **20,20** (Enter)	Places the first corner of the rectangle at ① (see fig. 5.1)

`Other corner: ` **`120,80`** Enter	Places the other corner at ② and draws the rectangle
`Command: ` *Choose Line (Draw, Line)*	Issues the LINE command
`From point: ` **`120,20`** Enter	Places the first point of the line at ③
`To point: ` **`167,29`** Enter	Places the endpoint of the line at ④
`To point: ` Enter	Finishes the line
`Command: ` Enter	Repeats the LINE command
`From point: ` **`120,80`** Enter	Places the first point of the line at ②
`To point: ` **`167,71`** Enter	Places the endpoint of the line at ⑤
`To point: ` Enter	Finishes the line
`Command: ` *Choose Arc Start End Radius (Draw, Arc)*	Issues the ARC command with the Start, End, and Radius options
`Center/<Start point>: ` **`167,29`** Enter	Places the arc start point at ④
`Endpoint: ` **`167,71`** Enter	Places the arc endpoint at ⑤
`Radius: ` **`25`** Enter	Specifies the radius and draws the arc

The following steps show you how to draw what is inside the toolplate: two circles, a rectangle, and a polygon.

`Command: ` *Choose Circle Center Radius (Draw, Circle)*	Issues the CIRCLE command
`3P/2P/TTR/<Center point>:` **`70,50`** Enter	Places the circle's center at ⑥
`Diameter/<Radius>: ` **`7.5`** Enter	Draws a circle with a radius of 7.5mm
`Command: ` *Choose Polygon (Draw, Polygon)*	Issues the POLYGON command
`Number of sides <4>: ` **`6`** Enter	Specifies a 6-sided polygon
`Edge/<Center of polygon>: ` **`30,38`** Enter	Places the center of the polygon at ⑦
`Inscribed in circle/Circumscribed about circle (I/C) <I>: ` Enter	Specifies the Inscribed option
`Radius of circle: ` **`5`** Enter	Specifies the radius and draws the polygon
`Command: ` *Choose Save (Standard Toolbar)*	Saves the drawing

Your drawing should look like the design shown in figure 5.1.

Figure 5.1

*The finished
toolplate.*

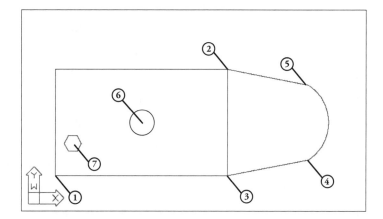

Creating Lines

Lines are the most common objects in a drawing. They are the simplest objects to draw and yet can serve many purposes. You can use lines to draw many of the objects in your design or as construction lines to aid in drawing other objects. Lines are created with the LINE command.

> **LINE.** The LINE command draws one or more straight line segments. Each line segment is a separate object.
> Toolbar: *Choose Line (Draw, Line)*
> Screen: *Choose* Draw1, LINE
> Alias: L

A line is defined by a start point and an endpoint. AutoCAD connects these two points to form a line. You can specify these two points either by using the pointing device or by entering coordinates at the keyboard.

The LINE Command Options

The LINE command has a number of options that help streamline the process of drawing lines. The LINE command has the following options:

- **From point.** This prompt specifies the first point of the line.

- **continue.** Press (Enter) at the From point: prompt to start the line from the endpoint of the most recently drawn line or arc.

- **To point.** This prompt specifies the point to which a line is drawn.

- **Undo.** This option enables you to undo the last line segment, stepping back to the previous point.

- **Close.** This option closes a series of two or more line segments.

By using the LINE command options, you can draw your design quickly and easily.

The following exercise shows how to use the LINE command's options to draw efficiently. In the exercise, you will begin to create a simple circuit board outline using the metric prototype drawing created in the Quick Tour exercise.

Drawing the CIRCUIT Perimeter

You begin by creating a new drawing named CIRCUIT.

Command: *Choose New (Standard Toolbar)*	Issues the NEW command and displays the Create New Drawing dialog box
Choose **P***rototype, and select the file* \AB\MET-PRO.DWG, *then choose* OK	Selects the drawing MET-PRO.DWG as the prototype drawing
In the New **D**rawing Name *edit box, type* **CIRCUIT**, *then choose* OK	Creates the new drawing CIRCUIT.DWG
Command: *Choose* **O***ptions,* **D***rawing Aids*	Issues the DDRMODES command and displays the Drawing Aids dialog box
In the Grid area, *double-click in the* X S**p**acing *text box, type* **5** (Enter)	Sets the grid spacing to 5mm and turns the grid on
In the Snap *area, place a check in the* On *box, then choose* OK	Turns on Snap and exits the dialog box
Command: *Double-click on* ORTHO *in the status bar*	Turns on ortho mode
Command: *Choose Line (Draw, Line)*	Issues the LINE command
From point: **20,20** (Enter)	Places the start of the line at ① (see fig. 5.2)
To point: **170,20** (Enter)	Places the end of the line at ②

continues

continued

```
To point: 170,90 (Enter)
```
Places the end of the line at ③

```
To point: (Enter)
```
Ends the LINE command

The following steps use the continue option to start a line from the last point. This is a good alternative to entering more coordinates.

```
Command: L (Enter)
```
Issues the LINE command using the command alias

```
From point: (Enter)
```
Places the start of the line at the last specified point

```
To point: Pick ④
```
Places the end of the line at 20,90

```
To point: Pick ①
```
Places the end of the line at 20,20

```
To point: (Enter)
```
Ends the LINE command

Next, you will create the connector at the bottom of the circuit board.

```
Command: (Enter)
```
Repeats the LINE command

```
From point: 155,15 (Enter)
```
Starts a line at ⑤

```
To point: Pick ⑥
```
Places the end of the line at 155,25

```
To point: Pick ⑦
```
Places the end of the line at 100,25

```
To point: Pick ⑧
```
Places the end of the line at 100,15

```
To point: Pick ⑨
```
Places the end of the line at 130,15

In the next step, you will intentionally make a mistake to see how the LINE command's Undo option works.

```
To point: 130,27 (Enter)
```
Draws a line too far up

```
To point: U (Enter)
```
Undoes the last line segment

```
To point: 130,17 (Enter)
```
Draws the line correctly at ⑩

After you have corrected the line, you can continue with the rest of the connector

```
To point: 135,17 (Enter)
```
Places the end of the line at ⑪

```
To point: 135,15 (Enter)
```
Places the end of the line at ⑫

```
To point: C (Enter)
```
Closes the connector and ends the LINE command

```
Command: Choose Save (Standard Toolbar)
```
Saves the drawing

Your drawing should now resemble figure 5.2.

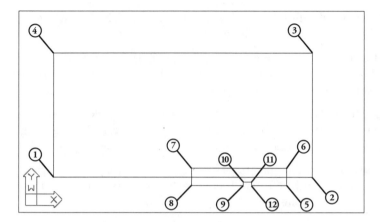

Figure 5.2

The outline of the circuit board.

Creating Circles and Arcs

Drawing circles and arcs is more complex than drawing lines. A line is drawn by two points. Circles and arcs can be drawn a number of ways: by any combination of the radius, diameter, included angle, start and end-points, and directions.

Understanding Circles

The circle is another basic object used in drawings. Circles commonly are drawn to represent holes, wheels, columns, and trees. You create circles with the CIRCLE command.

CIRCLE. The CIRCLE command can draw circles using a variety of geometric methods.
Toolbar: *Choose Circle 2 Point (Draw, Circle)*
Screen: *Choose DRAW 1, then* Circle
Alias: C

The CIRCLE Command Options

One of the advantages of using AutoCAD is its capability to create objects in a number of different ways. Circles are a good example of this concept;

there are five methods of drawing circles (see fig. 5.3). The following is a list of the CIRCLE command options:

- **Center point.** This option enables you to pick the center point by using the pointing device or entering coordinates of a point. Choosing this option directs you to specify the circle's diameter or radius.

- **Radius.** This option specifies the circle's radius by picking a point or typing a value. If you have previously drawn a circle, the previous circle's radius is given as the default.

- **Diameter.** This option specifies the circle's diameter by picking a point or typing a value. If you have previously drawn a circle, the previous circle's diameter will be given as a default.

- **3P.** This option constructs a circle by picking three points on the circumference.

- **2P.** This option constructs a circle by picking two points on the diameter.

- **TTR.** This option constructs a circle that is tangent to two objects and with a specific radius.

Figure 5.3

The five methods of drawing circles.

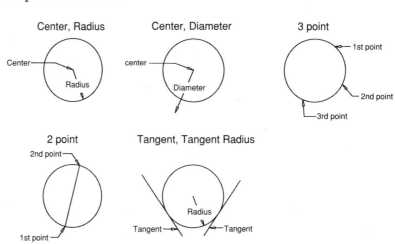

Typically, you create circles by picking the center point and specifying the radius. Often, you will not have such information, but will instead have other circle characteristics. AutoCAD gives you the ability to draw your circle based on the information you have. You can draw a circle, for example, if you know where the edges of the circle are located. You would then draw a circle using the 2-Point method. The following exercise shows you some of the available methods to draw circles.

Drawing Circles on the Circuit Board

Continue from the previous exercise.

Command: *Choose Circle Center Radius (Draw, Circle)*	Issues the CIRCLE command
3P/2P/TTR/<Center point>: **115,77** (Enter)	Sets the center at ① (see fig. 5.4)
Diameter/<Radius>: **7** (Enter)	Draws a circle with a radius of 7mm
Command: *Choose Circle Center Diameter (Draw, Circle)*	Issues the CIRCLE command with the Center and Diameter options
3P/2P/TTR/<Center point>: **@** (Enter)	Sets the center at the last specified point
Radius/<Diameter> <14.0000>: **10** (Enter)	Draws a circle with a diameter of 10mm
Command: *Choose Line (Draw, Line)*	Issues the LINE command
From point: **155,57** (Enter)	Places the start point at ②
To point: **69,57** (Enter)	Draws the line to ③
To point: (Enter)	Exits from the LINE command
Command: *Choose Circle 2 Point (Draw, Circle)*	Issues the CIRCLE command
First point on diameter: **@** (Enter)	Places the first point of the diameter at 69,57
Second point on diameter: **59,57** (Enter)	Places the second point at ④
Command: *Choose Line (Draw, Line)*	Issues the LINE command
From point: **115,70** (Enter)	Places the start point at ⑤
To point: **115,60** (Enter)	Draws the line to ⑥
To point: (Enter)	Exits the LINE command
Command: *Choose Circle Tan Tan Radius (Draw, Circle)*	Issues the CIRCLE command with the TTR option
Enter Tangent spec: *Pick* ⑦	Selects the first tangent
Enter second Tangent spec: *Pick* ⑧	Selects the second tangent

continues

continued

`Radius <5.0000>:` **Enter**   Accepts the default radius of the previous circle

`Command:` *Choose Save (Standard Toolbar)*   Saves the drawing

Your drawing now should look like figure 5.4.

Figure 5.4

Drawing circles with the CIRCLE command.

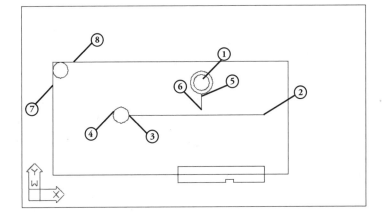

Understanding Arcs

You draw arcs much as you draw circles. Arcs, like circles, have a radius and a center point. Arcs also have a start point, endpoint, direction, chord length, and sweep angle. You can use any combination of these characteristics to draw your arc with the ARC command. You can, for example, set an arc to start at a specific point, specify where its center point is, and then give the arc a chord length. You can also draw an arc by setting three points which reside on the arc. By choosing which characteristics to use, you can work with what information you have instead of calculating other characteristics.

ARC. The ARC command draws a circular arc. Like the CIRCLE command, you can set the arc's characteristics by using the ARC command's options.
Toolbar: *Choose 3 Points (Draw, Arc)*
Screen: *Choose* DRAW 1, Arc
Alias: A

The ARC Command Options

Arcs are more complex than circles. As you learned in the previous section, arcs have more characteristics than circles. Because of their complexities, there are many methods you can use to draw arcs. It can be quite daunting to remember all of the options of the ARC command. A good approach to drawing arcs is to understand what combinations of data are needed to define an arc. Compare that to the information you have available and choose your method from there. You can specify an arc, for example, if you know its start point, radius, and endpoint. You then choose the options within the ARC command to enter the known information.

The following is a list of the ARC command options:

- **Start.** This (default) option enables you to specify the start point of an arc.

- **Center.** This option enables you specify the center point of an arc.

- **Second Point.** This option enables you to specify a point on the arc. This option is only available after you choose the start point of a 3-point arc.

- **End.** This option specifies the endpoint of the arc.

- **Angle.** This option enables you to enter a value for the arc's included angle or use the pointing device to pick a point for the angle.

- **Direction.** This option enables you to specify the direction of a line tangent to the start point of the arc. This option is only available after choosing the start point and endpoint of the arc.

- **Radius.** This option specifies the radius of an arc. You can either enter a value or use the pointing device to pick a radius point.

- **Length of Chord.** This option specifies the chord length of the arc. This option is only available after you choose the Start and Center options.

- **continue.** This option draws an arc tangent from the last line or arc drawn. You invoke this option by pressing (Enter) at the first arc prompt.

The ARC command is extremely flexible. By choosing a combination of options, you can construct an arc based on the information you have about it. Figure 5.5 shows arcs constructed by using 10 different methods.

5

Figure 5.5

Ten methods to draw arcs.

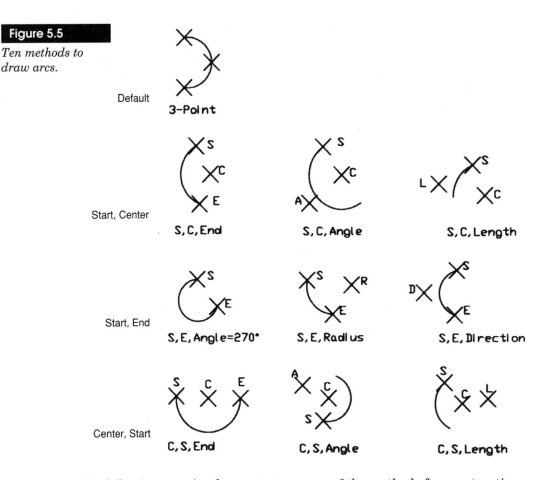

The following exercise demonstrates some of the methods for constructing arcs.

Drawing Simple Arcs

Continue from the previous exercise.

Command: *Choose Arc Start End Angle (Draw, Arc)*	Issues the ARC command with the Start, End, and Angle options
Center/<Start point>: **45,45** (Enter)	Places the start of the arc at ① (see fig. 5.6)
Endpoint: **70,45** (Enter)	Sets the endpoint at ②

Included angle: **45** (Enter)	Draws an arc with an included angle of 45 degrees
Command: (Enter)	Repeats the ARC command
Center/<Start point>: (Enter)	Places the start point of the arc tangent to ②
Endpoint: **71,43** (Enter)	Specifies the endpoint at ③
Command: *Choose 3 Points (Draw, Arc)*	Starts the ARC command again
Center/<Start point>: **@** (Enter)	Starts another arc
Center/End/<Second point>: **57,40** (Enter)	Specifies a point on the arc at ④
Endpoint: **44,43** (Enter)	Places the endpoint of the arc at ⑤
Command: *Choose Arc Continue (Draw, Arc)*	Issues the ARC command with the continue option
Endpoint: **45,45** (Enter)	Sets the endpoint at ①

The preceding steps showed you how you can use the continue option to create arcs that are tangent to one another. In the following steps, you will use the continue option with the LINE command.

Command: *Choose Line (Draw, Line)*	Issues the LINE command
From point: **170,75** (Enter)	Places the start point of the line at ⑥
To point: **160,75** (Enter)	Places the end of the line at ⑦
To point: (Enter)	Ends the LINE command
Command: *Choose Arc Continue (Draw, Arc)*	Issues the ARC command with the continue option and starts the arc tangent to the line at ⑦
Endpoint: **155,70** (Enter)	Sets the endpoint at ⑧ and draws the arc
Command: **L** (Enter)	Issues the LINE command with the alias
From point: (Enter)	Starts a line tangent to the arc at ⑧
Length of line: **25** (Enter)	Draws a line 25mm downward to ⑨
To point: (Enter)	Exits the LINE command
Command: *Choose Arc Continue (Draw, Arc)*	Issues the ARC command with the continue option and starts the arc tangent to the line at ⑨
Endpoint: **160,40** (Enter)	Sets the endpoint at ⑩ and draws the arc

continues

continued

Command: **L** (Enter)	Issues the LINE command with the alias
From point: (Enter)	Starts a line tangent to the arc at (10)
Length of line: **10** (Enter)	Draws a line 10mm to the right at (11)
To point: (Enter)	Exits the LINE command
Command: *Choose Save (Standard Toolbar)*	Saves the drawing

Your drawing now should resemble figure 5.6.

Figure 5.6

Using the ARC command.

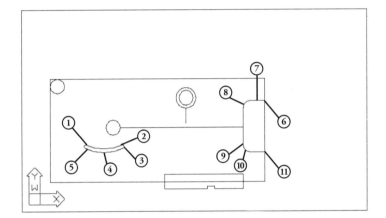

Understanding Rectangles and Polygons

With lines, arcs, and circles, you can create incredibly complex designs. The process of drawing line segments, however, can grow tedious. Fortunately, AutoCAD provides some shortcuts in the form of rectangles and polygons.

Creating Rectangles

Drawing a rectangle with the LINE command requires that you specify the location of each corner. AutoCAD greatly simplifies this process with the RECTANG command.

> **RECTANG.** The RECTANG command draws a rectangle specified
> by two corners of the rectangle.
> Toolbar: *Choose Rectangle (Draw, Polyline)*
> Screen: *Choose* DRAW 1, Rectang

Rectangles rival lines as the easiest objects to draw. The RECTANG
command simply prompts you for two diagonal corners. After specifying
the opposite corner, AutoCAD computes the locations of the other two
corners and draws the rectangle.

The following exercise shows you how to add chips to the circuit board by
using rectangles.

Drawing Rectangles

Continue from the previous exercise.

Command: *Choose Rectangle (Draw, Polygon)*	Issues the RECTANG command
First corner: **50,85** (Enter)	Specifies the upper left corner at ① (see fig. 5.7)
Other corner: **55,75** (Enter)	Specifies the lower right corner at ②
Command: (Enter)	Repeats the RECTANG command
First corner: *Pick* ③	Specifies the upper left corner at the coordinate 60,85
Other corner: *Pick* ④	Specifies the upper right corner at the coordinate 65,75
Command: *Choose Save (Standard Toolbar)*	Saves the drawing

You drawing now should resemble figure 5.7.

5

Figure 5.7

Drawing rectangles on the circuit board.

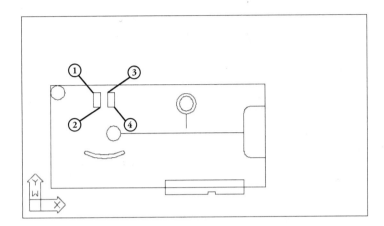

Creating Polygons

Polygons are another set of objects that represent closed shapes. The POLYGON command enables you to create regular (equilateral) polygons. You simply specify how many sides the polygon will have and then decide how large it will be.

> **POLYGON.** The POLYGON command draws regular polygon shapes with a specified number of sides.
> Toolbar: *Choose Polygon (Draw, Polygon)*
> Screen: *Choose* DRAW 2, Polygon

The POLYGON command first prompts you for the number of sides; you can enter any between 3 and 1,024. After specifying the number of sides, you have the following options:

- **Edge.** The Edge option enables you to specify two points as a segment of the polygon.

- **Center.** The Center option sets where the polygon will be located in the drawing.

- **Inscribed.** The Inscribed option draws a polygon from the center point to the point between the edges of the polygon.

- **Circumscribed.** The Circumscribed option draws a polygon from the center point to the polygon edge.

The Inscribed and Circumscribed options construct polygons based on an imaginary circle. Inscribed polygons are drawn inside the circle with the radius of the circle representing the distance from the center of the polygon to one of the corners (see fig. 5.8). Circumscribed polygons are drawn on the outside of the imaginary circle. The radius of the circle represents the distance from the center of the polygon to the midpoint of one of the sides (see fig. 5.8).

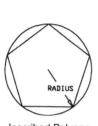 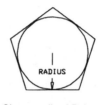

Inscribed Polygon   Edge Polygon   Circumscribed Polygon

Figure 5.8

Inscribed and circumscribed polygons.

The following exercise shows you how to use each method to draw the polygons on the circuit board.

Drawing Polygons

Continue from the previous exercise.

Command: *Choose Polygon (Draw, Polygon)*	Issues the POLYGON command
Number of sides <4>: **5** (Enter)	Specifies a 5-sided polygon
Edge/<Center of polygon>: **35,66** (Enter)	Specifies the center of the polygon at ① (see fig. 5.9)
Inscribed in circle/Circumscribed about circle (I/C) <I>: (Enter)	Accepts the default Inscribed option
Radius of circle: **5** (Enter)	Enters a radius for the circle that draws the polygon
Command: (Enter)	Repeats the POLYGON command
Number of sides <5>: **8** (Enter)	Specifies an 8-sided polygon
Edge/<Center of polygon>: **112,40** (Enter)	Specifies the center of the polygon at ②
Inscribed in circle/Circumscribed about circle (I/C) <I>: **C** (Enter)	Accepts the Circumscribed option

continues

continued

`Radius of circle: 10` (Enter)	Enters a radius for the circle to draw the polygon
`Command:` *Choose Polygon (Draw, Polygon)*	Issues the POLYGON command
`Number of sides <8>: 6` (Enter)	Specifies a 6-sided polygon
`Edge/<Center of polygon>: E` (Enter)	Selects the Edge option to draw a polygon
`First endpoint of edge: 30,25` (Enter)	Locates an endpoint of the polygon's edge at ③
`Second endpoint of edge: 30,28` (Enter)	Locates the other edge endpoint at ④

Note that where you set the two edge endpoints determines how the polygon is rotated and how large the polygon is drawn.

`Command:` *Choose Save (Standard Toolbar)*   Saves the drawing

Your drawing now should resemble figure 5.9.

Figure 5.9

The completed circuit board.

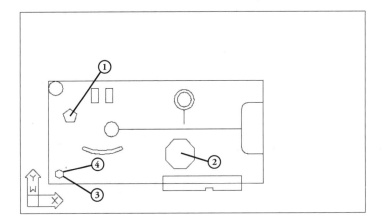

One of the advantages of using the RECTANG and POLYGON commands is that the shapes they create are a single object. When drawing with the LINE command, each line segment is a separate object. As your drawing becomes more populated, you will appreciate how easy it is to select a rectangle instead of four lines. When you move a polygon, for example, you save time by choosing one object instead of four.

Polygons and rectangles are a special type of line, called a *polyline*. A polyline can consist of several line or arc segments, but is a single object.

The following exercise demonstrates the difference between lines and polylines.

Selecting Lines and Polylines

Continue from the previous exercise.

Command: *Select the lines at* ①, ②, ③, *and* ④ — Selects the four separate line segments and displays their grips

Notice that each line segment is a separate object. These lines were drawn with the LINE command.

Command: *Press Esc twice* — Deselects the lines and clears the grips

Command: *Select the polygon at* ⑤ — Selects the polygon and displays its grips

Notice that when you select the polygon, all of the segments that make up the polygons are highlighted. The polygon is a single object.

Command: *Press Esc twice* — Deselects the polygon and clears the grips

Command: *Choose Save (Standard Toolbar)* — Saves the drawing

---

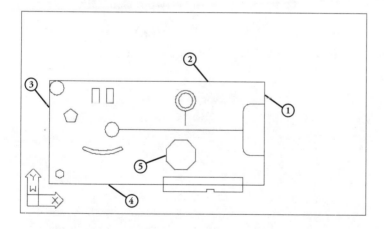

Figure 5.10

Selecting lines and polylines.

5

Polylines are very versatile objects that can significantly enhance your drawing efficiency. For a more detailed discussion of drawing polylines, see Chapter 9, "More Drawing Commands."

Summary

In this chapter, you learned how to draw lines, circles, arcs, rectangles, and polygons. You went through the commands and the options to draw these objects. By using these simple objects, you can create very complex designs.

Part of the aim of this chapter is to prepare you for more complex objects. Although the basic drawing objects are the ones you will use the most often, you will learn how using other, more complex objects can be more efficient for your design.

Now that you know the basics of drawing, the next chapter shows you how to control the way you look at your drawing.

Related Topics

- Inputting coordinates—Chapter 7, "Drawing Accurately"
- Using object snaps—Chapter 7, "Drawing Accurately"
- Creating polylines—Chapter 9, "More Drawing Commands"
- Other drawing objects—Chapter 9, "More Drawing Commands"
- Editing polylines—Chapter 12, "Constructive Editing"

This chapter covers the basics of the commands available to control how you view your drawing.

- Using the Aerial viewer effectively

- Working with the ZOOM command

- Managing the display using named views

- Displaying multiple views of your drawing with tiled viewports

- Understanding the basics of paper space and model space

This chapter covers drawing composition, display manipulation, and how to efficiently manage the graphics window, as well as the powerful features related to paper space and model space. At the end of the chapter, you generate another check plot of what you have created.

6

Controlling What You See

One of the most important aspects of working with any
CAD system is controlling what is displayed in the graphics window. AutoCAD provides you with a broad array of tools
and commands to make the process of changing your display to
fit your needs as easy as possible.

The following exercise will give you a quick overview on a few of
the things to be covered in this chapter. It uses the TOOLPLT
drawing that you created in Chapter 5, "The Basic Drawing
Commands," along with some of the AutoCAD Release 13
display features.

The Quick Tour

To begin, you will open the file TOOLPLT.DWG which is located in the \AB directory.

Command: *Choose Open (Standard Toolbar)* — Issues the OPEN command and displays the Select File dialog box

Select TOOLPLT *from the list, then choose* OK — Closes the dialog box and opens TOOLPLT.DWG

Command: *Choose Zoom Window (Standard Toolbar)* — Issues the ZOOM command with the Window option

First point: *Pick* ① *then* ② *as shown in figure 6.1* — Places a zoom window and updates the display

Command: *Choose Zoom Previous (Standard Toolbar)* — Updates the display with the Previous view

Command: *Choose Aerial View (Standard Toolbar, Tool Windows)* — Issues the DSVIEWER command and displays the Aerial View window

Command: *Choose Zoom (Aerial) then pick* ①, *then* ② *(see fig. 6.2)* — Draws the aerial zoom window and updates the drawing area

Command: *Choose Zoom All (Standard Toolbar, Zoom)* — Displays the current drawing limits

Command: *Choose Aerial View (Standard Toolbar, Tool Windows)* — Closes the Aerial View window

Command: *Double Click on* TILE *on the status bar* — Turns off TILEMODE, invokes paper space

Command: *Choose* **V**iew, Floatin**g** Viewports, **1** Viewport — Issues the MVIEW command

ON/OFF/Hideplot/Fit/2/3/4/Restore/ <First Point>: *Pick* ① *(see fig. 6.3)* — Places first corner of the viewport

Other corner: *Pick* ② — Creates a floating viewport

Command: ⌗Enter⌗ — Repeats the MVIEW command

ON/OFF/Hideplot/Fit/2/3/4/Restore/ <First Point>: *Pick* ③ — Places first corner of the viewport

Other corner: *Pick* ④ — Creates another floating viewport

Command: *Double-click on* PAPER *on the status bar* — Switches to model space

Command: *Choose Zoom Extents (Standard Toolbar, Zoom)*	Updates the second floating viewport display with the Extents of the objects in model space
Command: *Select anywhere in the first viewport*	Sets the first viewport current
Command: *Choose Zoom Scale (Standard Toolbar, Zoom)*	Issues the Scale option of ZOOM
`<Scale (X/XP)>:` **.8x** (Enter)	Reduces the display in the floating viewport
Command: *Double-click on* MODEL *on the status bar*	Switches to paper space
Command: *Double-click on* TILE *on the status bar*	Turns on TILEMODE and returns to model space
Command: *Choose Save (Standard Toolbar)*	Saves the drawing

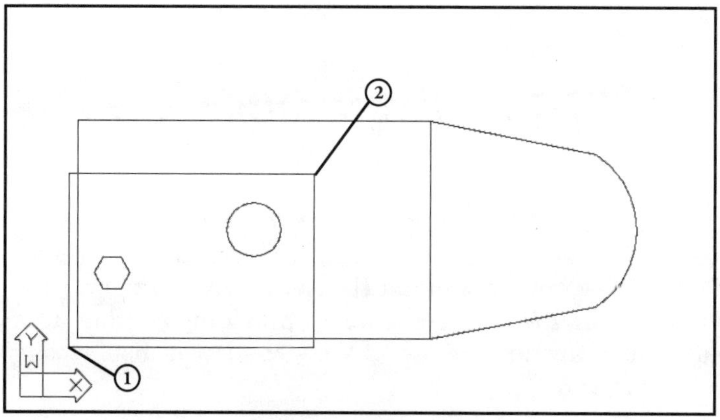

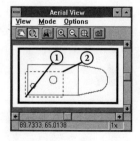

Figure 6.1

Zooming into the drawing.

6

Figure 6.2

Pick points for zoom window using the Aerial Viewer.

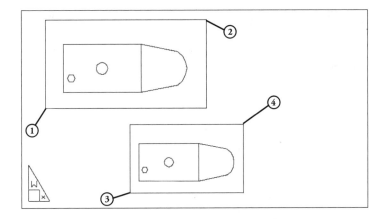

As you saw in the Quick Tour exercise, the Aerial view can be very helpful
in moving quickly about a drawing. This section presents several of the
Aerial view features in a series of exercises to help in your understanding
of this powerful display tool.

The Ins and Outs of the Aerial View Window

The Aerial View window (see fig. 6.4) provides a method by which you can
magnify and navigate about your drawing. The ZOOM and PAN commands provide these features as well but the Aerial View window is
separate from the graphics window, essentially providing another area in
which to display your drawing. The Aerial View window is displayed with
the DSVIEWER command.

'DSVIEWER. The DSVIEWER command provides a secondary
graphics window named Aerial View. By using the multiple display
tools available in this window, you can more efficiently move about
the drawing.
Toolbar: *Aerial View (Standard Toolbar)*

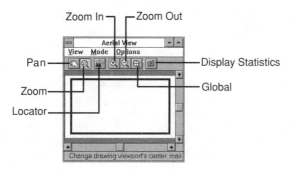

Figure 6.4

*The Aerial View
window.*

When using the Aerial View, remember that commands typed at the
command line act upon the application window drawing area, not the
display of the Aerial View window.

Access to the Aerial View window is only provided through use of the
accelerated display driver. See Appendix A, "Installation and Configuration," for more information on installing and configuring
AutoCAD.

The following list explains the function of the tools found on the Aerial
View toolbar. Although similar in function to the display tools and commands used when in the AutoCAD application window, these tools refer
only to the Aerial View window.

- **Pan.** The Pan tool provides you with a dynamic view box which can
  be positioned over any area of the drawing in the Aerial view. The
  display of the drawing area is updated when the position of the view
  box is picked but the display in the Aerial View window does not
  change.

- **Zoom.** The Zoom tool enables you to pick two corners to define the
  zoom window within the Aerial View. When the corners have been
  picked, the display of the drawing area is updated but the Aerial
  View window does not change.

- **Locator.** This tool provides you with a magnifier that magnifies the
  display of the drawing area. The default magnification is 100 percent
  (1×) and is changed using the Locator Magnification item of the

Aerial View Options menu. Whereas the Pan and Zoom tools do not change the display in the viewer, when using the Locator tool, the viewer displays in real-time the area of the drawing being magnified. The Locator tool can only be used in a press and drag mode. When the button is released upon locating the area to be magnified, the drawing area is updated with the magnified display and the Aerial View window returns to the original display.

- **Zoom In.** Similar in function to the Zoom In tool from the Standard Toolbar that is applied to the drawing area, this Zoom In tool magnifies the display in the Aerial View by 200 percent but does not affect the display in the drawing area.

- **Zoom Out.** The Zoom Out tool reduces the display of the Aerial view by 50 percent each time it is chosen. It does not affect the magnification of the display in the drawing area.

- **Global.** The Global tool displays the entire drawing in the Aerial View window.

- **Display Statistics.** The Display Statistics tool displays an informational dialog box giving you statistics relating to the amount of memory currently used by the display list driver.

In the following exercise, you create a simple office furniture layout using the ARCH-PRO prototype drawing created in Chapter 4, "Preparing Your Drawing," and then you open the Aerial View window.

Creating a Furniture Floor Plan

You start by creating a new drawing called FURNPLAN using the ARCH-PRO.DWG drawing located in the \AB directory.

Command: *Choose New (Standard Toolbar)*	Issues the NEW command
Choose **P**rototype *and select the file* ARCH-PRO.DWG *from the* \AB *directory*	Specifies the file ARCH-PRO.DWG as the prototype drawing
In the New **D**rawing Name *edit box,* *type* **FURNPLAN**, *then choose* OK	Creates a new drawing named FURNPLAN using the ARCH-PRO prototype drawing
Command: *Choose* **D**ata, Dr**a**wing limits	Issues the LIMITS command
Reset Model space limits: ON/OFF/ <Lower left corner> <0'-0",0'-0">: Enter	Accepts default value of 0,0 for the lower left corner

Upper right corner <288'-0",192'-0">: **60',40'** (Enter)	Sets limits area to 60'× 40'
Command: *Choose Zoom All (Standard Toolbar, Zoom)*	Updates the display with the area of the limits
Command: *Choose Line (Draw, Line)*	Issues the LINE command
From point: **4',4'** (Enter)	Starts the line at ① (see fig. 6.5)
To point: **4',34'** (Enter)	Draws the line to ②
To point: **54',34'** (Enter)	Draws the line to ③
To point: **54',22'** (Enter)	Draws the line to ④
To point: **39',22'** (Enter)	Draws the line to ⑤
To point: **39',4'** (Enter)	Draws the line to ⑥
To point: **C** (Enter)	Closes the line back to ①

This polyline represents the interior dimensions of the building. In the following steps, you create some furniture for the plan.

Command: From the *Layer Control drop-down list (Standard Toolbar), choose A-FURN*	Sets the current layer to A-FURN
Command: *Choose Rectangle (Draw, Polygon)*	Issues the RECTANG command
First corner: **41',31'** (Enter)	Places the first corner of the rectangle at ① (see fig. 6.6)
Other corner: **46',33'** (Enter)	Completes the rectangle at ②
Command: (Enter)	Repeats the RECTANG command
First corner: **46',31'** (Enter)	Places the first corner of the rectangle at ③
Other corner: **44',28'** (Enter)	Completes the rectangle at ④
Command: (Enter)	Repeats the RECTANG command
First corner: **46',33'** (Enter)	Places the first corner of the rectangle at ②
Other corner: **51',31'** (Enter)	Completes the rectangle at ⑤
Command: (Enter)	Repeats the RECTANG command
First corner: **46',31'** (Enter)	Places the first corner of the rectangle at ③

continues

6

continued

Other corner: **48',28'** (Enter)   Completes the rectangle at ⑥

Command: *Choose Aerial View (Standard*   Issues the DSVIEWER command and
Toolbar)   displays the Aerial View window

Command: *Choose Save (Standard Toolbar)*   Saves the drawing

Your drawing now should resemble figure 6.6.

Figure 6.5

*The completed
building shell.*

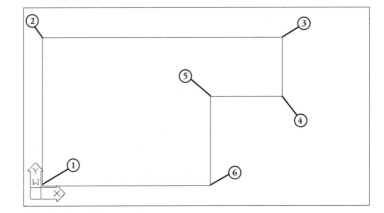

Figure 6.6

*The completed
desks.*

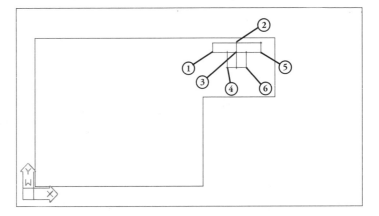

Moving around Your Drawing

By default, the Aerial View window displays the entire drawing. This allows you to see an overall view of your drawing while you are zooming and panning.

> If you find yourself with a different display than you expected, click on Zoom All on the Standard Toolbar and Global on the Aerial toolbar and just start again.

TIP

In the following exercise, you will use the Aerial View to move around your drawing.

Using Aerial View To Zoom about the Drawing

Continue from the previous exercise.

Command: *Choose Zoom Window (Aerial)*   Places the Aerial View in Zoom mode

Command: *Pick ① then ② (see fig. 6.7)*   Draws the aerial zoom window, then updates the drawing area

Notice that the result of that sequence modifies the graphics window but the Aerial View still displays the entire drawing.

Command: *Choose Pan (Aerial)*   Places the Aerial View in PAN mode

Place the pan window over the two desks in the Aerial View   Pans the drawing area to the new location

---

Figure 6.7

Zooming with the Aerial View.

6

When you choose Pan from the Aerial toolbar, it remains in effect until you choose Zoom. The Zoom In, Zoom Out, or Global tools do not affect the current mode.

The Aerial View Options

When working on a large drawing, you might want to magnify or pan the display in the Aerial View. The next exercise demonstrates the Aerial View toolbar's Zoom In and Zoom Out tools, as well as the scroll bars on the right and at the bottom.

Zooming and Panning within the Aerial View

Continue from the previous exercise.

Command: *Choose Zoom All (Standard Toolbar, Zoom)*	Updates both the drawing area and the Aerial View with the drawing limits
Command: *Choose Global (Aerial)*	Centers the limits of the drawing in the Aerial View
Command: *Choose Zoom In (Aerial)*	Magnifies the Aerial display by 2×
Click twice on the up arrow of the Aerial vertical scroll bar	Pans up the Aerial View display

The Aerial View's zooming and panning options are extremely useful as you position the Aerial View in the most effective location in the full graphics window.

TIP

As with all Windows applications, the Aerial View window can be sized up or down by dragging the edges and corners and relocated by dragging the title bar.

A feature that is most effective on large drawings is the Locator option. The Locator tool is a magnifier that can magnify up to 32 times as large as the image in the graphics window. The next exercise will review the process of using the locator at the default magnification of 1.

Using the Aerial View Locator Tool

Continue from the previous exercise

Command: *Choose Zoom All (Standard Toolbar, Zoom)*	Updates both the drawing area and the Aerial View with the drawing limits
Command: *Choose Global (Aerial)*	Centers the limits of the drawing in the Aerial Viewer
Press and drag the locator over the two desks and release	Dynamically displays the position of the locator in the Aerial View and zooms into the drawing (see fig. 6.8)
Press and drag the locator over the left desk and release	Dynamically displays the position of the locator in the Aerial View and zooms into the drawing (see fig. 6.9)
Command: *Choose Zoom All (Standard Toolbar, Zoom)*	Updates both the drawing area and the Aerial View with the drawing limits
Command: *Choose Aerial View (Standard Toolbar, Tool Windows)*	Issues the DSVIEWER command and closes the Aerial View window

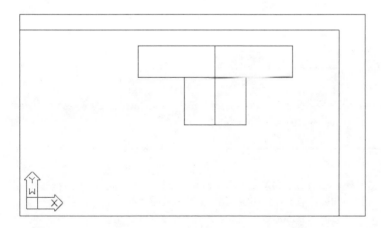

Figure 6.8

New display after using the Locator tool.

6

Figure 6.9

*Increased magnifi-
cation by repeating
the Locator.*

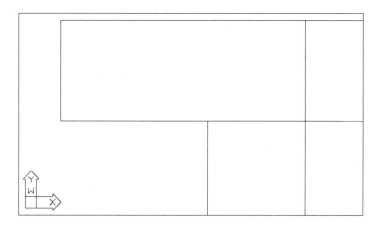

When used in combination with the scroll bars and the Locator magnifier, the Aerial View window provides some useful features for dynamically moving about the drawing.

When editing the drawing with the Aerial View enabled, the **O**ptions menu has a Dynamic Update that turns on or off the dynamic update of the Aerial window to reflect the edits. You should turn off this as you work on large drawings so that only the graphics window updates. The Aerial View window will update when you activate it.

The ZOOM Command

To make quick changes in your drawing that don't require a continual reference to the whole drawing (such as that provided by the Aerial View), the ZOOM command is the way to go.

'ZOOM. The ZOOM command is used to magnify or reduce the display of your drawing. ZOOM has several options by which you can be more specific in how your display is modified.

Tool:	*Choose Zoom Scale (Standard Toolbar, Zoom)*
Pull-down:	*Choose **V**iew, **Z**oom, **S**cale*
Screen:	*Choose VIEW, Zoom:*

The Zoom toolbar and the submenu are shown in the pull-down menu map and toolbar map at the back of the book. The **Z**oom submenu is located under the **V**iew pull-down menu and includes several items that begin a ZOOM command option. When you created the TV Remote in Chapter 3, "A Quick Drawing," you used some of the options for ZOOM by using the alias as well as some of the tools on the Standard Toolbar. The following list gives a brief explanation of each of the ZOOM command options.

- **All.** When you choose the All option, AutoCAD automatically updates the graphics window to the height and width values of the limits. If the drawing graphics extend beyond the drawing limits, the drawing fits into the graphics window. Do not confuse this option with Extents.

- **Center.** The Center option first prompts the user for a point that is to be the new center of the display. From that new center point the user is prompted for a magnification value (followed by an x) or the desired new height of the graphics window (from the bottom of the window to the top).

- **Dynamic.** The Dynamic option is similar in capabilities to the Aerial View but does not have as many features. The Dynamic option uses the AutoCAD drawing window to display an overview of the drawing along with a view box that represents your current viewport size. It then enables you to shrink or enlarge the view box and move it around the drawing as you wish to select a new view for your viewport. When finished with the display modifications in the dynamic view, AutoCAD returns to the drawing and updates the drawing window.

- **Extents.** The Extents option automatically fits the entire drawing into the graphics window. The drawing limits are not considered in the Extents option. Although not visible, the extents of objects on layers that are turned off are shown in the new display. Objects on layers that are frozen are ignored. This option always causes a regeneration of the drawing.

- **Left.** Though seldom used, the Left option first prompts the user to pick a point for the new lower left corner of the display. You are then prompted for the magnification or height of the window.

- **Previous.** The Previous option retains the last 10 displays from the graphics window, regardless of the method by which they were accomplished (Aerial View, scroll bar, PAN, ZOOM, and so on). When

6

the Previous option is chosen, AutoCAD updates the drawing with the previous window display. The command line notifies you if you have exhausted the 10 previous displays.

- **Vmax.** The Vmax option zooms as far away from the graphics as possible without incurring a drawing regeneration.

- **Window.** This is the default option for ZOOM. The Window option allows you to pick two diagonal points in the drawing to define a window area. After you pick the two corners, AutoCAD updates the graphics with what was bounded by the window.

- **<Scale(X/XP)>.** This option requires the user to enter a magnification factor for the new display and apply the factor to the area defined by the drawing limits. A value less than 1 will reduce the size of the graphics, a value greater than 1 will magnify the graphics. When the factor is followed by an X, the reduction or magnification is applied to the current display size. The XP option is covered in Chapter 16, "Composing and Plotting a Drawing," and relates exclusively to displays in floating viewports.

TIP

Because the zoom window always results in a new display, you should pick two points that are roughly the same proportion as the graphics window. Otherwise, you might get unexpected results.

The following exercise incorporates several options from ZOOM as you modify the display of the FURNPLAN drawing.

Using ZOOM Options To Change the Display

Continue from the previous exercise.

Command: *Choose Zoom All (Standard Toolbar, Zoom)*	Updates the drawing area with the drawing limits
Command: *Choose Zoom Window (Standard Toolbar)*	Issues the ZOOM commands with the Window option
First point: *Pick* ①, *then* ②	Places a zoom window and updates the drawing area as shown in figure 6.10
Command: (Enter)	Repeats the ZOOM command

`First point:` *Pick* ①, then ② *(see fig. 6.11)*	Places a zoom window, then updates the drawing area
`Command:` *Choose Zoom Previous (Standard Toolbar)*	Updates the graphics window with the previous display
`Command:` *Choose Zoom Previous (Standard Toolbar)*	Updates the graphics window with the previous display

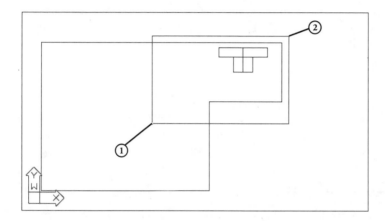

Figure 6.10

Pick points for a zoom window.

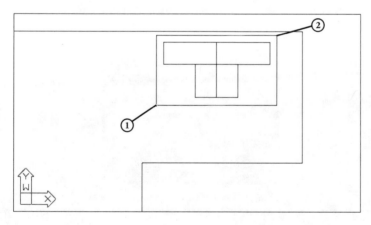

Figure 6.11

Pick points for another zoom window.

6

Saving and Restoring Named Views

During the course of a drawing session, you usually need to return to the previous display or view. The Previous option in ZOOM is helpful, but if the display you need to see was several zooms ago, Previous might not be the best solution.

You can save and restore a view by name with the DDVIEW command. By having a named view, one that shows the overall plan of the object or building, for example, you save it by name then restore that view when you need to see it.

'DDVIEW. The DDVIEW command allows you to save and restore named views by providing you with a dialog box for the view selection.

Tool: *Choose Named Views (Standard Toolbar, View)*
Pull-down: *Choose **V**iew, **N**amed views*
Screen: *Choose VIEW, Ddview:*

The DDVIEW command displays the View Control dialog box (see fig. 6.12) in which you can create a new view, restore and existing view, or delete a view from the list of views.

The View Control dialog box.

TIP

Because restoring a View does not normally require a drawing regeneration, it's a good idea to save a view of the whole drawing. This is especially handy if you are working on a large drawing.

In the following exercise, you save and restore some views.

Saving Named Views

Continue from the previous exercise.

`Command:` *Choose Zoom All (Standard Toolbar, Zoom)*	Displays the drawing limits
`Command:` *Choose Named Views (Standard Toolbar, View)*	Issues the DDVIEW command and displays the View Control dialog box
Choose **N**ew	Opens the Define New View dialog box
In the **N**ew Name *box, type* **ALL** *then choose* **S**ave View	Saves the view as ALL and adds it to the View Control list
Choose OK	Closes the View Control dialog box
`Command:` *Choose Zoom Window (Standard Window Toolbar)*	Issues the ZOOM command with the option
`First point:` *Pick* ①, *then* ② *(see fig. 6.13)*	Places a zoom window, then updates the display
`Command:` *Choose Named Views (Standard Toolbar, View)*	Issues the DDVIEW command and displays the View Control dialog box
Choose **N**ew	Opens the Define New View dialog box
In the **N**ew Name *box, type* **OFFICE** *then choose* **S**ave View	Saves the view as OFFICE and adds it to the View Control list
Choose OK	Closes the View Control dialog box
`Command:` *Choose Named Views (Standard Toolbar, View)*	Issues the DDVIEW command
Choose ALL *from the list, then choose* **R**estore, *and* OK	Restores the view ALL
`Command:` `Enter`	Issues the previous command
Choose OFFICE *from the list, then choose* **R**estore, *then* OK	Restores the view OFFICE
`Command:` *Choose Save (Standard Toolbar)*	Saves the drawing

6

Figure 6.13

Zoom window corners around the desks.

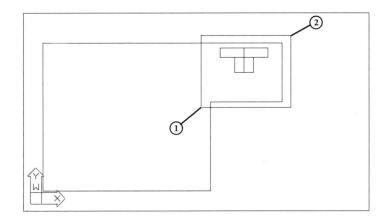

NOTE

> The command VIEW also enables you to create named views, but from the command line. Refer to *Inside AutoCAD Release 13 for Windows and Windows NT* or take a look at the *AutoCAD Reference Manual* for more information on the VIEW command.

When a view is saved, AutoCAD stores the X,Y coordinates for the lower left and upper right corners of the graphics window at the time the view is saved. No file is created from the process, just a couple coordinates that are saved with the name associated with those coordinates. When you restore the view, AutoCAD restores the lower left and upper right coordinates of the graphics window and updates the display.

A couple of added benefits are that named views are saved with the drawing and there is no limit to the number of saved views you can have in a drawing. Chapter 16, "Composing and Plotting a Drawing," covers plotting named views, which saves time and maintains consistency in plots.

Splitting the Display with Tiled Viewports

On occasion, you might need to see more than one area of a drawing at a time in the graphics window. This might be the case in engineering drawings or architectural floor plans when you need to not only see the overall object or floor plan, but also a detailed view of a specific area. In instances such as these, tiled viewports enable you to display more than just a single view of the drawing by splitting your screen into two or more viewports.

Tiled viewports get their name from the fact that they are viewports configured in much the same fashion as ceiling or floor tile: the display is divided into organized rectangles, edge to edge, fit within a specific area. Figure 6.14 illustrates an example of tiled viewports on the TV Remote drawing.

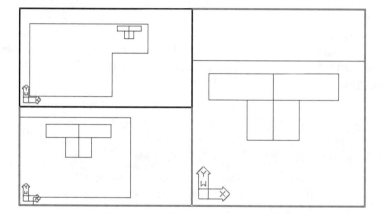

Figure 6.14

Tiled viewports.

With a split display, you can have an overall view of the drawing in one viewport and a close up view of the same drawing in two other viewports.

Selecting a Tiled Viewport Configuration

AutoCAD has several preset viewport configurations you can choose from in the Tiled Viewport dialog box. After the drawing area has been tiled by way of one of the selections, you may customize the divisions of each viewport, as well.

6

VPORTS. The VPORTS (or VIEWPORTS) command gives you several options by which to subdivide your display, thus enabling you to display multiple views of your drawing simultaneously.
Pull-down: *Choose* **V**iew, Tile**d** Viewports, *then a menu item*
Screen: *Choose* VIEW, Vports:

The following listing presents the options of the VPORTS command:

- **Save.** Similar in function to saving a named view, the Save option for the VPORTS command enables you to name the current tiled viewport configuration so that it may be restored when needed again.

- **Restore.** The Restore option will restore a previously saved tiled viewport configuration.

- **Delete.** The Delete option will simply delete a previously saved tiled viewport configuration from the list of those which can be restored.

- **Join.** This option enables you to join two existing viewports to make a single viewport. The only criteria is that the resulting viewport must form a rectangle. When joining viewports, the current viewport, by default, is considered to be the dominant viewport but you may select a different one if you wish. When selecting viewports to join, simply pick anywhere in the viewport.

- **SIngle.** Should you need to return to the standard, single view, graphics window, use the SIngle option. The SIngle option will set the current viewport to be displayed in the drawing area, regardless of the size of the display in the tiled viewport.

- **?.** This option enables you to see a listing of any saved tiled viewport configurations. After the list has been displayed, to restore a viewport configuration, use the Restore option.

- **2.** This option enables you to split the display into two horizontal or two vertical viewports. The default arrangement is for two vertical viewports.

- **3.** A configuration of 3 viewports is the default. One approach using this option is to split the screen into two viewports, then split one of those viewports. This configuration results in one large viewport and two smaller viewports. The large viewport can either be configured above, below to the right or to the left. The large viewport on the right is the default configuration. The alternative available is to split the screen into 3 equal viewport horizontally or vertically.

- **4.** This option simply splits the screen into four quadrants.

AutoCAD has several preset viewport configurations you can choose from in a dialog box. If you choose **V**iew, Tile**d** Viewports, **L**ayout, AutoCAD displays the Tiled Viewport Layout dialog box, which contains a number of preset viewport configurations.

The following exercise shows you how to select a tiled viewport configuration and how each viewport can contain a separate size view of the
drawing.

Selecting and Displaying Tiled Viewports

Continue from the previous exercise.

Command: *Choose Zoom All (Standard Toolbar, Zoom)*	Displays the drawing limits
Command: *Choose **V**iew, Tile**d** Viewports, then **L**ayout*	Displays the Tiled Viewports dialog box
From the list, choose vport-3r *then choose* OK	Configures the display for two small viewports on the left and a large viewport on the right (see fig. 6.15)
Command: *Pick anywhere in the upper left viewport*	Activates the upper left viewport
Command: *Choose Zoom Window (Standard Toolbar)*	Issues the ZOOM command with the Window option
First corner: *Place a window around the two desks*	Updates the viewport display
Command: *Pick anywhere in the lower left viewport*	Activates the lower left viewport
Command: (Enter)	Repeats the ZOOM command
First corner: *Place a window around the right wing of the building*	Updates the viewport display
Command: *Choose **V**iew, Tile**d** Viewports, then **1** Viewport*	Returns to a single viewport
Command: *Choose Save (Standard Toolbar)*	Saves the drawing

When using the ZOOM, PAN, or VIEW commands, you must activate
the viewport *before* choosing the command.

Figure 6.15

Tiled viewports.

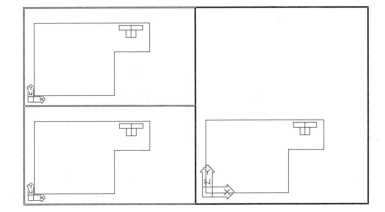

Because tiled viewports configure the display with multiple views of a single drawing, any edits that take place in one viewport are reflected in all viewports. As useful as this configuration might appear, the following are drawbacks to using tiled viewports:

- **The viewports cannot be moved or sized in the display.** Although you can choose from several preset configurations when you work with tiled viewports, you cannot change their shape or relationship to each other. The viewports are tiled and, by definition, must be next to each other.

- **Only one viewport is active at a time.** This restriction only becomes an issue when, for example, you need to have labeling or text go across more than one viewport for a title block or some other graphics designed for the whole drawing.

- **You cannot plot the display, only the active viewport.** The inability to plot the entire display can prove extremely disappointing, especially when you want to see all the views with their different plot scales on one sheet.

- **The layering is global.** If you want to view certain layers in one viewport, but not in the other viewports, this restriction will require extensive layer management.

Tiled viewports are useful as an editing and drawing tool to assist in your display manipulation. As a sheet composition technique, however, they have some critical shortcomings. To overcome the shortcomings of tiled viewports, Autodesk introduces the concept of paper space.

Paper Space Versus Model Space

The relationship between model space and paper space can most easily be presented by way of analogy. Act I of a play at the local theater comes to an end and the curtain comes down. As a good patron of the arts, you are sitting in the audience and now have a 2-dimensional environment (the curtain) between you and a 3-dimensional environment (the stage). The curtain is paper space, the stage whereon the actors move about 3 dimensionally, is model space. Though you don't see them, there are actors milling about on stage preparing for Act II. This is similar to what takes place in AutoCAD when you invoke paper space by turning off TILEMODE.

Paper space is a 2-dimensional environment. Model space is a 3-dimensional environment although you need not be working on anything in 3D to make use of this powerful tool. AutoCAD, by default, begins in model space. With respect to our analogy, there is no curtain by default, to separate you from the activity on the stage of model space. The system variable TILEMODE enables or disables paper space, it is the method by which the curtain is lowered or raised. If TILEMODE is set to 1 (ON), you are in model space, and the curtain is up, if TILEMODE is set to 0 (OFF), paper space is enabled and the curtain is down.

The word "tile" is used in reference to the way the display looks when configured with multiple tiled viewports as was presented in the previous exercise. The viewports automatically are placed neatly next to each other, just like ceiling tile or floor tile. The user can only select the number of viewports to be used and, to some extent, the configuration. But the viewports are always placed together or "tiled." Therefore, tiled viewports occur in model space when TILEMODE is on.

Returning to our analogy for a moment, when paper space is invoked and the curtain comes down, the objects in model space (the actors) are still there, they just can't be seen. To see them, viewports must be created in paper space, through which to see the objects in model space. The viewports can be created anywhere in paper space; they need not be next to each other. For this reason, viewports in paper space are referred to as "floating" viewports and can only be made when TILEMODE is off. Although you would suffer serious consequences were you to attempt this, if you were to cut a viewport in the stage curtain, you could see the actors and stage crew on stage, but I think you get the point.

In the next exercise, you will drop "the curtain" by turning off the TILEMODE variable, make some floating viewports and continue to edit the drawing by going back and forth between the two environments as the need arises.

6

Turning Off TILEMODE and Setting the Paper Space Limits

Continue from the previous exercise. Turn off grid, snap, and ortho. The results of this exercise might be disconcerting at first; just remember that Act I has come to an end. Notice that the status bar reads MODEL, indicating that model space is current.

Command: *Double-click on* TILE *on the status bar*	Turns off TILEMODE and invokes paper space
Command: *Choose* **D**ata, Dr**a**wing limits	Issues the LIMITS command
Reset Model space limits: ON/OFF/ <Lower left corner> <0'-0",0'-0">: (Enter)	Accepts default value of 0,0 for the lower left corner
Upper right corner <3'-0",2'-0">: **36,24** (Enter)	Sets limits area to 36"×24"
Command: *Choose Zoom All (Standard Toolbar, Zoom)*	Updates the display to the current limits
Command: *Choose Save (Standard Toolbar)*	Saves the drawing

You can set the paper space limits independently of the model space limits. By setting the paper space limits to 36"×24", you are setting up a D-size plot sheet.

Not to worry, the building shell is still in model space. The two-dimensional environment of paper space is now between you and model space. The following are a few things to notice when paper space is invoked.

- TILE on the status bar is grayed out (off).

- PAPER now appears on the status bar where MODEL had been.

- Paper space has a separate limits setting from model space. By default, the paper space limits is set to 12" × 9", which is the same default setting for model space.

- There is a different UCS icon for paper space.

- With no floating viewports yet in paper space, your drawing seems to have disappeared.

So far, so good. Now let's see what's happening on stage.

Creating a New Viewport in Paper Space

Now comes the time to "cut a hole" in the curtain of paper space. This is done with the MVIEW (which stands for Model space VIEWport) command. The MVIEW command allows you to create floating model space viewports in paper space.

MVIEW. The MVIEW command is the method by which floating viewports are created or "cut into" paper space. The display of the objects seen in the floating model space viewport is the display of the drawing area in model space prior to invoking paper space with the TILEMODE variable.

Pull-down: *Choose* **V**iew, Floatin**g** Viewports, *then a menu option*
Screen: *Choose* VIEW, Mview:

The MVIEW command has several options when creating floating model space viewports. Some of them are very similar to those found in the VPORTS command.

- **ON.** This option enables you to turn on a viewport previously turned off. Once turned back on, the viewport is editable as are any model space objects seen in the viewport.

- **OFF.** The OFF option enables you to temporarily turn off the selectability of the viewport as well as the visibility of any model space objects previously seen through the viewport.

- **Hideplot.** This option refers to the hidden lines of 3D objects in model space. It enables you to hide the lines of objects in the specified viewport when plotted that are hidden by opaque 3D faces.

- **Fit.** The Fit option automatically creates a single viewport that is fit to the existing drawing window.

- **2.** Similar in function to the 2 option for the VPORTS command, this option will automatically create two horizontal or two vertical floating viewports.

- **3.** The 3 viewport option enables you to create three equally sized viewports horizontally or vertically or a single large viewport on half the drawing area with two viewports dividing the other half. You determine whether the large viewport is placed above, below, to the left of or to the right of the other two viewports.

- **4.** This option creates four floating viewports that equally divide the drawing area into quadrants.

- **Restore.** The Restore option will restore a tiled viewport configuration that was saved using the Save option of the VPORTS command. The new viewports are floating viewports but the viewports are created in paper space in the same configuration as the tiled viewport configuration when saved in model space.

- **First Point.** The default option of First Point enables you to pick any two points to define the floating viewport.

Viewports are the holes in paper space, but when the drawing window background color is the same for both paper space and model space, however, it makes it impossible to see the viewports for editing. Fortunately, each viewport includes a selectable border so that you can edit the viewport's position or size later. In the next exercise, you create a VP layer, and then create floating viewports on that layer.

Looking into Model Space through a Floating Viewport

Continue from the previous exercise. So that the viewport frame can be turned off later, you must create a VP layer before making the viewport.

Command: *Choose Layers (Object Properties)*	Issues the DDLMODES command
In the edit box, type **VP**, *then choose* Ne**w**, *then* OK	Creates the VP layer
Command: *From the Layer Control drop-down list, choose* VP	Sets the VP layer current
Command: *Choose* **V**iew, Floatin**g** Viewports, **1** Viewport	Issues the MVIEW command
`ON/OFF/Hideplot/Fit/2/3/4/Restore/` `<First Point>`: *Pick* ① *(see fig. 6.16)*	Places first point of the viewport
`Other corner:` *Pick* ②	Makes viewport in paper space and ends the MVIEW command
Command: *Choose Save (Standard Toolbar)*	Saves the drawing

Simple! Now you see what is in model space through a floating viewport in paper space. The difference between floating and tiled viewports now is evident. While tiled viewports have to fill the entire drawing area, floating viewports can be placed anywhere on the screen and can be any size. Also, the cursor is free to move about the entire drawing area and is not limited to the floating viewport.

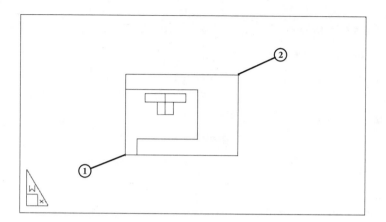

The first floating viewport in paper space.

The following are some things to remember about viewports and paper space:

- When using the Floating Viewports item from the View menu to create a viewport, paper space is still current after the viewport is created.

- While in paper space, you have a full screen cursor.

- The objects in model space are not selectable while paper space is current.

- The only editable objects in paper space are the objects that you created in paper space, such as the viewport frames. You learn more about adding other objects to paper space in Chapter 16, "Composing and Plotting a Drawing."

Currently, the FURNPLAN drawing is in paper space and there is a floating viewport in paper space through which you can see the objects in model space. Any command you issue at this point only addresses the paper space environment.

Switching between Paper Space and Model Space

The beauty of using paper space is that you can now work in either model space or paper space. Switching to model space is done easily from the status bar or by way of a command alias.

Switching to Model Space and Then Back to Paper Space

Continue from the previous exercise.

Command: *Double-click on* PAPER *on the status bar*	Switches to model space
Command: **PS** (Enter)	Switches to paper space
Command: **MS** (Enter)	Switches to model space
Command: *Choose Zoom Extents (Standard Toolbar, Zoom)*	Updates the floating viewport display with the extents of the objects in model space
Command: *Choose Zoom Previous (Standard Toolbar, Zoom)*	Returns to the previous model space display
Command: *Double-click on* MODEL *on the status bar*	Switches to paper space
Command: *Choose Zoom Extents (Standard Toolbar, Zoom)*	Updates the display with the extents of the objects in paper space
Command: *Choose Zoom Previous (Standard Toolbar, Zoom)*	Returns to the previous view in paper space
Command: *Choose Save (Standard Toolbar)*	Saves the drawing

AutoCAD makes it easy to switch between the two environments. Here are a few more pointers to add to your paper space/model space list:

- To switch between model space and paper space, you can type either MS (to switch to model space) or PS (to switch to paper space), or double-click on the MODEL/PAPER button on status bar.

- The UCS icon changes to reflect the active environment.

- When in model space, the cursor is only active in the current viewport.

- When in model space, all display commands you issue refer to the current viewport (although the result of a draw or edit command can be reflected in other viewports).

You now are able to invoke paper space, make a viewport, and switch between model space and paper space.

Changing the display in a viewport is quite simple and extremely helpful while editing. The next section covers *what* you see in each of the viewports now that you have defined the area of the drawing.

Viewport-Specific Layering Options

One of the most versatile features available when working with paper space is the capability to freeze layers by viewport. This gives you the ability to control the contents of each floating viewports. This can only be done when TILEMODE is off, it cannot be used in tiled viewports created using the VPORTS command.

You can manage the process of viewport-specific layering in a couple of ways. One way is by using the layer control tools in the DDLMODES command; the other way is by using the Layer Control tool on the Standard Toolbar.

The VPLAYER command gives you the ability to control layer visibility in multiple viewports. See *Inside AutoCAD Release 13 for Windows and Windows NT*, also published by New Riders Publishing, for more information on VPLAYER.

In the following exercise, you will turn off the A-FURN layer in the bottom viewport.

Freezing Layers in Floating Viewports

Continue from the previous exercise. Before beginning, make sure model space is active.

Command: *In the Layer Control drop-down list, click on the sun / rectangle icon for* A-FURN *and press Enter*	Changes the icon to a snowflake and turns off the layer A-FURN in the active viewport
Command: *Choose Save (Standard Toolbar)*	Saves the drawing

Remember that this sequence took place when a floating viewport was current. Keep in mind the following when using this method to freeze layers in a viewport:

6

- The sun/rectangle icon is the only icon in the drop-down list that relates to floating viewports.

- The drop-down list doesn't close until you either press Enter, pick a new current layer, or pick outside the drop-down list.

- You can select multiple layers to be frozen in the current viewport.

Text in Model Space and Paper Space

When there is text in model space, such as room names, lettering on machined parts, structural column bubble characters, and so forth, you should base the height of the text on the final output scale. Chapter 11, "Text," covers how to control the height of text in your drawing while Chapter 16, "Composing and Plotting a Drawing", covers the issue of plot scale and its relationship to text height more fully. It's important to know, however, that if the display of one floating model space viewport is at a greater magnification than another viewport, the height of the text magnifies accordingly.

Text in paper space acts differently than text in a floating model space viewport. Because paper space typically is plotted full scale, text placed in paper space should be full size.

When placing text in model space, however, the height of the text must be adjusted for the plot scale. If you want your model space text to appear 1/4" high when plotted at a scale of 1/4"=1'-0", for example, you must make the model space text 1' high.

In the following exercise, you add a line of text to the floating model space viewport.

Placing Text in a Model Space Floating Viewports

Continue from the previous exercise. Before starting, make sure model space is active and that the top viewport is current.

Command: *From the Layer Control drop-down list, choose* A-NOTES	Sets the A-NOTES layer current
Command: *Choose Dtext (Draw, Text)*	Issues the DTEXT command
_dtext Justify/Style/<Start point>: *Pick* ① *as shown in figure 6.17*	Establishes the start point for the text

`Height <0'-0 3/16">: 12 (Enter)`	Sets the text height to 12"
`Rotation angle <0>: (Enter)`	Accepts 0 for the rotation angle
`Text: ACCOUNTING (Enter)`	Enters the text
`Text: (Enter)`	Ends the DTEXT command

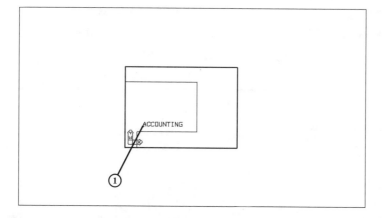

Figure 6.17

Starting point for text in the viewport.

The size of text in the previous exercise had a height of 12". When you assign the viewport a plot scale of 1/8"=1', for example, the text will plot 1/8" high. The text looks proportional in that viewport as well.

In the next exercise, you enter text in paper space. Bear in mind that paper space is plotted 1:1. The height of the text will be 1/2" as you add a label to the drawing before running a check plot.

Placing Text in Paper Space

Continue from the previous exercise.

`Command:` *Choose Layers (Object Properties)*	Issues the DDLMODES command
Select the layer A-FURN *from the* Layer Name *list and choose* Cur VP: **T**haw, *then* OK	Thaws the layer A-FURN in the current viewport
`Command:` *Double-click on* MODEL *in the status bar*	Switches to paper space
`Command:` *Choose Dtext (Draw, Text)*	Issues the DTEXT command

continues

6

continued

`_dtext Justify/Style/<Start point>:` *Pick ① as shown in figure 6.18*	Establishes the start point for the text
`Height <1'-0">:` **1/2** `(Enter)`	Sets the text height to 1/2"
`Rotation angle <0>:` *Press Enter*	Accepts 0 for the rotation
`Text:` **Second Floor** `(Enter)`	Enters the first line of text
`Text:` **Large Scale Plans** `(Enter)`	Enters the second line of text
`Text:` Press Enter	Ends the DTEXT command
`Command:` *Choose Save (Standard Toolbar)*	Saves the drawing

Figure 6.18

Text added in paper space.

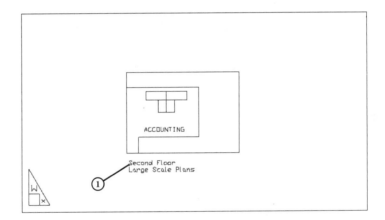

Recommended Paper Space Contents

Often the question, "What should be in paper space and what should be in model space?" is asked. The contents of paper space might include objects such as the title block, legends, revisions, and general sheet notes. The contents of model space, on the other hand, would contain the primary objects of the drawing, as well as the dimensions, room names and numbers, construction notes particular to a certain area of the drawing, column lines, and section cuts, to name a few.

Summary

AutoCAD Release 13 has several ways to manage your display. From the simple commands, such as ZOOM, PAN, and VIEW, to the new Aerial window, to the more sophisticated capabilities provided in paper space with floating model space viewports. When used in combination, these features can improve your efficiency in producing your final drawing by using the quickest way to modify your display.

Related Topics

- Working with layers—Chapter 4, "Preparing Your Drawing"
- Numeric accuracy in drawing—Chapter 7, "Drawing Accurately"
- Using grips—Chapter 8, "Editing with Grips"
- Drawing with polylines—Chapter 9, "More Drawing Commands"
- Plotting to scale and Zoom/XP—Chapter 16, "Composing and Plotting a Drawing"
- Drawing composition—Chapter 16, "Composing and Plotting a Drawing"

6

Chapter Snapshot

Accuracy is everything when it comes to creating documents. This chapter covers the following features that enable you to create accurate drawings with AutoCAD Release 13:

- Entering numeric coordinates for accurate lines and circles

- Manipulating the User Coordinate System

- Snapping to objects for accurate placement and positioning

- Advanced geometry location techniques using point filters

7

Drawing Accurately

Computer aided design has been likened to an Etch-A-Sketch for grown-ups. When you turn the dials, you get lines on the screen just like when you draw lines with the mouse or digitizer. It's a lot of fun, but doesn't lend itself to creating the accurate drawings that are frequently needed in the real world. Fortunately, AutoCAD offers several tools to help ensure drawing accuracy.

In the following Quick Tour exercise, you draw a floppy disk from days gone by—the 5.25" size. As you work through this exercise, you are introduced to several of the features that will be covered in this chapter.

The Quick Tour

To begin, create a new drawing named FLOPPY using the default ACAD.DWG prototype drawing. Create a new layer named DISK and set it current.

Command: *Choose Rectangle (Draw, Polygon)*	Issues the RECTANG command
First corner: *Pick* ① *(see fig. 7.1)*	Places the first corner of the rectangle at the point 2,2
Other corner: **@5.25,5.25** (Enter)	Creates rectangle, ends the command
Command: *Choose Circle Center Radius (Draw, Circle)*	Issues the CIRCLE command
3P/2P/TTR/<Center point>: *Choose .X (Standard Toolbar, Point Filters)*	Selects the .X point filter
.x of *Choose Snap to Midpoint (Standard Toolbar, Object Snap)*	Starts the Midpoint object snap
mid of *Pick* ②	Specifies the X coordinate of the circle
(need YZ): *Choose Snap to Midpoint (Standard Toolbar, Object Snap)*	
mid of *Pick* ③	Specifies the Y and Z coordinates of the circle
Diameter/<Radius>: **.5625** (Enter)	Draws the circle
Command: (Enter)	Repeats the CIRCLE command
3P/2P/TTR/<Center point>: *Choose Snap to Center (Standard Toolbar, Object Snap)*	Starts the CENter object snap
cen of *Pick* ④	Places the center of the circle
Diameter/<Radius> <0.5625>: **.7813** (Enter)	Draws the circle
Command: *Choose Line (Draw, Line)*	Issues the LINE command
From point: *Choose Snap From (Standard Toolbar, Object Snap)*	Starts the FROM modifier
Base point: *Choose Snap to Midpoint (Standard Toolbar, Object Snap)*	Starts the MIDpoint object snap
mid of *Pick* ②	Places the FROM base point at the midpoint of the line
<Offset>: **@-.25,.375** (Enter)	Places the start of the line at ⑤
To point: **@.875<90** (Enter)	Places the end of the line at ⑥

To point: (Enter)	Ends the LINE command
Command: (Enter)	
From point: @.5<0 (Enter)	Places the start of the line at ⑦
To point: @.875<270 (Enter)	Places the end of the line at ⑧
To point: (Enter)	Ends the LINE command
Command: *Choose Running Object Snap (Standard Toolbar, Object Snap), turn on* **E**ndpoint, *and choose* OK	Issues the DDOSNAP command and sets a running endpoint object snap
Command: *Choose Arc Start End Radius (Draw, Circle)*	Issues the ARC command with the Start, End, and Radius options
Center/<Start point>: *Pick* ⑦	Places the start of the arc at ⑦
End point: *Pick* ⑥	Places the end of the arc at ⑥
Radius: .25 (Enter)	Draws a .25 radius arc
Command: *Choose Arc Start End Radius (Draw, Circle)*	Issues the ARC command with the Start, End, and Radius options
Center/<Start point>: *Pick* ⑤	Places the start of the arc at ⑤
End point: *Pick* ⑧	Places the end of the arc at ⑧
Radius: .25 (Enter)	Draws a .25 radius arc
Command: *Choose Running Object Snap (Standard Toolbar, Object Snap), choose* Clear All, *and choose* OK	Clears the running object snap
Command: *Choose Save (Standard Toolbar)*	Saves the drawing

Your drawing now should resemble figure 7.1.

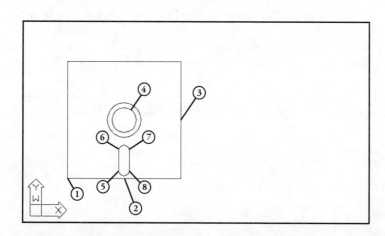

Figure 7.1

The floppy disk.

7

Using Coordinate Entry for Drawing Accuracy

Entering coordinates from the Command: line is the most basic means by which you can draw and edit accurately in AutoCAD. AutoCAD provides a number of ways to specify coordinates. The following list is a brief explanation of the three types of coordinate entries covered in this section.

- **Absolute Coordinate Entry.** The absolute method uses coordinates that are based upon the current coordinate system. The coordinates are entered at the prompt in the format X,Y.

- **Relative Coordinate Entry.** When using relative coordinate entry, the coordinates are preceded by the @ sign in the format @x,y. This entry sequence draws or edits the object from the last point selected.

- **Polar Coordinate Entry.** Similar to the relative entry mode, polar coordinate entry requires a distance and an angle to be entered in the format @dist<angle. This entry also draws or edits the selection set from the last point picked, such as a base point.

Figure 7.2 indicates the coordinate entry at the command line for the various methods indicated. After picking a start point for the LINE command, the resulting line is based upon the entry given in the figure.

Absolute Coordinate Entry

Absolute coordinate entry is the simplest method for entering points. As you move your cursor, the status bar coordinates reflect the crosshair position from absolute 0,0 of the current coordinate system.

This chapter's exercises step you through the process of drawing a building plaza with three wings extending from a central atrium. The exercises use the ACADISO.DWG metric prototype and use millimeters as the default unit. The first exercise of the series creates the orthogonal wing.

Creating the Orthogonal Wing of the Building Plaza

Begin by creating a new drawing named 3WING using the ACADISO.DWG prototype drawing, which is located in the \ACADR13\COMMON\SUPPORT directory. Create two layers named PLAN and ELEVATION and set the PLAN layer current.

Command: *Choose* **D**ata, Dr**a**wing Limits   Issues the LIMITS command

`ON/OFF/<Lower left corner>` `<0.0000,0.0000>:` (Enter)	Accepts the default 0,0 for the lower left corner
`Upper right corner <420.000,297.000>:` **`100000,100000`** (Enter)	Places the upper right limits corner at 100000,100000
Command: *Choose Zoom All (Standard Toolbar, Zoom)*	Displays the area defined by the limits
Command: *Choose Line (Draw, Line)*	Issues the LINE command
`From point:` **`45350,53300`** (Enter)	Begins the line at ① (see fig. 7.3)
`To point:` **`45350,94700`** (Enter)	Draws the line to ②
`To point:` **`67550,94700`** (Enter)	Draws the line to ③
`To point:` **`67550,53300`** (Enter)	Draws the line to ④
`To point:` **`C`** (Enter)	Closes the line back to ①

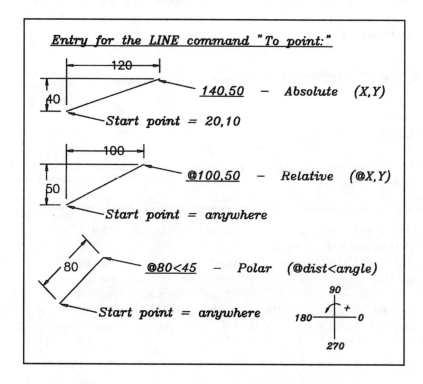

Figure 7.2

The various methods of coordinate entries.

Figure 7.3

The orthogonal building wing.

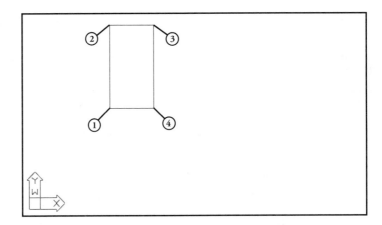

Absolute coordinate entry is best used when you are working from a drawing labeled with coordinates or if you can transfer a drawing on grid paper into AutoCAD. In most other cases, a more convenient method is relative coordinate entry.

Relative Coordinate Entry

Relative coordinate entry is probably the most common method because it only requires you to know the location of the last point placed in the drawing. Like absolute coordinates, relative coordinates are entered in the X,Y format but are preceded by the @ (at sign). This sign indicates that you want to go a specified distance from where you are *at*, improper grammar notwithstanding.

TIP

The F6 function key not only turns on and off the display of the coordinates that track the current position of the crosshairs, but when a point is picked, it also enables the display of the relative position and the angle of the line being drawn or the object being edited. Press F6 three times to see each of the features, then move the cursor slowly across the display to see how each of them works. You also can cycle through the features of the display coordinates by double-clicking on them in the status bar.

The following exercise uses relative entry to create the connecting structure between the primary building and the atrium.

Adding a Connecting Structure Using Relative Coordinate Entry

Continue from the previous exercise.

Command: *Choose Line (Draw, Line)*	Issues the LINE command
From point: **50000,53300** (Enter)	Begins the line at ① (see fig. 7.4)
To point: **@0,-3300** (Enter)	Draws the line to ②
To point: **@12900,0** (Enter)	Draws the line to ③
To point: **@0,3300** (Enter)	Draws the line to ④
To point: (Enter)	Ends the LINE command
Command: *Choose Save (Standard Toolbar)*	Saves the drawing

Your drawing now should resemble figure 7.4.

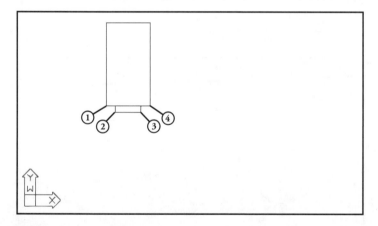

Figure 7.4

The connecting structure.

Polar Coordinate Entry

The polar coordinate entry function is similar in concept to relative coordinate entry in that it continues from the last point placed in the drawing. The difference, as shown in figure 7.2, is that polar coordinates are entered with a distance and an angle.

In the following exercise you use polar coordinate entry to create the six-sided atrium. Keep in mind that the X and Y axes, which define the 0, 90, 180 and 270 degree positions, do not rotate after each entry but are always constant.

Creating the Atrium Using Polar Coordinate Entry

Continue from the previous exercise.

Command: *Choose·Line (Draw, Line)*	Issues the LINE command
From point: **50000,50000** (Enter)	Begins the line at ① (see fig. 7.5)
To point: **@6600<240** (Enter)	Draws the line to ②
To point: **@12900<300** (Enter)	Draws the line to ③
To point: **@6600<0** (Enter)	Draws the line to ④
To point: **@12900<60** (Enter)	Draws the line to ⑤
To point: **@6600<120** (Enter)	Draws the line to ⑥
To point: (Enter)	Ends the LINE command
Command: *Choose Redraw (Standard Toolbar)*	Redraws the display
Command: *Choose Save (Standard Toolbar)*	Saves the drawing

Figure 7.5

The atrium created using polar coordinate entry.

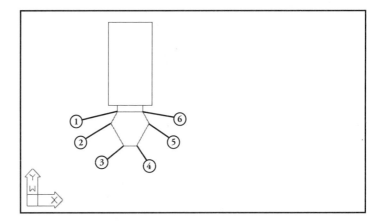

User Coordinate Systems

As was discussed in Chapter 4, "Preparing Your Drawing," the default point where the X and Y axes intersect is absolute 0,0 and frequently is called the origin. The default coordinate system is referred to as the World Coordinate System (WCS).

The majority of the time, the World Coordinate System is sufficient for locating objects in the drawing. There are times, however, when it would be convenient to change the location of the origin or rotate the X and Y axes.

The UCS Command

AutoCAD gives you the ability to create a custom coordinate system, known as the User Coordinate System (UCS), anywhere in a drawing with the UCS command.

UCS. The UCS command enables you to create a custom coordinate system by relocating the origin and rotating either the X, Y, or Z axis.

Toolbar: *Choose World UCS (Standard Toolbar, UCS)*

Pull-down: *Choose **V**iew, **S**et UCS, then a menu option*

Screen: *Choose VIEW, UCS:*

The UCS command is useful in 2D drawings for a couple reasons. The first is to relocate the origin for easier coordinate entry. In the case of the previous exercise using absolute coordinate entry, relocation of the UCS would have meant that the coordinates entered could have been the actual values for the sides of the rectangle created.

The second strategic application for UCS in 2D is with regard to rotation of the X,Y plane. If you create a drawing that is rotated 60 degrees from horizontal, for example, it's helpful to be able to rotate the UCS by 60 degrees. This simplifies coordinate entry as you create the drawing.

The UCS command has 14 options, some of which are used only in 3D applications. The following is a list of the options useful in 2D applications:

- **Origin.** The Origin option enables you to reposition the UCS origin. The origin is where the X and Y axes intersect.

- **3point.** The 3point option enables the user to pick three points to define the X,Y plane. The three prompts are for the origin point, a second point to define the X axis, and a point anywhere in the positive portion of the X,Y plane.

- **OBject.** This option prompts you to select an object with which you want the UCS to align. The resulting orientation of the UCS is based upon the direction in which the object was drawn.

7

- **Z.** Using the Z option is the method by which the X,Y plane is rotated. Keep in mind the right-hand thumb rule, a positive rotation is counterclockwise.

- **Previous.** AutoCAD can store a maximum of 10 unnamed UCS positions. The Previous option relocates the UCS to the previous UCS position.

- **Restore.** Used in conjunction with the Save option, Restore restores the position of a named UCS.

- **Save.** The Save option enables you to save the current UCS position by name.

- **Delete.** The Delete option deletes an existing UCS name.

- **?.** Similar to the question mark found in the options for several other commands, this option enables you to see a listing of existing UCS names.

- **World.** World is the default. This option sets the coordinate system to the World Coordinate System position.

By default, the UCS icon is on and displayed at the lower-left corner of the display. When not changing the position of the coordinate system, the icon can be turned off. When manipulating the coordinate system, however, it might be advantageous to show the UCS icon at the origin. The display of the UCS icon can be controlled with the UCSICON command.

UCSICON. The UCSICON command enables you to alter the visibility and position of the UCS icon usually seen in the lower-left corner of the display.
Screen: *Choose* OPTIONS, UCS icon:

The UCSICON command has some unique characteristics that you will see in the next exercise. The following is a list of the UCSICON options:

- **ON.** This option turns on the visibility of the UCS icon.

- **OFF.** This option turns off the visibility of the UCS icon.

- **All.** This option addresses the visibility of the UCS icon in all viewports.

- **Noorigin.** This option essentially is the opposite of the Origin option. Selecting this option causes the UCS icon to remain in the lower-left corner of the display, even though you have relocated the coordinate system origin.

- **Origin.** The Origin option causes the UCS icon to be positioned at the origin of the current UCS from the default icon position in the lower-left corner of the display. If the icon is unable to be entirely displayed at the current origin, it remains in the default position.

  The next exercise relocates the coordinate system and repositions the UCS icon. The UCS icon has a couple of unique characteristics you should be aware of going into this exercise.

- The W that appears as part of the UCS icon means that the World Coordinate System is current. When you use the UCS command to relocate the origin, the W goes away, implying there is now a *user* coordinate system current.

- The UCS icon has a (+) at the origin *only* if the UCS icon is currently positioned at the origin.

Relocating the UCS Origin

Continue from the previous exercise.

Command: *Choose* **O**ptions, **U**CS, Icon Ori**g**in	Issues the UCSICON command with the ORigin option
Command: *Choose Origin UCS (Standard Toolbar, UCS)*	Issues the UCS command with the Origin option
Origin/ZAxis/3point/OBject/View/X/Y/Z/ Prev/Restore/Save/Del/?/<World>: _o Origin point <0,0,0>: **50000,50000** (Enter)	Sets the UCS origin at ① (see fig. 7.6)
Command: *Choose Save UCS (Standard Toolbar, UCS)*	Issues the UCS command with the Save option
Origin/ZAxis/3point/OBject/View/X/Y/Z/ Prev/Restore/Save/Del/?/<World>: _s Desired UCS name: **BLDG1** (Enter)	Saves the UCS as BLDG1
Command: *Choose Save (Standard Toolbar)*	Saves the drawing

7

Placement of the origin is relatively simple and, once the UCS icon has been placed on a new origin, it automatically follows to any subsequent relocations.

Figure 7.6

The origin point for the UCS.

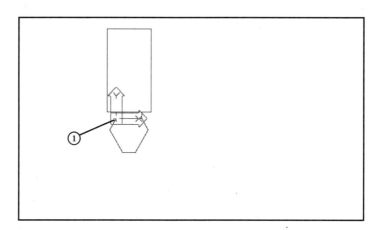

Rotation of the UCS

Rotation of the User Coordinate System in a two-dimensional plane takes place about Z axis. When assigning a rotation value, remember that a positive rotation is in a counterclockwise direction.

In the next exercise, you rotate the UCS to draw another wing of the building.

Previous, Saved, and Rotated UCS Positions

Continue from the previous exercise.

Command: *Choose Origin UCS (Standard Toolbar, UCS)*	Issues the UCS command with the Origin option

`Origin/ZAxis/3point/OBject/View/X/Y/Z/`
`Prev/Restore/Save/Del/?/<World>: _o`
`Origin point <0,0,0>:` *Choose Snap to Endpoint (Standard Toolbar, Object Snap)*
	Specifies the ENDpoint object snap

`endp of` *Pick* ① *(see fig. 7.7)*	Positions the UCS origin at the end of the line
Command: *Choose Z Axis Rotate UCS (Standard Toolbar, UCS)*	Issues the UCS command with the Z option

`Origin/ZAxis/3point/OBject/View/X/Y/Z/`
`Prev/Restore/Save/Del/?/<World>: _z`
`Rotation angle about Z axis <0>:`
`-30` (Enter)
	Rotates the UCS –30 degrees about the Z axis

Command: *Choose Save UCS (Standard Toolbar, UCS)*	Issues the UCS command with the Save option
`Origin/ZAxis/3point/OBject/View/X/Y/Z/` `Prev/Restore/Save/Del/?/<World>: _s` `Desired UCS name:` **BLDG2** (Enter)	Saves the UCS as BLDG1
Command: *Choose Save (Standard Toolbar)*	Saves the drawing

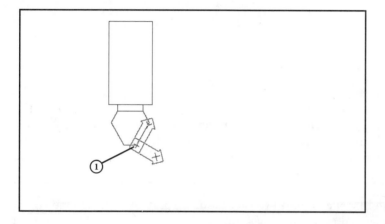

Figure 7.7

The rotated UCS.

Although the crosshairs can be rotated using the Rotate option from the SNAP command, the UCS does not reflect that rotation, which can cause some confusion. For this reason, it is recommended that rotation of the UCS about the Z axis be used for such needs.

In the previous exercises, you saved the current UCS by using the Save option of the UCS command. The DDUCS command displays the UCS Control dialog box, which enables you to see the named UCSs. The UCS Control dialog box (see fig. 7.8), also enables you delete a named UCS or list the numeric position of the UCS Origin and the X,Y, and Z axes.

'DDUCS. The DDUCS command enables you to assign a name to the current UCS, set a named UCS to current, or rename a saved UCS through the UCS Control dialog box.
Toolbar: *Choose Named UCS (Standard Toolbar, UCS)*
Pull-down: *Choose **V**iew, Named U**CS***
Screen: *Choose View, Dducs:*

Figure 7.8

The UCS Control
dialog box.

Aligning the Display with the UCS

Position and rotation of the UCS are both very important, but it would be
significantly more convenient if the drawing were placed squarely within
the display window. The PLAN command is designed to regenerate the
display such that the current X axis is oriented horizontally in the display.
By doing so, further drawing and editing can be done much more easily.

PLAN. The PLAN command reorients the display to align the view
with the specified coordinate system.

Pull-down: *Choose* **V**iew, 3D V**i**ewpoint Presets, **P**lan View, *then*
              one of the menu options

Screen: *Choose* VIEW, Plan:

The PLAN command is the most efficient tool to use when you need to
reorient the display after rotating the coordinate system. The PLAN
command has the following options:

- **Current UCS.** This is the default option. When using the Current
  UCS option, AutoCAD reorients the display so the X axis is horizontal.

- **Ucs.** This option prompts for a named UCS against which to horizontally align the X axis.

- **World.** The X axis of the World Coordinate System is aligned horizontally when this option is selected.

In the following exercise, you use the PLAN command to reorient the
drawing area to make it more convenient to draw the next wing of the
building.

Using the PLAN Command To Orient the Drawing

Continue from the previous exercise.

Command: *Choose* **V**iew, 3D V**i**ewport Presets, **P**lan View, **C**urrent	Issues the PLAN command with the Current option
Command: *Choose Rectangle (Draw, Polygon)*	Issues the RECTANG command
First corner: **0,0** (Enter)	Places first corner of the rectangle
Other corner: **3300,12900** (Enter)	Draws the rectangle
Command: *Choose Origin UCS (Standard Toolbar, UCS)*	Issues the UCS command with the Origin option
Origin/ZAxis/3point/OBject/View/X/Y/Z/ Prev/Restore/Save/Del/?/<World>: _o Origin point <0,0,0>: **3300,-4650** (Enter)	Places the UCS origin 3300 mm to the right and 4650 mm below the current UCS origin (see fig. 7.9)
Command: *Choose Rectangle (Draw, Polygon)*	Issues the RECTANG command
First corner: **0,0** (Enter)	Places first corner of the rectangle
Other corner: **41400,22200** (Enter)	Draws the rectangle
Command: *Choose Save (Standard Toolbar)*	Saves the drawing

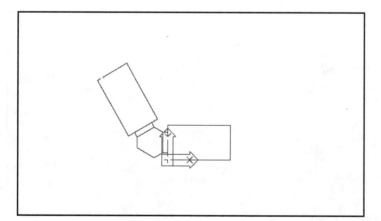

Figure 7.9

Building one and building two.

7

You now should have a pretty good idea of when to manipulate the UCS in a two-dimensional drawing. The convenience of saving a UCS position by name is a real time-saver when you need to perform edits on a drawing created with multiple UCS positions.

Object Snaps

Object snaps are another feature that enables you to place and edit linework accurately. Object snaps enable you to exactly pick geometric points (such as endpoints and midpoints) on objects. Whether it involves drawing new objects or editing existing objects, the use of object snaps is paramount in maintaining drawing accuracy.

Whenever you encounter a prompt requesting a point or a corner, such as the first point of a line, a base point, or the corner of a rectangle, you can specify an object snap and select the object. AutoCAD then snaps to the desired point and continues with the command.

When an object snap option has been selected, an "aperture" box appears at the center of the crosshairs. When the aperture is positioned over the snap position of the object, the cursor snaps to that position.

Snap Locations on Existing Objects

Figure 7.10 shows the object snap locations for some common AutoCAD objects. The figure indicates where a possible pick position might be and the location of the snap.

Figure 7.10

Object snap positions for AutoCAD objects.

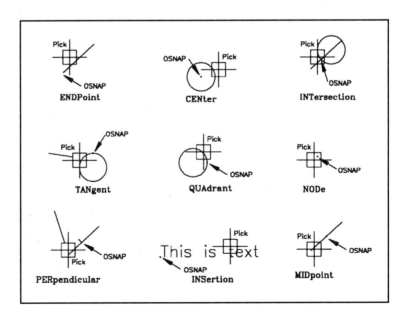

The Object Snap flyout from the Standard Toolbar can be found in Appendix F. The following is a brief explanation of the 14 object snap modes.

- **From.** The From object snap enables you to pick a dummy point from which you can specify an offset coordinate. Once the offset coordinate has been entered, the current command continues from the offset point.

- **ENDPoint.** This object snap snaps the cursor to the closest endpoint of the object that falls within the aperture.

- **MIDpoint.** This object snap snaps to the midpoint of the object picked.

- **CENter.** The CENter object snap snaps to the center of a circle, arc, or ellipse when the edge is picked.

- **NODe.** The NODe snap snaps to a point object. A point is created using the POINT command and can be configured to several preset graphics and a user-specified size. For a more extensive review of the POINT command, refer to *Inside AutoCAD Release 13 for Windows and Windows NT*.

- **QUAdrant.** The QUAdrant object snap selects the 12, 3, 6, and 9 o'clock positions of circles, arcs, and ellipses. When using the quadrant object snap, the cursor snaps the quadrant closest to the aperture box.

- **INTersection.** By definition, an intersection is where two lines cross. The INTersection object snap snaps the cursor to an intersection that falls within the aperture.

- **INSertion.** This object snap snaps to the insertion point of both text and blocks. It is the only object snap option that snaps to text.

- **PERpendicular.** The PERpendicular object snap picks a point that is perpendicular to the object picked.

- **TANgent.** Similar to the perpendicular snap for orthogonal objects, the TANgent object snap picks a point tangent to a circle, arc, or ellipse.

- **NEArest.** The NEArest object snap snaps the cursor to the point on an object closest to the center of the aperture box.

7

- **APParent.** New to Release 13, the APParent intersection snap calculates the intersection point of nonparallel, nonintersecting lines and picks that point. The prompt requires that the lines with the apparent intersection be selected.

- **QUIck.** The QUIck object snap must be used in conjunction with other object snaps. By using QUIck, the cursor snaps to the first eligible snap position based upon the current object snaps.

- **NONe.** The NONe object snap typically is invoked when a running object snap is not desired for a single pick point. It also is what you use to turn off any running object snaps.

When picking endpoints or midpoints of lines, AutoCAD finds the closest snap point as long as the aperture box falls on the line to be snapped to.

Accessing and Using a Temporary Object Snap

Temporary object snaps are used for "single shot" applications where it isn't necessary to have an object snap activated or "running" for all operations. You can invoke a temporary object snap in several ways:

- You can type the capitalized letters from the preceding object snap list for the one you want to use.

- You can choose the object snap from the Object Snap flyout of the Standard Toolbar.

- You can choose from the items listed in the cursor menu.

The cursor menu (see fig. 7.11) is invoked by holding down the shift key, then clicking the Enter (right) button on your mouse. This process is noted as Press Shift+Enter button. If you are using a digitizer, button 2 opens the cursor menu as well. If your input device does not respond in this fashion, refer to Appendix A, "Installation and Configuration," or the *AutoCAD Installation Guide*.

For those of you with a three-button mouse, the middle button might invoke the cursor menu. Should the cursor menu not appear in response to the middle button, press Shift + right click to invoke the cursor menu.

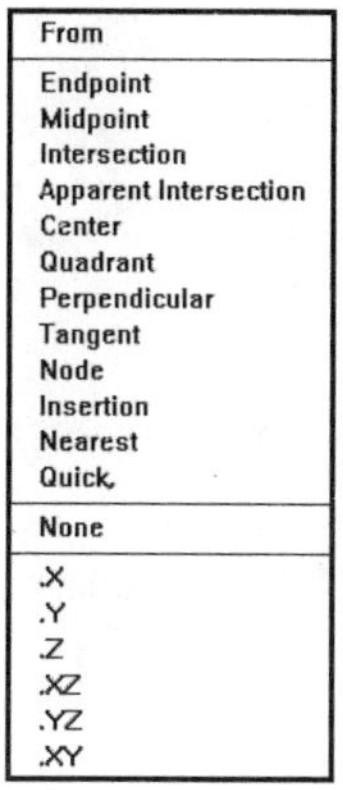

Figure 7.11

The cursor menu.

The cursor menu contains all the object snap options as well as point filters (which are covered later in this chapter).

The following exercise uses object snaps along with coordinate entry to add some detail to the building.

Adding Objects Using a Temporary Object Snap

Continue from the previous exercise.

Command: *Choose Rectangle (Draw, Polygon)*	Issues the RECTANG command
First corner: *Press Shift+Enter button and select* From	Specifies the FROM object snap
Base point: *Press Shift+right click and select* Midpoint	Specifies the MIDpoint object snap
mid of *Pick* ① *(see fig. 7.12)*	Selects the midpoint of the line as the base point of the offset
<Offset>: **@4200<90** (Enter)	Starts the rectangle 4200 mm above the base point
Other corner: **@2800,-8400** (Enter)	Draws the rectangle
Command: *Choose Line (Draw, Line)*	Issues the LINE command
From point: *Choose From (Standard Toolbar, Object Snap)*	Specifies the FROM object snap
from Base point: *Choose Snap to Endpoint (Standard Toolbar, Object Snap)*	Specifies the ENDpoint object snap

continues

continued

endp of *Pick* ②	Specifies the endpoint of the line as the base point of the offset
<Offset>: @0,-10350 (Enter)	Starts the line 10350mm below the base point
To point: *Choose Snap to Perpendicular (Standard Toolbar, Object Snap)*	Specifies the PERPendicular object snap
per to *Pick* ③	Draws the line perpendicular to the line at ③
To point: (Enter)	Ends the LINE command
Command: (Enter)	Repeats the LINE command
From point: @1500<270 (Enter)	Starts the line 1500mm below the last point
To point: *Choose Snap to Perpendicular (Standard Toolbar, Object Snap)*	Specifies the PERPendicular object snap
per to *Pick* ①	Draws the line perpendicular to the line at ①
To point: (Enter)	Ends the LINE command
Command: *Choose Save (Standard Toolbar)*	Saves the drawing

Your drawing should now resemble figure 7.12.

Figure 7.12

Drawing with object snaps.

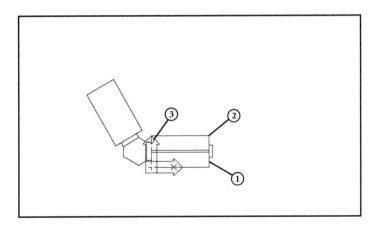

As seen in the previous exercise, temporary object snaps only are active for a single prompt; you needed to choose an object snap each time you need to snap to an object.

In early releases of AutoCAD Release 13, choosing a tool from the Object Snap Toolbar does not set an object snap during AutoLISP defined commands, such as RECTANG. If choosing an object snap from the Toolbar does not work, try choosing the object snap from the cursor menu.

Establishing a Running Object Snap

A running object snap is a semi-permanent object snap. The running object snap retains the setting(s) you choose until you clear the running object snap. You can set a running object snap with the DDOSNAP command.

'DDOSNAP. The DDOSNAP command allows you to set running object snaps as well as control the size of the aperture box.

Toolbar:	*Choose Running Object Snap (Standard Toolbar, Object Snap)*
Pull-down:	*Choose **O**ptions, Running **O**bject Snap*
Screen:	*Choose ASSIST, Osnap:, DDosnap*

The DDOSNAP command displays the Running Object Snap dialog box as shown in figure 7.13.

Figure 7.13

The Running Object Snap dialog box.

7

One of the more frequent applications of a running object snap would be when editing an existing drawing. As you edit, you frequently need to hold or snap to the end or center of one object to relocate it to another point.

Dimensioning requires frequent snapping to objects and is another prime example of the benefit of setting a running object snap.

In early versions of AutoCAD Release 13 you can set a running object snap by choosing a tool from the Object Snap toolbar at the Command: prompt. For example, choosing Snap to Endpoint (Standard Toolbar, Object Snap) at the Command: prompt will set a running endpoint object snap. This feature was dropped in the AutoCAD Release 13_c2. Choose **H**elp, **A**bout AutoCAD to see what version of AutoCAD you have.

A running object snap overrides any coordinate entry. This means that if the result of a coordinate entry specifies a point within the aperture box range of an existing object while a running object snap is on, the cursor snaps to the object snap, not to the specified coordinate.

The following exercise presents the DDOSNAP dialog box used to set a running object and shows how to change the size of the aperture.

Setting a Running Object Snap

Continue from the previous exercise. Before beginning, zoom into the drawing so that the view matches figure 7.14.

Command: *Choose Running Object Snap (Standard Toolbar, Object Snap)*	Issues the DDOSNAP command
Place an X in the **C**enter *check box*	Sets a running center object snap
Click once on the left arrow in Aperture Size *area, then choose* OK	Reduces the size of the aperture by 1 pixel
Command: *Choose Circle Center Radius (Draw, Circle)*	Issues the CIRCLE command
3P/2P/TTR/<Center point>: **6900,7400** (Enter)	Places the center of the circle at ① (see fig. 7.14)
Diameter/<Radius>: **300** (Enter)	Draws a 300mm radius circle
Command: (Enter)	Repeats the circle command
3P/2P/TTR/<Center point>: **@6900<0** (Enter)	Places the center of the circle at ②

`Diameter/<Radius> <300.0000>:` (Enter)	Accepts the default 300mm radius
`Command:` *Choose Copy (Modify, Copy)*	Issues the COPY command
`Select objects:` *Select the circle at* ②	Highlights the circle
`Select objects:` (Enter)	Ends the selection process
`Base point or displacement>` `/Multiple:` `M` (Enter)	Specifies the Multiple option
`Base point:` *Pick* ①	Establishes the base point at the center of the first circle
`Second point of displacement:` *Pick* ②	Copies the circle to ③
`Second point of displacement:` *Pick* ③	Copies the circle to ④
`Second point of displacement:` *Pick* ④	Copies the circle to ⑤
`Second point of displacement:` (Enter)	Ends the COPY command
`Command:` (Enter)	Repeats the COPY command
`Select objects:` *Select the 5 circles at* ①, ②, ③, ④, *and* ⑤	Selects the five circles to be copied
`Select objects:` (Enter)	Ends the selection process
`<Base point or displacement>` `/Multiple:` `0,7400` (Enter)	Specifies the displacement
`Second point of displacement:` (Enter)	Copies circles
`Command:` *Choose World UCS (Standard Toolbar, UCS)*	Issues the UCS command with the World option
`Command:` *Choose **V**iew, 3D V**i**ewport Presets, **P**lan View, **C**urrent*	Issues the PLAN command with the Current option
`Command:` *Choose Zoom All (Standard Toolbar, Zoom)*	Issues the ZOOM command with the All option
`Command:` *Choose Running Object Snap (Standard Toolbar, Object Snap), and choose C**l**ear All, then OK*	Clears the running object snap
`Command:` *Choose Save (Standard Toolbar)*	Saves the drawing

Your drawing now should now look like figure 7.15.

Throughout the remainder of this book, you will encounter running object snaps as well as temporary object snaps. The use of object snaps, whether running or temporary, is one of the primary concepts in working with AutoCAD and is of extreme importance as you create drawings.

7

Figure 7.14

Copying the circle with a running object snap.

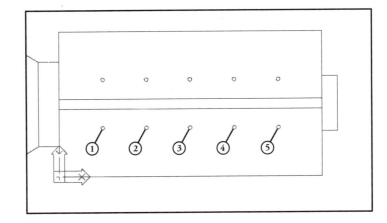

Figure 7.15

The completed wing.

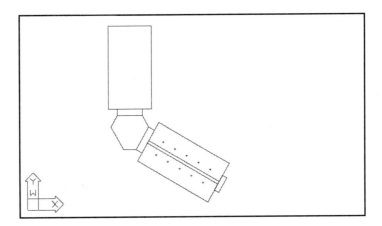

Choosing more than one running object snap from the dialog box is possible. It's best to use just two or three at the most, though, to avoid lengthy calculations on the part of AutoCAD.

Definition and Applications of Point Filters

A point filter is a process rather than a command. Using a point filter enables you to construct points by selecting the X, Y, and Z coordinates from existing objects. A point filter can be specified for a point in either the X, Y, or Z axis or any combination of the three. In a two-dimensional application, the filters typically use only the X and Y axes though you will be prompted for Z as well.

When creating an architectural elevation, for example, the vertical lines generated in the elevation relate to points on the floor plan. If working on the drafting board, to draw the vertical line in elevation of a change in the wall line in the floor plan, you place your triangle so that the vertical edge aligns with the dogleg in the plan view and draw the vertical line. Point filters act in much the same way and are most easily explained by way of an exercise.

To initiate the use of a point filter for either X or Y, you might choose the required filter from the Standard Toolbar or enter the filter to be used, preceded by a (.) point. The following is a list of point filters:

- **.X.** When you enter .X at a command prompt, the .X filter allows you to specify the horizontal coordinate (along the X axis) of the point you want to place. You can use any existing object on which to identify this point, the identification of which is most effectively done with the assistance of an object snap. When the position along the X axis has been picked, you are prompted for the YZ position, at which time you identify the vertical position of the desired point.

- **.Y.** Acting in much the same fashion as the .X point filter, the .Y point filter enables you to identify the vertical position of the point you wish to place first, then prompts for the XZ position.

- **.Z.** The Z point filter is used in 3D applications in the same fashion in which the X and Y filters function.

- **.XY.** Because all points in a 2D application lie in the XY plane, use of the XY point filter to indicate a point whose X and Y coordinates are the same as the point to be placed is unnecessary. This could more efficiently be done by using an object snap to place the point.

- **.XZ.** Used primarily in 3D applications, the XZ point filter enables you to pick an object whose X and Z coordinates are the same as the point to be placed.

- **.YZ.** The YZ point filter is also used in 3D applications when you wish to choose a point whose Y and Z coordinates are the same as the point you wish to place.

The following exercise creates a partial elevation of the central atrium of the building shell.

7

Using Point Filters To Create a Partial Elevation

Continue from the previous exercise.

Command: *Choose Running Object Snap (Standard Toolbar, Object Snap), choose* **E**ndpoint, *then* OK	Sets a running endpoint object snap
Command: *Click twice on the down arrow of the drawing area's vertical scroll bar*	Pans the screen down
Command: *Choose Line (Draw, Line)*	Issues the LINE command
From point: *Choose .X (Standard Toolbar, Point Filters)*	Specifies a .X point filter
.x of *Pick* ① *(see fig. 7.16)*	Specifies the X coordinate at the endpoint of the line
(need YZ): *Pick a point near* ②	Specifies the Y and Z coordinate of ②
To point: *Choose .X (Standard Toolbar, Point Filters)*	Specifies a .X point filter
.x of *Pick* ③	Specifies the X coordinate at the endpoint of the line
(need YZ): @ (Enter)	Specifies the Y and Z coordinates of the last point picked
To point: **@9900<90** (Enter)	Draws a line 9900mm up
To point: *Choose .X (Standard Toolbar, Point Filters)*	Specifies a .X point filter
.x of *Pick* ②	Specifies the X coordinate at the endpoint of the line
(need YZ): @ (Enter)	Specifies the Y and Z coordinates of the last point picked
To point: **C** (Enter)	Closes the line segments
Command: (Enter)	Repeats the LINE command
From point: *Choose .X (Standard Toolbar, Point Filters)*	Specifies a .X point filter
.x of *Pick* ④	Specifies the X coordinate at the endpoint of the line
(need YZ) *Pick* ⑤	Specifies the Y and Z coordinates of the endpoint of the line picked

To point: *Choose Snap to Perpendicular (Standard Toolbar, Object Snap)*	Issues a PERpendicular object snap
per to *Pick* ② **Enter**	Draws the line perpendicular to the selected line
Command: **Enter**	Repeats the LINE command
From point: *Choose .X (Standard Toolbar, Point Filters)*	Specifies a .X point filter
.x of *Pick* ⑥	Specifies the X coordinate at the endpoint of the line
(need YZ) *Pick* ⑤	Specifies the Y and Z coordinates of the endpoint of the line picked
To point: *Choose Snap to Perpendicular (Standard Toolbar, Object Snap)*	Issues a PERpendicular object snap
per to *Pick* ② *and press* **Enter**	Draws the line perpendicular to the selected line
Command: *Choose Snap to None (Standard Toolbar, Object Snap)*	Clears the running object snap
Command: *Choose Save (Standard Toolbar)*	Saves the drawing

Your drawing should now look like figure 7.16.

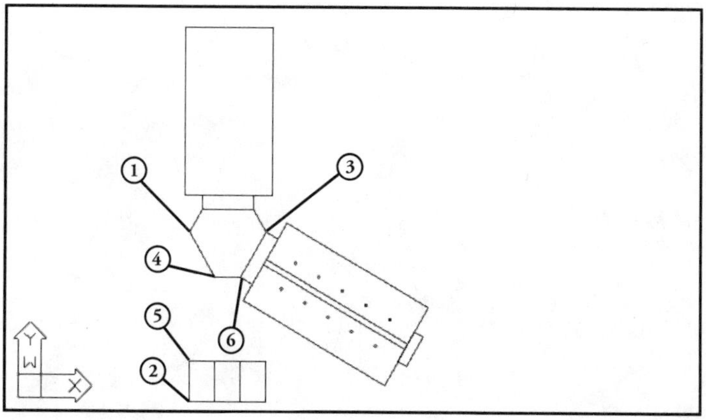

Figure 7.16

Drawing with point filters.

Used in combination with the running object snap, point filters are a useful tool in creating quick elevations. Although a simple application, many situations exist where the point filters can cut drafting time significantly in lieu of more time-consuming techniques.

Summary

During the course of this chapter, you were introduced to several methods that assist in creating accurate drawings. The coordinate entry modes enable you to enter coordinates at the prompt line in either absolute, relative, or polar entry, depending upon the angles and distances required by the drawing. In the case of non-orthogonal drawings or portions of a drawing, using the UCS command enables you to reorient and relocate the coordinate system to more efficiently accomplish the task. Once you have existing objects in the drawing, you can accurately snap to various locations by using one of the several object snap features.

Related Topics

- Zooming around the drawing—Chapter 6, "Controlling What You See"

- Copying objects with the COPY command—Chapter 8, "Editing with Grips"

- Building selection sets—Chapter 10, "Selecting and Editing Objects"

Chapter Snapshot

Introduced in Release 12, object grips are extremely powerful and enable you to make changes to existing objects in your drawing quickly and easily. Because you can choose any of six primary editing commands from a single grip choice, you can efficiently edit your selection.

This chapter will present several grip features, including the following concepts and applications:

- Grip locations for AutoCAD objects

- Displaying and clearing grips

- Grip modes and their options

- Options when creating selection sets

- Selecting objects to be edited with grips

- Controlling grip graphics: Enabling grips, setting their size and color

Editing with Grips

In the previous few chapters, you learned how to create objects and manipulate the drawing area. This chapter presents the benefits of using grips to edit your drawing. Just as a tool from a toolbar provides immediate access to a command and the Aerial View window presents a more effective means to modify the display of the drawing area, grips enable you to more easily edit your drawing.

This chapter presents how to stretch, move, rotate, scale, mirror, and copy objects using grips. You also will review the various means by which you can select objects and the related object selection dialog box. The following Quick Tour exercise gives you an overview of editing with grips.

The Quick Tour

To begin, create a new drawing named BRACKET by using the default ACAD.DWG prototype drawing. Create a layer called OBJECT and set it as current. Set the grid spacing to 1, the snap spacing to .125, and turn on grid and snap.

Command: *Choose Line (Draw, Line)*	Issues the LINE command
From point: *Pick* ① *(see fig. 8.1)*	Places the first point of the line
To point: **@5<0** (Enter)	Draws the line to ②
To point: (Enter)	Ends the LINE command
Command: *Choose Circle Center Radius (Draw, Circle)*	Issues the CIRCLE command
3P/2P/TTR/<Center point>: *Using the From and Midpoint object snaps, pick* ③	Places the center point of the circle
<Offset>: **@1.25<90**	Locates the center of the circle
Diameter/<Radius>: **1** (Enter)	Draws the circle
Command: (Enter)	Repeats the CIRCLE command
3P/2P/TTR/<Center point>: **@2<0** (Enter)	Places the center point of the circle
Diameter/<Radius>: **.25** (Enter)	Draws the circle
Command: *Choose Arc Start End Radius (Draw, Arc)*	Issues the ARC command with the Start, End, and Radius Options
Center/<Start point>: *Using the Endpoint object snap, pick* ②	Places the start point of the arc
End point: **@2.5<90** (Enter)	Places the end of the arc
Radius: **2.5** (Enter)	Draws the arc

You now have the basic shapes to create the bracket. Your drawing should look like figure 8.1. In the following steps, you will use grips to complete the bracket.

Command: *Select the circle*	Highlights the circle and displays its grips
Command: *Select the right quadrant grip at* ① *(see fig. 8.2)*	Makes the grip hot and starts the grip editing
** STRETCH ** <Stretch to point>/Base point/ Copy/Undo/eXit: **C** (Enter)	Specifies the Copy option of Stretch mode
** STRETCH (multiple) ** <Stretch to point>/Base point /Copy/Undo/eXit: **@.25<180** (Enter)	Copies the circle

`** STRETCH (multiple) **`
`<Stretch to point>/Base point`
`/Copy/Undo/eXit:` *Press Esc three times*
	Ends grip editing, deselects the circle, and turns off the grips

Command: *Select the line and the arc*	Highlights the objects and displays their grips
Command: *Hold down Shift and select the arc*	Deselects the arc; the grips remain visible
Command: *On the line, pick the right endpoint grip*	Makes the grip hot and starts the grip editing

`** STRETCH **`
`<Stretch to point>/Base point`
`/Copy/Undo/eXit:` (Enter)
	Switches to move mode

`** MOVE **`
`<Move to point>/Base point`
`/Copy/Undo/eXit:` **C** (Enter)
	Specifies the Copy option of move mode

`** MOVE (multiple) **`
`<Move to point>/Base point`
`/Copy/Undo/eXit:` *Pick* ②
	Copies the line to ②

`** MOVE (multiple) **`
`<Move to point>/Base point`
`/Copy/Undo/eXit:` *Press Esc three times*
	Ends grip editing, deselects the objects, and turns off their grips

Command: *Select the two lines, the arc, and the small circle*	Highlights the objects and displays their grips
Command: *Hold down Shift and select the two lines*	Deselects the objects, their grips remain visible
Command: *On the arc, pick the right quadrant grip*	Makes the grip hot and starts the grip editing

`** STRETCH **`
`<Stretch to point>/Base point`
`/Copy/Undo/eXit:` **MI** (Enter)
	Switches to mirror mode

`** MIRROR **`
`<Second point>/Base point`
`/Copy/Undo/eXit:` **C** (Enter)
	Specifies the Copy option of mirror mode

`** MIRROR (multiple) **`
`<Second point>/Base point`
`/Copy/Undo/eXit:` **B** (Enter)
	Specifies the Base point option of mirror mode

`Base point:` *Pick the midpoint grip of the bottom line*	Specifies the base point of the mirror line

continues

8

continued

`** MIRROR (multiple) **`
`<Second point>/Base point`
`/Copy/Undo/eXit:` *Pick the midpoint grip*
of the top line
	Specifies the second point of the
	mirror line

`** MIRROR (multiple) **`
`<Second point>/Base point`
`/Copy/Undo/eXit:` *Press Esc three times*
	Ends grip editing, deselects the objects,
	and turns off their grips

`Command:` *Choose Save (Standard Toolbar)*	Saves the drawing

Your drawing now should resemble figure 8.2.

Figure 8.1

*The basic bracket
shapes.*

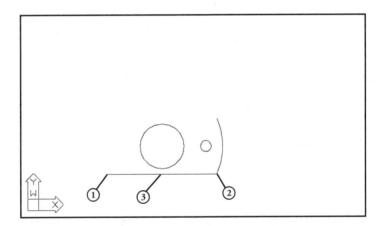

Figure 8.2

*The finished
bracket.*

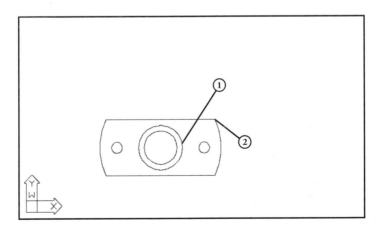

The Basic Principle of Grips

Grips provide a quick and easy way of editing objects in a drawing. When grips are enabled, you can select and edit an object without ever issuing a command. Grips are intended as an expedient means of editing objects and frequently prove to be a valuable tool, as you will see in this chapter.

Grip Locations

As you saw in the Quick Tour exercise, to display an object's grips, you simply select the object. By default, the object is highlighted and blue grips appear at the grip positions of the object. Figure 8.3 shows the grip locations for various AutoCAD objects:

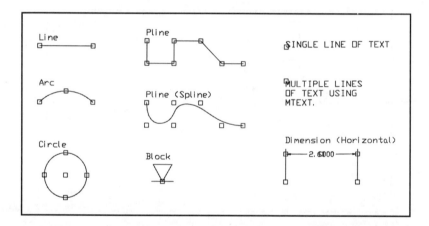

Figure 8.3

Object grip positions.

When a grip is picked, that grip changes to a solid color and is referred to as a *hot grip*. To clear an object's grips, press Esc until the grip boxes disappear. Depending upon the grips' status, you might need to press Esc up to three times.

The following exercise steps you through the process of displaying and clearing grips.

Displaying and Clearing an Object's Grips

To begin, create a new drawing named REMOTE2 using the \AB\TVREMOTE.DWG drawing created in Chapter 3 as the prototype. Turn on TILEMODE to return to model space, and turn off grid and snap. Your drawing should look like figure 8.4.

continues

8

continued

Command: *Pick* ① *as shown in figure 8.5*	Highlights the object and displays the object's grips
** STRETCH ** <Stretch to point>/Base point/ Copy/Undo/eXit: *Pick* ②	Makes the grip hot and starts the grip editing process
** STRETCH ** <Stretch to point>/Base point/ Copy/Undo/eXit: *Press Esc*	Releases the hot grip
Command: *Press Esc*	Clears the selection set
Command: *Press Esc*	Clears the grips

Figure 8.4

The REMOTE2 drawing.

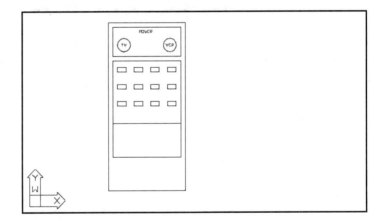

Figure 8.5

Displaying the grips.

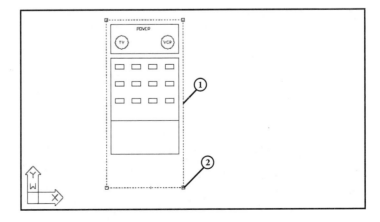

Selecting Multiple Objects

The most obvious way to select more than one object is to pick all the objects individually, one at a time. Should there be several objects in one area, you might want to use either the window or crossing methods of selecting objects.

Window and Crossing Selections

The window and crossing selection methods enable you to select objects by dragging a box around the objects you want to select. By default, if you drag a box from right to left, you define a window selection; if you drag a box from left to right, you define a crossing selection. The following is an explanation of each:

- **Window.** A window selection must totally enclose all of the objects to be selected. If, for example, an endpoint of a line is not within the window, that line will not be selected. By default, this method is implemented by moving the cursor to the right to define the window. The rectangle that defines the window is a solid line.

- **Crossing.** A crossing selection selects whatever it crosses or encloses. If an object is touched by any of the four edges of the crossing window, those objects will be selected. Any objects that fall totally within the window also will be selected. By default, the crossing selection method is implemented by moving the cursor to the left to define the crossing window. As a visual clue of the windowing method used, the crossing window is defined by a dashed rectangle.

The following exercise demonstrates the window and crossing selection methods.

Selecting Objects with a Window and Crossing

Continue from the previous exercise.

Command: *Pick* ① *(see fig. 8.6)*	Starts a selection window
Other corner: *Pick* ②	Drags a window selection and selects the objects

Notice that only the objects that were totally within the window selection are selected. Also notice that the window selection box is a solid line.

8

continues

continued

Command: *Press Esc twice*	Deselects the objects and clears the grips
Command: *Choose Redraw (Standard Toolbar, Redraw)*	Refreshes the display
Command: *Pick ① (see fig. 8.7)*	Starts a selection window
Other corner: *Pick ②*	Drags a crossing selection and selects the objects

Notice, this time, that anything that touches the edge of the crossing box, or is inside the box is selected. Also notice that the crossing selection box is a dotted line.

Command: *Press Esc twice*	Deselects the objects and clears the grips
Command: *Choose Redraw (Standard Toolbar, Redraw)*	Refreshes the display

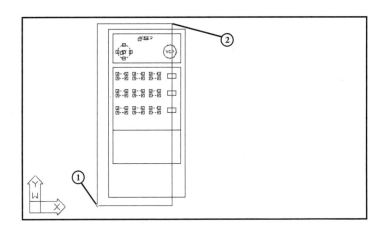

Figure 8.6

Selecting objects with a window.

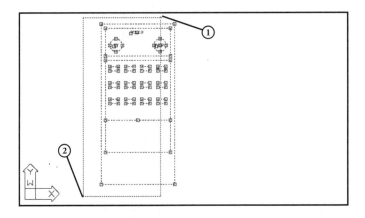

Figure 8.7

Selecting objects with a crossing.

Building a Selection Set

The process of selecting objects is called *building a selection set*. When doing any type of editing, AutoCAD requires you to build a selection set of the objects you want to edit. As you experienced in the previous exercise, one way to clear a selection set is to press Esc. The only problem with this is that pressing Esc clears the entire selection set. What if you only wanted to remove one or two objects from the selection set? AutoCAD gives you a number of ways of building and controlling the selection process.

Removing Objects from the Selection Set

One way to remove objects from a selection set is with the Shift key. By default, holding down Shift while selecting objects removes objects from the selection set. If you select an object without pressing Shift, the objects are *added* to the selection set. The following exercise demonstrates this.

Removing Objects from a Selection Set

Continue from the previous exercise.

Command: *Pick* ① *(see fig. 8.8)* Starts a selection window

Other corner: *Pick* ② Drags a window selection and selects the objects

Command: *Hold down the Shift key and pick* ③ Starts a selection window

Other corner: *Hold down the Shift key key and pick* ④ Drags a window selection and deselects the objects; the grips remain

Command: *Hold down the Shift key and pick* ③ Starts a selection window

Other corner: *Hold down the Shift key key and pick* ④ Drags a window selection and turns off the grips of the selected objects

Command: *Press Esc twice* Deselects the objects and clears the grips

Command: *Choose Redraw (Standard Toolbar, Redraw)* Refreshes the display

---

8

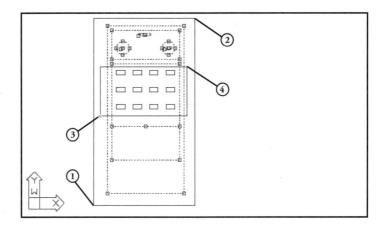

Using DDSELECT

If you have used other Windows CAD or graphics programs, or even a
word processing program in Windows, you might be familiar with using
the press-and-drag method of selecting objects or pressing the Shift key to
add objects to a selection set. In many Windows word processing packages,
holding down the mouse button and dragging it across the document
highlights text until you release the button. If you want to select additional text, you can hold down the Shift key and continue to select text.
AutoCAD can be set up to work in a similar fashion with the DDSELECT
command.

> **'DDSELECT.** The DDSELECT command opens the Object Selection
> Settings dialog box, which enables you to control the way objects are
> selected.
> Pull-down: *Choose* **O**ptions, **S**election
> Screen: *Choose* Options, DDselec

This chapter covers two of the selection options from the Object Selection
Settings dialog box (see fig. 8.9). Chapter 10, "Selecting and Editing
Objects," covers the remaining options.

Figure 8.9

*The Object Selection
Settings dialog box.*

The following are two of the selection options presented in the
DDSELECT dialog box:

- **Use Shift to Add.** When this option is on, you must press the Shift
  key to add objects to the selection set after selecting the first object.
  If you fail to press the Shift key when selecting a second object, the
  first object is deselected and the second object is the only object in
  the selection set.

- **Press and Drag.** This option requires you to keep the mouse button
  pressed after placing the first point for a window and dragging the
  cursor to the other corner, and then release the button. This process
  will then define the window. This windowing method only applies to
  the process of defining a selection set. It is not necessary to use this
  method when defining a zoom window.

Chapter 10, "Selecting and Editing Objects," reviews the other
options available from the Object Selection Settings dialog box.

The following exercise demonstrates the **U**se Shift to Add and **P**ress and
Drag options. These options will be turned on and will remain on as the
default for the rest of this book.

Changing the Selection Options with DDSELECT

Continue from the previous exercise.

Command: *Choose* **O**ptions, **S**election   Issues the DDSELECT command

8

continues

continued

Place an X in the **U**se Shift to Add *and the* **P**ress and Drag *boxes, and choose* OK	Turns on the options
Command: *Press and drag from* ① *to* ② *(see fig. 8.10)*	Drags a window selection and highlights the objects
Command: *Hold the Shift key down and press and drag from* ③ *to* ④	Drags a crossing selection and deselects the objects from the selection set
Command: *Pick anywhere away from the drawing*	Removes the highlighted objects from the selection set
Command: *Pick anywhere away from the drawing*	Removes the grips
Command: *Choose Save (Standard Toolbar)*	Saves the drawing

Figure 8.10

Building a selection set.

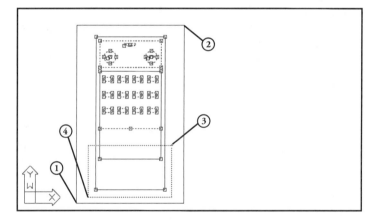

As you can see, you have a great deal of flexibility in building a selection set.

 The options in Object Selection Settings dialog box are system settings. This means that, once set, they apply to all AutoCAD sessions, even if you quit from a session and come back later.

Now that you know how to display and clear the grips, you move to the editing modes and how to cycle through them.

Grip Editing Modes

The five editing modes are presented in sequence at the prompt line whenever a grip is picked (which makes it a hot grip). To cycle to the next mode in the sequence, press Enter.

- **Stretch.** The Stretch mode repositions a hot grip, effectively stretching the object. The Stretch mode only moves the object if a grip is picked that is not at an endpoint of the object or the edge of a circle, such as the midpoint of a line or the center of a circle. Although you may have several objects displaying grips in a selection set, the Stretch mode only operates on the object that has the hot grip. Blocks and text are the object types that cannot be stretched but are moved when using the Stretch mode on a grip.

- **Move.** The Move mode moves the entire selection set. The base point for the selection set is the hot grip.

- **Rotate.** When rotating with the Rotate mode, you have the option of either entering a rotation angle or graphically rotating the selection set by moving the cursor to rotate the objects. The hot grip is the point about which the selection set is rotated.

- **Scale.** The Scale mode also enables you to graphically or numerically increase or decrease the scale of the selected objects. You can use the Scale mode, for example, to make an object 50 percent smaller. Similar to the rotation process, the hot grip is the point from which the selection set is scaled.

- **Mirror.** The Mirror mode enables you to mirror the selection set to create a reflected image, as in the right hand versus left hand image of an object. The Mirror mode enables you to dynamically position the mirror line from the hot grip.

As you use the grip editing modes, you will see various options on the Command: line. The following is a list of the grip editing options:

- **Base point.** By default, the base point for editing is the hot grip. The Base point option enables you to pick another location as the base point for the editing process. There is a Base point option for all grip modes.

- **Copy.** When you choose the Copy option, a copy of the selection set is made when the edit process is completed. After selecting the Copy option, the word (multiple) will appear in parentheses next to the grip mode. There is a Copy option for all grip modes.

8

- **Undo.** If you make a mistake while editing with grips, the Undo option will undo the edit. After you choose Undo, you need to reselect the objects and the hot grip if you want to continue editing with grips.

- **Reference.** The Reference option is available in the rotate and scale modes. This option enables you to rotate or scale the selection set with reference to another object's rotation angle or scale.

- **eXit.** Choosing the eXit option is the same as pressing Esc once when a hot grip is displayed. The eXit option clears the hot grip, but the selection set and grips are still displayed.

For a more complete review of the AutoCAD edit commands found here as grip options, refer to Chapter 10.

Stretching with Grips

There might be occasions when you need to make a line shorter, or a rectangle wider or higher. This editing process, in which part of the object stays in place while another part is lengthened or shortened, is referred to as stretching the object.

> Chapter 12, "Constructive Editing," illustrates the STRETCH command and the LENGTHEN command, which are other effective methods by which to stretch objects.

In the exercise titled "Displaying and Clearing an Objects Grips," you picked a grip to make it hot. There are occasions in which having more than one hot grip is desirable in the editing process. You can select multiple hot grips by pressing the Shift key *before* picking the grips you want to make hot.

In the following exercise you work with the Stretch mode and use two hot grips.

> If you happen to cycle past the grip mode you want to use, keep pressing Enter. The five grip modes are in a continuous loop for easy access.

Editing with Grips Using Stretch, Move, and Copy

Continue from the previous exercise.

Command: *Pick ① , the TV remote outline rectangle, as shown in figure 8.11*	Highlights the rectangle and displays the four rectangle grips
Command: *Press Shift and pick the two bottom grips of the rectangle, ② and ③*	Displays hot grips
Command: *Pick ② again*	Begins the grip editing cycle
** STRETCH ** <Stretch to point>/Base point/ Copy/Undo/eXit: **@0,.5** (Enter)	Stretches the bottom of the drawing down 0.5"
Command: *Press Esc twice*	Deselects the rectangle and clears the grips
Command: *Choose Save (Standard Toolbar)*	Saves the drawing

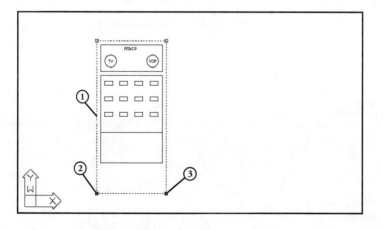

Figure 8.11

Pick points for multiple hot grips.

As was the case in the previous chapter on drawing accuracy, once a base point is selected when editing objects, relative coordinate entry can be used for accurate placement. This also is applicable when editing with grips, as you just learned in the previous exercise.

8

Moving and Copying with Grips

When moving an object or a group of objects with grips, the hot grip is the point by which the selection set is held by the cursor and you can either dynamically move the selection set to the desired location or enter a numeric distance. One of the multiple benefits of editing with grips is the ability to copy the selection set from each of the grip modes. When the Copy option is used with Move, the selection set remains in the original position and a copy is placed in the new position.

In the following exercise, you use the Move mode alone and in combination with the Copy option to create some new buttons.

Moving and Copying with Grips

Continue from the previous exercise.

Command: *Select the text "POWER"* | Highlights the text, and displays the text grips

Command: *Pick the middle grip* | Displays a hot grip

```
** STRETCH **
<Stretch to point>/Base point/
Copy/Undo/eXit: (Enter)
```
Cycles to the Move mode

```
** MOVE **
<Move to point>/Base point/Copy/
Undo/eXit: @0,-.5 (Enter)
```
Moves the selection set down 0.5"

Command: *Press and drag from* ① *to* ② *as shown in figure 8.12* | Deselects the text, selects the four buttons and their grips

Command: *Pick* ③ | Displays a hot grip

```
** STRETCH **
<Stretch to point>/Base point/
Copy/Undo/eXit: (Enter)
```
Cycles to the Move mode

```
** MOVE **
<Move to point>/Base point/Copy/
Undo/eXit: C (Enter)
```
Issues the Copy option

```
** MOVE (multiple) **
<Move to point>/Base point/Copy/
Undo/eXit: @.125<270 (Enter)
```
Places copy of the selection set

Command: *Press Esc three times*	Clears the hot grip, clears the selection set, clears the grips
Command: **R** (Enter)	Issues the REDRAW command
Command: *Choose Save (Standard Toolbar)*	Saves the drawing

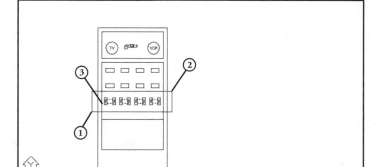

Figure 8.12

The new buttons.

Rotating Objects Using Grips

When rotating an object in AutoCAD, you are prompted for a point about which to rotate the selection set—basically, where you are going to "pin it down." When using grips, this point is the hot grip. Grips are perfect for the rotate routine because of the various points you can choose as a rotation base point.

In the following exercise you rotate the buttons of the TV remote drawing.

Rotating the Buttons Using Grips

Continue from the previous exercise. Keep in mind that the press and drag mode is still on.

Command: *Press and drag the cursor from* ① *to* ②, *as shown in figure 8.13*	Highlights the channel buttons and displays all grips
Command: *Pick* ③	Displays a hot grip and begins the grip cycle

`** STRETCH **`
`<Stretch to point>/Base point/`
`Copy/Undo/eXit:` *Press* (Enter) *twice*
	Cycles to the Rotate mode

8

continues

continued

`** ROTATE **`
`<Rotation angle>/Base point/Copy/`
`Undo/Reference/eXit: B` (Enter)
	Issues the Base point option

`Base point:` *Pick* ④	Establishes a new base point for the rotation

`** ROTATE **`
`<Rotation angle>/Base point/Copy/`
`Undo/Reference/eXit: 90` (Enter)
	Rotates the selection set 90° about the base point

`Command:` *Pick the lower left grip*	Displays a hot grip

`** STRETCH **`
`<Stretch to point>/Base point/`
`Copy/Undo/eXit:` (Enter)
	Cycles to the Move mode

`**MOVE**`
`<Move to point>/Base point/`
`Copy/Undo/eXit: @-.3,-.5` (Enter)
	Moves the selection set down by 0.3"and to the left by 0.5"

`Command:` *Press Esc*	Clears the selection set, grips remain
`Command:` *Press and drag the cursor from* ① *to* ② *as shown in figure 8.14*	Defines the new selection set of four buttons
`Command:` *Pick* ③	Displays a hot grip

`** STRETCH **`
`<Stretch to point>/Base point/`
`Copy/Undo/eXit:` (Enter)
	Cycles to the Move mode

`**MOVE**`
`<Move to point>/Base point/Copy/`
`Undo/eXit: C` (Enter)
	Issues the Copy option

`**MOVE (multiple) **`
`<Move to point>/Base point/`
`Copy/Undo/eXit: B` (Enter)
	Issues the Base point option

`Base point:` *Pick* ④	Establishes the new base point for the copy routine

`**MOVE (multiple) **`
`<Move to point>/Base point/`
`Copy/Undo/eXit:` *Pick* ③
	Places a copy of the selection set

`**MOVE (multiple) **`
`<Move to point>/Base point/`
`Copy/Undo/eXit: X` *Enter*
	Clears the hot grip

Command: *Press Esc twice*	Clears the selection set, clears the grips
Command: *Choose Save (Standard Toolbar)*	Saves the drawing

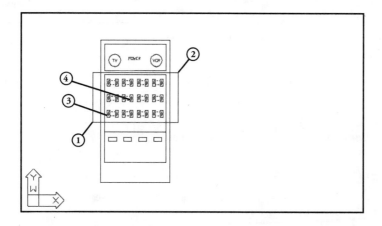

Figure 8.13

Pick points to select and rotate the channel buttons.

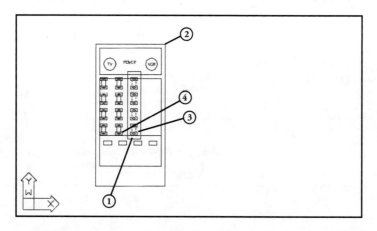

Figure 8.14

Defining the new selection set and copy points.

Scaling Objects Using Grips

The Scale grip mode provides the editing method required to increase or decrease the size of the selection set proportionally. This is done by entering a scale factor by which the selection set is to be scaled or by dynamically scaling the selection set by moving your cursor to a new

8

position that will scale the objects as desired. You might, for example, need to use this mode to increase the size of a countersink by a factor of 1.5 in a mechanical drawing or to dynamically change the scale of a tree symbol in an architectural drawing.

In the following exercise, you make the remote larger using the scale mode.

Scaling the Remote

Continue from the previous exercise.

Command: *Press and drag the cursor from* ① *to* ②, *as shown in figure 8.15*
Highlights the objects crossed or included in the crossing window, displays all grips

Command: *Press Shift and pick* ③, *then* ④ *to select the line and the rectangle*
Adds the line and the rectangle to the selection set

Command: *Pick* ⑤
Displays a hot grip

`** STRETCH **`
`<Stretch to point>/Base point/`
`Copy/Undo/eXit:` *Press* (Enter) *three times*
Cycles to the Scale mode

`**SCALE**`
`<Scale factor>/Base point/Copy/`
`Undo/Reference/eXit:` *Move your cursor to see the effect of dynamic scaling*
Graphically scales the selection set

`**SCALE**`
`<Scale factor>/Base point/Copy/`
`Undo/Reference/eXit:` **1.2** (Enter)
Scales the selection set by a factor of 1.2

Command: *Press Esc twice*
Clears the selection set, clears the grips

Command: *Choose Save (Standard Toolbar)*
Saves the drawing

Mirroring Objects Using Grips

Object mirroring is a great time saver when opposite-hand or reflected objects are required—for example, stair wells at opposite ends of a building, reflected workstation configurations, or numerous other applications. To get a reflected image when using the grips Mirror mode, you must use the Copy option.

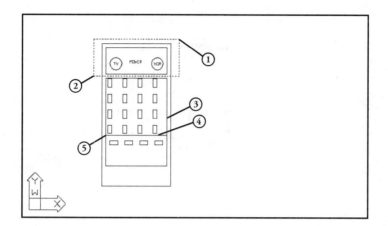

Figure 8.15

*Pick points to select
and scale the TV
remote.*

In the following exercise, you encounter a case in which text is included in
the selection set to be mirrored. To keep the text from mirroring, you set
the MIRRTEXT variable to 0 prior to mirroring the TV remote.

> NOTE
>
> If you intend to use the Copy *and* Base point options from the same
> grip mode, choose Copy first because the Base point option continues
> with the editing routine.

Creating His and Hers TV Remotes Using Mirror with Grips

Continue from the previous exercise.

Command: **MIRRTEXT** (Enter)	Accesses the MIRRTEXT system variable
New value for MIRRTEXT <1>: **0** (Enter)	Sets the variable to 0
Command: *Select all objects*	Highlights the objects, displays the grips
Command: *Pick the lower right grip on the TV remote*	Displays a hot grip
** STRETCH ** <Stretch to point>/Base point/ Copy/Undo/eXit: *Press* (Enter) *four times*	Cycles to the mirror mode
** MIRROR ** <Second point>/Base point/Copy/ Undo/eXit: **C** (Enter)	Issues the Copy option

continues

8

continued

`** MIRROR (multiple) **`
`<Second point>/Base point/Copy/`
`Undo/eXit:` **B** (Enter)
	Issues the Base point option

`Base point:` **@1,0** (Enter)	Places the first point of the mirror line 1" to the right of the hot grip

`** MIRROR (multiple) **`
`<Second point>/Base point/Copy/`
`Undo/eXit:` *Make sure Ortho*
mode is on and pick ① *as*
shown in figure 8.16
	Places the second point to define the
	mirror line

`** MIRROR (multiple) **`
`<Second point>/Base point/Copy/`
`Undo/eXit:` **X** (Enter)
	Clears the hot grip

`Command:` *Press Esc twice*	Clears the selection set, clears the grips

Figure 8.16

*Pick point for the
second point of
the mirror line.*

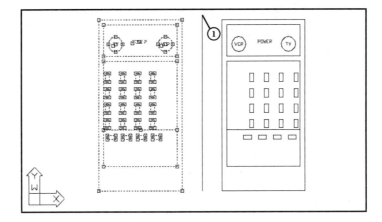

From the previous exercise, you can see that the new TV remote is a
reflected image of the original with the power buttons in reversed positions. You now should have a really good handle on using grips.

Controlling the Look of the Grips

Grips, by default, are blue and perhaps a bit large for certain objects. You
can control the color and size of grips with the DDGRIPS command.

> **'DDGRIPS.** The DDGRIPS command opens the Grips dialog box, which provides several options relating to grips and their display.
> Pull-down: *Choose* **O**ptions, **G**rips
> Screen: *Choose* Options, DDgrips

The DDGRIPS command displays the Grips dialog box (see fig. 8.18). The Grips dialog box has the following options:

- **Enable Grips.** When the Enable Grips item is on, object grips will be displayed when an object is selected.

- **Enable Grips Within Blocks.** By default, the Enable Grips Within **B**locks option is off and a blocks grip is displayed at the insertion point. When on, the grips of the objects within a block are displayed when the block is selected but there is no grip displayed at the insertion point of the block.

- **Unselected.** When this item is chosen, you can choose a new color for unselected grips from a color palette. By default, the color is blue.

- **Selected.** When you choose **S**elected, you can choose a color for the hot grips if you want to have something other than the default color of red.

- **Grip Size.** The **G**rip Size item provides you with a Min/Max scroll bar. You can either press and drag the scroll box to the desired size or use the left or right arrows to increase or decrease the size of the object grips.

Figure 8.17

The Grips dialog box.

In the following exercise, you are given the opportunity to choose colors and a size for the grips.

8

Personalizing and Sizing Grips

Continue from the previous exercise.

Command: *Choose* **O**ptions, **G**rips	Opens the Grips dialog box
Choose **S**elected	Opens the Select Color dialog box for a hot grip
Click on a color, then choose OK	Sets the color for a hot grip, closes the dialog box
Choose **U**nselected	Opens the Select Color dialog box for unselected grips
Click on a color, then choose OK	Sets the color for a grip, closes the dialog box
Click once on the right arrow	Increases the size of the grip boxes
Choose OK	Closes the Grips dialog box
Command: *Pick the left TV remote outline rectangle*	Highlights the rectangle, displays the grips
Command: *Press Shift and pick the two bottom grips*	Displays two hot grips

`** STRETCH **`
`<Stretch to point>/Base point/`
`Copy/Undo/eXit:` *Pick the bottom left grip*
	Initializes the grip modes

`** STRETCH **`
`<Stretch to point>/Base point/`
`Copy/Undo/eXit:` `@0,.5` (Enter)
	Stretches the bottom of the TV remote up by 0.5"

Command: *Press Esc twice*	Clears the selection set, clears the grips
Command: *Choose Save (Standard Toolbar)*	Saves the drawing

Your drawing now should look like figure 8.18.

Should you decide to disable the grips for any reason, turn off the Enable Grips setting in the Grips dialog box. You also can set the GRIPS variable to 0 to accomplish the same end result.

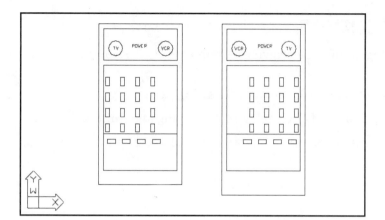

Figure 8.18

The completed remotes.

Summary

This chapter introduced you to the power of editing using grips. From the five grip modes to nearly all the options, you were able to stretch, move, rotate, scale, mirror, and copy objects without ever choosing a tool from the Modify toolbar. The Base option, which enables you to define a new base point, is a powerful feature of grips, as is the easy way in which you can cycle through the various modes by pressing the Enter button. You can use grips in combination with other editing tools, such as numeric coordinate entry, when making copies and placing base points.

This chapter also presented the dynamics of selecting objects, and you were able to experiment with customizing your selection process. The window and crossing selection methods enable you to select objects by dragging a box around the objects you want to select. Prior to confirming a selection set, you can press the Shift key and pick any objects you want to remove from the selection set. All of these features prove to be valuable tools in identifying and modifying the selection set.

As you work with AutoCAD, you will find numerous occasions to utilize grips and experiment with the most effective method of selecting objects. The remainder of this book uses the selection set procedures presented in this chapter.

8

Related Topics

- Zooming around the drawing—Chapter 6, "Controlling What You See"
- Coordinate entry—Chapter 7, "Drawing Accurately"
- Editing commands—Chapter 10, "Selecting and Editing Objects"
- Building selection sets—Chapter 10, "Selecting and Editing Objects"

PART III

Advanced Drawing and Editing

Chapter Snapshot

By now, you have learned the basics to creating a simple drawing. This chapter introduces more objects available in AutoCAD Release 13. As you create more complex drawings, you can use these objects to better manage your drawing and to give you features not available to the basic drawing commands.

This chapter shows you the following:

- How to draw polylines

- How to draw ellipses

- How to set up and use multiple lines

9

More Drawing Commands

Part of learning about AutoCAD is understanding how to use the various drawing commands. Like tools in a toolbox, AutoCAD Release 13 has many tools for you to use in the design process. In certain situations, some tools are better than others. An important part of being productive in AutoCAD is deciding which tools to use and when to use them.

The commands in this chapter build upon the basic drawing skills you have learned so far. The drawing commands covered in this chapter give you more drawing power as well as the ability to form your drawing intelligently. By learning how to use polylines, ellipses, and multiple lines, you can streamline your design process.

The following Quick Tour exercise gives an overview of the drawing commands explored in this chapter. In the exercise, you will create a simple load gate.

The Quick Tour

Begin this exercise by creating a new drawing named LOADGATE using the default ACAD.DWG. Set the grid spacing to .5 units, the snap to .125 units, and turn grid and snap on. The first step is to draw the logic gate. To do this, you will draw a polyline to represent the logic gate.

Command: *Choose Polyline (Draw, Polyline)*	Issues the PLINE command
From point: **6,7.5** (Enter)	Starts a polyline at coordinates ① (see fig. 9.1)
Current line-width is 0.0000 Arc/Close/Halfwidth/Length/Undo/ Width/<Endpoint of line>: **@1<270** (Enter)	Draws a line segment to ②
Arc/Close/Halfwidth/Length/Undo/ Width/<Endpoint of line>: **@1.5<0** (Enter)	Draws another line segment at ③
Arc/Close/Halfwidth/Length/Undo/ Width/<Endpoint of line>: **A** (Enter)	Switches to arc mode
Angle/CEnter/CLose/Direction/Halfwidth /Line/Radius/Second pt/Undo/Width/ <Endpoint of arc>: **@1<90** (Enter)	Draws an arc segment at ④
Angle/CEnter/CLose/Direction/Halfwidth /Line/Radius/Second pt/Undo/Width/ <Endpoint of arc>: **L** (Enter)	Switches back to line mode
Arc/Close/Halfwidth/Length/Undo/ Width/<Endpoint of line>: **C** (Enter)	Closes the polyline
Command: *Choose Ellipse Axis End (Draw, Ellipse)*	Issues the ELLIPSE command
Arc/Center/<Axis endpoint 1>: *Using the Midpoint object snap,* *pick* ⑤	Starts an ellipse at the midpoint of the arc
Axis endpoint 2: **@.75<0** (Enter)	Continues the axis .75 units to the right
<Other axis distance>/Rotation: **@.2<90** (Enter)	Draws the ellipse

Use a multiline to draw a circuit line.

Command: *Choose Multiline (Draw, Polyline)*	Issues the MLINE command

`Justification = Top, Scale = 1.00,`
`Style = STANDARD`
`Justification/Scale/STyle/`
`<From point>: S (Enter)`
	Specifies the Scale option

`Set Mline scale <1.00>: .5 (Enter)`	Sets the scale to .5

`Justification = Top, Scale = 0.50,`
`Style = STANDARD`
`Justification/Scale/STyle/`
`<From point>: J (Enter)`
	Specifies the Justification option

`Top/Zero/Bottom <top>: Z (Enter)`	Sets the justification to zero

`Justification = Top, Scale = 1.00,`
`Style = STANDARD`
`Justification/Scale/STyle/`
`<From point>:` *Using the Midpoint,*
object snap pick ⑥
	Starts a multiline object at the midpoint of the line

`<To point>: @4<180 (Enter)`	Draws a multiline segment
`Undo/<To point: (Enter)`	Ends the MLINE command
`Command:` *Choose Save (Standard Toolbar)*	Saves the drawing

Your drawing now should resemble figure 9.1.

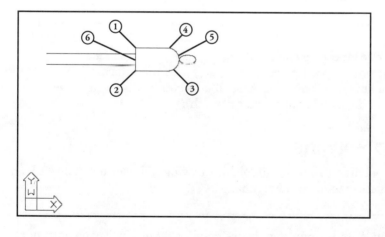

Figure 9.1
The LOADGATE drawing.

Polylines, ellipses, and multilines enable you to create very complex designs. The exercises in this chapter show you how to use these objects to draw a topographic map.

Understanding Polylines

A polyline is a single object that can contain both line and arc segments. In Chapter 5, "The Basic Drawing Commands," you were introduced to the RECTANG and POLYGON commands. These two commands created rectangles and polygons, which are two types of polylines. Figure 9.2 shows several other types of polylines.

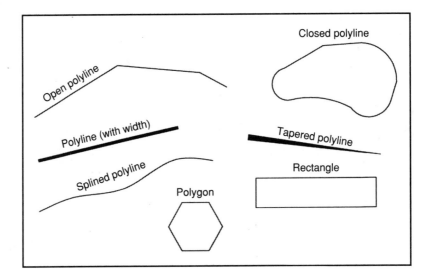

The endpoint connecting each polyline segment is called a *vertex*. AutoCAD stores the vertex locations along with the information about the segments in between the vertices (such as whether it's a line or arc segment, and its starting and ending width).

Creating a Polyline

Drawing a polyline can be as simple as drawing a line or arc. The PLINE command is used to draw a polyline.

PLINE. The PLINE command draws polylines. Polylines can contain line and arc segments.
Toolbar: *Choose Polyline (Draw, Polyline)*
Screen: *Choose DRAW 1, Pline:*
Alias: PL

When you first invoke the PLINE command, you are in line mode. In this mode, you draw the line segments of the polyline. When you are ready, you can switch to the arc mode. You use the arc mode to draw the arc segments of the polyline. You can switch between each mode to draw as many arc and line segments as needed.

Because a polyline is more complex than a line, the PLINE command has many options available to it. The following is a list of the PLINE command options:

- **Endpoint of line.** Specifies the endpoint of the current line segment. This is the default option.

- **Arc.** Switches between drawing line segments and arc segments in a polyline.

- **Close.** Draws a closed polyline. Like the Line command's Close option, this option draws a segment from the last endpoint to the starting point and then exits from the PLINE command.

- **Halfwidth.** Sets the polyline width by specifying the distance from the center to the polyline's edges (half the actual width).

- **Width.** Sets the total polyline width. You are prompted for a Starting width: and an Ending width:. You can draw tapered polylines by specifying a different starting and ending width. When you continue to the next segment, the ending width is used. The default width for polylines is 0 (no width).

- **Length.** Asks for the length of a new polyline segment. The new polyline segment is drawn at the same angle as the last polyline segment or tangent to the last arc segment.

- **Undo.** Reverses the last action done.

The following exercise illustrates how the polyline options are used to draw a polyline. The exercise shows you how to draw the building in figure 9.3.

Drawing a Building as a Polyline

To begin, create a new drawing named TOPO.DWG using the default ACAD.DWG as a prototype. Create four layers named CONTOUR, OBJECTS, ROAD, and SURFACE. Choose appropriate colors for the layers and assign the linetype DASHED2 to the CONTOUR layer. Set the SURFACE layer current. Set the LTSCALE to 40, set the limits to 0,0 and 960,720, and finally, zoom to the drawing limits. In this exercise, 1 unit will be equal to 1'.

continues

continued

Command: *Choose Polyline (Draw, Polygon)*	Issues the PLINE command
From point: **650,375** (Enter)	Starts a polyline at ① (see fig. 9.3)
Current line-width is 0.0000 Arc/Close/Halfwidth/Length/ Undo/ Width/<Endpoint of line>: **@100<0** (Enter)	Draws a polyline line segment
Arc/Close/Halfwidth/Length/Undo/ Width/<Endpoint of line>: **@100<270** (Enter)	Draws a polyline line segment
Arc/Close/Halfwidth/Length/Undo/ Width/<Endpoint of line>: **@10<0** (Enter)	Draws a polyline line segment
Arc/Close/Halfwidth/Length/Undo/ Width/<Endpoint of line>: **@100<270** (Enter)	Draws a polyline line segment
Arc/Close/Halfwidth/Length/Undo/ Width/<Endpoint of line>: **@110<180** (Enter)	Draws a polyline line segment
Arc/Close/Halfwidth/Length/Undo/ Width/<Endpoint of line>: **C** (Enter)	Closes the polyline back to ①
Command: (Enter)	Repeats the PLINE command
From point: **200,450** (Enter)	Starts the polyline at ②
Current line-width is 0.0000 Arc/Close/Halfwidth/Length/Undo/ Width/<Endpoint of line>: **@150<0** (Enter)	Draws a polyline line segment
Arc/Close/Halfwidth/Length/Undo/ Width/<Endpoint of line>: **@100,90** (Enter)	Draws a polyline line segment
Arc/Close/Halfwidth/Length/Undo/ Width/<Endpoint of line>: **@150<180** (Enter)	Draws a polyline line segment
Arc/Close/Halfwidth/Length/Undo/ Width/<Endpoint of line>: **C** (Enter)	Closes the polyline

Next, draw a concrete pad using the LINE command.

Command: *Choose Line (Draw, Line)*	Issues the LINE command
First point: **100,200** (Enter)	Sets the starting point of the concrete pad at ③
To point: **@100<90** (Enter)	Draws a 100-foot line to the right

To point: **@100<0** (Enter)	Draws a 100-foot line upward
To point: **@100<270** (Enter)	Draws a 100-foot line to the left
To point: **C** (Enter)	Draws a 100 × 100 foot concrete pad

One way polylines are different from normal lines in that a polyline is one object with many line segments. A line is a single line segment. In the next steps, you move one of the concrete pads.

Command: *Click on the rectangle at* ②	Displays grips on the polyline
Command: *Pick the grip at* ②	Selects a grip as a base point and displays the grip editing options
STRETCH <Stretch to point>/Base point/Copy/ Undo/eXit: **MO** (Enter)	Switches to the move grip edit mode
MOVE <Move to point>/Base point/Copy/ Undo/eXit: **@300<0** (Enter)	Moves building to 300' to the left
Command: *Press Esc twice*	Deselects the polyline and turns off the grips
Command: *Choose Save (Standard Toolbar)*	Saves the drawing

Your drawing now should look like figure 9.4.

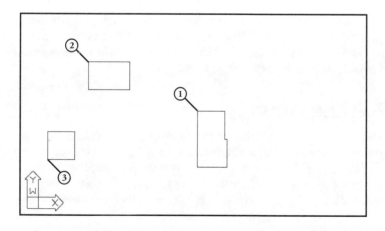

Figure 9.3

Drawing the buildings with polylines.

Polylines have unlimited uses. They can be used to draw plotting borders, contour lines, toolplates, and shapes for symbols and many other things. The potential uses are many. The key to using polylines is being aware of how they differ from lines.

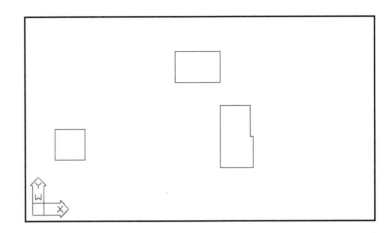

Figure 9.4

The completed building outlines.

Polylines Versus Lines

Using polylines can add a great deal of power and flexibility to your drawing. Polylines have features not available with normal lines and arcs. You can control how the polyline looks, for example. You can draw a polyline as a thick line or have the width change over the length (refer to figure 9.2). The polyline's width can be used to place emphasis in a drawing or as a convenient way to draw a thick line. Polylines can contain arcs, but lines cannot.

Another advantage is that because a polyline is one object, you can perform one action for the entire polyline. As you saw in the previous exercise, you only had to select a single polyline to move it, while you would have had to select all four lines to move them.

Creating Polyline Arcs

Drawing an arc in a polyline is similar to drawing a normal arc. You can define an arc by its center, endpoints, included angle, direction, or radius. The only real difference is that a normal arc is drawn using the ARC command, while a polyline arc is drawn using the Arc options of the PLINE command. The following list displays the PLINE command's Arc options:

- **Endpoint of arc.** Specifies the endpoint of the current arc segment. This is the default.

- **Angle.** Specifies the included angle of the arc. A negative value draws the arc clockwise.

- **Center.** Specifies the arc's center point.

- **Close.** Closes the polyline's last endpoint and starting point with an arc segment and then exits the PLINE command.

- **Direction.** Specifies the tangent direction of an arc segment.

- **Halfwidth.** Specifies the arc's width from the polyline center to the edge. This option is the same as in line mode.

- **Line.** Switches you back to line mode to draw line segments.

- **Radius.** Specifies the arc's radius.

- **Second pt.** Specifies the second point of a three-point arc.

- **Undo.** Reverses the last action done.

- **Width.** Specifies the width for the arc segment. This option is the same as the line mode.

Drawing polyline arc segments is similar to drawing arcs with the ARC command. In the following exercise, you draw some contour polylines with line and arc segments.

Drawing the Contours

Continue from the previous exercise. Set the CONTOUR layer current before proceeding with this exercise.

Command: *Choose Polyline (Draw, Polygon)*   Issues the PLINE command

From point: **45,450** (Enter)   Sets starting point of the polyline at ①
(see fig. 9.5)

Current line-width is 0.0000   Switches to arc mode
Arc/Close/Halfwidth/Length/Undo/
Width/<Endpoint of line>: **A** (Enter)

Angle/CEnter/CLose/Direction/Halfwidth/   Specifies the Second pt option
Line/Radius/Second pt/Undo/Width/
<Endpoint of arc>: **S** (Enter)

Second point: **160,530** (Enter)   Sets the second point of the arc at ②

End point: **230,640** (Enter)   Sets the endpoint of the arc at ③

Angle/CEnter/CLose/Direction/Halfwidth/   Ends the PLINE command
Line/Radius/Second pt/Undo/Width/
<Endpoint of arc>: (Enter)

continues

continued

This second contour is a bit more complex. You will draw both line segments and arc segments in the contour.

Command: (Enter)	Repeats the PLINE command
From point: **45,150** (Enter)	Sets starting point of polyline at ④
Current line-width is 0.0000 Arc/Close/Halfwidth/Length/Undo/ Width/<Endpoint of line>: **A** (Enter)	Switches to arc mode
Angle/CEnter/CLose/Direction/Halfwidth/ Line/Radius/Second pt/Undo/Width/ <Endpoint of arc>: **R** (Enter)	Specifies the Radius option
Radius: **500** (Enter)	Sets the arc radius to 500'
Angle/<End point>: **290,230** (Enter)	Sets the endpoint at ⑤
Angle/CEnter/CLose/Direction/Halfwidth/ Line/Radius/Second pt/Undo/Width/ <Endpoint of arc>: **L** (Enter)	Switches to line mode
Arc/Close/Halfwidth/Length/Undo/ Width/<Endpoint of line>: **460,380** (Enter)	Draws a line segment to ⑥
Arc/Close/Halfwidth/Length/Undo/ Width/<Endpoint of line>: **A** (Enter)	Switches to arc mode
Angle/CEnter/CLose/Direction/Halfwidth/ Line/Radius/Second pt/Undo/Width/ <Endpoint of arc>: **600,430** (Enter)	Draw the arc segment tangent to the previous line segment at ⑦
Angle/CEnter/CLose/Direction/Halfwidth/ Line/Radius/Second pt/Undo/Width/ <Endpoint of arc>: **750,480** (Enter)	Draws an arc segment tangent to the previous arc segment at ⑧
Arc/Close/Halfwidth/Length/Undo/ Width/<Endpoint of line>: (Enter)	Ends the PLINE command
Command: *Choose Save (Standard Toolbar)*	Saves the drawing

Now that you have a feel for drawing polylines, you can change their looks by assigning a width.

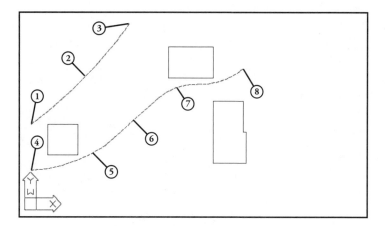

Figure 9.5

Drawing polylines with arc segments.

9

Adding Width to Polylines

To add weight and emphasis to your drawing, you can draw polylines with width. This feature is not available to normal lines and arcs. You can taper the polyline width or keep the width constant throughout the polyline.

To control how polyline widths are displayed on AutoCAD's screen, use the FILL command. If FILL is off, objects are shown as outlines. If FILL is on, objects are shown filled-in. If FILL is off, AutoCAD does not have to work as hard because there is less on the display to show.

FILL. The FILL command sets AutoCAD to display solids, polylines, and traces to single-line outlines of their boundaries. The FILL command is either on or off.

Pull-down: *Choose* **O**ptions, **D**isplay, S**o**lid Fill
Screen: *Choose* OPTIONS, DISPLAY, Fill:

The exercise below shows you how to draw wide and tapered polylines.

Drawing the Highlight Contours and Pipelines

Continue from the previous exercise. The following polyline you will draw is the highlight contour. You will assign the highlight contour a width to distinguish it from the other contour lines.

Command: *Choose Polyline (Draw, Polygon)*   Issues the PLINE command

continues

continued

From point: **45,60** (Enter)	Sets the polyline starting point at ① (see fig. 9.6)
Current line-width is 0.0000 Arc/Close/Halfwidth/Length/Undo/ Width/<Endpoint of line>: **W** (Enter)	Specifies the Width option
Starting width <0.0000>: **1.5** (Enter)	Sets a width of 1.5'
Ending width <1.5000>: (Enter)	Keeps the polyline width constant
Arc/Close/Halfwidth/Length/Undo/ Width/<Endpoint of line>: **320,100** (Enter)	Draws a line segment at ②
Arc/Close/Halfwidth/Length/Undo/ Width/<Endpoint of line>: **A** (Enter)	Switches to arc mode
Angle/CEnter/CLose/Direction/Halfwidth/ Line/Radius/Second pt/Undo/Width/ <Endpoint of arc>: **560,240** (Enter)	Draws an arc segment at ③
Angle/CEnter/CLose/Direction/Halfwidth/ Line/Radius/Second pt/Undo/Width/ <Endpoint of arc>: **650,300** (Enter)	Draws an arc segment at ④
Angle/CEnter/CLose/Direction/Halfwidth/ Line/Radius/Second pt/Undo/Width/ <Endpoint of arc>: (Enter)	Ends the PLINE command

The next polyline here is a pipeline connecting the concrete pad and the building. You'll change the polyline width over the polyline length. Set the layer OBJECT current before drawing the pipeline.

Command: *Choose Polyline (Draw, Polygon)*	Issues PLINE command again
From point: *Using the Midpoint object snap, pick* ⑤	Sets starting point for new polyline
Arc/Close/Halfwidth/Length/Undo/ Width/<Endpoint of line>: **W** (Enter)	Specifies the Width option
Starting width <1.5000>: **5** (Enter)	Assigns a width of 5' to the polyline
Ending width <5.0000>: (Enter)	Keeps polyline width constant over length
Arc/Close/Halfwidth/Length/Undo/ Width/<Endpoint of line>: **@50<0** (Enter)	Draws a line segment at ⑥
Arc/Close/Halfwidth/Length/Undo/ Width/<Endpoint of line>: **W** (Enter)	Specifies the Width option
Starting width <5.0000>: **10** (Enter)	Changes polyline width to 10'

9

`Ending width <10.0000>:` (Enter)	Keeps polyline width constant
`Arc/Close/Halfwidth/Length/Undo/` `Width/<Endpoint of line>:` **`@100<270`** (Enter)	Draws a line segment at ⑦
`Arc/Close/Halfwidth/Length/Undo/` `Width/<Endpoint of line>:` **`W`** (Enter)	Specifies the Width option
`Starting width <10.0000>:` (Enter)	Keeps the previous width
`Ending width <10.0000>:` **`25`** (Enter)	Changes ending width to make polyline wider over the length

`Arc/Close/Halfwidth/Length/Undo/`
`Width/<Endpoint of line>:`
Using the Perpendicular object snap,
pick ⑧
	Draws a line segment to the building

`Angle/CEnter/CLose/Direction/Halfwidth/`
`Line/Radius/Second pt/Undo/Width/`
`<Endpoint of arc>:` (Enter)
	Ends the PLINE command

Command: *Choose* **O**ptions, **D**isplay, S**o**lid Fill	Turns off solid fill
Command: **REGEN** (Enter)	Regenerates the drawing

After regenerating, the solid fill is turned off. Your drawing now should resemble figure 9.7. Notice that although the solid fill is turned off, you still see the miter joints at the vertices.

Command: *Choose* **O**ptions, **D**isplay, S**o**lid Fill	Turns on solid fill
Command: **REGEN** (Enter)	Regenerates the drawing
Command: *Choose Save (Standard Toolbar)*	Saves the drawing

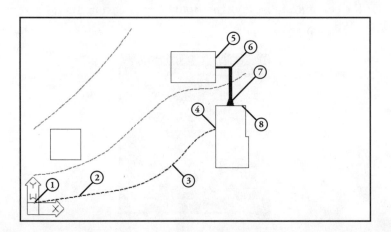

Figure 9.6

Using width in a drawing.

Figure 9.7

Using FILL with polylines.

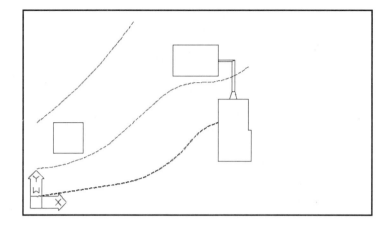

Creating a Boundary

As you start drawing more complex designs, some polylines are difficult to draw using the PLINE command. AutoCAD provides an easy way to create polylines from existing objects. The BOUNDARY command enables you to create a polyline by picking a point within an enclosed area.

> **BOUNDARY.** The BOUNDARY command creates a polyline from a set of existing objects that form an enclosed area. This command formerly was known as BPOLY.
> Toolbar: *Choose Boundary (Draw, Polyline)*
> Screen: *Choose* Constrct, Boundar:

The BOUNDARY command displays the Boundary Creation dialog box, as shown in figure 9.8.

Figure 9.8

The Boundary Creation dialog box.

The following exercise shows you how to draw a polyline using the BOUNDARY command.

Enclosing an Area and Drawing a Boundary

Continue from the previous exercise.

Command: *Choose Line (Draw, Line)*	Issues LINE command
From point: *Using the Endpoint object snap, pick ① (see fig. 9.9)*	Starts a line from the lower left corner of the concrete pad
To point: `@100<270` (Enter)	Draws a line, which encloses an area between the concrete pad and the contour line
To point: (Enter)	Ends the LINE command
Command: *Choose Boundary (Draw Polygon)*	Issues the BOUNDARY command
Choose **P**ick Points	Lets you choose a point within an enclosed area
`_boundary` `Select internal point:` *Pick ②*	Selects the enclosed area to draw the boundary

`Selecting everything...`
`Selecting everything visible...`
`Analyzing the selected data...`
`Analyzing internal islands...`	

`Select internal point:` (Enter)	Finishes selecting the pick points
`BOUNDARY created 1 polyline`	Draws the polyline and ends the BOUNDARY command
Command: *Pick the line at ③*	Highlights the line and displays its grips
Command: *Choose Erase (Modify)*	Issues ERASE command and erases the line
Command: *Choose Redraw (Standard Toolbar, Redraw)*	Issues the REDRAW command and refreshes the display
Command: *Pick the polyline at ④*	Displays the grips on the polyline created by the BOUNDARY command
Command: *Click on upper left grip*	Selects a grip as a base point

`** STRETCH **`
`<Stretch to point>/Base point/Copy/`
`Undo/eXit:` `MO` (Enter)
	Switches to move mode

continues

continued

`** MOVE **`
`<Move to point>/Base point/Copy/`
`Undo/eXit: @355<270` (Enter)
	Moves the polyline boundary to a location where it can be seen better

Command: *Press Esc twice*	Clears the grips
Command: *Choose Save (Standard Toolbar)*	Saves the drawing

Your drawing now should look like figure 9.10.

Figure 9.9

Drawing a boundary.

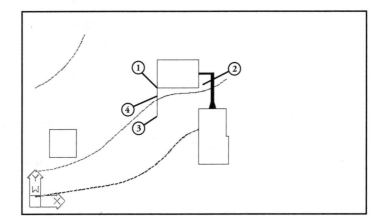

Figure 9.10

The new boundary polyline.

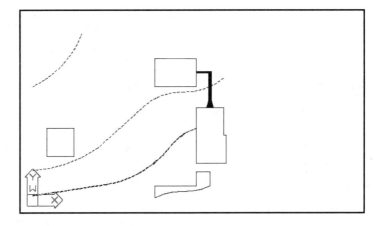

Understanding Ellipses

In AutoCAD, an ellipse is described by one center and the major and minor axes (see fig. 9.11). You use these characteristics to draw the ellipse.

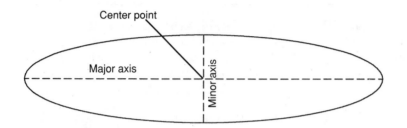

Center point

Major axis

Minor axis

Figure 9.11

The parts of an ellipse.

Ellipses are created with the ELLIPSE command.

ELLIPSE. The ELLIPSE command draws a true ellipse.
Toolbar: *Choose Ellipse Axis End (Draw, Ellipse)*
Screen: *Choose DRAW 1, Ellipse:*

The following list describes the options of the ELLIPSE command:

- **Arc.** Draws an elliptical arc (a partial ellipse). After specifying the Arc option and defining the ellipse, you have the following options:

  - **Start angle.** Specifies a starting angle on the ellipse. AutoCAD draws an assisting ellipse and you specify where the elliptical arc starts and ends. The angle is measured from the start point of the major axis. After specifying a start angle, you can specify either an ending angle or an included (total) angle.

  - **Start parameter.** Similar to the Start angle, AutoCAD prompts you for the starting angle on the ellipse but uses a different equation for deriving the ellipse. See the *AutoCAD Command Reference* for more on creating elliptical arcs.

- **Center.** Specifies the center of the ellipse.

- **Axis endpoint 1.** Specifies the endpoints of the first axis. After specifying a start point, you are prompted for Axis endpoint 2:. You then have the following options:

- **Other axis distance.** Specifies the endpoints of the second axis.

- **Rotation.** Specifies the rotation angle of the ellipse. This enables you to define an ellipse as if it were a circle viewed from an angle.

> An ellipse in AutoCAD 13 can be a true ellipse or a polyline that simulates an ellipse. You can specify a simulated ellipse by setting the system variable PELLIPSE to 1. The default value of PELLIPSE is 0, which sets ellipses to be drawn as true ellipses.

Drawing an ellipse is nothing more than telling AutoCAD where the ellipse is located and what its characteristics are. You select the options to use based on what information you have about the ellipse. The following exercise shows you how to draw an ellipse when you know the center point and the length of the major and minor axes.

Drawing Ellipses

Continue from the previous exercise. The first ellipse is drawn by specifying its center point and its major and minor axes.

Command: *Choose Ellipse Center (Draw, Ellipse)*	Issues the ELLIPSE command with the Center option
Center of ellipse: **705,275** (Enter)	Sets the center of the ellipse at ① (see fig. 9.12)
Axis endpoint: **@40<90** (Enter)	Sets the major axis to 40'×2=80'
\<Other axis distance>/Rotation: **@24<180** (Enter)	Sets minor axis to 24'×2=48' and draws the ellipse
Command: *Choose Ellipse Axis End (Draw, Ellipse)*	Issues ELLIPSE command
Arc/Center/\<Axis endpoint 1>: **530,500** (Enter)	Sets the major axis endpoint at ②
Axis endpoint 2: **@80<0** (Enter)	Draws a major axis of 80'
\<Other axis distance>/Rotation: **@25<270** (Enter)	Draws a minor axis of 50'
Command: *Click Ellipse Elliptical Arc (Draw, Ellipse)*	Issues ELLIPSE command with the Arc option

`<Axis endpoint 1>/Center:` *Using the Endpoint object snap, pick* ③	Sets the starting point of major axis
`Axis endpoint 2:` *Using the Endpoint object snap, pick* ④	Sets the length of the major axis
`<Other axis distance>/Rotation:` `@30<100` (Enter)	Sets the length of the minor axis
`Parameter/<start angle>:` `0` (Enter)	Sets the starting angle
`Parameter/Included/<end angle>:` `180` (Enter)	Draws the elliptical arc
`Command:` *Choose Save (Standard Toolbar)*	Saves the drawing

Your drawing now should look like figure 9.12.

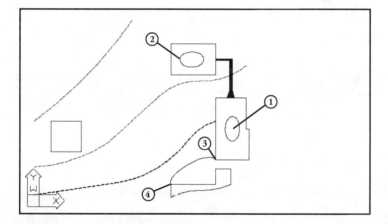

Figure 9.12

Drawing ellipses.

Creating Multilines

A *multiline* is an object that contains two or more parallel lines. The parallel lines are called elements. Each element has a distance (called an *offset*) from the origin (or *zero offset*) of the multiline. Multilines are useful for drawing objects such as roads, borders, or any object requiring the use of parallel lines. Multilines might look like separated lines, but they act as a single object. Figure 9.13 shows a typical multiline.

There are two steps to creating multilines. The first part consists of setting up the multiline style. This involves defining the number of elements, their offset distances, and how each element will look. A multiline with three elements at an offset of 30 feet, for example, can represent a 60-foot-wide road with a centerline at the zero offset.

Figure 9.13

An example of a multiline.

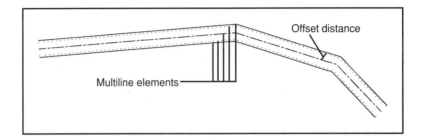

Creating Multiline Styles

Multiline styles have many features available. You can assign different colors and linetypes to each element in a multiline . You also can specify various line or arc end caps for the multilines. Multiline styles are defined with the MLSTYLE command.

MLSTYLE. The MLSTYLE command displays the Multiline Style dialog box. This dialog box enables you to define up to 16 multiline elements as well as specify a color and linetype for each element. You also can specify starting and ending caps as well a adding a solid fill to the multiline.

Toolbar: *Choose Multiline Style (Object Properties)*
Pull-Down: *Choose **D**ata, **M**ultiline style*
Screen: *Choose DRAW 1, Mline:, MLstyle:*

The MLSTYLE command displays the Multiline Style dialog box as shown in figure 9.14.

Figure 9.14

The Multiline Styles dialog box.

The Multiline Styles dialog box has two dialog boxes of its own. The first is the Element Properties dialog box (see fig. 9.15). In this dialog box, you can add or delete elements of a multiline style. Each element can be assigned a color and a linetype.

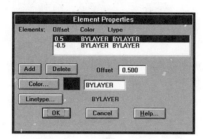

Figure 9.15

The Element Properties dialog box.

The second dialog box is the Multiline Properties dialog box (see fig. 9.16). You can set a multiline to draw a line or arcs at the start or end of a multiline. You also can assign a Fill color to the multiline.

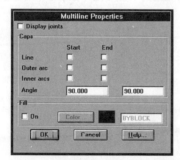

Figure 9.16

The Multiline Properties dialog box.

In the following exercise, you set up a multiline style for a road. The road will be named ROAD60 and will be 60 feet wide. The multiline will have three elements—two elements for the edge of the road and one element for the centerline of the road.

Creating the ROAD60 Multiline Style

Continue from the previous exercise.

Command: *Choose Multiline Style (Object Properties)*

Issues the MLSTYLE command

Choose Element Properties

Displays the Element Properties dialog box

continues

In the Offset *text box, type* **30** (Enter), *then choose the* Add *button*	Changes the offset to 30' and adds a zero offset element
Click on the −0.5 *offset element, then in the* Offset *text box, type* **-30** (Enter)	Adds an element −30' from the center
Click on the 0.00 *offset element, then choose* Linetype	Displays the Select Linetype dialog box
Load the CENTER2 *linetype, then select* CENTER2, *choose* OK	Selects the CENTER2 linetype for the 0 offset element
Choose OK	Exits to Multiline Styles dialog box
In the Name *text box, type* **ROAD60**	Names the multiline style
In the Description *text box, type* **60' wide road**, *then choose* Add	Describes the multiline style and adds it to the set of multiline styles
Choose OK	Exits to Multiline Styles dialog box

The multiline style is now created.

Drawing Multilines

The second part of creating a multiline is the actual drawing of the multiline itself. You can set how the multiline's origin is oriented, set the scale factor applied to the multiline, and choose the style of the multiline. You use the MLINE command to draw the multiline.

> **MLINE.** The MLINE command draws a set of 1 to 16 parallel lines. Each parallel line has an offset value from the multiline origin. You can choose the multiline style and then draw the multiline.
> Toolbar: *Choose Mline (Draw, Polyline)*
> Screen: *Choose DRAW 1, Mline:*

The MLINE command has the following options:

- **Justification.** This option specifies the origin of the multiline.

- **Scale.** This option applies a scale factor to a multiline style. Scale is useful for drawings of different plot scale factors.

- **Style.** This option chooses the multiline style to draw.

- **From point.** This option sets the starting point of the multiline.

- **Undo.** This option reverses the last drawing action. Undo is similar to the LINE command's Undo option.

- **Close.** This option draws a multiline segment back to the starting point. Close is similar to the LINE command's Close option.

The following exercise shows you how to draw a multiline as a 60' wide road. The ROAD60 multiline style was set up in the earlier exercise.

Drawing the 60' Road

Continue with the previous exercise. Set the layer ROAD current before continuing.

Command: *Choose Multiline (Draw, Polyline)*	Issues the MLINE command
Justification = Top, Scale = 1.00, Style = ROAD60 Justification/Scale/STyle/ <From point>: **J** (Enter)	Specifies the Justification option
Top/Zero/Bottom <top>: **Z** (Enter)	Selects the Zero element as the origin
Justification = Zero, Scale = 1.00, Style = ROAD60 Justification/Scale/STyle/ <From point>: **100,580** (Enter)	Starts the multiline at ① (see fig 9.17)
<To point>: **360,360** (Enter)	Draws a multiline segment at ②
Undo/<To point>: **360,50** (Enter)	Draws a multiline segment at ③
Close/Undo/<To point>: (Enter)	Finishes multiline
Command: *Choose Save (Standard Toolbar)*	Saves the drawing

Your drawing now should look like figure 9.17.

Multilines are a powerful drawing feature. You have scratched only the surface of creating multilines and multiline styles. For more about creating multilines, see *Inside AutoCAD Release 13 for Windows and Windows NT.*

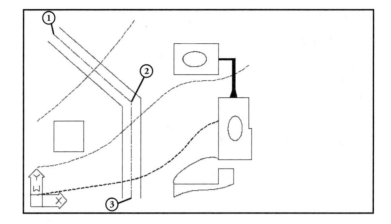

Figure 9.17

*The TOPO
drawing.*

Summary

As your drawing becomes more complex, you should employ the right tools
to get the job done. For some drawings, using lines is difficult and
polylines might be easier to use. By using the new drawing objects in this
chapter, you are able to access features not available to the basic drawing
commands. It is important to examine when to use polylines, multilines,
and ellipses in your drawing.

This concept becomes more important in later chapters. You will learn
how to draw objects from existing objects and how much easier it is to edit
one polyline instead of several lines.

At this point, you are quite skilled in the use of drawing objects to complete your design in AutoCAD. The next step is to explore how editing
commands can help build your design as well. The next chapter, "Selecting
and Editing Objects," teaches you about more editing commands and
selection options. As your drawing holds more objects, selecting and
editing them becomes more critical.

Related Topics

- Rectangles and polygons—Chapter 5, "The Basic Drawing
  Commands"

- Grips and grip editing—Chapter 8, "Editing with Grips"

Chapter Snapshot

Never being wrong means never having to edit. While drawing your design, more than likely you'll change how your drawing looks, move objects around, and make copies. This chapter shows you how the editing commands work and how they can help you when you need to make changes to your drawing.

In this chapter, you will do the following:

- Learn to move, copy, rotate, stretch, and scale objects

- Draw new objects from existing objects with the OFFSET, ARRAY, and MIRROR commands

- Explore noun-verb editing

- Learn the various methods of building a selection set

- Change an object's properties

Selecting and Editing Objects

N o matter how much care you put into your drawing, you always will need to make changes to it. Editing is an integral part of drawing in AutoCAD. Using the editing commands, you can save time and effort by working with what objects you have and changing them.

The editing basics were introduced to you in Chapter 8, "Editing with Grips." You used grips and the grip options to edit objects. This chapter introduces you to some of AutoCAD's other editing commands and advanced object selection options. The following Quick Tour exercise gives you an overview of some of the concepts presented in this chapter.

The Quick Tour

Begin by creating a new drawing named MTPLATE using the default ACAD.DWG prototype drawing. Create a layer named PLATE and set it current. Set the grid spacing to 1, the snap spacing to .125 and turn both grid and snap on.

Command: *Choose Polyline (Draw, Polyline)*	Issues the PLINE command
Draw a polyline from the point **2,2** *to* **@5<0**, **@1<90**, **@2<0**, **@2<90**, **@2<180**, **@1<90**, **@5<180**, *then* Close	Draws the mounting plate at ① (see fig. 10.1)
Command: *Choose Offset (Modify, Copy)*	Issues the OFFSET command
Offset distance or Through <Through>: **.25** (Enter)	Sets the offset distance to .25"
Select object to offset: *Select the polyline*	Selects the polyline
Side to offset? *Pick anywhere outside the polyline*	Creates another polyline .25" away from the original polyline at ②
Select object to offset: (Enter)	Ends OFFSET command
Command: *Choose Circle Center Radius (Draw, Circle) and draw a circle with a center point at* **5,4** *and a radius of* **.5**	Issues the CIRCLE command and draws the circle at ③
Command: *Choose Copy Object (Modify, Copy)*	Issues the COPY command
Select objects: **L** (Enter)	Selects the last circle drawn
Select objects: (Enter)	Ends object selection
<Base point or displacement>/Multiple: **M** (Enter)	Specifies the Multiple option
Base point: *Using the Center object snap, pick the circle at* ③	Begins dragging the circle from its center
Second point of displacement: **@2<180** (Enter)	Copies the circle to ④
Second point of displacement: **@2<0** (Enter)	Copies the circle to ⑤
Second point of displacement: (Enter)	Ends the COPY command
Command: *Choose Scale (Modify, Resize)*	Issues the SCALE command
Select objects: **P** (Enter)	Reselects the previously selected circle
Select objects: (Enter)	Ends object selection

Base point: *Using the Center object snap, pick the circle at* ③	Begins scaling the circle from its center
<Scale factor>/Reference: **.5** (Enter)	Changes size of circle to half-size
Command: *Choose Line (Draw, Line) and draw a line from* **5,4.25** *to* **5,4.75**	Issues the LINE command and draws the line at ① (see fig. 10.2)
Command: *Choose Array Polar (Modify, Copy)*	Issues the ARRAY command with the Polar option
Select objects: **L** (Enter)	Selects the last line drawn
Select objects: (Enter)	Ends object selection
Center point of array: *Using the Center object snap, pick the circle at* ②	Specifies the center of the array
Number of items: 8 (Enter)	Specifies the total number of objects to be copied
Angle to fill (+=ccw, -=cw) <360>: (Enter)	Accepts the default full circle option
Rotate objects as they are copied? <Y> (Enter)	Accepts the default and creates eight copies of the line around the edge of the circle
Command: *Choose Save (Standard toolbar)*	Saves the drawing

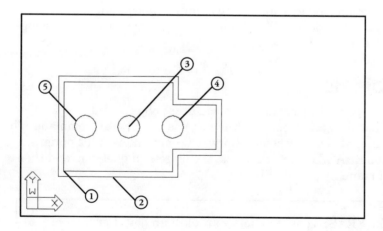

Figure 10.1

The mounting plate outline.

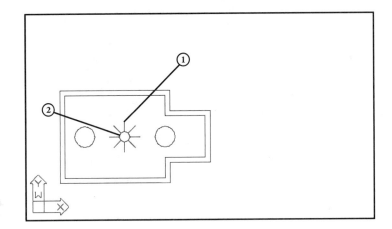

Figure 10.2

*The completed
MTPLATE
drawing.*

Editing Objects

In AutoCAD, editing is a matter of deciding what needs to be done, choosing the appropriate editing commands, and selecting the objects to edit. If you need to correct a mistake, you can move, stretch, or scale them to your satisfaction. You can duplicate existing geometry or create new objects from existing objects. You change only the objects that need changing. This saves considerable time and effort.

In the next section, you explore how to manipulate existing objects to gradually draw your design. This build-up process is how most drawings are done.

Erasing Objects

The easiest way to edit your drawing is to erase objects and re-create them. To remove objects from the drawing, use the ERASE command. The ERASE command is a very straightforward command with no options. You issue the ERASE command, select the objects in question, and then exit the command by pressing Enter.

ERASE. The ERASE command lets you select an object or a set of objects and remove them from the drawing.
Toolbar: *Choose Erase (Modify)*
Screen: *Choose* MODIFY, Erase:
Alias: E

Moving Objects

In manual drafting, if you need to relocate an object, you have to erase the object and redraw it in its new location. In AutoCAD, this process changes—you select the object(s) and use the MOVE command to relocate to the new location.

MOVE. The MOVE command changes the location of an object(s) in AutoCAD's coordinate space.
Toolbar: *Choose Move (Modify)*
Screen: *Choose* MODIFY, Move:
Alias: M

The MOVE command asks you to select the objects to be moved, and then how and where to move the objects by presenting you with the following prompts:

- **Base point or displacement.** This prompt asks for the base point with which to move the objects. You can pick a base point or specify a displacement using absolute (X,Y) coordinates. The displacement specifies the distance to move the object from its current location.

- **Second point of displacement.** This prompt asks for the new location of the base point. If you specified a displacement, you can simply press (Enter) to move the objects.

Previously, you explored how to move objects before using an object's grips. The MOVE command is very similar to that. The following exercise shows you how to use the MOVE command to relocate a circle to a new location. In the exercise, you begin to create a photogrammetric aerial camera.

Drawing and Moving Objects

To begin this exercise, create a new drawing named AERCAM using the default ACAD.DWG prototype drawing. Create two layers named CAM-INT and CAM-EXT and select colors for each of them. Assign the linetype DASHED2 to layer CAM-INT and set the layer CAM-EXT current. Finally, set the limits to 22,17 and zoom to the drawing limits.

Command: *Choose Polyline (Draw, Polyline)*   Issues the PLINE command

continues

continued

From point: *Draw a polyline from* **8,2** *to the points* **@2.5<90, @5<135, @5<90, @1.5<45, @8<0, @1.5<-45, @5<270, @5<225,** *and end it at* **@2.5<270**	Draws the exterior shell of the aerial camera in the form of a polyline
Command: *Choose Circle Center Radius (Draw, Circle) and draw a circle centered at* **6,12** *with a radius of* **1**	Issues the CIRCLE command and draws the circle at ① (see fig. 10.3)
Command: *Choose Circle Center Radius (Draw, Circle) and draw a circle centered at* **2,2** *with a radius of* **.25**	Issues the CIRCLE command and draws the circle at ②
Command: *Choose Move (Modify)*	Issues the MOVE command
Select Objects: *Pick* ②	Selects the circle to be moved
Select Objects: (Enter)	Ends object selection
Base point: *Using the Center object snap, pick the circle at* ②	Begins dragging the circle from its center
Second point of displacement: **6,10.75** (Enter)	Selects the new location of the circle
Command: (Enter)	Repeats the MOVE command
Select Objects: *Pick* ①	Selects the circle to be moved
Select Objects: (Enter)	Ends object selection
Base point: **1,0** (Enter)	Specifies a displacement of 1,0
Second point of displacement: (Enter)	Moves the circle 1" to the right
Command: *Choose Save (Standard Toolbar)*	Saves the drawing

Your drawing now should resemble figure 10.4.

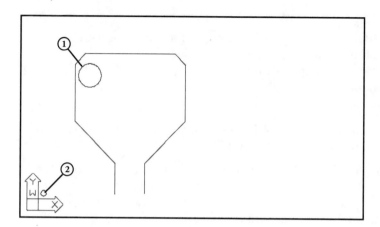

Figure 10.3
Moving the circles.

10

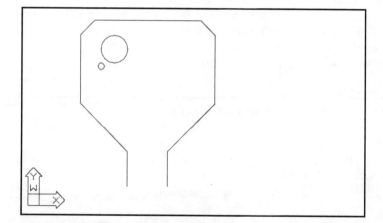

Figure 10.4
The camera outline.

Making Multiple Copies

In previous exercises, you also explored how to copy objects with grips.
The process of using the basic COPY command is similar to using the
MOVE command. While the MOVE command relocates an object from one
location to another, the COPY command leaves the object in its original
location.

COPY. The COPY command makes a copy of an object or set of objects in another location.
Toolbar: *Choose Copy Object (Modify, Copy)*
Screen: *Choose* CONSTRCT, Copy:

The COPY command has the same selection options as the MOVE command. One unique option for the COPY command is the Multiple option.

The Multiple option makes several copies of the original object(s). Using this option, you can make as many copies as you need of objects without selecting the objects again. After you have drawn enough copies, you can end the command by pressing Enter or Esc.

The Multiple option is useful when you are making copies of a set of objects and placing each copy in a different location. This process is easier than having to invoke the COPY command each time, select the objects, and then place the new objects over and over. The following exercise shows you how to use the COPY command's Multiple option.

Making Multiple Copies

Continue from the previous exercise.

Command: *Choose Line (Draw, Line)* *and draw a line from point* **9,12** *to* **10,12**	Issues the LINE command, draws the line
Command: *Choose Copy Object (Modify, Copy)*	Issues the COPY command
Select objects: *Pick the line*	Selects the new line to make copies from
Select objects: (Enter)	Ends object selection
<Base point or displacement>/Multiple: **M** (Enter)	Selects the Multiple option of the COPY command
Base point: *Using the Endpoint object snap, pick* ① (see fig. 10.5)	Selects the base point for copying
Second point of displacement: **@1<90** (Enter)	Copies the line to ②

Notice that the original line is still in place.

Second point of displacement: **@0.5<90** (Enter)	Copies the line to ③

`Second point of displacement:` `@0.5<270` (Enter)	Copies the line to ④
`Second point of displacement:` `@1<270` (Enter)	Copies the line to ⑤
`Second point of displacement:` (Enter)	Ends the COPY command
Command: *Choose Save (Standard Toolbar)*	Saves the drawing

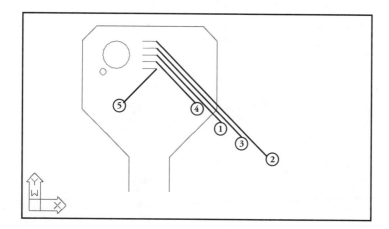

Figure 10.5

Making copies.

10

Rotating Objects

While the MOVE command changes the location of an object, the ROTATE command changes the angular orientation of an object. When you use the ROTATE command, you first select the objects to rotate, select a base point, and then enter a rotation angle. The rotation angle is an absolute value, based on the current user coordinate system. If a negative rotation angle is entered, the selected objects are rotated clockwise. If a positive rotation angle is entered, the objects are rotated counterclockwise.

ROTATE. The ROTATE command rotates an object or a set of objects from a base point. You can enter a rotation angle or an angle from a reference direction.

Screen: *Choose MODIFY, Rotate:*

Toolbar: *Choose Rotate (Modify, Rotate)*

The ROTATE command has only one option—the Reference option.

The Reference option enables you to select a relative rotation angle by either typing an angle or picking two points. By default, AutoCAD measures the rotation angle from 0°. You then can enter a rotation angle measured from the reference angle.

The Reference option is useful when you don't know the angle of a direction, and you want to make rotations from it.

Rotating the Camera Lens

Continue from the previous exercise.

Command: *Choose Polyline (Draw, Polyline)*	Issues the PLINE command
From point: **9.5,5.5** (Enter)	Places the start of the polyline
<Endpoint of line>: **@.5<0** (Enter)	Draws a line segment
<Endpoint of line>: **A** (Enter)	Switches to arc mode
<Endpoint of arc>: **R** (Enter)	Specifies the Radius option
Radius: **3** (Enter)	Specifies the arc radius
Angle/<End point>: **@2<270** (Enter)	Draws the arc segments
<Endpoint of arc>: **L** (Enter)	Switches to line mode
<Endpoint of line>: **@.5<180** (Enter)	Draws a line segment
<Endpoint of line>: **C** (Enter)	Closes the polyline
Command: *Choose Rotate (Modify, Rotate)*	Issues the ROTATE command
Select objects: *Pick the new polyline at* ① *(see fig. 10.6)*	Selects the lens to rotate
Select objects: (Enter)	Ends object selection
Base point: *Using the Midpoint object snap, pick the line at* ②	Begins dragging the circle from its center

Move pointing device around to see the lens rotate.

<Rotation angle>/Reference: **270** (Enter)	Rotates the lens

The next rotation shows you how to use the Reference option of the ROTATE command. You will draw the outline of the inner cone and correct it by rotating it.

Command: **LINE** (Enter)	Issues LINE command
From point: *Using the Endpoint object snap, pick* ① *(see fig. 10.7)*	Places the start of the line

`To point: @5<50` (Enter)	Draws the line at an intentionally wrong angle
`To point:` (Enter)	Ends the LINE command
`Command:` *Choose Rotate (Modify, Rotate)*	Issues the ROTATE command
`Select objects:` *Pick line at* ①	Selects new line to rotate
`Select objects:` (Enter)	Ends object selection
`Base point:` *Using the Endpoint object snap, pick* ①	Specifies the base point of the rotation
`<Rotation angle>/Reference: R` (Enter)	Selects Reference option
`Reference angle <0>:` *Using the Endpoint object snap, pick the line at* ①	Picks the first point of the reference angle
`Second point:` *Using the Endpoint object snap, pick* ②	Defines the reference angle
`New angle: 120` (Enter)	Rotates the line to an angle of 120°
`Command:` *Choose Save (Standard Toolbar)*	Saves the drawing

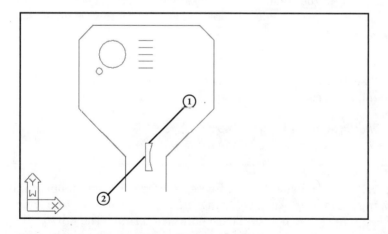

Figure 10.6

Using the ROTATE command.

You should keep a few things in mind when using the ROTATE command:

- The base point's location affects how the object looks after the rotation. If you select a base point on the object, the object rotates about itself. If the base point is located off the object, the object actually is displaced to another location.

- For certain objects, it's easier to draw them and then rotate them. It's easier, for example, to draw a rectangle and then rotate it than it is to type the coordinates of a polyline.

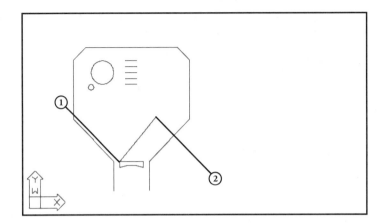

Figure 10.7

The finished rotation.

Creating Mirror Images

Learning how to use existing geometry is an important skill in AutoCAD Release 13. By working with the objects you already have, you don't have to spend a lot of time recreating or redrawing objects. The MIRROR command is a useful tool that lets you work with existing geometry. The MIRROR command inverts selected objects, creating a mirror image of the selected objects.

MIRROR. The MIRROR command draws a mirror image of selected objects around a mirror line. The original objects can be deleted or kept.
Toolbar: *Choose Mirror (Modify, Copy)*
Screen: *Choose* CONSTRCT, Mirror:

The MIRROR command enables you to create mirror images of objects, in effect, flipping them over. After selecting the objects you want to mirror, you are asked to pick two points. These points determine the mirror line, and the objects are inverted around that line. After defining the mirror line, you have the option of keeping the original objects or deleting them.

TIP

Turning on ORTHO while picking the second point of the mirror line ensures that the mirrored objects are either horizontally or vertically aligned with the original objects.

The following exercise shows you how to use the MIRROR command to create the film magazine on the other side of the aerial camera.

10

Using MIRROR To Draw the Film Magazine

Continue from the previous exercise.

Command: *Choose Line (Draw, Line)* — Issues the LINE command

Using the Quadrant object snap, draw a — Draws a line
line from coordinates ① to ② (see fig. 10.8)

Command: *Choose Mirror (Modify, Copy)* — Issues the MIRROR command

Select objects: *Press and drag from* — Selects the objects to mirror
③ to ④

4 found

Select objects: (Enter) — Ends object selection

First point of mirror line: *Using the* — Selects the first point of the mirror line
Midpoint object snap, pick ⑤

Second point: *Using the Midpoint* — Sets the mirror line and creates a
object snap, pick ⑥ — new set of objects

Where you place the mirror line determines how far away the two sets of objects are from each other. The mirror line is exactly halfway between the two sets of objects.

Delete old objects? <N> (Enter) — Keeps old objects

Command: *Choose Save (Standard Toolbar)* — Saves the drawing

Your drawing now should resemble figure 10.9.

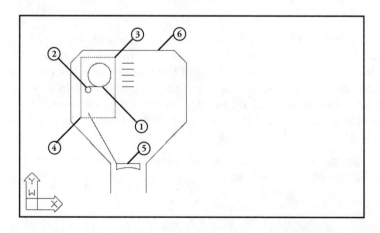

Figure 10.8

Drawing the second film reel.

Figure 10.9

The mirrored objects.

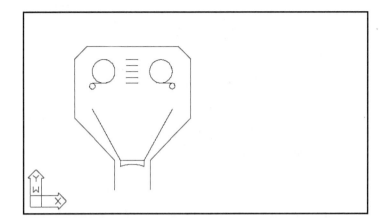

Stretching Objects

The STRETCH command modifies existing objects by changing their endpoints. You can, for example, select a new endpoint of an existing line instead of re-creating the line. The other endpoint of the line maintains its connection to other objects, while the new endpoint is changed. The STRETCH command is a convenient tool to edit your drawing and is another example of editing only what you need to change.

> **STRETCH.** The STRETCH command stretches objects from one point to a new point by using a crossing window. Any objects having endpoints inside the crossing are stretched.
> Toolbar: *Choose Stretch (Modify, Resize)*
> Screen: *Choose* MODIFY, Stretch:

The STRETCH command is similar to the MOVE command. The difference is that instead of moving the entire object, you move selected points on objects. This enables you to push and pull the points to modify the shape of the objects. The points on the objects must be selected in a crossing window. Any points that lie within the crossing window are stretched. After selecting the points to be stretched, you then select a base point and move the selected points to a new location.

The following exercise shows you how to use the STRETCH command to draw the focal plane of the aerial camera.

Stretching the Inner Cone

Continue from the previous exercise.

Command: *Choose Rectangle (Draw, Polygon)*	Issues the RECTANG command
First corner: **5,10.5** `Enter`	Sets first corner of focal plane
Other corner: **@9,-.5** `Enter`	Draws the focal plane as a rectangle
Command: *Choose Stretch (Modify, Resize)*	Issues the STRETCH command
Select objects to stretch by crossing -window or -polygon...	
Select objects: *Press and drag from* ① *to* ② *(see fig. 10.10)*	Selects the points to stretch
Select objects: `Enter`	Ends object selection
Base point or displacement: *Using the Endpoint object snap, pick the line at* ③	Begins stretching the lines
Second point of displacement: *Using the Perpendicular object snap, pick the rectangle at* ④	Begins stretching the lines
Command: *Choose Save (Standard toolbar)*	Saves the drawing

Your drawing now should look like figure 10.11.

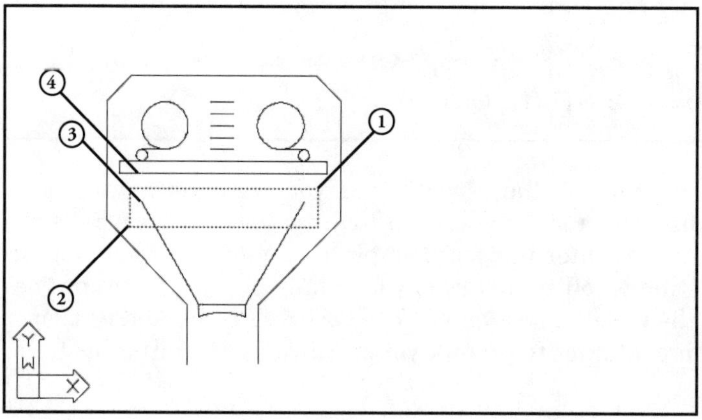

Figure 10.10

Stretching the inner cone.

The STRETCH command can take some getting used to. Some objects (such as circles, text, and blocks) do not stretch; they are moved instead.

Figure 10.11

The completed inner cone.

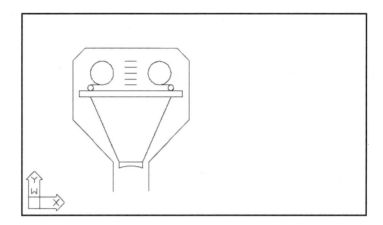

Using OFFSET To Create Parallel Objects

Another technique you can use to draw from existing geometry is the OFFSET command. The OFFSET command creates parallel objects from existing objects. When you use the OFFSET command on a circle, for example, you create a new circle that is either larger or smaller. Both circles have the same center point, layer, and other properties. The only real difference between the two circles is each circle's size.

OFFSET. The OFFSET command creates objects parallel to a selected object.
Toolbar: *Choose Offset (Modify, Copy)*
Screen: *Choose* CONSTRCT, Offset

There are two ways to offset an object. First, you can enter a numerical value for the offset distance. If you want to draw the 30' edge offsets of a road from the road's centerline, for example, you enter an offset distance of 30'. After setting an offset distance, you simply pick any point on the side you want the offset to be created. The OFFSET command is a repeating command; it continues to prompt you until you press either Enter or Esc.

The other method of offsetting objects is with the Through option. This method is more graphical. After selecting the object to offset, you choose where on the drawing you want the offset to be located. This is convenient when you don't know what the distance is between the two objects.

The following exercise shows you how to use the OFFSET command to create the aerial camera's interior shell.

Drawing the Interior Shell Using OFFSET

Continue from the previous exercise.

Command: *Choose Offset (Modify, Copy)*	Issues the OFFSET command
Offset distance or Through <Through>: **.25** (Enter)	Sets an offset distance of 0.25 inches
Select object to offset: *Pick* ① *(see fig. 10.12)*	Selects the outer shell of the aerial camera
Side to offset? *Pick any point inside the polyline*	Draws an offset object inside the aerial camera
Select object to offset: (Enter)	Ends the OFFSET command
Command: *Choose Save (Standard Toolbar)*	Saves the drawing

Your drawing now should look like figure 10.12.

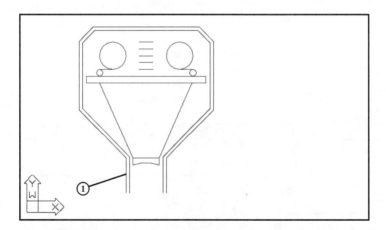

Figure 10.12

The interior shell of the aerial camera.

The OFFSET command does have some limitations. Only one object can be selected at a time, and some types of objects cannot be offset (such as text and blocks). In addition, offsetting a large distance from a small arc can result in a negative radius, and AutoCAD will fail to perform the offset.

Changing Object Size with SCALE

While objects in AutoCAD are drawn full-size, sometimes you might want an object's size to be smaller or larger. Some drawn objects, for example, are not sized correctly. You can scale the objects' sizes to correct it. Another example is when you make copies of an object and each copy's size needs to be adjusted. To change the size of an object, you use the SCALE command.

SCALE. The SCALE command changes the size of an object about a base point by a scale factor or by referencing one distance to another.
Toolbar: *Choose Scale (Modify, Resize)*
Screen: *Choose* MODIFY, Scale:

When you use the SCALE command, you select the objects you want to scale, select a base point, and enter a scale factor. You can enter a scale factor by specifying a numerical value or by picking two points. For scale factor values less than one, objects get smaller. For values more than one, objects get larger.

Like the ROTATE command, the SCALE command has a Reference option. With the SCALE command, the Reference option enables you to specify two distances either by typing them in or by picking points. AutoCAD then determines the ratio between the two distances and uses it as the scale factor. This is useful when you don't know the size of the objects or don't know the scale factor.

The following exercise shows you what the SCALE command can do. In this exercise, you will change the size of the lens.

Scaling the Lens

Continue from the previous exercise.

Command: *Choose Scale (Modify, Resize)*   Issues the SCALE command

Select objects: *Pick ① (see fig. 10.13)*   Selects the lens

Select objects: (Enter)   Ends object selection

Base point: *Using the Midpoint object snap, pick ②*   Selects the base point around which to scale

`<Scale factor>/Reference:` **`.9`** `(Enter)`	Shrinks the lens to 90 percent of its original size
`Command:` *Choose Save (Standard Toolbar)*	Saves the drawing

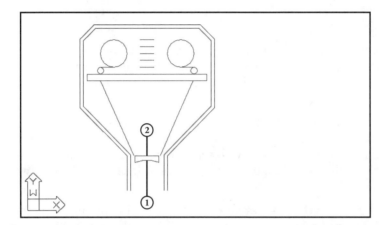

Figure 10.13
Shrinking the lens.

10

The SCALE command behaves like other commands. Like the ROTATE command, selecting a base point can displace the object's location. Like the OFFSET command, you can enter a value by typing it or by selecting two points graphically.

Creating Objects in a Pattern with Array

Arranging objects in a pattern can be fairly frustrating. One method is to use the COPY command and its Multiple option to lay out the pattern. You have to take care to locate each copy properly to create the pattern. This can be a tedious and time-consuming procedure. For patterns with a large number of objects, finding another way to make patterns easier is important. Luckily, AutoCAD provides such a technique with the ARRAY command.

ARRAY. The ARRAY command makes copies of selected objects in a rectangular or a circular pattern.
Toolbar: *Choose Array (Modify, Copy)*
Screen: *Choose CONSTRCT, Array:*

The ARRAY command is aptly named—it draws objects in a pattern quickly and easily. The ARRAY command has the following prompts and options:

- **Rectangular.** This option draws new objects and arranges them along rows and columns. The rectangle option has the following prompts:

  - **Number of rows (---) <1>.** This prompt asks for the number of rows in the rectangular array. Using this prompt, you can specify the number of objects to be drawn from the top to bottom.

  - **Number of columns (| | |) <1>.** This prompt asks for the number of columns in a rectangular array. You use this prompt to specify how many array objects are to be drawn from the left to the right. A rectangular array needs at least two rows or two columns.

  - **Unit cell or distance between rows (---).** This prompt asks for the distance between the rows. A positive value copies objects in the positive Y axis direction (up). Negative values copy the objects in the negative Y axis direction (down). You can enter a numerical value or pick two points in the drawing to specify the distance between both the rows and the columns. Picking two points defines a rectangle and AutoCAD uses the horizontal length of the rectangle as the distance between the rows and the vertical length as the distance between the columns.

  - **Distance between columns (| | |).** This prompt appears only if you enter a numerical value for the distance between the rows and set the distance between the vertical columns. Positive values copy the objects in the positive X axis direction (to the right). Negative values copy objects in the negative X axis direction (to the left).

- **Polar.** This option draws new objects and arranges them along a circular pattern. The Polar option has the following prompts:

  - **Center point of array.** This prompt asks for a center point for the circular array. The objects are copied in a circular pattern around the center point.

  - **Number of items.** This prompt asks for the total number of objects to be drawn in the array. You can enter a positive number or press Enter.

- **Angle to fill (+-ccw, -=cw) <360>.** This prompt asks what angle to fill with the array objects. The default 360, for example, lets you draw an array all around the center point. You also can set an angle of 180 degrees to draw an array around the top of the circular pattern. Positive values copy the objects in a counterclockwise direction, while negative values copy the objects in a clockwise direction.

- **Angle between items.** This prompt only appears if you press Enter for the number of items. This prompt allows you to specify the angle between the array objects.

- **Rotate objects are they are copied? <Y>.** This prompt asks if you want the array objects to be rotated around the center point.

10

To use the polar ARRAY option, you need to know three things: the center point to rotate objects around, the number of array objects to be drawn, and what angle to fill up. You can fill the whole circle around the center point or copy only along a circle angle. The number of objects and the angle to fill determine how wide the space is between objects.

Drawing Patterns with ARRAY

Continue from the previous exercise. Before beginning, zoom your display to match figure 10.14.

Command: *Choose Circle Center Radius (Draw, Circle)*	Issues the CIRCLE command
Draw a circle with a center point at **7,11.25** *and a radius of* **.10** *inches*	Draws the circle at ① (see fig. 10.14)
Command: *Choose Line (Draw, Line)*	Issues the LINE command
Draw a line from **7,11.15** *to* **7,11**	Draws a line at ②
Command: *Choose Polar Array (Modify, Copy)*	Issues the ARRAY command with the Polar option
Select objects: *Pick* ① *(see fig. 10.14)*	Selects the circle
Select objects: *Pick* ②	Selects the line
Select objects: (Enter)	Ends object selection

continues

continued

`Center point of array:` *Using the Center object snap, pick* ③	Selects the center of the circle about which to draw the array
`Number of items:` **5** Enter	Enters total number of objects in the array
`Angle to fill (+=ccw, -=cw) <360>:` **180** Enter	Draws the array along the right half of the film reel circle
`Rotate objects as they are copied? <Y>` Enter	Rotates the array objects about the center of the circle
`Command:` *Choose Polygon (Draw, Polygon)*	Issues the POLYGON command
Draw a **6** *sided inscribed polygon at* **11.5, 12.25** *with a radius of* **.10** *inches*	Draws a polygon symbol in film reel at ④
`Command:` *Choose Rectangular Array (Modify, Copy)*	Issues the ARRAY command with the Rectangular option
`Select objects:` *Pick* ④	Selects the polygon just drawn to build an array pattern around
`Select objects:` Enter	Ends object selection
`Number of rows (---) <1>:` **2** Enter	Sets up an array of two horizontal rows
`Number of columns (¦¦¦) <1>:` **2** Enter	Sets up a square array of two vertical columns
`Unit cell or distance between rows (---):` **-0.5** Enter	Enters the distance between rows
`Distance between columns (¦¦¦):` **0.5** Enter	Enters the distance between columns
`Command:` *Choose Zoom Previous (Standard Toolbar, Zoom)*	Returns to the previous view
`Command:` *Choose Save (Standard Toolbar)*	Saves the drawing

In previous exercises, you picked objects and then invoked an editing command. Editing one or two objects at a time can be fairly time-consuming. In this next section, you learn how to collect objects to edit using the selection options.

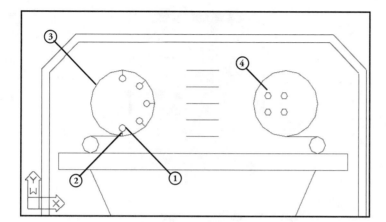

Figure 10.14

Using the ARRAY command.

10

Building a Selection Set

Chapter 8, "Editing with Grips," introduced you to the concept of building a selection set using the window and crossing selection methods, as well as the **U**se Shift to Add and **P**ress and Drag options of the DDSELECT command. Every editing command requires you to build a selection set of objects before carrying out an editing command.

Noun-Verb Editing

There are two ways to select and edit objects in AutoCAD. One method is called *verb-noun editing*. You issue an editing command (the verb), and AutoCAD asks you to build a selection set (the nouns). Throughout this chapter, you have been using verb-noun editing.

The second method is called *noun-verb editing*, in which you select the objects (nouns) and then issue the editing command (verb). Grip editing works this way. You first must select the objects before you can edit. In fact, building a selection set actually starts the grip editing process.

You can disable or enable noun-verb editing by using the Object Selection Settings dialog box (see fig. 10.15), which is displayed with the DDSELECT command. When enabled, all of AutoCAD's editing commands can use noun-verb editing.

The following exercise shows you how to select which process (noun-verb or verb-noun) to use by changing the settings in the Object Selection Settings dialog box.

Figure 10.15

The Object Selection Settings dialog box.

Setting the Editing Mode

Continue from the previous exercise.

Command: *Pick any circle in the drawing*   Highlights the circle and displays its grips

Command: *Choose Move (Modify)*   Issues the MOVE command

Notice that AutoCAD skips the Select objects: prompt and proceeds directly to the next prompt. This is noun-verb editing.

Base point or displacement: *Press Esc*   Cancels the MOVE command

Command: *Choose **O**ptions, **S**election*   Issues the DDSELECT command

*Remove the X from the **N**oun/Verb Selection box and choose OK*   Disables noun-verb editing

Command: *Pick any circle in the drawing*   Highlights the circle and displays its grips

Command: *Choose Move (Modify)*   Issues the MOVE command

Notice that AutoCAD deselects the circle and prompts you to Select objects:. This is verb-noun editing.

Select objects: *Press Esc*   Cancels the MOVE command

Command: *Choose **O**ptions, **S**election*   Issues the DDSELECT command

*Place an X in the **N**oun/Verb Selection box and choose OK*   Enables noun-verb editing

Command: *Choose Save (Standard Toolbar)*   Saves the drawing

The Selection Options

For most editing, the selection options you have used so far are adequate. You can pick single objects and use window and crossing selections to select most objects and use Shift to add and remove objects from the selection set. But, as your drawings become more complex and the number of objects increase, you might find it difficult to precisely select the objects you want to edit. Not to worry, AutoCAD has a number of selection options to help you.

The following is a list of options when selecting objects. These options are available whenever you see the Select Objects: prompt.

10

- **Window.** This option selects objects inside a window you specify. Any objects that are entirely within the window are added to the selection set. This is the same as pressing and dragging your cursor to the right.

- **Last.** This option selects the most recently created object in the current view.

- **Crossing.** This option selects objects that are touched by a window you specify. Like the Window option, Crossing selects any object inside the window, but also all objects that the window intersects. This is the same as pressing and dragging your cursor to the left.

- **ALL.** This option selects all objects in the drawing that are not on frozen or locked layers.

- **Fence.** This option enables you to draw an open polyline to select objects. All objects that touch the polyline are be added to the selection set.

- **WPolygon.** This option enables you to draw an irregular closed polygon to select objects. Like the Window option, this option selects all objects within the irregular polygon.

- **CPolygon.** This option lets you draw an irregular closed polygon to select objects. Like the Crossing option, this option selects all objects within and touching the irregular polygon.

- **Add.** This option returns you to the Add objects mode. If you used the Remove objects option, you can add more objects to the selection set by returning to the Add objects mode.

- **Remove.** This option switches you to the Remove objects mode. The Remove objects mode enables you to select objects to remove from the selection set.

- **Multiple.** This option enables you to pick multiple objects in close proximity. This option speeds up selection by enabling multiple selections without highlighting or prompting.

- **Previous.** This option selects all the objects in the preceding selection set. It is useful when you want to perform several editing commands on the same objects.

- **Undo.** This option reverses the last selection operation.

The most commonly used selection options can be accessed through the Select Objects flyout on the Standard Toolbar; however, usually it's convenient to type them. The following exercise gives you a taste of how some of the selection options work.

Building a Selection Set

Continue from the previous exercise.

Command: *Choose Move (Modify)*	Issues the MOVE command
Select objects: **ALL** (Enter)	Selects all the objects in the drawing
31 found	
Select objects: **R** (Enter)	Enters Remove objects mode
Remove objects: *Press and drag from ① to ② (see fig. 10.16)*	Selects a window to remove objects
5 found, 5 removed	
Remove objects: (Enter)	Ends object selection
Base point or displacement: **.25<270**	Specifies the displacement
Second point of displacement: (Enter)	Moves the selected object downwards
Command: (Enter)	Repeats the MOVE command
Select objects: **F** (Enter)	Specifies the Fence option
First fence point: *Pick ①* *(see fig. 10.17)*	Specifies the first fence point
Undo/<Endpoint of line>: *Pick ②*	Specifies the next fence point

`Undo/<Endpoint of line>:` *Pick* ③	Specifies the next fence point
`Undo/<Endpoint of line>:` (Enter)	Ends the fence and selects the objects
`3 found`	
`Select objects:` (Enter)	Ends object selection
`Base point or displacement:` **.25<270**	Specifies the displacement
`Second point of displacement:` (Enter)	Moves the selected object downwards
`Command:` *Choose Save (Standard Toolbar)*	Saves the drawing

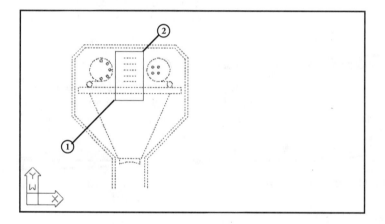

Figure 10.16

Building a selection set.

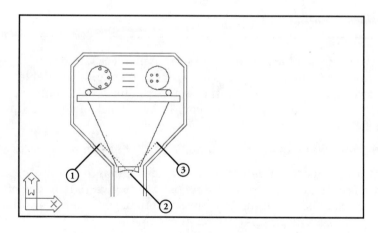

Figure 10.17

Building a fence selection.

10

Object Selection Cycling

For drawings with many objects on top of each other, selecting objects becomes more difficult. Perhaps using the Window or Crossing options is not feasible because you only need to select one object. AutoCAD has provided for that with object selection cycling.

Object selection cycling is a new AutoCAD Release 13 feature with which you can pick at an area of the drawing populated with objects. You activate this feature by pressing and holding the Ctrl key and picking at the area. You then keep clicking the pick button on the pointing device. Each click of the pick button highlights a possible object to select. When the desired object is highlighted, press Enter to select the highlighted object.

Grouping Objects Together

The GROUP command is another new feature in AutoCAD Release 13. The GROUP command has the capability to bind objects together so that they can be selected as a single object. The previously separate objects now act as one.

GROUP. The GROUP command displays the Object Grouping dialog box. The Object Grouping dialog box enables you to select objects that will act as a single object.
Toolbar: *Choose Group (Standard Toolbar)*
Screen: *Choose* ASSIST, Group:

Setting up groups is similar in concept to setting up blocks. Groups, however, cannot be transferred across drawings and are only available within a drawing. You can access all the groups you have named and set up by using the Object Grouping dialog box. To keep track of your groups, you use the following Name and Description options:

- **Name.** This option lets you give a name to a set of grouped objects.

- **Description.** This option lets you enter a description to a group. Sometimes the name of a group is not enough to give you an idea of what the group is. Using the Description option, you can differentiate between the various groups with similar names.

The other Group options are discussed thoroughly in *Inside AutoCAD Release 13 for Windows and Windows NT*.

The GROUP command displays the Object Grouping dialog box as shown in figure 10.18

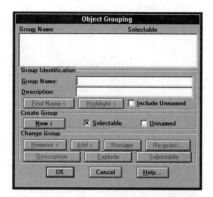

Figure 10.18

The Object Group-ing dialog box.

10

The following exercise shows you how to form the group REEL-LEFT. You select the objects for the film reel and set them up as a group.

Grouping Objects

Continue from the previous exercise. Before beginning, zoom to the view shown in figure 10.19.

Command: *Choose Object Group (Standard Toolbar)*	Issues the GROUP command
In the **G**roup Name: *text box, type* **REEL-LEFT**	Names the new group to be created
In the **D**escription: *text box, type* **Left film reel**	Enters a description for the group
Choose **N**ew	Creates the new group
Select objects for grouping:	Exits Object Grouping dialog box to select the objects for the group
Select objects: *Press and drag from* ① *to* ② *(see fig. 10.19)*	Selects the objects
12 found	
Select objects: **Enter**	Ends object selection and returns to the Object Grouping dialog box

continues

continued

*In the **G**roup Name: text box, type* **REEL-RIGHT**	Names the new group to be created
*In the **D**escription: text box, type* **Right film reel**	Enters a description for the group
*Choose **N**ew*	Creates the new group
Select objects for grouping:	Exits Object Grouping dialog box to select the objects for the group
Select objects: *Press and drag from* ③ *to* ④	Selects the objects
Choose OK	Saves changes to group list
Command: *Choose Move (Modify)*	Issues the MOVE command
Select objects: *Pick* ⑤ *and* ⑥	Selects the two groups
Base point or displacement: **.5<270**	Sets the displacement
Second point of displacement: (Enter)	Moves the two reels
Command: *Choose Zoom Previous (Standard Toolbar, Zoom)*	Returns to the previous view
Command: *Choose Save (Standard Toolbar)*	Saves the drawing

Grouping objects.

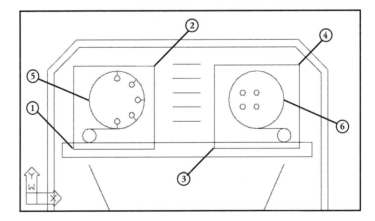

Changing an Object's Characteristics

In this chapter, you've explored how to move objects around and how to replicate objects in your drawing. The last aspect of editing is changing the actual characteristics of an object.

If you use proper care, changing an object's properties might not be necessary. Layers, with their assigned colors and linetypes, are the best tool to manage objects and their properties. Sometimes, however, you draw an object on the wrong layer accidentally or you need an object to be assigned a specific color. In these examples, you need to use the DDCHPROP and DDMODIFY commands.

Using the DDCHPROP Command

For most objects, you assign it properties by placing it on a specific layer. By controlling the layer characteristics, you can control how all the objects on that layer look. Sometimes, you need to change the color or linetype of a specific object on a layer. The DDCHPROP command enables you to change the layer, color, linetype, linetype scale and elevation of a selection set.

DDCHPROP. The DDCHPROP command displays the Change Properties Dialog Box. This dialog box enables you change the color, linetype, and layer of objects.

Toolbar: *Choose Properties (Object Properties)*
Pull-down: *Choose **E**dit, **P**roperties*
Screen: *Choose MODIFY, DDchpro:*

The DDCHPROP command displays the Change Properties dialog box as shown in figure 10.20.

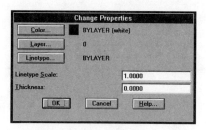

The Change Properties dialog box.

The Change Properties dialog box helps you assign a color and linetype to a set of specific objects. You also can change an object's layer using this dialog box. To change the properties of several objects, invoke the DDCHPROP command, select the objects, and then make the changes in the Change Properties dialog box.

The following exercise walks you through the change properties process. You will change the offset of the exterior shell and the lines representing the inner cones to dashed line.

Changing Object Properties

Continue from the previous exercise.

Command: *Click Properties (Object Properties)*	Begins object selection
Select Objects: *Pick* ① *(see fig. 10.21)*	Lets you select objects by a window
Other corner: *Pick* ②	Selects the inner cone lines and the inner shell offset
In the Change Properties *dialog box, click on* **L**ayer, *then select the layer* CAM-INT, *and choose* OK	Changes the line and polyline to layer CAM-INT
Command: *Choose Save (Standard Toolbar)*	Saves the drawing

Figure 10.21

The AERCAM drawing with linetypes.

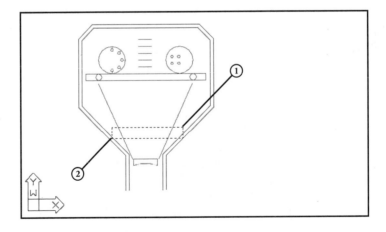

Using the DDMODIFY Command

To change the very nature of an object, you can use the DDMODIFY command. The DDMODIFY command enables you to change any part of an object including point locations, circle and arc radii, and text styles. The DDMODIFY command only acts on one object at a time.

10

DDMODIFY. The DDMODIFY command displays the Modify Properties dialog box. This dialog box lets you set any characteristic of an object.

Toolbar: *Choose Properties (Object Properties)*
Pull-down: *Choose **E**dit, **P**roperties*
Screen: *Choose MODIFY, Modify:*

If you select only one object while using the Properties tool (Object Properties), AutoCAD assumes you want to use the DDMODIFY command. If you select more than one object, AutoCAD issues the DDCHPROP command.

NOTE

The DDMODIFY command displays the Modify object toolbar. The actual dialog box changes with each type of object. You can set a circle's radius, for example, but no such option will show when you use the DDMODIFY command on a polyline. The Modify Polyline dialog box, for example, is shown in figure 10.22 because a polyline was selected.

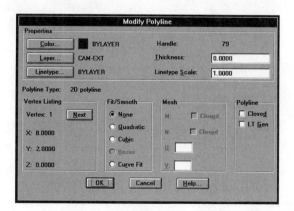

Figure 10.22

The Modify Polyline dialog box.

The following exercise shows you how to use the DDMODIFY command.

Modifying Objects

Continue from the previous exercise.

Command: *Click Properties (Object Properties)*	Begins object selection
Select Objects: *Pick* ① *(see fig. 10.23)*	Selects the line
Select Objects: (Enter)	Ends object selection and issues the DDMODIFY command
In the From Point *area, in the* **X** *text box, type* **5.5**	Changes the starting point of the line
In the To Point *area, in the* **X** *text box, type* **13.5**	Changes the ending point of the line
Choose OK	Sets the changes to the drawing
Command: *Choose Save (Standard Toolbar)*	Saves the drawing

Your drawing now should look like figure 10.23.

Figure 10.23

The AERCAM drawing.

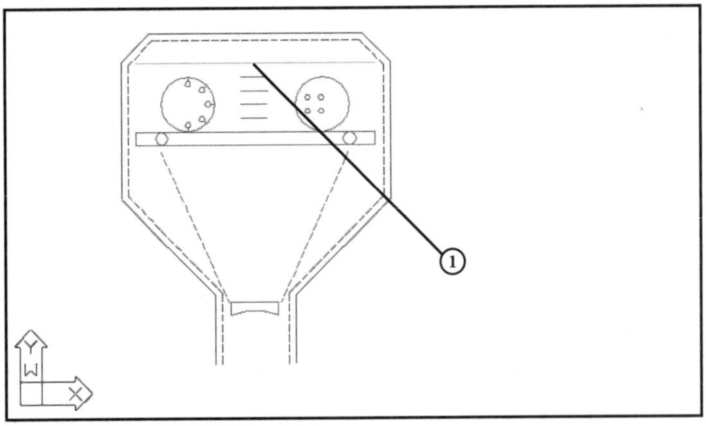

Summary

In this chapter, you learned how to work with the existing objects in your drawing. You moved and rotated objects around your drawing. You changed the size of objects and stretched them. You learned how to replicate existing objects instead of tediously drawing them again. You then found techniques for selecting objects efficiently. You removed undesired objects from a selection set and explored some of the selection options.

Editing requires much practice. As you experiment with the editing commands, you will learn how they help you manage complex drawings. Keep in mind what you want to do and then choose the appropriate editing command.

The next chapter shows you techniques for using text in your drawing. You will learn how to place and edit text, and how to use the special characters. By annotating your drawing, you can add some final detail to your design.

Related Topics

- Drawing constructively—Chapter 12, "Constructive Editing"
- Trimming and extending objects—Chapter 12, "Constructive Editing"
- Using blocks—Chapter 13, "Blocks and Overlays"
- Organizing your drawing—Chapter 4, "Preparing Your Drawing"
- Using grips—Chapter 8, "Editing with Grips"

Chapter Snapshot

Text, a powerful way to convey meaning in your drawing, is essential to any design. In previous chapters, you didn't fully explore how to use text in your drawing. In this chapter, you learn how to add text to your drawing.

This chapter covers the following topics:

- Setting up text styles

- Creating single line text and multiline text objects

- Editing text

- Formatting text

- Check your spelling

Text

The primary purpose of a drawing is to communicate information. So far, you have used graphic objects to represent your designs. Text is another powerful tool you can use to help you communicate.

By using text, you can provide more information in your drawing. Text makes drawings easier to understand and also conveys information not easily represented by graphic objects, such as exact dimensions, tolerances, and project notes.

In this chapter, you will learn how to add and control text. You use dynamic text and multiline text to add detail to your drawing. The following Quick Tour exercise gives you a quick primer on the text commands used in this chapter. In the exercise, you create two traffic signs.

The Quick Tour

To begin, create a new drawing named TRAFFIC using the default ACAD.DWG proto-type. Set the grid spacing to 1 and the snap spacing to .25. Turn on both the grid and snap.

`Command:` *Choose Polygon (Draw, Polygon)*	Issues the POLYGON command
Draw an 8-sided inscribed polygon with the center point at **4,5** *and a radius of* **3**	Creates the outline of the STOP sign at ① (see fig. 11.1)
`Command:` *Choose Rectangle (Draw, Polygon)*	Issues the RECTANG command
Draw a rectangle from **8,1** *to* **14,8**	Creates the outline of the speed limit sign at ②
`Command:` *Choose Offset (Modify, Copy)*	Issues the OFFSET command
`Offset distance or Through <Through>:` **.25** (Enter)	Sets an offset distance of .25
Offset the octagon and the rectangle to the inside of each shape and press (Enter)	Creates the sign borders

Next, you set up a text style of the traffic signs. You use one of the PostScript fonts in the text style.

`Command:` *Choose* **D**ata, **T**ext Style	Issues the STYLE command
`Text style name (or ?) <STANDARD>:` **TRAFFIC** (Enter)	Defines a new text style named TRAFFIC and displays the Select Font File dialog box
Select Font (*.PFB) *from the* **L**ist Files of Type *drop-down list, then choose* SASB____.PFB *from the* File **N**ame *list box, and choose* OK	Displays the PostScript *.PFB font files and selects the font for the text style
`Height <0.0000>:` (Enter)	Accepts the default text height
`Width factor <1.0000>:` (Enter)	Accepts the default width factor
`Obliquing angle <0>:` (Enter)	Accepts the default obliquing angle
`Backwards? <N>` (Enter)	Leaves text as normal (forward)
`Upside-down? <N>` (Enter)	Keeps the text as right-side-up
`Vertical? <N>` (Enter)	Leaves the text horizontal and ends the STYLE command

TRAFFIC is now the current text style.

Now that the text style is defined, you can place some text. Keep in mind that when entering text you must press the Enter key on your keyboard when you see (Enter). The spacebar and the Enter button on your mouse do not work as an carriage return when creating and editing text.

Command: *Choose Dtext (Draw, Text)*	Issues the DTEXT (Dynamic Text) command
Justify/Style/<Start point>: **J** (Enter)	Selects the Justify option
Align/Fit/Center/Middle/Right/TL/TC/ TR/ML/MC/MR/BL/BC/BR: **M** (Enter)	Middle-justifies the text
Center point: **4,5** (Enter)	Places the middle point of the text at ③
Height <0.2000>: **1.5** (Enter)	Sets a text height of 1.5 units
Rotation angle <0>: (Enter)	Accepts the default rotation angle of 0
Text: **STOP** (Enter)	Labels the STOP sign
Text: (Enter)	Ends the DTEXT command and draws the text as middle-justified
Command: *Choose Properties (Object Properties)*	Begins the object selection process
Select objects: **L** (Enter)	Selects the text, which was the last object created
Select objects: (Enter)	Ends object selection and issues the DDMODIFY command
*Change the value in the **W**idth Factor edit box to **.8** and choose* OK	Changes the width of the text
Command: *Choose Text (Draw, Text)*	Issues the MTEXT (Multiline Text) command
Attach/Rotation/Style/Height/ Direction/<Insertion point>: **H** (Enter)	Specifies the Height option
Height <1.5000>: **.75** (Enter)	Sets the default text height to .75 units
Attach/Rotation/Style/Height/ Direction/<Insertion point>: **A** (Enter)	Specifies the Attach option
TL/TC/TR/ML/MC/MR/BL/BC/BR: **TC** (Enter)	Selects the Top Center attachment option
Attach/Rotation/Style/Height/ Direction/<Insertion point>: **11,7.25** (Enter)	Locates the start point for the multiline text at ④

continues

continued

`Attach/Rotation/Style/Height/`
`Direction/Width/2Points/`
`<Other corner>:` **W** (Enter)
	Specifies the Width option

`Object width:` **10** (Enter)	Sets the width of the multiline text box
In the Select Font dialog box, *select the font* ARIAL *from the* *drop-down list, then choose* OK	Selects a font to use while editing the multiline text and displays the Edit MTextdialog box
In the dialog box, type **55** (Enter) **SPEED** (Enter) **LIMIT**	Enters the multiline text
Place your cursor at the start of the *first line of text, press and drag* *your cursor over the text*	Highlights the text to change its height
In the Height edit box type **2.5** (Enter)	Changes the height of the highlighted text to 2.5 units
Choose OK	Ends the MTEXT command and places multiline text into the drawing
`Command:` *Choose Save (Standard Toolbar)*	Saves the drawing

Your drawing now should look like figure 11.1.

Figure 11.1

The completed
traffic signs.

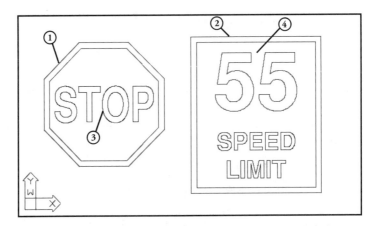

The exercises in this chapter show you how to use text to its fullest capabilities.

Placing Text in Your Drawing

There are two types of text objects in AutoCAD Release 13. *Line text* is a single line of text. Each line of text is a separate object by itself and is not associated with other text objects. The other type of text object is called *multiline (or paragraph) text*. A new addition to Release 13, multiline text is a paragraph instead of one line of text (see fig. 11.2). The relationship between multiline text and line text is similar to the relationship between polylines and lines. If your need is simple, use lines and line text objects. For complex uses, use polylines and multiline text objects.

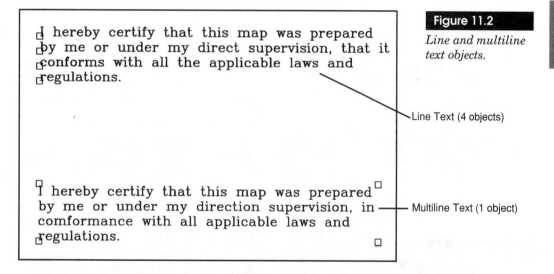

Figure 11.2

Line and multiline text objects.

11

As a rule, line text is useful when you need only a short line of text, such as titles and labels. Line text is more difficult to use when you have to enter a large amount of text.

You should use multiline text when you need to add a large amount of text. A paragraph of notes and descriptions are good applications for multiline text. No matter how much text there is in a multiline text object, the entire paragraph acts as a single object.

Text Size and Plotting

One thing to consider when creating text is the final output scale. The majority of objects in AutoCAD are drawn full-size and then assigned an output (plot) scale at the time they are printed. When placing text in model space, however, you must take into account the final output scale and adjust the text size accordingly. See Chapter 4, "Preparing Your Drawing," for information on how to use the plot scale factor to calculate your text size.

Creating Line Text with the DTEXT command

In many cases, you might simply need to place a short note or label a section of your drawing. For those situations, single line text is the answer. You place single line text with the DTEXT command.

DTEXT. The DTEXT command creates single line text objects in the drawing, showing the text dynamically as it is being typed.
Toolbar: *Choose Dtext (Draw, Text)*
Screen: *Choose DRAW 2, Dtext*

One of the advantages of the DTEXT (Dynamic Text) command is that it enables you to place text at multiple locations in your drawing without exiting the command. At any time while using the DTEXT command, you can pick a point to relocate the cursor and continue typing.

The DTEXT command has the following options:

- **Start point.** This option selects the insertion point of the line text. After selecting a start point, you are prompted for the following.

- **Height.** This sets the text height of your text. This option will appear if the text style you are using has a height value of 0. The Height option is useful when you want to be able to change text height every time you invoke the DTEXT command.

- **Rotation angle.** This option specifies the rotation angle of the text. You can enter an angle value or pick two points to indicate an angle. Your text will be rotated.

- **Style.** This option selects the current text style. See the section "Understanding Text Styles" later in this chapter for more information on creating text styles.

- **Justify.** This option sets the justification of the text. It is similar to the concept of right, left, or center justified in word processors. See the section "Justifying Text" later in this chapter for more information on this option.

While entering text, keep in mind that the spacebar is active, meaning you can't use the spacebar as an (Enter). In fact, the only way to issue a (Enter) while placing text is by pressing the Enter key on the keyboard.

In the following exercise, you create a title block for a C-size (18×24) engineering drawing. You begin by creating the borders for the title block and then add some text.

Adding Single Line Text

Start with a new drawing named C-TITLE using the prototype drawing ACAD.DWG. Create the layers TITLE-TEXT with the color red, and TITLE-OBJ with the color blue. Set the snap spacing to 0.25 and the grid spacing to 1.00. Set the limits to 0,0 and 24,18 and then zoom to the drawing limits. Finally, set your current layer to TITLE-OBJ.

Command: *Choose Rectangle (Draw, Polygon)*	Issues the RECTANG command
Draw two rectangles, one from point **0,0** *to point* **24,18** *and another from point* **2,1** *to* **23,17**	Draws the title block borders at ① and ② (see fig. 11.3)
Command: *Choose Line (Draw, Line)*	Issues the LINE command
Draw a line from the point **18,1** *to the point* **18,17**	Draws a line segment at ③
Command: (Enter)	Repeats the LINE command
Draw a line from coordinates **18,14** *to coordinates* **23,14**	Draws a line segment at ④
Command: *From the* Layer Control *drop-down list, select* TITLE-TEXT	Makes layer TITLE-TEXT current
Command: *Choose Dtext (Draw, Text)*	Issues the DTEXT command
Justify/Style/<Start point>: **19,13** (Enter)	Places the starting point of the text at ⑤
Height <0.2000>: (Enter)	Accepts the default text height
Rotation angle <0>: (Enter)	Accepts the default rotation angle
Text: **VICINITY MAP** (Enter)	Enters a line of text
Text: **Not to scale** (Enter)	Enters a line of text
Text: *Pick the point 19,10*	Places the starting point of the next line of text at ⑥
Text: **NOTES** (Enter)	Enters a line of text

continues

continued

Text: (Enter)	Ends the DTEXT command
Command: (Enter)	Repeats the DTEXT command
Justify/Style/<Start point>: *Pick the point 17.75,7.25*	Sets the starting point of the text at ⑦
Height <0.2000>: (Enter)	Accepts the default text height
Rotation angle <0>: **90** (Enter)	Rotates the text 90 degrees
Text: **Rotation angle** (Enter)	Enters a line of text
Text: (Enter)	Ends the DTEXT command
Command: *Choose Save (Standard Toolbar)*	Saves the drawing

Figure 11.3

Adding line text to the title block.

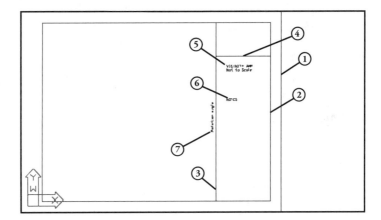

The DTEXT command gives you an easy way to place text in your drawing. It does have some drawbacks, however. Because each line of text is a separate object, editing text that spans two or more lines becomes difficult. Also, the formatting of the text applies to the entire line of text; you cant have different fonts or text sizes in the same line of text. AutoCAD, however, helps you overcome these drawbacks with paragraph text.

The TEXT command performs the same functions as the DTEXT command. The two use the same options and methods to add text to your drawing. The TEXT command does not show text in your drawing as it is being entered at the command line. The DTEXT command, however, does show text as it is being created on the screen. Also, the TEXT command will place only a single line of text at a time. For more on the TEXT command, see *Inside AutoCAD Release 13 for Windows and Windows NT.*

Creating Paragraph Text with the MTEXT Command

In previous versions of AutoCAD, only single line text was available. If you wanted to type a paragraph of text, it required several single-line text objects. Managing large amounts of text became difficult.

Multiline text objects are new to AutoCAD Release 13. By using multiline text, you gain the control and capabilities found in most Windows word processors. You can create underline text, use different fonts within the multiline text, as well as create stacked text.

You create multiline text objects with the MTEXT command.

11

> **MTEXT.** The MTEXT command adds a paragraph text object to the drawing. The paragraph text object can have multiple lines of text and still behave as one object.
> Toolbar: *Choose Text (Draw, Text)*
> Screen: *Choose* DRAW 2, Mtext
> Alias: T

The MTEXT command has the following options:

- **Attach.** This option sets the justification of the paragraph text. This setting is similar to the Justify option of the DTEXT command.

- **Rotation.** This option selects the rotation angle of the paragraph text. It is the same as the Rotation option of the DTEXT command.

- **Style.** This option enables you to select the default text style for the paragraph text. The text style settings can be overridden in the Edit Mtext dialog box.

- **Height.** This option sets the default text height of the paragraph text. This setting can be overridden in the Edit Mtext dialog box.

- **Direction.** This option sets the multiline text object as vertical (top-to-bottom) or horizontal (left-to-right). This option is similar to the STYLE command's Vertical option.

- **Insertion point.** This option sets the starting point of the paragraph text. This option also begins the process of defining the width (or line length) of the multiline text object. After specifying the insertion point, you have the following three additional options to determine the width of the mtext object:

  - **Other point.** This is the default option and enables you to define the width of the mtext object by dragging a window from the insertion point to another point in the drawing. The distance from the insertion point to the other point defines the width of the text object.

  - **Width.** Width enables you to enter the width of the text from the keyboard.

  - **2Points.** This option sets the width of the mtext object by selecting two points. The distance between the two points defines the width of the mtext.

After you define the location and width of the mtext, the Edit Mtext dialog box appears (see fig. 11.4). This dialog box actually is a little word processor. In it, you can type and format the text, as well as control its placement, and even import ASCII text files into AutoCAD. See the section "Editing Multiline Text" later in this chapter for more information on formatting mtext.

Figure 11.4

The Edit Mtext dialog box.

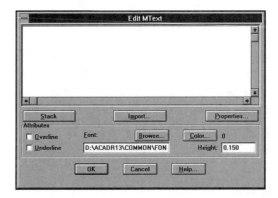

The Edit MText dialog box is a Windows word processor that uses standard Windows fonts to display the text while you are editing it. Because AutoCAD is capable of using a number of different font files, the Edit MText dialog box is not always capable of showing the true AutoCAD font. When this happens, AutoCAD displays the Select Font dialog box and asks you to select one of the available Windows fonts to use while editing the mtext. Simply select a Windows font that approximates the current AutoCAD font and continue to edit your text.

The following exercise shows you how to add multiline text to your drawing.

Adding Multiline Text

Continue from the previous exercise. Before beginning, zoom to the area shown in figure 11.5.

Command: *Choose Text (Draw, Text)*	Issues the MTEXT command
Attach/Rotation/Style/Height/Direction /<Insertion point>: **18.25,9** (Enter)	Enters the starting point of the multiline text at ① (see fig. 11.5)
Attach/Rotation/Style/Height/Direction /Width/2Points/<Other corner>: **22.75,6.5** (Enter)	Sets the second point of the text, defining the boundary of the multiline text, then displays the Edit Mtext dialog box
Type the following: **I hereby certify that this map was drawn by me or under my direct supervision, in conformance with all applicable laws and regulations.**	Enters a paragraph of text
Choose OK	Places the paragraph text on the drawing
Command: *Choose Save (Standard Toolbar)*	Saves the drawing

Multiline text can be extremely useful when you have a lot of text in your drawing. Now that youre familiar with the methods to add multiline text and line text to your drawing, you can explore how to control text with the Justify and Attach options.

Figure 11.5

Adding multiline text.

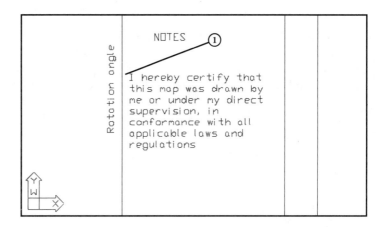

Justifying Text

When adding text to your drawing, you can control how it's formatted in your drawing. The Justify option in the DTEXT command and the Attach option in the MTEXT command enable you to specify how to justify your text.

The following are the methods you can use to justify text. The Align, Fit, Center, and Middle justification methods are only available for line text. Figure 11.6 shows how the various justification points for single line text. Figure 11.7 shows the justification points on multiline text.

- **Align.** This option enables you to select the starting and ending points of a baseline. The text height is scaled between these two points, drawn proportionately to the length of the baseline.

- **Fit.** This option enables you to select the starting and ending points of a baseline. The text width is scaled to fit between these two points but the height is not changed.

- **Center.** This option sets text as centered.

- **Middle.** This option sets text as middle justified. Text is drawn from a center point and will fill equally in the vertical and horizontal directions.

- **Right.** This option sets text as right justified.

The following justification options are available for both line text and multiline text.

- **TL.** This option specifies the top left point of the text. This is the default for multiline text objects.

- **TC.** This option specifies the top center point of the text.

- **TR.** TR specifies the top right point of the text.

- **ML.** ML specifies the middle left point of the text.

- **MC.** MC specifies the middle center point of the text. This is the same as the Middle option for single line text.

- **MR.** This option specifies the middle right point of the text.

- **BL.** BL specifies the bottom left point of the text. This is the default option for single line text.

- **BC.** This option specifies the bottom center point of the text. This is the same as the Center option for single line text.

- **BR.** This option specifies the bottom right point of the text. This is the same as the Right option for single line text.

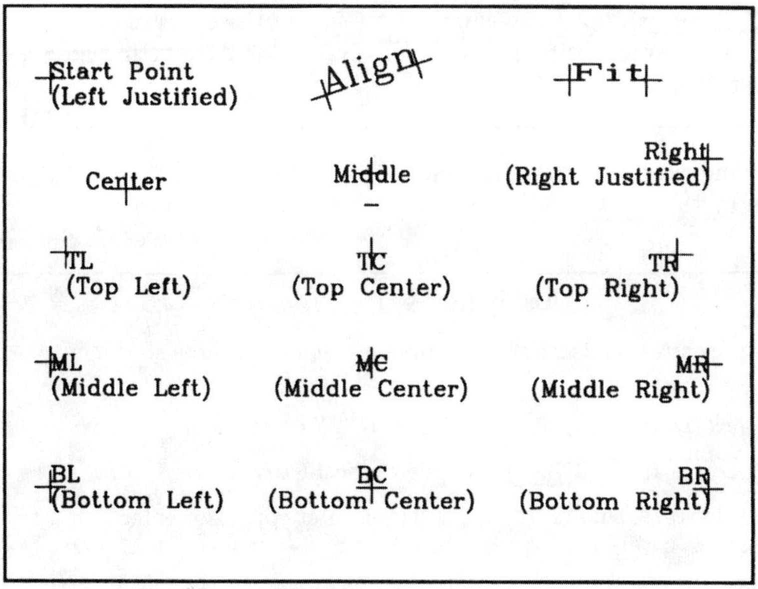

Figure 11.6

The Justify options for single line text.

Figure 11.7

*The Attach options
for multiline text.*

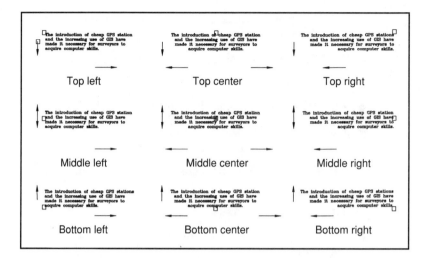

TIP

If you know what type of justification you want to use, you can type it at the MTEXT Insertion point: or DTEXT Start point: prompts. Using DTEXT, for example, you can type **C** (Enter) at the Start point: prompt to draw center justified text. This way, you don't have to type **J** for the Justify option.

In the following exercise, you add some more text using some of the justification methods.

Justifying Text

Continue from the previous exercise. Before beginning, zoom to the area shown in figure 11.8.

Command: *Choose Dtext (Draw, Text)*	Issues DTEXT command
Justify/Style/<Start point>: **J** (Enter)	Selects the Justify option
Align/Fit/Center/Middle/Right/TL/TC/ TR/ML/MC/MR/BL/BC/BR: **C** (Enter)	Selects Center option to center-justify text
Center point: **20.5,4.5** (Enter)	Sets the center point at ① (see fig. 11.8)
Height <0.2000>: (Enter)	Retains the current text height
Rotation angle <90>: **0** (Enter)	Retains the rotation angle of 0

Text: **SUBDIVISION SURVEY MAP** (Enter)	Enters a line of text

Notice that the text is not justified. When you end the DTEXT command, the text will be center justified.

Text: **OF** (Enter)	Enters another line of text
Text: **PROJECT NAME** (Enter)	Enters a line of text
Text: **TAMUNING, GUAM** (Enter)	Enters a line of text
Text: (Enter)	Ends the DTEXT command and justifies the text
Command: *Choose Text (Draw, Text)*	Issues the MTEXT command
Attach/Rotation/Style/Height/Direction /<Insertion point>: **H** (Enter)	Selects the Height option
Height <0.2000>: **.1** (Enter)	Sets the default text height to 0.1 units
Attach/Rotation/Style/Height/Direction /<Insertion point>: **A** (Enter)	Selects the Attach option
TL/TC/TR/ML/MC/MR/BL/BC/BR: **TR** (Enter)	Selects the TR option
Attach/Rotation/Style/Height/ Direction/<Insertion point>: *Pick the point 22.75, 6.5*	Picks the first point of multiline text boundary at ②
Attach/Rotation/Style/Height/Direction/ Width/2Points/<Other corner>: *Pick the point 18.25, 5.00*	Sets the width of the multiline text object and displays the Edit Mtext dialog box
In the Edit Mtext dialog box, type **D.B. Grey** (Enter) **Surveyor** (Enter)(Enter) **M.B. Summers** (Enter) **Architect** (Enter) (Enter) **J.F. Manabat** (Enter) **Civil Engineer**	Enters the multiline text

Notice that the text is being right-justified as you type it.

Choose OK	Adds the multiline text to the drawing
Command: *Choose Save (Standard Toolbar)*	Saves the drawing

The justification options are just one way to control the look of your text. Another way to control the look of text is through the use of text styles.

Figure 11.8

Justified single line and multiline text.

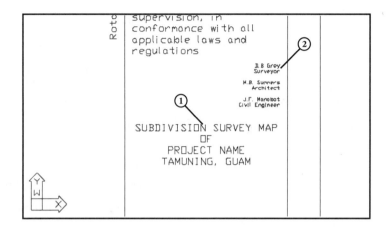

Understanding Text Styles

Text styles are collections of text settings that define how the text is displayed. You can have a text style with a large text height for large bold text, for example, and another text style that contains the settings for smaller line text.

Text styles contain several settings: text height, text file (font file), width factor, obliquing angle, and whether the text appears backward, forward, upside-down, or vertical. By using these settings, you can control exactly how your text looks in the drawing. This section shows you how to specify these settings and helps you get your text to look the way you want it to.

Controlling the Look of Text with Text Styles

To set up a text style, you need some idea of how you want your text to look. Is it a title text style that needs large italic letters? Or do you want a different text style for the main default text?

Text styles are very convenient for keeping text formats in your drawing. You can create as many text styles as you need. You issue the STYLE command to create text styles.

STYLE. The STYLE command creates and edits text styles. Text styles are collection of text settings such as text height, width, and text font file.
Pull-down: *Choose* **D**ata, **T**ext style
Screen: *Choose* DRAW 2, Style:

The STYLE command has the following options:

- **Text style name (or ?).** This prompt allows you to specify the name of the text style. Entering **?** at this prompt will list all of the currently defined text styles.

- **Text file.** This option selects which text font file to use in the text style. The font controls how the individual alphabetic characters and symbols look. The font files are files that have the extensions *.SHX (AutoCAD shape files), *.PFA (PostScript type A fonts), *.PFB (PostScript type B fonts), and *.TTF (TrueType fonts).

- **Height.** Height sets the height of the text. If you specify a height of 0 (the default), AutoCAD prompts you for the height of the text when creating line text objects. If you specify a height greater than 0, AutoCAD skips the Height: prompt when creating line text objects and uses the text style height.

- **Width factor.** This option sets how condensed or separated text letters are from each other. For width factors less than 1.0, words are condensed. If you set the width factor greater than 1.0, words are displayed with more space between letters.

- **Obliquing angle.** This option sets the slant angle for the text. A negative value slants the text to the left. A positive value slants the text to the right. An obliquing angle of 30 approximates italic text.

- **Backwards.** This option displays text backward. It is useful for plotting on the back of plot sheets for template borders.

- **Upside-down.** This option displays text upside-down.

- **Vertical.** This option displays characters vertically. The second character is displayed below the first character, and so on.

Figure 11.9 shows how the various settings affect the appearance of text.

So far in this chapter you have been using the STANDARD text style, which uses the TXT.SHX font file. Although this text style works, it is not very attractive. In the following exercise, you set up the text style TITLE, which is used for title text; and NORMAL, which is used for notes and small type.

11

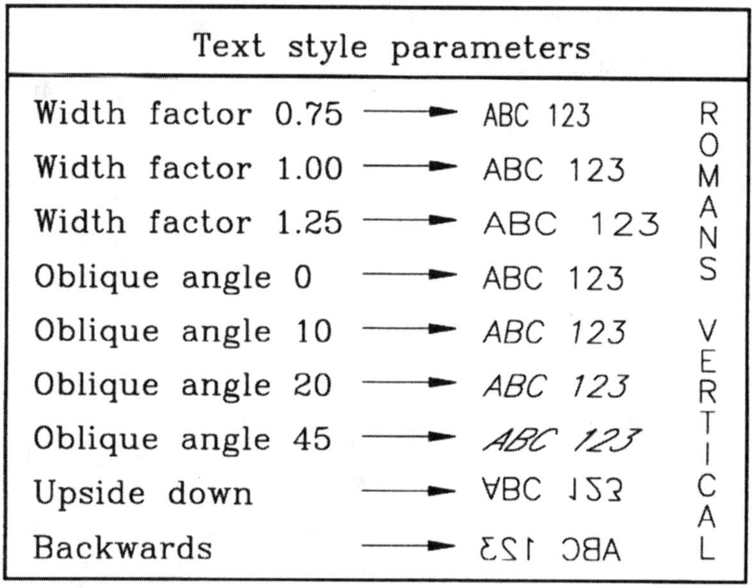

Figure 11.9

Examples of text style settings.

```
                    Text style parameters

        Width  factor  0.75  ───────►  ABC 123           R
                                                         O
        Width  factor  1.00  ───────►  ABC 123           M
                                                         A
        Width  factor  1.25  ───────►  ABC  123          N
                                                         S
        Oblique  angle  0   ───────►  ABC 123
                                                         V
        Oblique  angle  10  ───────►  ABC 123            E
                                                         R
        Oblique  angle  20  ───────►  ABC 123            T
                                                         I
        Oblique  angle  45  ───────►  ABC 123            C
                                                         A
        Upside  down    ───────►  ∀BC ⅃2ꓭ                L
        Backwards       ───────►  ꓱ⌁⌵ ⌵2ꓭ  ⌵8∀
```

Setting Up Text Styles

Continue from the previous exercise.

Command: *Choose* **D**ata, *then* **T**ext Style	Issues STYLE command
`Text style name (or ?)<STANDARD>:` **TITLE** (Enter)	Creates a new style named TITLE and displays the Select Font File dialog box
Select **F**ont (*.TTF) *from the* **L**ist Files of Type *drop-down list, then choose* DUTCH.TTF *from the* File **N**ame *list box, and choose* OK	Displays the TrueType (*.TTF) font files and selects the font for the text style
`Height <0.0000>:` (Enter)	Accepts the text height of 0 units
`Width factor <1.0000>:` (Enter)	Retains the current width factor
`Obliquing angle <0>:` (Enter)	Retains obliquing angle of 0
`Backwards? <N>` (Enter)	Leaves text as left-to-right
`Upside-down? <N>` (Enter)	Retains text as right-side-up
`Command:` (Enter)	Repeats STYLE command
`Text style name (or ?) <TITLE>:` **NORMAL** (Enter)	Creates a new text style named NORMAL and displays the Select Font File dialog box

In the Select Font File dialog box, select the file ROMANS.SHX, *and choose* OK	Sets the font file for the text style NORMAL
Height <0.0000>: `Enter`	Accepts the text height of 0 units
Width factor <1.0000>: `Enter`	Keeps current width factor
Obliquing angle <0>: `Enter`	Obliquing angle left at 0
Backwards? <N> `Enter`	Leaves text as left-to-right
Upside-down? <N> `Enter`	Keeps text right-side up
Vertical? <N> `Enter` NORMAL is now the current text style.	Sets text direction to horizontal and exits the STYLE command
Command: *Choose Dtext (Draw, Text)*	Issues the DTEXT command
Justify/Style/<Start point>: *Pick* 18.25,2.75	Sets the starting point for the line text at ① (see fig. 11.10)
Height <0.1000>: **.08** `Enter`	Specifies the height of the text
Rotation Angle <0>: `Enter`	Accepts the default rotation angle
Text: **PROJECT NAME** `Enter`	Creates a line of text
Text: **CLIENT** `Enter`	Creates a line of text
Text: **DATE** `Enter`	Creates a line of text
Text: `Enter`	Exits the DTEXT command
Command: *Choose Text (Draw, Text)*	Issues the MTEXT command
Attach/Rotation/Style/Height/Direction /<Insertion point>: **S** `Enter`	Selects the Style option
Style name (or ?) <NORMAL>: **TITLE** `Enter`	Selects the TITLE style
Attach/Rotation/Style/Height/Direction /<Insertion point>: **H** `Enter`	Selects the Height option
Height <0.0800>: **.2** `Enter`	Specifies the height of the text
Attach/Rotation/Style/Height/Direction /<Insertion point>: *Pick 18.25,2.0*	Specifies upper left corner of multiline text at ②
Attach/Rotation/Style/Height/Direction/ Width/2Points/<Other corner>: *Pick the point 22.75,2.0*	Sets the lower right corner of multiline text at ③ and displays Edit Mtext dialog box

continues

continued

In the Edit Text dialog box, type **A.T. & L.U. Engineering Services**	Enters text into MTEXT object
Choose OK	Draws the text onto the drawing
`Command:` *Choose Save (Standard Toolbar)*	Saves the drawing

Figure 11.10

Using text styles and adding text.

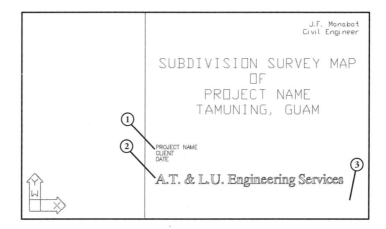

For most purposes, you use text styles to control the text font. The Backwards, Upside-down, and Vertical options are rarely used. By using a combination of the text settings, you can create some truly unique and complex effects. If you need to make changes to that text style, you can invoke the STYLE command again and redefine the text style with new settings.

TIP

TrueType and PostScript fonts use fill patterns that can slow down your display. You can speed up your display by choosing **O**ptions, **D**isplay, and then either **O**utline Text or **T**ext Frame Only from the pull-down menu. The **O**utline Text option turns off the fill pattern, and the **T**ext Frame Only option replaces text with a rectangular text frame that simply marks the position of the text.

You also can speed up your display by defining your text style with a very simple font (one that doesn't require much regeneration) while you're working on the drawing. When you're ready to plot the drawing, you can redefine the text style using a more complex font file and regenerate the drawing with the REGEN command.

Typically, you set up text styles at the beginning of a drawing project. You should set the text styles at the same time you set up your limits, scale, and layers. If you use the same text style settings for other drawings, you can add the text styles to your prototype drawing. Your text styles are then automatically included and already set up when you begin a new drawing.

Now that you have properly set up your text styles, you can learn how to edit the text that you have placed in your drawing.

Editing Single Line Text

Making changes to your text objects involves more than just changing what the text says. You can change the alignment, style, insertion point, color, and layer of the text. In this section, you explore using the commands to change and correct your text.

Changing and Correcting Line Text

If you need to change what your text says, look no further than the DDEDIT command.

DDEDIT. The DDEDIT command enables you to edit both line text and multiline text objects through one of two dialog boxes. If you select a line text object, the Edit Text dialog box is displayed. If a multiline text object is selected, the Edit MText dialog box is shown.
Toolbar: *Choose Edit Text (Modify, Special Edit)*
Screen: *Choose* MODIFY, DDedit

The Edit Text dialog box (see fig. 11.11) appears when you pick a single line text object to edit. Editing single line text is nothing more than making changes in the Edit Text dialog box and choosing OK.

In the next exercise, you select a line text object and make corrections to it.

Figure 11.11

The Edit Text dialog box.

Editing Single and Multiline Text

Continue from the previous exercise. Before beginning, zoom your display to the area shown in figure 11.12.

Command: *Choose Edit Text (Modify, Special Edit)*	Issues the DDEDIT command
<Select a TEXT or ATTDEF object>/Undo: *Pick ①*	Selects the NOTE text object to edit and displays the Edit Text dialog box
Press the End key and spacebar, then type **AND CERTIFICATION** *and choose* OK	Adds the words "AND CERTIFICATION" to the text object
<Select a TEXT or ATTDEF object>/Undo: (Enter)	Ends the DDEDIT command
Command: *Choose Save (Standard Toolbar)*	Saves the drawing

Your drawing now should look like figure 11.12.

Figure 11.12

The modified text.

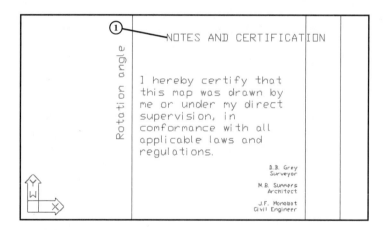

When you first enter the Edit Text dialog box, all the text is highlighted for you. If you start typing, any text within that dialog box is replaced by what you entered. You can use the pointing device to pick a place to start and make edits.

TIP

> You can use Ctrl+X to cut, Ctrl+C to copy, and Ctrl+V to paste within the dialog boxes. You can easily cut and paste within the dialog box as well as between AutoCAD Release 13 and another Windows word processor.

Formatting Single Line Text

AutoCAD provides a number of formatting options for single line text by way of special text characters. When AutoCAD encounters special text characters in single line text objects, it replaces them with the appropriate formatting or symbols.

Figure 11.13 shows the special text characters available. You can use these characters to underline and overscore characters, and to create degree, diameter, or plus/minus symbols.

Character	Function	Example of Use	Result
%%o	Turns overscore on or off	%%oOver%%o	Over
%%u	Turns underline on or off	%%uUnder%%u	Under
%%d	Degrees symbol	70%%d	70°
%%p	Plus/minus symbol	3%%p.002	3±.002
%%c	Diameter symbol	%%c4	⌀4
%%nnn	Displays ASCII character	15%%181	15μ
%%%	Single percent symbol	85%%%	85%

Figure 11.13

Special text characters.

The following exercise shows you how to use the special text characters to change how your text looks.

Formatting Single Line Text

Continue from the previous exercise.

Command: *Choose Edit Text (Modify, Edit Special)*	Issues the DDEDIT command
<Select a TEXT or ATTDEF object>/Undo: *Pick ① (see fig. 11.14)*	Selects a text object to edit and displays Edit Text dialog box
Press the Home key and type **%%u** *then choose* OK	Underlines the title NOTES AND CERTIFICATION
<Select a TEXT or ATTDEF object>/Undo: Enter	Ends the DDEDIT command

Figure 11.14

The underlined text.

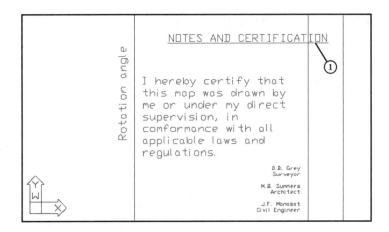

Using DDMODIFY To Edit Text

Chapter 10, "Selecting and Editing Objects," introduced you to the DDMODIFY command, which enables you to change virtually any aspect of an object. DDMODIFY is especially useful with text objects in that it enables you to change the value of the text, the insertion point, justification, text style, and any aspect of the text style, through the Modify Object dialog box.

The following exercise shows you how to edit existing text with the DDMODIFY command.

Modifying Line Text

Continue from the previous exercise.

Command: *Choose Properties (Object Properties)*	Enables you to pick an object to modify
Select objects: *Pick* ① *(see fig. 11.15)*	Selects the title label to modify
Select objects: (Enter)	Ends object selection and displays the Modify Text dialog box
In the **J**ustify *drop-down list, select* Center	Center-justifies the text
In the Sty**le** *drop-down list, select* TITLE	Changes the text style for the text object

In the Origin *area, choose the* **P**ick Point *button*	Enables you to select another location for the insertion point of the text object
`Insertion point:` *Pick 20.50,10.00*	Selects a new insertion point at ②
Choose OK	Makes changes to the text object and returns you to the drawing editor
`Command:` *Choose Save (Standard Toolbar)*	Saves the drawing

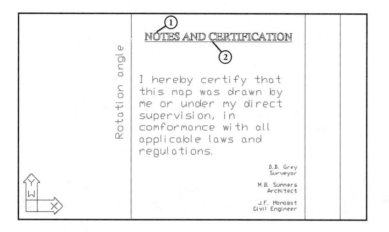

Figure 11.15

Modifying line text by using DDMODIFY.

11

Editing Multiline Text

You edit multiline text with the DDEDIT command as well, but if you choose a multiline text object, AutoCAD displays the Edit MText dialog box (see fig. 11.4). This is the same dialog box used when creating multiline text. The Edit MText dialog box has the following options:

- **Overline.** This option draws a line over selected text.

- **Underline.** This option draws a line under selected text.

- **Font.** This option assigns a font to the selected text.

- **Color.** This option assigns a color to the selected text.

- **Height.** This option changes the height of the selected text.

- **Properties.** This option changes the style, justification, rotation, and width of the multiline text.

- **Import.** This option lets you add text to a multiline text object through external text files.

- **Stack.** This option draws text on top of each other on the same line. This option is useful for drawing fractions and tolerances.

In the following exercise, you add some formatting enhancements to multiline text.

Formatting Multiline Text

Continue from the previous exercise.

`Command:` *Choose Edit Text (Modify, Special Edit)*	Issues the DDEDIT command.
`<Select a TEXT or ATTDEF object>/Undo:` *Pick ① (see fig. 11.16)*	Selects a multiline text object and displays Edit Mtext dialog box
Highlight the words D.B. Grey, *then click on the* **O**verline *check box*	Overlines the words D.B. Grey
Highlight the words Civil Engineer, *then click on the* **U**nderline *check box*	Underlines the words Civil Engineer
Choose OK	Returns you to the drawing editor
`<Select a TEXT or ATTDEF object>/Undo:` *Pick ②*	Selects a multiline text object to change
In the text area box, highlight the words hereby *through* regulations	Highlights the words to change
In the **H**eight *text box, type* .1 *and press* (Enter)	Changes the text height of the selected words
In the text area box, highlight the first I (as in I hereby...)	Highlights a word to change
Choose the **B**rowse *button*	Displays the Change Font dialog box
In the Change Font *dialog box, change to the directory COMMON\FONTS, select* SWISSB.TTF, *and choose* OK	Changes the font file for the text

If you have not installed the font SWISSB.TTF as a Windows font using the Control Panel, AutoCAD will display the Select Font dialog box. This enables you to specify a substitute font to use while editing the text. If you have installed the font in Windows, the dialog box will not appear and you can skip the following step.

In the Select Font *dialog box, click on the* Font *drop-down list, and select the font* Bookman Old Style	Selects a substitute font for the text and returns to the Edit MText dialog box

Click on the **B***old and* **I***talic check boxes and press* (Enter)	Applies boldface and italics to the text
Choose the **C***olor button*	Displays the Select Color dialog box
Click on color blue and choose OK	Selects the color blue for the word
Choose OK	Finishes edits to the multiline text
`<Select a TEXT or ATTDEF object>/Undo:` *Press* (Enter)	Exits the DDEDIT command
`Command:` *Choose Text (Draw, Text)*	Issues the MTEXT command
`Attach/Rotation/Style/Height/Direction/` `<Insertion point>:` **S** (Enter)	Selects the Style option
`Style name (or ?) <TITLE>:` **NORMAL** (Enter)	Changes the MTEXT style to NORMAL
`Attach/Rotation/Style/Height/Direction/` `<Insertion point>:` *Pick 18.25,7.75*	Sets the upper left corner of the MTEXT object at ③
`Attach/Rotation/Style/Height/Direction/` `Width/2Points/<Other corner>:` *Pick* *22.75,6.75*	Sets the lower right corner of the MTEXT object at ④
Type `1. Contour intervals are within 1/2 of` `the true value.` (Enter)(Enter) `2. Building tolerances are` `1.000 +0.005^-0.005` (Enter)	Enters text into multiline text

The / in 1/2 and the ^ in +0.005^-0.005 denote where the stacking will occur.

Highlight 1/2, then choose **S***tack*	Stacks the fraction
Highlight +0.005^-0.005, then choose **S***tack*	Stacks the text
Choose OK	Accepts the changes

Your drawing should look like figure 11.16.

> There are other special codes in the multiline text objects. They are for use when importing text files into multiline text objects or when using AutoCAD 13 for DOS or Unix. Consult your *AutoCAD User's Guide* or *Inside AutoCAD 13 for Windows and Windows NT* for more information.

Figure 11.16

*Changing the notes
of the title block.*

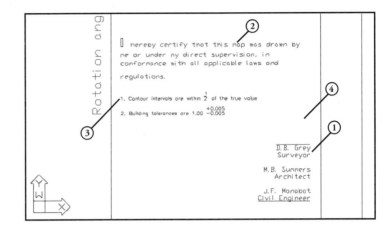

Checking Your Spelling in AutoCAD

One of the best additions to AutoCAD Release 13 is the SPELL command. The SPELL command offers you the ability to spell-check your text within AutoCAD.

SPELL. The SPELL allows you to check the spelling of text in your drawing. The Check Spelling dialog box displays suspect words and suggests the alternatives.

Toolbar: *Choose Spelling (Standard Toolbar)*
Pull-down: *Choose **T**ools, **S**pelling*
Screen: *Choose TOOLS, Spell*

After you select the text you want to check, AutoCAD searches through the selected text. If it finds a word not in the dictionary, the SPELL command displays the Check Spelling dialog box. You can ignore suspect words, or have AutoCAD suggest alternatives for spelling. You also have the ability to create custom dictionaries that enable you to add words and abbreviations that are specific to your application. Figure 11.17 shows you the Check Spelling dialog box and its options.

In the following exercise, you check the spelling of the words in several text objects. You learn how to invoke the SPELL command, how to create a custom dictionary, and how to add words to the custom dictionary.

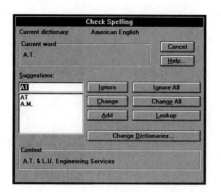

Figure 11.17

The Check Spelling dialog box.

11

Checking the Spelling of Text

Continue from the previous exercise.

Command: *Choose Spell (Standard Toolbar)*	Issues the SPELL command
Select objects: **All** (Enter)	Selects all of the object in the drawing
Select objects: (Enter)	Ends object selection and displays the Check Spelling dialog box

AutoCAD ignores any object that is not a line text or multiline text object. The SPELL command searches the text and the word %%uNotes, and the proper names (A.T., L.U., D.B., Grey, M.B., J.F., Manabat, and TAMUNING) are shown as words not recognized.

*Choose the **I**gnore button eight times for each unrecognized word*	Ignores the spelling of the unrecognized words and completes the spell check
Choose OK	Ends the SPELL command
Command: *Choose Zoom All (Standard Toolbar, Zoom)*	Displays the drawing limits
Command: *Choose Save (Standard Toolbar)*	Saves the drawing

Your drawing now should look like figure 11.18.

Editing and spell-checking your text are an important part of using text. The ability to create and modify spelling dictionaries enables you to build application-specific dictionaries.

Figure 11.18

The completed title block.

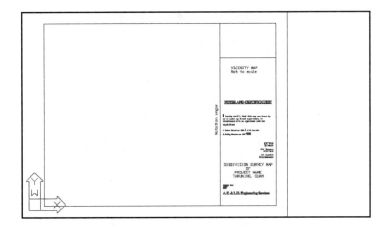

Summary

In this chapter, you learned how to use text to add detail to your drawing. You learned when to use line text and multiline text, and how to edit existing text. You used the special characters to enhance your text and design, as well as how to check your spelling.

The preliminaries are over. At this stage, you are familiar with practically all the drawing commands that you will ever use. What's left is to put all of your skills together into one drawing.

The next chapter shows you how to streamline your editing process with constructive editing techniques.

Related Topics

- Using DDMODIFY and DDCHPROP—Chapter 10, "Selecting and Editing Objects"
- Using colors and layers—Chapter 4, "Preparing Your Drawing"
- Constructive editing—Chapter 12, "Constructive Editing"
- Drawing blocks—Chapter 13, "Blocks and Overlays"
- Using the plot scale factor to set up your text styles—Chapter 4, "Preparing Your Drawing"
- Using paper space—Chapter 7, "Drawing Accurately"

Chapter Snapshot

There are some tools in AutoCAD that you just can't do without, regardless of the frequency with which they're used. This chapter presents the following constructive editing tools that come in handy for just about any AutoCAD session:

- Lengthening lines and arcs

- Trimming and extending objects

- Cutting corners: rounded, squared, or angled

- Converting lines and arcs into polylines

- Using PEDIT to assign a numeric width to a polyline

Constructive Editing

The editing commands you have encountered so far have enabled you to rotate, copy, mirror, erase, and move. You have modified existing objects and have, with the exception of erasing and stretching, left the objects in their original shape. Constructive editing involves using AutoCAD tools as you would tools from a toolshop. You use tools such as a saw to create a chamfer or trim a board, a sander or router to round off a square edge, or a torch and welding rod to weld several pieces of steel together to make one continuous object. These procedures take existing objects and change their shape and condition. That's the concept of constructive editing that this chapter covers.

In the following Quick Tour exercise, you draw a few objects and then use several of the editing commands presented in this chapter to create a rather unique drawing.

The Quick Tour

To begin, create a new drawing named CADEDIT by using the default ACAD.DWG prototype drawing. Create a layer called EDIT and set it as current.

Command: *Choose Circle Center Radius (Draw, Circle)*	Issues the CIRCLE command
Draw a circle centered at **4,4** *with a radius of* **1.1**	Draws the circle
Command: *Choose Rectangle (Draw, Polygon)*	Issues the RECTANG command
Draw a rectangle from **5.4,3** *to* **7.4,5**	Draws the rectangle (see fig. 12.1)
Command: *Choose Copy Object (Modify, Copy)*	Issues the COPY command
Select objects: **L** (Enter)	Selects the last object placed
Select objects: (Enter)	Ends object selection
<Base point or displacement>/Multiple: **2.4,0** (Enter)	Specifies the displacement
Second point of displacement: (Enter)	Copies the rectangle to the right
Command: *Choose Line (Draw, Line)*	Issues the LINE command
Draw a line from **4,4.3** *to* **8,4.3**	Draws the line
Command: *Choose Copy (Modify, Copy)*	Issues the COPY command
Select objects: **L** (Enter)	Selects the last object placed
Select objects: (Enter)	Ends object selection
<Base point or displacement>/Multiple: **0,-.5** (Enter)	Copies the line down
Second point of displacement: (Enter)	Copies the line down
Command: *Choose Trim (Modify, Trim)*	Issues the TRIM command
Select cutting edges: Select objects: *Select the 2 lines and the middle rectangle, then press* (Enter)	Selects the cutting edges
<Select object to trim>/Project/Edge/ Undo: *Pick* ①, ②, ③, ④, *and* ⑤	Trims the selected objects (see fig. 12.1)
<Select object to trim>/Project/Edge/ Undo: (Enter)	Ends the TRIM command
Command: *Choose Redraw (Standard Toolbar, Redraw)*	Redraws the display

Command: *Choose Chamfer (Modify, Chamfer)*	Issues the CHAMFER command
Polyline/Distance/Angle/Trim/Method/ <Select first line>: **D** (Enter)	Issues the Distance option
Enter first chamfer distance: **1** (Enter)	Sets the first distance to 1
Enter second chamfer distance <1.0000>: (Enter)	Accepts the default second distance equal to the first
Command: (Enter)	Repeats the CHAMFER command
Polyline/Distance/Angle/Trim/Method/ <Select first line>: *Pick ①, then ② (see fig.12.2)*	Chamfers the corner defined by the lines selected
Command: (Enter)	Repeats the CHAMFER command
Polyline/Distance/Angle/Trim/Method/ <Select first line>: *Pick ③, then ④*	Chamfers the corner
Command: *Choose Fillet (Modify, Fillet)*	Issues the FILLET command
Polyline/Radius/Trim/<Select first object>: **R** (Enter)	Issues the Radius option
Enter fillet radius: **.75** (Enter)	Sets the radius to .75"
Command: (Enter)	Repeats the FILLET command
Polyline/Radius/Trim/<Select first object>: *Pick ⑤, then ⑥*	Applies a fillet to the corner defined by the lines selected
Command: (Enter)	Repeats the FILLET command
Polyline/Radius/Trim/<Select first object>: *Pick ⑦, then ⑧*	Applies a fillet to the corner defined by the lines selected
Command: *Choose Explode (Modify, Explode)*	Issues the EXPLODE command
Select objects: *Pick the middle rectangle, then press* (Enter)	Identifies the objects to be exploded
Command: *Choose Erase (Modify, Erase)*	Issues the ERASE command
Select objects: *Pick the top and bottom horizontal line of the middle rectangle, then press* (Enter)	Erases the objects, and then ends the command
Command: *Choose Redraw (Standard Toolbar, Redraw)*	Redraws the display
Command: *Choose Save (Standard Toolbar)*	Saves the drawing

Your drawing now should look like figure 12.3.

12

Figure 12.1

Trimming the lines and the circle.

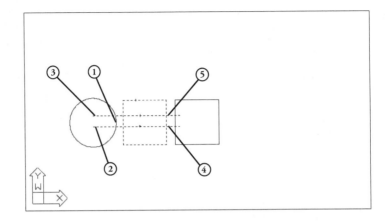

Figure 12.2

Adding the chamfers and fillets.

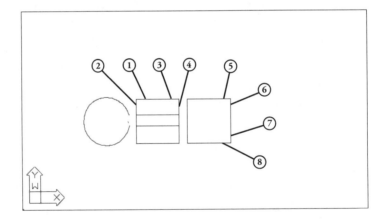

Figure 12.3

The finished drawing.

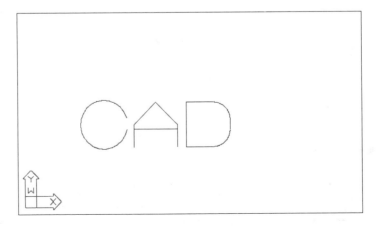

Trimming, Extending, and Lengthening Existing Objects

When editing existing objects, there are numerous occasions in which a line's position is okay, but you just need to make it longer or shorter. The TRIM, EXTEND, and LENGTHEN commands are the best tools in the editing toolshop to use for these occasions.

The TRIM and EXTEND Commands

TRIM. The TRIM command removes portions of objects that cross selected cutting edges. You can use lines, arcs, circles, polylines, ellipses, and splines as cutting edges. An object can be both a cutting edge and an object to trim.
Toolbar: *Choose Trim (Modify, Trim)*
Screen: *Choose* MODIFY, Trim

12

The TRIM command acts as a pair of scissors in cutting or trimming objects. It requires two selection sets: the first to identify the cutting edges, the second to identify the objects to be trimmed. You can use any selection routine to identify the two selection sets. You also can identify an "implied" cutting edge where the object to be trimmed does not actually intersect the cutting edge.

The TRIM command shortens or removes sections from existing objects. The opposite of TRIM is the EXTEND command.

EXTEND. The EXTEND command extends objects to selected boundary edges. You can use lines, arcs, circles, polylines, ellipses, and splines as boundary edges.
Toolbar: *Choose Extend (Modify, Trim)*
Screen: *Choose* MODIFY, Extend

Similar to TRIM, the EXTEND command also requires two selection sets: the first to identify the boundary edges, the second to identify the objects to be extended. When extending objects, you can use any selection routine to identify the two selection sets. You also can identify an "implied" boundary when the object to be extended does not intersect that boundary.

TIP

Use the Fence selection method when selecting the objects to trim or extend. Anything that touches the fence line will be trimmed or extended to the nearest edge.

Both of these commands have similar options. The Project, Edge, and Undo options become available after the first selection set has been identified. Each of these functions are explained in the following list:

- **Project.** The Project option enables you to choose how the objects will be trimmed or extended in 3D space. For 2D applications, the default position of the User Coordinate System (UCS) is used.

- **Edge.** The Edge option enables you to control whether the objects to be trimmed or extended actually must intersect the cutting or boundary edges. If you select Extend mode, AutoCAD trims or extends the objects to their apparent intersection with the cutting or boundary edges. If you select No Extend, the objects actually must touch the edge after they are trimmed or extended.

- **Undo.** The Undo option undoes the previous trim or extend results. This enables you to correct a mistake without exiting the command. If you continue to choose the Undo option, it will sequentially undo all previous edits during that session.

When selecting the object to extend, pick on the portion of the object that is closest to the boundary line. This will indicate the direction the object is to be extended. When selecting objects to trim, pick on the portion of the object you want to delete. The object will be trimmed to the nearest cutting edge(s).

In the following exercise, you expand upon the partial elevation in the 3WING.DWG drawing created in Chapter 7, "Drawing Accurately."

Developing an Elevation Using TRIM and EXTEND

Begin by creating a new drawing called ELEV using the \AB\3WING.DWG file as a prototype. You will begin by adding the third wing to the building.

Command: *Choose Mirror (Modify, Copy)*   Issues the MIRROR command

Select objects: *Drag a window from* ① *to* ② *(see fig. 12.4) then press* **Enter**	Highlights the selection set
First point of mirror line: *Using the Midpoint object snap, pick* ③	Places the first point of the mirror line
Second point: *Using the Midpoint object snap, pick* ④	Places the second point of the mirror line
Delete old objects? <N> **Enter**	Copies the objects about the mirror line
Command: *Choose Copy Object (Modify, Copy)*	Issues the COPY command
Select objects: *Pick the top horizontal line of the elevation, then press* **Enter**	Highlights the line
<Base point or displacement>/Multiple: **0,3600** **Enter**	Copies the line up 3600mm
Second point of displacement: **Enter**	Copies the line down
Command: *Choose Extend (Modify, Trim)*	Issues the EXTEND command
Select boundary edges: Select objects: **L** **Enter**	Highlights the last object created, the line, then goes to the next prompt
Select objects: **Enter**	Ends object selection
<Select object to extend>/Project/ Edge/Undo: **F** **Enter**	Issues the Fence selection option
First fence point: *Draw a fence from* ⑤ *to* ⑥ *and press* **Enter**	Extends the four lines
<Select object to extend>/Project/ Edge/Undo: **Enter**	Ends the EXTEND command
Command: *Choose Trim (Modify, Trim)*	Issues the TRIM command
Select cutting edges: Select objects: *Pick* ① *and* ② *(see fig. 12.5) and press* **Enter**	Selects the cutting edges
<Select object to trim>/Project/ Edge/Undo: *Pick* ③*, then press* **Enter**	Trims the horizontal line between the cutting edges
Command: *Choose Save (Standard Toolbar)*	Saves the drawing

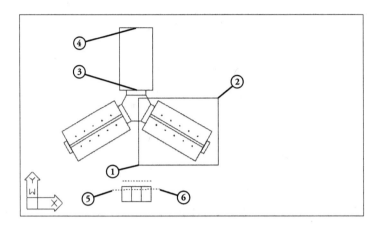

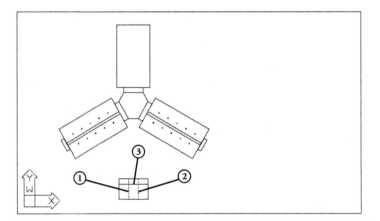

The LENGTHEN Command

The LENGTHEN command is similar in function to the TRIM and EXTEND commands.

LENGTHEN. The LENGTHEN command enables the user to lengthen (or shorten) a line or polyline.
Toolbar: *Choose Lengthen (Modify, Resize)*
Screen: *Choose* MODIFY, Lengthn:

Although the end result is similar to that of TRIM or EXTEND, the LENGTHEN command does not require a cutting edge or boundary and provides the user with several editing options. The LENGTHEN editing options can only be used to edit lines, open polylines, or arcs. The following is a list of the LENGTHEN options:

- **DElta.** This option enables you to enter a positive or negative value by which to lengthen (or shorten) the selected object. The command continues to prompt for objects to edit until you press Enter to end the sequence. DElta also provides the option for a positive or negative angle value by which to edit existing arcs. The value given is applied to the end of the line nearest the pick point.

- **Percent.** If an object needs to be edited by a percentage of the current length, the Percent option prompts for the percentage of the current object to be applied (default=100). The value given is applied to the end of the line nearest the pick point.

- **Total.** In the event you mistakenly enter a relative length for a line, the Total option provides you with a method by which you can simply enter the desired total length of the line selected. As with the other options, the procedure is applied to the end of the line nearest the pick point.

- **DYnamic.** The DYnamic option enables you to drag a line or arc to a specified point and still maintain the vector or angle of the object selected.

- **Select object.** The default mode of Select object returns the length of an object and included angle of an arc.

The LENGTHEN command returns the length of the object selected at the prompt line. For some queries, therefore, it can be more efficient to use LENGTHEN instead of LIST, which flips to the text screen.

TIP

This chapter takes you through a couple of the more intuitive options for LENGTHEN. For a more in depth explanation of all the LENGTHEN options, refer to *Inside AutoCAD Release 13 for Windows and Windows NT*.

In the following exercise, you use the LENGTHEN command to lengthen some of the lines of the elevation by snapping to the endpoint of an existing object. Because there are several times when the Endpoint object snap is used, Endpoint is set to be the running object snap.

Using LENGTHEN To Create a Full Elevation

Continue from the previous exercise.

Command: *Choose Running Object Snap (Standard Toolbar, Object Snap), choose* **E**ndpoint, *and choose* OK	Sets a running endpoint object snap
Command: *Choose Lengthen (Modify, Resize)*	Issues the LENGTHEN command
DElta/Percent/Total/DYnamic/ <Select object>: **DY** Enter	Issues the DYnamic option
Specify new end point.	
<Select object to change>/Undo: *Pick* ① *(see fig. 12.6)*	Identifies the line to lengthen
<Select object to change>/Undo: *Pick* ② *on the right side of the plan*	Lengthens the line
<Select object to change>/Undo: *Pick* ③ *on the middle horizontal line*	Identifies the line to lengthen
<Select object to change>/Undo: *Pick* ④ *on the left side of the plan*	Lengthens the line
<Select object to change>/Undo: Enter	Ends the LENGTHEN command
Command: *Choose Save (Standard Toolbar)*	Saves the drawing

Figure 12.6

Lengthen points for a horizontal elevation line.

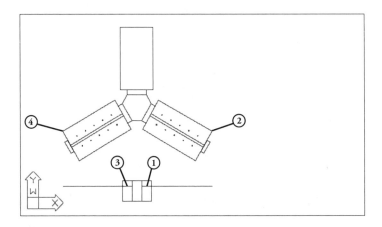

The DYnamic option of LENGTHEN is the easiest to implement, especially when there are reference points that can be selected (as was done in the previous exercise). Although virtually identical in the end result accomplished by the EXTEND command, LENGTHEN only requires a point to which to lengthen the line, whereas EXTEND requires a boundary line. As you continue to use AutoCAD, you will find that there are many ways to accomplish a given task.

Constructing Fillets and Chamfers

The FILLET and CHAMFER commands enable you to create square, rounded, and mitered corners on objects. The commands are similar to the TRIM and EXTEND commands but also create the transitional lines or arcs between two objects.

The FILLET Command

The FILLET command rounds a corner, much like a router or sander rounds a corner of wood. The filleted corner in AutoCAD is defined by an arc. The FILLET command enables you to choose the objects between which you wish to have the arc and you may choose any line-arc combination as the two objects for the fillet. The arc radius can be equal to or greater than 0. After a radius has been set, you simply pick two objects and AutoCAD smoothes the intersection of the objects with the specified radius.

12

FILLET. The FILLET command creates an arc between two lines or arcs, or an arc segment between two polyline segments. Although typically used on non-parallel lines or arcs, a semi-circle results if you pick two lines that are parallel.
Toolbar: *Choose Fillet (Modify, Feature)*
Screen: *Choose CONSTRCT, Fillet*

The FILLET command has the following three options for defining the fillet:

- **Polyline.** The FILLET command requires the selection of two lines, arcs, or polyline segments on which to apply the fillet. The Polyline option enables you to apply the specified fillet radius to all corners of an open or closed polyline.

- **Radius.** The Radius option defines the size of the round. The default radius is 0 (which creates square corners). After you specify a radius, that radius remains in effect until another radius is specified by choosing the option again. The radius value is saved with the drawing and need not be respecified each time you open the drawing. After setting the radius, you must restart the command.

- **Trim.** The Trim option provides you with a choice of fillet results of either a trimmed corner (Trim) or No trim, which leaves the lines selected for the radius in their original state after the fillet is applied. The default setting is Trim.

The CHAMFER Command

The CHAMFER command cuts a straight corner at any angle much like cutting the corner from some wood with a saw or a piece of fabric with a pair of scissors. In AutoCAD, the edges between which the chamfer is applied are lines or polyline segments, although the FILLET command can apply a fillet between any combination of lines and arcs. The CHAMFER command enables you to define the distance from the corner for the cut of the chamfer or specify the angle of the chamfer.

CHAMFER. The CHAMFER command creates an angled corner between two non-parallel lines. You can define the angle of the cut by specifying two cut distances or a cut distance and an angle.
Toolbar: *Choose Modify, Chamfer*
Screen: *Choose CONSTRCT, Chamfer*

The CHAMFER command options are similar to the FILLET options. Because you can accomplish a straight cut across a corner by either defining the cut distances from the corner or specifying the angle of the cut, the Distance and Angle options enable you to specify these values. The following list explains the options available with the CHAMFER command:

- **Polyline.** The Polyline option is the same as the FILLET Polyline option. The CHAMFER command requires the selection of two lines or polyline segments on which to apply the chamfer. The Polyline option enables you to apply the chamfer to all corners of an open or closed polyline.

- **Distance.** The Distance option refers to the distance of the chamfer cut from the nearest endpoint of the lines selected (default = 10). The first chamfer distance is the distance from the nearest endpoint of the first line selected. This distance becomes the default for the second distance or a different second distance can be specified. As with the FILLET command, after setting the distance(s), you must reselect the command.

- **Angle.** The Angle option enables you to define the cut with an angle and a distance. The distance is measured along the first selected line.

- **Trim.** The Trim option provides you with a choice of chamfer results. You can choose either Trim, which removes the trimmed line segments, or No trim, which leaves the lines selected for the chamfer in their original state after the chamfer is applied. The default setting is Trim.

- **Method.** The Angle or Distance choices presented in the Method option enable you to switch between defining the chamfer with the two distances or with the distance and angle. Angle is the default.

The following exercises present some common ways in which to use these two commands. The first exercise introduces you to their basic application.

Applying Chamfers and Fillets to the Elevation

Continue from the previous exercise.

Command: *Choose Fillet (Modify, Feature)*	Issues the FILLET command
Polyline/Radius/Trim/<Select first object>: **R** (Enter)	Issues the Radius option
Enter fillet radius <0.0000>: **3600** (Enter)	Sets the fillet radius to 3600mm
Command: (Enter)	Repeats the FILLET command
Polyline/Radius/Trim/<Select first object>: *Pick ①, then ② as shown in figure 12.7*	Applies the fillet to the lines selected
Command: (Enter)	Repeats the FILLET command
Polyline/Radius/Trim/<Select first object>: **P** (Enter)	Issues the Polyline option

continues

continued

Select 2D polyline: *Pick* ①	Applies the fillet to all corners of the selected polyline
Command: (Enter)	Repeats the FILLET command
Polyline/Radius/Trim/<Select first object>: **P** (Enter)	Issues the Polyline option
Select 2D polyline: *Pick* ③	Applies the fillet to all corners of the selected polyline

For the next steps, zoom your display to match the view shown in figure 12.8

Command: *Choose Chamfer (Modify, Feature)*	Issues the CHAMFER command
Polyline/Distance/Angle/Trim/Method/ <Select first line>: **D** (Enter)	Specifies the Distance option
Enter first chamfer distance: **1800** (Enter)	Sets the distance from the endpoint of the first line to 1800mm
Enter second chamfer distance <1800>: (Enter)	Accepts the default second distance of 1800mm
Command: (Enter)	Repeats the CHAMFER command
Polyline/Distance/Angle/Trim/Method/ <Select first line>: *Pick* ①, *then* ② *as shown in figure 12.8*	Applies a chamfer to the selected lines
Command: (Enter)	Repeats the CHAMFER command
Polyline/Distance/Angle/Trim/Method/ <Select first line>: *Pick* ③, *then* ④	Applies a chamfer to the selected lines
Command: *Choose Save (Standard Toolbar)*	Saves the drawing

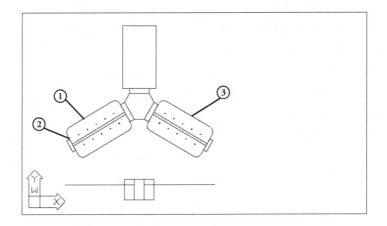

Figure 12.7

Pick points for fillet applications.

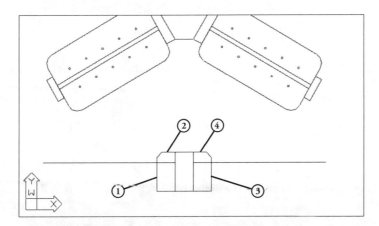

Figure 12.8

Lines to chamfer.

12

The following exercise introduces another way in which a fillet can be used to edit objects. In the exercise, you create the elevation views of the two building wings.

Additional Uses for CHAMFER and FILLET

Continue from the previous exercise.

Command: *Choose Line (Draw, Line)*	Issues the LINE command
From point: *Pick ① (see fig. 12.9)*	Begins the line
To point: *Using the Perpendicular object snap, pick ② then press* (Enter)	Draws a vertical line
Command: (Enter)	Repeats the LINE command
From point: *Pick ③*	Begins the line
To point: *Using the Perpendicular object snap, pick ④ then press* (Enter)	Draws a vertical line
Command: *Choose Fillet (Modify, Feature)*	Issues the FILLET command
Polyline/Radius/Trim/<Select first object>: **R** (Enter)	Issues the Radius option
Enter fillet radius <3600.0000>: **0** (Enter)	Sets the fillet radius to 0, ends the command
Command: (Enter)	Repeats the FILLET command
Polyline/Radius/Trim/<Select first object>: *Pick ⑤, then ⑥*	Fillets the selected lines to a 0 radius
Command: (Enter)	Repeats the FILLET command
Polyline/Radius/Trim/<Select first object>: *Pick ⑦, then ⑧*	Fillets the selected lines to a 0 radius
Command: (Enter)	Repeats the FILLET command
Polyline/Radius/Trim/<Select first object>: *Pick ⑧, then ④*	Fillets the selected line to a 0 radius
Command: (Enter)	Repeats the FILLET command
Polyline/Radius/Trim/<Select first object>: *Pick ②, then ⑤*	Fillets the selected line to a 0 radius
Polyline/Radius/Trim/<Select first object>: (Enter)	Ends the FILLET command
Command: *Choose Save (Standard Toolbar)*	Saves the drawing

Your drawing now should look like figure 12.10.

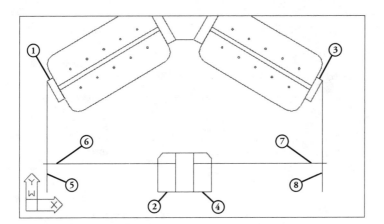

Figure 12.9

Filleting the lines.

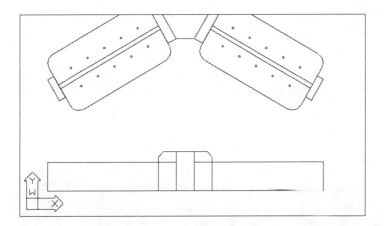

Figure 12.10

*The building
outlines.*

12

The next exercise presents you with a new feature of FILLET: the capability of placing a fillet on non-parallel lines. This turns out to be a semicircle. You also update the elevation based on the new filleted corners of the building wings by using the TANgent object snap in placing a new line.

Capping the Atrium with a Fillet

Continue from the previous exercise.

Command: *Choose Fillet (Modify, Feature)*	Issues the FILLET command
Polyline/Radius/Trim/<Select first object>: *Pick ①, then ② as shown in figure 12.11*	Creates an arc between the two lines
Command: *Choose Trim (Modify, Trim)*	Issues the TRIM command
Select objects: *Pick the arc as the cutting edge, then press* **Enter**	Highlights the arc
<Select object to trim>/Project/Edge/ Undo: *Pick ③*	Trims out the horizontal line
Command: *Choose Line (Draw, Line)*	Issues the LINE command
LINE From point: *Using the Tangent object snap, pick ④*	Begins the line tangent to the fillet curve
To point: *Using the Perpendicular object snap, pick ⑤, then press* **Enter**	Draws a line tangent to the fillet curve perpendicular to the horizontal line
Command: **Enter**	Repeats the LINE command
LINE From point: *Using the Tangent object snap, pick ⑥*	Begins the line tangent to the fillet curve
To point: *Using the Perpendicular object snap, pick ⑦, then press* **Enter**	Draws a line tangent to the fillet curve perpendicular to the horizontal line
Command: *Choose Fillet (Modify, Feature)*	Issues the FILLET command
Polyline/Radius/Trim/<Select first object>: *Pick ①, then ② (see fig. 12.12)*	Fillets the corner to a 0 radius
Command: **Enter**	Repeats the FILLET command
Polyline/Radius/Trim/<Select first object>: *Pick ③, then ④*	Fillets the corner to a 0 radius
Command: *Choose Save (Standard Toolbar)*	Saves the drawing

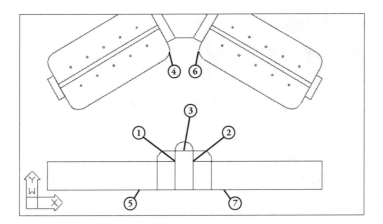

Figure 12.11

Adding a fillet to the dome.

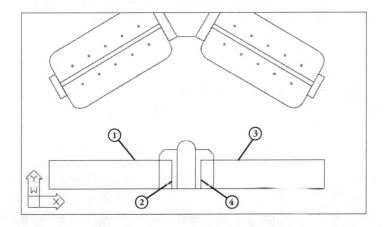

Figure 12.12

Creating a vertical line from a tangent point.

12

Converting Lines to Polylines

In Chapter 5, "The Basic Drawing Commands," you learned about lines and polylines and the differences between the two objects' types. One of the advantages of using polylines is the ability to assign a width to the polyline segments, while lines and arcs are easy to create and edit. AutoCAD enables you to convert lines and arcs to polylines and add segments to polylines with the PEDIT command.

The PEDIT Command

The PEDIT command initially prompts you to Select polyline:. If you select a line or an arc, AutoCAD asks if you want to turn it into a polyline. After you have created a polyline, all the editing options are at your disposal.

PEDIT. The PEDIT command enables you to modify existing polylines as well as convert lines and arcs to polylines.
Toolbar: *Choose Edit Polyline (Modify, Special Edit)*
Screen: *Choose* MODIFY, Pedit

The PEDIT command has several options that enable you to accomplish simple or complex edits on 2D or 3D polylines. The following list presents the basic PEDIT options. For a review of all 2D and 3D polyline editing options, refer to *Inside AutoCAD Release 13 for Windows and Windows NT*.

- **Close.** The Close option adds a polyline segment between the beginning and ending endpoints of the open polyline, thus turning the object into a closed polyline. This option does not appear if a closed polyline has been selected for editing.

- **Open.** If you select a closed polyline for editing, the Open option essentially erases the last segment drawn of the closed polyline. The result is an open polyline, and the replacement of the Open option with the Close option.

- **Join.** The Join option enables you to add line or arc segments to an existing open polyline. You can select lines, arcs, or other polylines to add. The new objects must have connecting endpoints. If the endpoints do not match exactly, the object will not be joined.

- **Width.** The Width option enables you to change the width of the polyline. The width is applied to the entire polyline.

- **Undo.** The Undo option undoes the most recent edit applied while the command is active.

- **eXit.** (Default) The eXit option ends the PEDIT command.

TIP

> When selecting several lines to convert to polylines, window the area containing the lines to be joined when prompted to select the objects. Only those lines that are contiguously connected at the endpoints will be selected to be joined together as a polyline.

The following exercise steps you through converting existing lines to polylines, one of the more frequently used applications of the PEDIT command.

Converting Some Elevation Lines to Polylines

Continue from the previous exercise.

Command: *Choose Edit Polyline (Modify, Special Edit)*	Issues the PEDIT command
Select polyline: *Pick* ① *(see fig. 12.13)*	Selects the line
Object selected is not a polyline Do you want to turn it into one? <Y> (Enter)	Accepts the option to turn the line into a polyline
Close/Join/Width/Edit vertex/Fit/ Spline/Decurve/Ltype gen/Undo/eXit <X>: **J** (Enter)	Specifies the Join option
Select objects: *Press and drag a window from* ② *to* ③, *then press* (Enter)	Selects the lines in the elevation
6 segments added to the polyline Close/Join/Width/Edit vertex/Fit/ Spline/Decurve/Ltype gen/Undo/eXit <X>: (Enter)	Exits from the PEDIT command
Command: *Choose Trim (Modify, Trim)*	Issues the TRIM command
Select objects: *Pick* ①, *then press* (Enter)	Highlights the polyline
<Select object to trim>/Project/ Edge/Undo: *Pick* ④, *then* ⑤	Trims the lines from the elevation

continues

12

continued

`<Select object to trim>/Project/` `Edge/Undo:` (Enter)	Ends the TRIM command
`Command:` *Choose Edit Polyline (Modify, Special Edit)*	Issues the PEDIT command
`Select polyline:` *Pick* ⑥	Selects the building wing

`Close/Join/Width/Edit vertex/Fit/`
`Spline/Decurve/Ltype gen/Undo/eXit`
`<X>:` **W** (Enter)
	Specifies the Width option

`Enter new width for all segments:` **120** (Enter)	Changes the width of the entire polyline

`Close/Join/Width/Edit vertex/Fit/`
`Spline/Decurve/Ltype gen/Undo/eXit`
`<X>:` (Enter)
	Ends the PEDIT command

`Command:` (Enter)	Repeats the PEDIT command
`Select polyline:` *Pick* ⑦	Selects the building wing

`Close/Join/Width/Edit vertex/Fit/`
`Spline/Decurve/Ltype gen/Undo/eXit`
`<X>:` **W** (Enter)
	Specifies the Width option

`Enter new width for all segments:` **120** (Enter)	Changes the width of the entire polyline

`Close/Join/Width/Edit vertex/Fit/`
`Spline/Decurve/Ltype gen/Undo/eXit`
`<X>:` (Enter)
	Ends the PEDIT command

`Command:` *Choose Save (Standard Toolbar)*	Saves the drawing

The EXPLODE Command

Having a polyline is very efficient when trimming intersecting lines because the entire polyline is considered to be a cutting edge. There are occasions, however, when having a polyline is not a desirable condition. You can convert polylines into lines and arcs with the EXPLODE

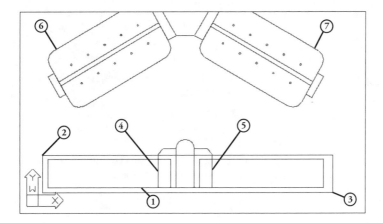

Figure 12.13
Pick points to convert and trim the elevation lines.

command.

> **EXPLODE**. The EXPLODE command converts complex objects
> (polylines, blocks, dimensions, hatches, solids, and meshes) back into
> their component objects
> Toolbar: *Choose Explode (Modify, Explode)*
> Screen: *Choose* MODIFY, Explode

The EXPLODE command essentially takes apart a polyline by converting
it to a series of line segments. When a polyline with a width greater than
0 is exploded, all of the width information is lost because lines and arcs
cannot have a width.

In the following exercise, you want to lengthen the bottom horizontal line
because, as the ground line, it extends beyond the building elevation.
Before you can lengthen the horizontal line, however, you must disassoci-
ate it from the polyline. (Keep in mind that the object containing the
bottom horizontal line is integrally a polyline.)

Converting the Polyline Back to Lines

Continue from the previous exercise.

Command: *Choose Explode (Modify, Explode)*   Issues the EXPLODE command

continues

continued

Select objects: *Pick* ① *(see fig. 12.14)*	Selects the polyline
Select objects: **Enter**	Explodes the selected object and ends the command
Command: *Pick* ②	Displays the line's grips
Command: *Pick the left grip*	Displays a hot grip
** STRETCH ** <Stretch to point>/Base point/Copy/ Undo/eXit: *Turn ortho on and pick a new point to the left of the building elevation*	Stretches the line to the new position and clears the hot grip
Command: *Pick the right grip*	Displays a hot grip
** STRETCH ** <Stretch to point>/Base point/Copy/ Undo/eXit: *Pick a new point to the right of the building elevation*	Stretches the line to the new position and clears the hot grip
Command: *Press Esc twice and turn off ortho*	Clears the selection set and clears the grips
Command: *Choose Zoom Previous (Standard Toolbar, Zoom)*	Updates the display
Command: *Choose Save (Standard Toolbar)*	Saves the drawing

Figure 12.14

Stretching the ground line.

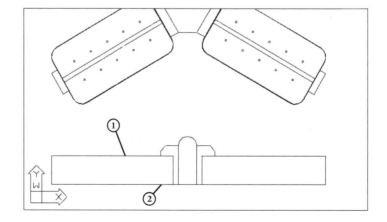

Breaking Lines and Polylines

The BREAK command is another method by which lines and polylines can be trimmed or have existing objects opened. BREAK does not require specific cutting edges as does the TRIM command. Therefore, you can use it in a broader range of situations. For specific point identification, use the BREAK command with any of the object snaps.

BREAK. The BREAK command cuts a segment from an object between two selected points.
Toolbar: *Choose Break 2 Points (Modify, Break)*
Screen: *Choose* MODIFY, Break:

The BREAK command has the following prompts:

- **Select Object.** Because you can only break one object at a time, you must pick a point on the object itself. All of the other selection methods are disabled during the command.

- **Enter Second Point (or F for first point).** By default, the point you picked when selecting the object is the start point of the break. You can either pick a second point to break the objects, or use the F option to respecify the first point.

Although it seems simple enough, you actually can create a number of different effects with the BREAK command. By specifying @ for the second point, you can "snap" an object in two. The object won't look any different, but it actually will be broken into two objects. You also can trim an object by specifying a second break point past the end of the object.

In the next exercise, you break an existing polyline, the rectangular staircase, and a portion of the left wing of the floor plan between two endpoints.

Breaking and Trimming Polylines

Continue from the previous exercise. Zoom your display to match the view shown in figure 12.15.

Command: *Choose 2 Points Select (Modify,*   Issues the BREAK command with the
Break)   First point option

continues

continued

Select object: *Pick ① (see fig. 12.15)*	Selects the object to break
Enter first point: *Pick ②, then ③*	Breaks the polyline between the two pick points and ends the command
Command: *Choose Redraw (Standard Toolbar, Redraw)*	Issues the REDRAW command

Notice that there still is a section of small rectangle overlapping the polyline.

Command: *Choose 2 Points Select (Modify, Break)*	Issues the BREAK command with the First point option
Select object: *Pick ④*	Selects the object to break
Enter first point: *Pick ⑤, then ⑥*	Breaks the polyline between the two pick points and ends the command
Command: *Choose Redraw (Standard Toolbar, Redraw)*	Issues the REDRAW command
Command: *Choose Save (Standard Toolbar)*	Saves the drawing

Figure 12.15

The trimmed polyline and broken staircase.

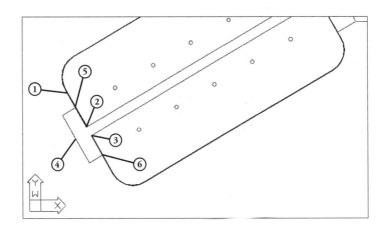

Summary

Constructive editing typically is the process by which you manipulate and create objects from existing objects. The routines of rounding corners with FILLET, or applying a straight angle to a corner using CHAMFER is the CAD equivalent of using tools in a workshop to get the same result. The TRIM, EXTEND, LENGTHEN, and BREAK commands enable you to adjust the length of objects.

Constructively editing polylines using PEDIT further equips you to edit your drawing effectively by enabling you to assign a width to polylines, as well as the ability to join multiple lines or polylines together into a single object. When you need to erase or edit a single segment or series of segments within a polyline, the EXPLODE command converts the polyline to separate lines.

Related Topics

12

- Drawing polylines—Chapter 5, "The Basic Drawing Commands"

- Drawing accurately—Chapter 7, "Drawing Accurately"

- Editing with grips—Chapter 8, "Editing with Grips"

- Additional editing commands—Chapter 10, "Selecting and Editing Objects"

- AutoCAD blocks—Chapter 13, "Blocks and Overlays"

Chapter Snapshot

Many issues are involved in working with
blocks. This chapter covers the basic features and presents several exercises designed to convey the important concepts of
using blocks. These concepts include the
following:

- Understanding block concepts

- Creating block definitions

- Creating block reference objects

- Redefining an existing block in a
  drawing

- Writing blocks to external files

Blocks and Overlays

This chapter introduces two of the most powerful features of AutoCAD: blocks and the new overlay external reference. Blocks can be thought of as symbols or parts placed repetitively in a drawing. In this chapter, you learn to use the BLOCK and WBLOCK commands to create blocks and when each would be used. You also learn to use the DDINSERT command, which enables you to place blocks in a drawing by way of the Insert dialog box.

The external reference overlay is a new option of the XREF command that enables you to overlay a drawing over the current drawing for reference purposes.

In the following Quick Tour exercise, you create a simple block to represent a valve, then insert it into the drawing.

The Quick Tour

Begin a new drawing named BLOKTEST using the default ACAD.DWG prototype drawing, turn on grid, and set snap to .25.

Command: *Choose Polyline (Draw, Polyline)*	Issues the PLINE command
From point: **2,7** (Enter)	Places the polyline start point
Arc/Close/Halfwidth/Length/Undo/ Width/<Endpoint of line>: **2,7.5** (Enter)	Places the next point
<Endpoint of line>: **3,7** (Enter)	Places the next point
<Endpoint of line>: **3,7.5** (Enter)	Places the next point
<Endpoint of line>: **C** (Enter)	Closes the polyline
Command: *Choose Line (Draw, Line)*	Issues the LINE command
From point: *Turn on ortho and pick* (1), *then* (2) *(see fig. 13.1), and press* (Enter)	Places 2 points for the line, ends the command
Command: *Choose Block (Draw, Block)*	Issues the BLOCK command
Block name (or ?): **VALVE** (Enter)	Names the block
Insertion base point: *Using the Midpoint object snap, pick* (3)	Identifies the insertion point of the block
Select objects: *Pick* (3)	Specifies the object(s) to block
Select objects: (Enter)	Ends the command and erases the selected objects
Command: **OOPS** (Enter)	Unerases the previous selection set
Command: *Choose Insert Block (Draw, Block)*	Issues the DDINSERT command, opens the Insert dialog box
*Choose **B**lock*	Opens the Defined blocks dialog box
Select VALVE, then choose OK	Identifies the block to insert, closes the dialog box
Choose OK	Closes the Insert dialog box
Insertion point: *Using the Nearest object snap, pick* (4)	Places the block at the end of the line
Insertion point: X scale factor <1>/ Corner / XYZ: (Enter)	Accepts the default X scale factor of 1

`Y scale factor (default=X):` (Enter)	Accepts the default Y scale factor
`Rotation angle <0>:` (Enter)	Accepts the default 0 rotation
`Command:` *Choose 2 Points Select (Modify, Break)*	Issues the BREAK command with the First point option
`Select object:` *Pick the horizontal line*	Identifies the object to break
`Enter first point:` *Using the Intersection object snap, pick* ④	Specifies the first break point
`Enter second point:` *Using the Intersection object snap, pick* ⑤	Specifies the second break point
`Command:` *Choose Polyline Edit (Modify, Special Edit)*	Issues the PEDIT command
`Select polyline:` *Pick the polyline at* ③	Identifies the polyline to edit
`Close/Join/Width/Edit vertex/Fit/ Spline/Decurve/Ltype gen/Undo/eXit <X>:` `W` (Enter)	Issues the Width option
`Enter new width for all segments:` `.05` (Enter)(Enter)	Sets the width of the selected polyline to .05 units
`Command:` *Choose Block (Draw, Block)*	Issues the BLOCK command
`Block name (or ?):` **VALVE** (Enter)	Specifies the block name
`Block VALVE already exists. Redefine it? <N>` `Y` (Enter)	Begins process to redefine the VALVE block
`Insertion base point:` *Using the Midpoint object snap, pick* ③	Identifies the insertion point of the block
`Select objects:` *Pick* ③	Specifies the object(s) to block
`Select objects:` (Enter)	Updates all block references, ends the command, and erases the selected objects
`Command:` *Choose Save (Standard Toolbar)*	Saves the drawing

Your drawing should look like figure 13.2.

13

The valve block.

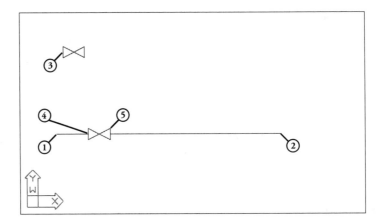

The completed valve drawing.

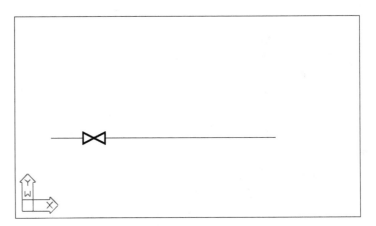

Understanding Blocks

Much of the work you do in a typical drawing duplicates something you have already done. Most drawings use standard parts and symbols that appear on other drawings. You use standard title blocks over and over again. An entire drawing, such as a shop drawing, might be similar to other drawings. If you have to redraw each part, symbol, title block, and drawing from scratch, AutoCAD doesn't save much time over manual drawing.

AutoCAD uses blocks to help you make use of standard parts and symbols from drawing to drawing. A *block* is a collection of objects combined into a single entity. A block also can be just a single object, such as the polyline in the previous quick tour exercise. When defined, blocks are inserted into the drawing using the DDINSERT or the INSERT command.

There are two main reasons for using blocks in your drawings: convenience and efficiency. Even if a block contains one object, such as the valve polyline in the quick tour exercise, blocks are more convenient. To copy the valve to another location in the drawing, for example, you might need to use the COPY, ROTATE, SCALE, and MOVE commands or cycle through multiple grip editing modes. When inserting a block, however, you are prompted for the location, scale, and rotation within a single command, thereby reducing the number of steps required to place the valve.

Blocks are more efficient than copying objects because the objects that make up a block are stored only once in a drawing as a block definition. A *block definition* is a group of objects that have been collected, given a name, and stored in the drawing. Block definitions are not visible in a drawing. You insert a reference to a block definition into the drawing whenever you need it.

A block definition might contain a thousand lines, circles, and arcs, but a block reference is only one entity. Using one block reference object to access a stored block definition becomes more efficient every time you create another block reference object. You can move, erase, or otherwise manipulate the block reference as a whole.

Creating a Block

The BLOCK command combines separate objects into a single named object. Blocks help reduce the amount of effort needed to draw repetitive objects and reduce the size of the drawing. The objects that make up a block are stored as a block definition. When a block definition is created, blocks are inserted into a drawing with the INSERT command.

13

BLOCK. The BLOCK command is the method by which you create a block definition that then can be inserted into the current drawing. You also can use BLOCK to view the block definitions that are in the current drawing as well as any external reference overlays.
Toolbar: *Choose Block (Draw, Block)*

When defining a block, you are presented with three prompts. As you learn the sequence of these prompts, it is important to watch the command line closely for what is being requested at each prompt. After issuing the BLOCK command, you are prompted for the following information:

- **Block name.** The block name can be up to 31 characters in length and should be indicative of what the block's function is in the drawing. For a listing of existing blocks in the drawing, type a **?** at the prompt. To see all existing blocks in the drawing, press Enter to accept the wild-card (*) default. You can use any of AutoCAD's standard wild cards at this prompt to display specific groups of block definitions.

- **Insertion base point.** At this prompt, specify a base point, relative to the objects being blocked, that is convenient for inserting the block. You can use any of the AutoCAD object snap features to specify this point.

- **Select objects.** Select the objects you want to block at this prompt. After selecting the desired objects and pressing Enter, AutoCAD erases them.

The first item of information AutoCAD requests is the block's name. The name under which AutoCAD creates the block definition is the name you use later to insert visible block references to the block in your drawing.

Next, AutoCAD prompts you for an insertion base point. This is the point by which AutoCAD references the block and the point at which the block is placed on the cursor when inserted. The location of a block's insertion point is important because it determines where the block will be located in relation to the rest of the drawing. It also is the point about which the block is scaled if you specify scale factors other than 1, and about which it rotates if you specify a nonzero rotation. If you have two parts that must fit together when they are inserted, create them with coordinated insertion base points. Then, both parts can be inserted at the same coordinates and will fit together properly. In general, endpoints, centers, midpoints, or other object snap points are good insertion base points.

After you specify the insertion base point, AutoCAD prompts you to select objects. As it does with any command that generates the object selection prompt, AutoCAD is building a selection set. The selection set is the group of entities that will be placed in the block definition. When you finish selecting entities, press Enter. The entities disappear as AutoCAD places them in the block definition.

> The block is created relative to the current UCS, so be sure the correct UCS is current, particularly if you are using 0,0 as the insertion base point.

Before a block can be created, you need to have something drawn that you want to turn into a block. In the following exercise, you create a simple floor plan and an office desk with a return, which you use to create a block.

Creating Furniture Blocks

Start a new drawing FURNBLOK using the US_ARCH drawing in the \ACADR13\COMMON\SUPPORT\ directory as a prototype. Then create the layers PLAN, LAYOUT, CHAIRS, and FURNITURE and set the layer colors to your liking. Make the PLAN layer current.

Command: *Choose Running Object Snap (Standard Toolbar, Object Snap), choose* **E**ndpoint, *then choose* OK	Sets endpoint as the running object snap
Command: *Choose Polyline (Draw, Polyline)*	Issues the PLINE command
From point: **15',15'** (Enter)	Begins the polyline
Current line-width is 0'-0" Arc/Close/Halfwidth/Length/Undo/Width/ <Endpoint of line:> **@0,30'** (Enter)	Draws the next segment 30' up
<Endpoint of line:> **@50',0** (Enter)	Draws a segment 50' to the right
<Endpoint of line:> **@0,-12'** (Enter)	Draws a segment 12' down
<Endpoint of line:> **@-15',0** (Enter)	Draws a segment 15' to the left
<Endpoint of line:> **@0,-18'** (Enter)	Draws a segment 18' down
<Endpoint of line:> **C** (Enter)	Closes the polyline and ends the PLINE command

Zoom to the view shown in figure 13.3.

Command: *Set the* FURNITURE *layer current*

Command: *Choose Rectangle (Draw, Polygon)*   Issues the RECTANG command

continues

continued

First corner: *Pick* ① *(see fig. 13.2)*	Places the first corner of the rectangle
Other corner: **@60,30** (Enter)	Draws a 5'×2'6" rectangle
Command: (Enter)	Issues the previous command
First corner: *Pick* ①	Places the first corner
Other corner: **@18,-30** (Enter)	Draws a 1'6"×2'6" rectangle
Command: *Choose Block (Draw, Block)*	Issues the BLOCK command
Block name (or ?): **DESK-L** (Enter)	Names the new block
Insertion base point: *Pick* ②	Identifies the base point
Select objects: Select both rectangles	Highlights the objects
Select objects: (Enter)	Makes an internal block, erases the selection set, ends the command
Command: *Choose Save (Standard Toolbar)*	Saves the drawing

Figure 13.3

Creating a block for the left-hand return desk.

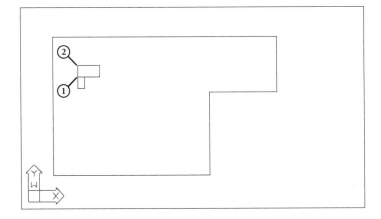

After a block is created, the objects that were selected to define the block are erased. The objects can be unerased using the OOPS command, but they still are just individual objects, not the block. They're the cookie cutter, not the cookie.

OOPS. The OOPS command unerases the last selection set that was erased. You can issue the OOPS command at any time in a drawing session to unerase the most recently erased objects. Unlike U or UNDO, which will sequentially undo the effects of the previous AutoCAD commands, the OOPS command only addresses erased objects and can only be issued once after an erasure is completed.
Toolbar: *Choose OOPS! (Miscellaneous)*
Screen: Choose MODIFY, Oops:

Inserting a Block

To place a block reference into the drawing, the command DDINSERT is used. This command displays the Insert dialog box so that you can easily specify any block available in the drawing and all the insert parameters. All of the insert parameters are specified on-screen (as opposed to in the dialog box) by default. When you select a block to insert and choose OK, you specify the parameters specified on-screen as follows:

- **Insertion point.** This prompt asks you to specify a point to place the block. The insertion base point defined in a block is placed at the point you specify. You can use any object snap mode or the From modifier when specifying an insertion point.

- **X scale factor.** By default, the block is inserted at the same size it was created (an X scale factor of 1). This prompt enables you to enter a different scale factor for the block insertion. A negative value (–1) mirrors the object about the X axis. You also can specify a scale by picking two points to specify a distance. Blocks that are drawn at actual size, such as the desk in the previous exercise, usually are not scaled when inserted.

- **Y scale factor.** The default scale factor for the Y scale factor is the same as that specified for the X scale factor. This enables you to easily specify an equally scaled block. Enter a negative value (–1) to mirror the object about the Y axis. As with the X scale factor, you can specify a scale by picking two points to specify a distance as a scale factor.

- **Rotation angle.** This prompt enables you to rotate the block at insertion time. The rotation angle default value of 0 inserts a block at the same orientation as when it was created. You can specify a positive or negative rotation angle or graphically rotate the block.

13

TIP

Turning on ORTHO when inserting blocks enables you to quickly specify rotation angles at 90° increments.

DDINSERT. The DDINSERT command opens the Insert dialog box, which enables you to specify a block name or a drawing file name to insert into your drawing. You also can use the Insert dialog box to specify an insertion point, scale, and rotation angle for the block.
Toolbar: *Choose Insert Block (Draw, Block)*
Screen: *Choose DRAW 2, DDINSERT*

The desk block you created in the previous exercise is asymmetrical. If you want to insert a desk with an opposite return, you could create another block and name it DESK-R for the right hand return, or you could insert DESK-L again but use a negative value for the Y scale factor. This eliminates the need to make a separate block definition for a right-hand return.

In the following exercise, you create a desk chair block, then insert the desk and the chair into the drawing. You also insert the desk block using a negative scale factor to draw a mirrored insertion of the desk block.

Inserting a Furniture Block into the Drawing

Continue from the previous exercise.

Command: *Set the CHAIRS layer current*

Command: *Choose Zoom In (Standard Toolbar) twice*   Magnifies the graphics display by 400 percent

Command: *Choose Rectangle (Draw, Polygon)*   Issues the RECTANG command

First corner: *Pick* ① *(see fig. 13.4)*   Begins the rectangle

Other corner: **@20,-20** (Enter)   Draws the rectangle, ends the command

Command: *Choose Fillet (Modify, Feature)*   Issues the FILLET command

Polyline/Radius/Trim/<Select first   Issues the Radius option
object>: **R** (Enter)

Enter fillet radius <0'-0">: **3** (Enter)   Sets the fillet radius to 3"

Command: *Press the spacebar*   Issues the previous command

`Polyline/Radius/Trim/<Select first object>:` **P** (Enter)	Issues the Polyline option
`Select 2D polyline:` *Pick the rectangle*	Applies a 3" fillet to all corners, ends the command
`Command:` *Choose Explode (Modify, Explode)*	Issues the EXPLODE command
`Select objects:` **L** (Enter)	Selects the last object created
`Select objects:` (Enter)	Explodes the selected object
`Command:` *Press and drag from ② to ③*	Selects the objects and displays their grips
`Command:` *Pick the top left grip*	Displays a hot grip

`** STRETCH **`
`<Stretch to point>/Base point/Copy/`
`Undo/eXit:` **MI** (Enter)
	Switches to mirror mode

`** MIRROR **`
`<Second point>/Base point/Copy/Undo/`
`eXit:` **C** (Enter)
	Issues the Copy option

`** MIRROR (multiple)**`
`<Second point>/Base point/Copy/Undo/`
`eXit:` *Pick the top right grip*
	Places the second point of the mirror line, copies the selection set

`** MIRROR **`
`<Second point>/Base point/Copy/Undo/`
`eXit:` *Press Esc three times*
	Clears the hot grip, then the selection set, then the grips

`Command:` *Choose Block (Draw, Block)*	Issues the BLOCK command
`Block name (or ?):` **CHAIR** (Enter)	
`Insertion base point:` *Using the Midpoint object snap, pick ④*	Establishes the base point to be used when the block is inserted
`Select objects:` *Use a window to select all the objects that comprise the chair, then press* (Enter)	Highlights the objects, creates the block, erases the selection set
`Command:` *Choose Zoom Previous (Standard Toolbar) twice*	Updates the display
`Command:` *Set the LAYOUT layer current*	
`Command:` *Choose Insert Block (Modify, Block)*	Issues the DDINSERT command, and opens the Insert dialog box
*Choose **B**lock*	Opens the Defined Blocks dialog box

13

continues

continued

Select DESK-L, *then choose* OK	Specifies block to insert
Choose OK	Closes the Insert dialog box and continues insertion process
Insertion point: *Pick* ① *(see fig. 13.5)*	Places the base point for the block insertion
X scale factor <1>/Corner/XYZ: (Enter)	Accepts the default
Y scale factor (default=X): (Enter)	Accepts the default
Rotation angle <0>: (Enter)	Accepts the default
Command: (Enter)	Repeats the DDINSERT command, opens the Insert dialog box
Choose **B**lock	Opens the Defined Blocks dialog box
Select CHAIR, *then choose* OK	Specifies block to insert
Choose OK	Closes the Insert dialog box and continues insertion process
Insertion point: *Pick* ②	Specifies the insertion point for the chair
X scale factor <1>/Corner/XYZ: (Enter)	Accepts the default X scale
Y scale factor (default=X): (Enter)	Accepts the default Y scale
Rotation angle <0>: (Enter)	Accepts the default rotation angle
Command: (Enter)	Repeats the DDINSERT command, opens the Insert dialog box
Choose **B**lock	Opens the Defined Blocks dialog box
Choose DESK-L, *then* OK	Sets DESK-L as the selection, closes the dialog box
Choose OK	Accepts DESK-L as the block to be inserted, closes the Insert dialog box
Insertion point: *Pick* ①	Places the base point for the block insertion
X scale factor <1>/Corner/XYZ: -1 (Enter)	Specifies a negative X scale factor
Y scale factor (default=X): 1 (Enter)	Specifies a positive Y scale factor

Rotation angle <0>: **Enter**	Accepts the default rotation angle
Command: *Choose Save (Standard Toolbar)*	Saves the drawing

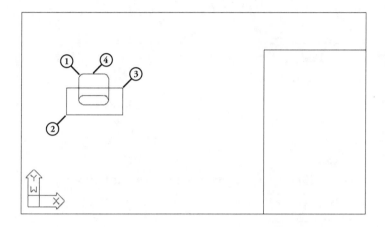

Creating and inserting the furniture blocks.

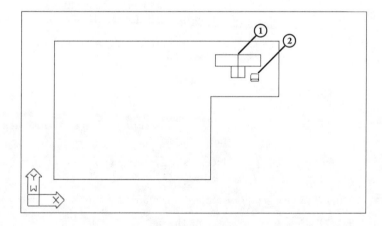

Inserting the DESK-L and CHAIR blocks.

13

Renaming an Existing Block

Because you mirrored the desk block to create the right-hand return desk, the name DESK-L is no longer appropriate. A better name is the more generic DESK. The DDRENAME command enables you to edit a block name that may have been entered incorrectly or, as with the current situation, requires a different name to more accurately describe the block.

In the following exercise, you use DDRENAME to change the DESK-L block name to DESK. Then you insert another desk to confirm the change.

Renaming the DESK-L Block and Inserting Another DESK

Continue from the previous exercise.

Command: *Choose* **D**ata, **R**ename	Issues the DDRENAME command, opens the Rename dialog box
Select Block *from the* Named Objects *list*	Displays block names in the Items list
Select DESK-L *from the* Items *list*	Places DESK-L in the **O**ld Name edit box
Type **DESK** *in the* Rename To *edit box, then choose the* **R**ename To *button*	Renames DESK-L to DESK
Choose OK	Closes the dialog box and renames all instances of DESK-L to DESK
Command: *Choose Insert Block (Draw, Block)*	Issues the DDINSERT command and displays the Insert dialog box
Choose **B**lock	Opens the Defined Blocks dialog box
Select DESK, *then choose* OK	Specifies block to insert
Choose OK	Closes the Insert dialog box and continues insertion process
Insertion point: *Pick* ① *(see fig. 13.6)*	Specifies the insertion point for as shown the desk
X scale factor <1>/Corner/XYZ: (Enter)	Accepts the default X scale
Y scale factor (default=X): (Enter)	Accepts the default Y scale
Rotation angle <0>: (Enter)	Accepts the default rotation angle
Command: *Choose Save (Standard Toolbar)*	Saves the drawing

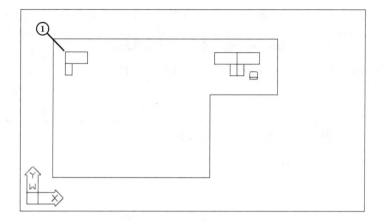

*Placement position
of the block DESK.*

Using Blocks and Layers

As you learned in Chapter 4, "Preparing Your Drawing," all objects have
properties such as layer, color, and linetype. Properties such as color and
linetype can be explicit (RED, DASHED, and so forth) or BYLAYER.
BYLAYER properties take on the settings of the object's layer. Explicit
properties ignore the settings of the object's layer.

Until this point, you have treated the layer property as if it were always
explicit. This is true for all objects except for blocked objects created on
layer 0. Blocked objects created on layer 0 take on the layer property of
the block reference's layer.

If the properties of a blocked object created on layer 0 are set to
BYLAYER, the properties take on the settings of the block reference's
layer. It doesn't matter if the properties for new objects are set explicitly;
the current layer settings are still used. If, however, the blocked object's
properties are set explicitly, it retains the explicit settings when inserted
as a block.

In this chapter's exercises, you created blocks with objects on explicit
layers (CHAIRS and FURNITURE) and then inserted them on the
LAYOUT layer. When you inserted the block references, the color of the
blocked objects did not take on the color of the current layer because the
blocked objects were created on layers other than 0.

While the interaction of object properties and layers within blocks can
seem confusing, it is possible to keep things simple and predictable. As a

general rule, blocks should be created from objects created on layer 0 with BYLAYER property settings. Blocked objects with explicit layers can be a powerful tool, but this requires careful planning and block design.

The following exercise creates a new desk on layer 0, then inserts the desk on the FURNITURE layer.

Using Blocks Drawn on Layer 0

Continue from the previous exercise.

Command: *Copy the left desk to a clear area as shown in figure 13.7*	
Command: *Choose Explode (Modify, Explode)*	Issues the EXPLODE command
Select objects: *Select the copied desk and press* (Enter)	Selects the object to explode
Command: *Choose **E**dit, P**r**operties, then select the exploded objects and press* (Enter)	Opens the Change Properties dialog box and selects the objects to modify
*In the Change Properties dialog box, choose the **L**ayer button*	
Select layer 0 in the Select Layer dialog box, then click on OK twice	Changes the polylines to layer 0
Command: *Choose Block (Draw, Block)*	Issues the block command
Block name (or ?): **NEWDESK** (Enter)	Specifies the block name
Insertion base point: *Pick* ① *(see fig. 13.7)*	Specifies the insertion base point at the corner of the desk
Select objects: *Select the two desk polylines* (Enter)	Specifies the objects to block, creates the block and erases the polylines
Command: *Choose Insert Block (Draw, Block),specify the* NEWDESK *block, and choose* OK	Issues the DDINSERT command and specifies the block to insert
Insertion point: *Pick point at* ①	Specifies insertion point
X scale factor <1> / Corner / XYZ: (Enter)	Accepts default X scale factor
Y scale factor (default=X): (Enter)	Accepts default Y scale factor
Rotation angle <0>: (Enter)	Accepts default rotation angle
Command: *Choose Save (Standard Toolbar)*	Saves the drawing

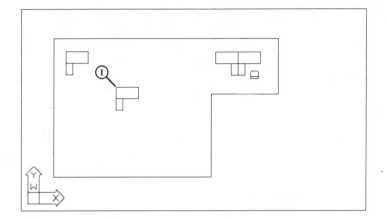

Figure 13.7

Block with layer 0 objects inserted on the LAYOUT layer.

For more extensive exercises that illustrate the power of layers and blocks, refer to *Inside AutoCAD Release 13 for Windows and Windows NT* from New Riders Publishing.

Editing Blocks

After a block is created and inserted into the drawing, you might find occasionally that it doesn't meet the needs of every situation. The position of a block might need to change because of design changes, the size of a blocked part might change, or you might want to change a block's orientation or its layer. You can use any of AutoCAD's basic editing tools, such as COPY, MOVE, SCALE, ROTATE, and DDCHPROP, on the entire block but not on individual blocked objects. The STRETCH command, however, has no effect on blocked objects.

You even can use grip editing with blocks. By default, the grips of blocked objects are not highlighted when a block is selected for grip editing; only the grip at the block's insertion point is displayed. You can turn on the grips of blocked objects by turning on the Enable Grips Within **B**locks feature in the Grips dialog box. You access the Grips dialog box with the DDGRIPS command or by choosing **O**ptions, **G**rips. As with the standard editing commands, the grip editing modes only affect the entire block, and the STRETCH autoediting mode does not have an effect on blocked objects.

You can use any of AutoCAD's object snaps with blocks and blocked objects. You can use object snaps to position a block or to draw new objects that snap to a block's objects.

13

If you want to edit the objects that make up a block, you first must use the EXPLODE command on the block. The EXPLODE command, when used on a block, deletes the block reference object and replaces it with a copy of the actual objects that make up a block definition. When you are done editing the exploded block's objects, you can leave them as they are, you can use them to create a new block, or you can use them to redefine the original block.

In the following exercise, you enable the grips within the chair block to rotate its position, then explode a DESK block to edit the rectangles.

Exploding and Editing Blocks

Continue from the previous exercise and zoom to the view in figure 13.8 to get a better view of the two desks and the chair.

Command: *Choose* **O**ptions, **G**rips	Opens the Grips dialog box
Turn on Enable Grips Within **B**locks, *then click on* OK	Turns on grip display for blocked objects
Command: *Pick the chair*	Selects CHAIR block for grip editing
Command: *Pick* ① *(see fig. 13.8)*	Enters grip editing mode
`** STRETCH **` `<Stretch to point>/Base point/Copy/` `Undo/eXit:` `RO` (Enter)	Switches to rotate mode
`** ROTATE **` `<Rotation angle>/Base point/Copy/` `Undo/Reference/eXit:` `45` (Enter)	Rotates the block 45 degrees
Command: Press Esc twice	Clears the selection set, then the grips
Command: *Choose Explode (Modify, Explode)*	Issues the EXPLODE command
`Select objects:` *Select the rectangle at* ② *and press* (Enter)	Explodes the DESK block into the original rectangles
Command: *Pick* ③	Displays the rectangle's grips
Command: *Press Shift and pick* ④, *then* ⑤	Makes two grips hot
Command: *Pick* ④ *again*	Initiates the grip editing mode
`** STRETCH **` `<Stretch to point>/Base point/Copy/` `Undo/eXit:` `@0,-6` (Enter)	Stretches the rectangle down 6"

Command: *Choose **O**ptions, **G**rips*	Opens the Grips dialog box
Turn off Enable Grips Within **B**locks, *then choose* OK	Turns off grip setting for blocks, closes the dialog box
Command: *Choose Zoom Previous (Standard Toolbar, Zoom)*	Returns to the previous display
Command: *Choose Save (Standard Toolbar)*	Saves the drawing

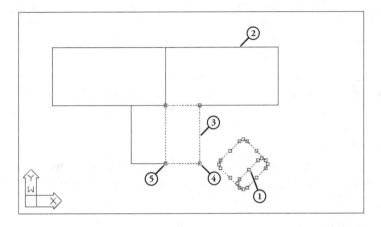

Figure 13.8

Rotating the chair and editing the desk.

When you exploded the desk block, the rectangles remained on the FURNITURE layer. If the rectangles were created on layer 0, they would have returned to layer 0 when exploded.

Redefining Blocks

The capability to redefine a block definition is one of AutoCAD's most powerful features. When a block is redefined, all blocks based on the original definition are automatically updated to the new block definition. Because blocks are automatically updated when redefined, you don't have to go through the tedium of erasing existing blocks and then reinserting them.

A block is redefined with the BLOCK command and specifying an existing block name. AutoCAD then asks you if you want to redefine the existing block. If you answer yes, the standard block prompts are displayed to enable you to create the new block definition.

You should keep in mind the following things as you go through the sequence of redefining an existing block:

- **Explode the block to be redefined.** This avoids creating a block from another block with the same name, which will cause an internal error. You may wish to insert a separate reference of the block rather than using one that has already been inserted. Once exploded, select the objects used to create the block.

- **The base point for the redefined block should be the same as the original block.** If you forget where the insertion base point is located, reinsert the block. You might want to turn on BLIPMODE prior to inserting the block to assist you in locating the base point.

- **The name of the redefined block must be the same as the block it is replacing.** When a block name that already exists is entered, AutoCAD will prompt you to redefine the block. This indicates that you are effectively redefining an existing block and that you gave it the right name.

- **The drawing will automatically regenerate after a block has been redefined.** This occurs so that you have the most current reference of each block definition in the drawing

In the following exercise, you use the desk objects you modified in the previous exercise to redefine all of the DESK blocks. The NEWDESK object is unaffected because it has a different name.

Redefining a Block

Continue from the previous exercise.

Command: *Choose Block (Draw, Block)*	Issues the BLOCK command
_block Block name (or ?): **DESK** (Enter)	
Block DESK already exists. Redefine it? <N> Y (Enter)	Asks you to confirm redefinition
Insertion base point: *Use ENDPoint to pick ① (see fig. 13.9)*	Specifies the base point
Select objects: *Select both rectangles and press* (Enter)	Selects the desk objects to be the block, redefines all instances of DESK, erases the selection set, and ends the command
Command: *Choose Insert Block (Draw, Block)*	Issues the DDINSERT command

Choose **B**lock	Opens the Defined Blocks dialog box
Select DESK, *then choose* OK	Specifies block to insert and closes the dialog box
Choose OK	Accepts DESK as the block to be inserted, and closes the Insert dialog box
`Insertion point:` *Pick* ①	Specifies the insertion point
`X scale factor <1>/Corner/XYZ:` (Enter)	Accepts the default
`Y scale factor (default=X):` (Enter)	Accepts the default
`Rotation angle <0>:` (Enter)	Accepts the default
`Command:` *Choose Save (Standard Toolbar)*	Saves the drawing

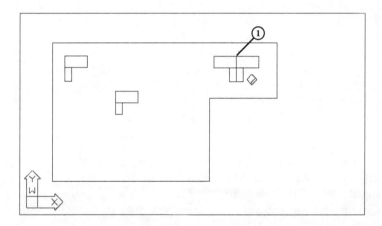

Figure 13.9

The redefined DESK blocks.

13

> It's extremely important that you do not create a new block definition from a block of the same name. It will cause a block definition to reference itself, which will result in an internal error and cause AutoCAD to close.

Sharing Blocks with Other Drawings

The BLOCK command only defines blocks in the current drawing; you can't insert blocks created with the BLOCK command from another drawing. To share blocks with other drawings, AutoCAD provides the WBLOCK command (WBLOCK stands for Write BLOCK). The WBLOCK command exports a block or selected objects to a separate drawing file. You can open and edit any drawing file created with the WBLOCK command as a normal drawing.

After you start the WBLOCK command, the Create Drawing File dialog box opens to enable you to specify a file name for the new drawing. Once you have specified a file name, the `Block name:` prompt displays. You can enter the name of an existing block at this prompt to create a drawing from the existing block. If you specify an existing block name at this prompt, AutoCAD writes the block to disk and ends the command. You also can press Enter at the `Block name:` prompt. If you press Enter, you see the usual BLOCK command prompts.

WBLOCK. The WBLOCK command enables you to create a drawing file from a block, a selection set, or an entire drawing, which makes the block accessible to other drawing files. The WBLOCK command is very similar to the BLOCK command, except that the WBLOCK command does not create a block definition in the current drawing and asks you to specify a filename and a block name to export.
Pull-down: *Choose* **F**ile, **E**xport
Screen: *Choose* FILE, EXPORT, Wblock:

The WBLOCK command does not create a block definition in the current drawing or the exported drawing. The block definition is created when the drawing created with WBLOCK is inserted into a drawing with the DDINSERT command. In fact, you can insert any drawing as a block into any other drawing with the DDINSERT command.

Be careful when inserting drawings not created with the WBLOCK command. Drawing files created by saving a drawing have an insertion base point of 0,0,0 by default. You can use the BASE command to specify a new insertion base point in a drawing.

The following are some of the benefits of using WBLOCK instead of the SAVE command (which also writes a file to the disk, of course).

● The SAVE command only asks for a file name.

● The WBLOCK command enables you to pick a specific insertion base point.

- You can use any of the selection options to select objects when using WBLOCK to create a file.

In the following exercise, you use WBLOCK to save a cluster of desks as a separate drawing and then insert the cluster from disk into the drawing.

Creating a Drawing File Using WBLOCK

Continue from the previous exercise.

Command: *Choose Copy Object (Modify, Copy) and copy the 2 desks and the chair in the upper right corner of the plan to the lower right corner as shown in figure 13.10*

Command: *Press and drag from ① to ②*   Highlights the three blocks, displays their grips

Command: *Pick the grip at ③*   Makes grip hot and enters grip editing mode

```
** STRETCH **
<Stretch to point>/Base point/Copy/
Undo/eXit: RO (Enter)
```
Switches to rotate mode

```
** ROTATE **
<Rotation angle>/Base point/Copy/
Undo/Reference/eXit: C (Enter)
```
Issues the Copy option

```
** ROTATE (multiple) **
<Rotation angle>/Base point/Copy/
Undo/Reference/eXit: 180 (Enter)
```
Rotates and copies the selection set

```
** ROTATE (multiple) **
<Rotation angle>/Base point/Copy/
Undo/Reference/eXit: Press Esc twice
```
Ends the grip editing and deselects the objects

Command: *Press Shift, then pick both chairs*   Highlights both chairs

Command: *Pick the grip at ③ and change to MIRROR autoedit mode*   Begins grip editing

```
** MIRROR **
<Second point>/Base point/Copy/Undo/
eXit: C (Enter)
```
Issues the Copy option

continues

continued

`** MIRROR (multiple)**`
`<Second point>/Base point/Copy/Undo/`
`eXit: @60,0` (Enter)
	Places the second point of the mirror line and copies the selection set

`Command:` **WBLOCK** (Enter)	Starts the WBLOCK command and opens the Create Drawing File dialog box
Enter **DESKQUAD** *in the* File **N**ame *edit box and choose* OK	Closes the dialog box
`Block name:` (Enter)	Skips using an existing block
`Base point:` *Use ENDPoint and pick* ① *(see fig. 13.11)*	Specifies the base point
`Select objects:` *Use a window to select the 4 desks and 4 chairs* (Enter)	Highlights the selection set, creates DESKQUAD.DWG, erases the selection set
`Command:` *Choose Insert Block (Draw, Block)*	Issues the DDINSERT command
Choose **F**ile	Opens the Select Drawing File dialog box
Select DESKQUAD.DWG, *then choose* OK	Specifies the file to be inserted
Choose OK	Accepts the dialog box settings
`Insertion point:` *Pick* ① *again*	Specifies the insertion point
`X scale factor <1>/Corner/XYZ:` (Enter)	Accepts the default
`Y scale factor (default=X):` (Enter)	Accepts the default
`Rotation angle <0>:` (Enter)	Accepts the default
`Command:` *Choose Save (Standard Toolbar)*	Saves the drawing

NOTE

If you choose **F**ile, **E**xport to export a block, select Drawing (*.DWG) from the List files of Type drop-down list, and enter a valid drawing name. The EXPORT command operates exactly like the WBLOCK command.

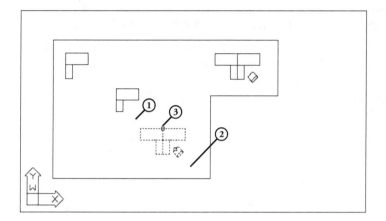

Figure 13.10

Copied desks and chairs.

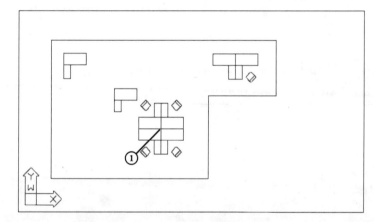

Figure 13.11

The DESKQUAD block.

13

Redefining Block Definitions Using Drawings

Previously in this chapter, you learned how to redefine an existing block within the current drawing. You also can redefine any block using any other drawing. If an external drawing inserted as a block is updated, the block can be redefined easily. The process is exactly the same as inserting a drawing as a block, except you tell AutoCAD that you want to redefine an existing block.

Redefining a Block Definition Using an External Drawing

Continue from the previous exercise. Open the DESKQUAD drawing, erase all the chairs, save the drawing, and reopen the FURNBLOCK drawing. You might have to zoom to the extents of the drawing to see the desks and chairs.

Notice that the DESKQUAD block reference still shows the chairs. The original block definition still contains the chairs.

Command: *Choose Insert Block (Draw, Block)*	Issues the DDINSERT command
Choose **F**ile	Opens the Select Drawing File dialog box
Select DESKQUAD.DWG, *then click on* OK	Specifies the file to be inserted
Choose OK	Accepts the dialog box settings
Choose OK *in the* Warning *dialog box*	Closes the Warning dialog box, redefines all existing instances of DESKQUAD
Insertion point: *Press Esc*	Cancels insertion, but keeps new block definition
Command: *Choose Save (Standard Toolbar)*	Saves the drawing

Your drawing now should resemble figure 13.12.

Figure 13.12

New definition of DESKQUAD.

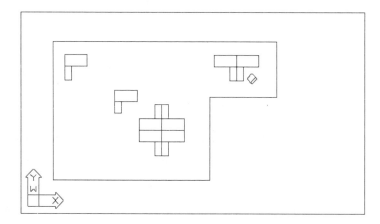

As demonstrated in the previous exercise, the process of redefining a block with an external drawing is quite similar to redefining a block within the current drawing. Because the block redefinition takes place prior to specifying an insertion point, it is not necessary to actually place a redefined block in the drawing; all block references that refer to the redefined block definition automatically are updated.

Understanding External References

Because block definitions don't have automatic links to external files and they are fully defined within a drawing, they are not well suited for sharing information between drawings or between design groups. While you can redefine blocks when they are updated, there isn't an easy way to ensure that the inserted block is current. To provide links between external drawing files, AutoCAD uses an external reference or xref for short.

An external reference is a special block reference. It is similar to a standard block reference except that the referenced objects are stored in an external drawing file rather than as a block definition. Because xrefs don't use stored internal block definitions, AutoCAD reads the externally referenced drawing file every time it opens a drawing that contains an xref. This ensures that the latest version of the referenced file is always loaded.

An xref behaves much like a block that can't be exploded. Like a block, an xref is a single object that contains other objects. Objects drawn on layer 0 with BYLAYER object properties in external reference files take on the properties of the xref layer. The differences between blocks and xrefs are beyond the scope of this book.

External references are inserted with the XREF command. The XREF command can create two types of xrefs: attached and overlaid. Overlaid xrefs are much more flexible and easy to use. This chapter focuses on overlaid xrefs for this reason.

13

> **XREF.** The XREF command enables you to attach, overlay, bind, or update external reference drawings. The xref's data resides entirely in the external drawing's database, and only a reference to the external file is placed in the current drawing's database.
> Toolbar: *Choose Overlay (External Reference)*
> Screen: *Choose* FILE, Xref:, Overlay

There are several uses for overlaid xrefs. Overlaid xrefs are useful for simplifying the drawing process. You can use overlaid xrefs for drawing elements that are relatively static, but might change occasionally. Also, you can use overlaid xrefs to see the way your current drawing relates to drawings of others in a concurrent-design workgroup. Overlaid xrefs enable each designer in the workgroup to see any other designer's drawings without worrying about creating circular xrefs or inflexible drawing interdependencies.

Using the XREF Overlay Option

The Overlay (External Reference) tool starts the XREF command and specifies the Overlay option for you. Overlaid xrefs do not display nested, overlaid xrefs; an overlaid xref is not visible in a drawing if it is more than one attached or overlaid xref-level deep.

In the following exercise, you save the building shell as a separate drawing that will be overlaid to begin a new furniture layout. To understand the linkage between the drawing and an overlay, you will edit the building shell and then open the furniture layout.

Overlaying a Building Shell for Reference in the Layout

Continue from the previous exercise.

Command: *Choose Offset (Modify, Copy)*	Issues the OFFSET command
Offset the building polyline 6" to the outside	Offsets the polyline
Command: **WBLOCK** (Enter)	Starts the WBLOCK command and opens the Create Drawing File dialog box
Use **BLDGSHEL** *as the file name and choose* OK	Specifies the new drawing file name
Block name: (Enter)	Accepts the default for no preexisting block definition
Base point: *Pick* ① *(see fig. 13.13)*	Specifies a base point for the drawing file
Select objects: *Select both polylines that define the building shell and press* (Enter)	Specifies the selection set, creates BLDGSHEL.DWG, and erases the selection set

Start a new drawing named LAYOUT using US_ARCH.DWG as a prototype. Do not save the changes to FURNBLOCK.

Command: **XREF** (Enter)	Issues the XREF command

`?/Bind/Detach/Path/Reload/Overlay/ <Attach>: O` (Enter)	Issues the Overlay option, opens Select file to overlay dialog box
Choose BLDGSHEL.DWG *from the* \AB *directory, then* OK	Closes the dialog box, places the insertion base point of BLDGSHEL on the crosshairs
`Insertion point: 10',10'` (Enter)	Places the insertion point 10' up and over from absolute 0,0
`X scale factor <1>/Corner/XYZ:` (Enter)	Accepts the default
`Y scale factor (default=X):` (Enter)	Accepts the default
`Rotation angle <0>:` (Enter)	Accepts the default
`Command:` *Choose Insert Block (Draw, Block)*	Issues the DDINSERT command
Choose **F**ile	Opens the Select Drawing File dialog box
Select DESKQUAD.DWG, *then click on* OK	Specifies the file to be inserted
Choose OK	Accepts the dialog box settings
`Insertion point:` *Pick* ① *(see fig. 13.14)*	Places a block reference of DESKQUAD
`X scale factor <1>/Corner/XYZ:` (Enter)	Accepts the default
`Y scale factor (default=X):` (Enter)	Accepts the default
`Rotation angle <0>:` (Enter)	Accepts the default
`Command:` *Copy the DESKQUAD block to* ②	
Save the drawing and open BLDGSHEL.DWG	
`Command:` *Choose Stretch (Modify, Resize)*	Issues the STRETCH command
`Select objects:` *Specify a crossing window from* ①, *to* ② *as shown in figure 13.15* (Enter)	
`Base point or displacement: 5',0` (Enter)	Specifies displacement
`Second point of displacement:` (Enter)	Accepts displacement

Save the drawing and open LAYOUT.DWG. When the LAYOUT drawing is opened, AutoCAD automatically loads the updated BLDGSHEL.DWG external reference.

13

Figure 13.13

Placement points for the furniture.

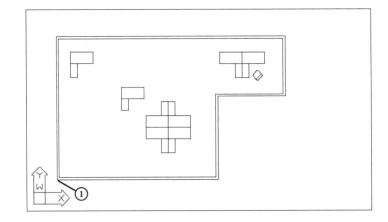

Figure 13.14

Stretch window to edit the BLDGSHEL drawing.

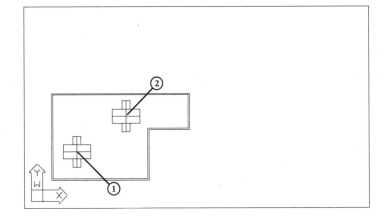

Figure 13.15

Stretching the building shell.

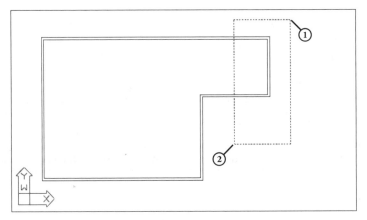

Summary

In this chapter, you learned how to use the BLOCK, DDINSERT, and WBLOCK commands to create blocks to increase drawing efficiency. Blocks save time as well as drawing file size. Blocks also enable you to update an entire drawing quickly if a blocked part changes.

You also learned how to use external references to share drawing data and further simplify your drawings.

Related Topics

- Using the DDRENAME command—Chapter 4, "Preparing Your Drawing"
- Using the EXPLODE command—Chapter 12, "Constructive Editing"

13

PART IV

Annotation and Plotting

Chapter Snapshot

This chapter presents the dimensioning basics that are integral to every dimensioning situation. Understanding these basic concepts enables you to more work more efficiently and effectively when dimensioning the drawing and prepares you for the more advanced concept of dimensioning styles in Chapter 15. The following are some of the important concepts covered in this chapter:

- Dimensioning terminology used by AutoCAD

- Creating horizontal and vertical dimensions using the DIMLINEAR command

- Defining placement variables and techniques for creating continued and baseline dimensions

- Generating dimensions for non-orthogonal objects and angles

- Using a dimension leader to annotate the drawing

- Editing dimensions by using grips

Dimensioning

Historically, the dimensioning of a drawing was a job that few people wanted. With each release of AutoCAD, however, the task is made easier and more intuitive, and Release 13 is no exception. The dialog boxes encountered in this chapter enable the new AutoCAD user to easily dimension the most complex drawing. Another improvement to the dimensioning process is the addition of the dimensioning toolbar from which many of the commands in this chapter are issued.

In the following exercise, you create a small plate to which you add several dimensions from the Dimensioning toolbar.

The Quick Tour

To begin, create a new drawing named BOX4DIMS by using the default ACAD.DWG prototype drawing. Create two new layers called BOX and DIMS and set BOX current.

Command: *Choose Rectangle (Draw, Polygon)*	Issues the RECTANG command
Draw a rectangle from **6,2** *to* **11,5**	Draws the rectangle from ① to ② (see fig. 14.1)
Command: *Choose Circle Center Radius (Draw, Circle)*	Issues the CIRCLE command
Draw a circle centered at **7,3** *with a radius of* **.5**	Draws the circle at ③
Command: *Choose Chamfer (Modify, Feature)*	Issues the CHAMFER command
Polyline/Distance/Angle/Trim/ Method/<Select first line>: **A** (Enter)	Issues the Angle option
length on the first line <0.0000>: **1.25** (Enter)	Sets the first chamfer length
Enter chamfer angle from the first line <0.0000>: **30** (Enter)	Sets the angle of the chamfer from the first line
Command: (Enter)	Repeats the CHAMFER command
<Select first line>: *Pick* ④, *then* ⑤	Chamfers the corner

Now that you have the basic geometry for the plate, you can add some dimensions. Before beginning, set the layer DIMS current.

Command: *Choose* **T**ools, **T**oolbars, **D**imensioning	Displays the Dimensioning toolbar
Command: *Choose Linear Dimension (Dimensioning)*	Issues the DIMLINEAR command
Select object to dimension: *Using the Endpoint object snap, pick* ① *(see fig. 14.2)*	Places the start point of the extension line
Second extension line origin: *Using the Quadrant object snap pick,* ②	Places the second point of the extension line
Dimension line location (Text/ Angle/Horizontal/Vertical/ Rotated):	Places the dimension line and ends the command

*Move the cursor to down and place
the dimension as shown in figure 14.2*

Command: *Choose Baseline Dimension (Dimensioning)*	Issues the DIMBASELINE command
`Second extension line origin or RETURN to select:` *Using the Endpoint object snap pick ③*	Places a baseline dimension
`Second extension line origin or RETURN to select:` *Press Esc*	Ends the DIMBASELINE command
Command: *Choose Linear Dimension (Dimensioning)*	Issues the DIMLINEAR command
`First extension line origin or RETURN to select:` (Enter)	Enables you to pick the object to be dimensioned
`Select object to dimension:` *Pick ④*	Selects the line to be dimensioned
`Dimension line location (Text/ Angle/Horizontal/Vertical/Rotated):` *Move the cursor to the left and place the dimension as shown in figure 14.2*	Places the dimension line
Command: *Choose Continue Dimension (Dimensioning)*	Issues the DIMCONTINUE command
`Second extension line origin or RETURN to select:` *Using the Endpoint object snap, pick ⑤*	Places a continued dimension
`Second extension line origin or RETURN to select:` *Press Esc*	Ends the DIMCONTINUE command
Command: *Choose Angular Dimension (Dimensioning)*	Issues the DIMANGULAR command
`Select arc, circle, line, or RETURN:` *Pick the line at ④*	Selects the first defining line
`Second line:` *Pick the line at ⑥*	Selects the second defining line
`Dimension arc line location (Text/Angle):` *Move the cursor to up and place the dimension as shown in figure 14.2*	Places the angular dimension
Command: *Choose Diameter Dimension (Dimensioning, Radial Dimension)*	Issues the DIMDIAMETER command

continues

continued

`Select arc or circle:` *Pick the circle at* ②	Selects the circle to dimension
`Dimension line location (Text/Angle):` *Move the cursor to the right and place the dimension as shown in figure 14.2*	Places the diameter dimension
`Command:` *Choose Save (Standard Toolbar)*	Saves the drawing

Figure 14.1

Drawing the block.

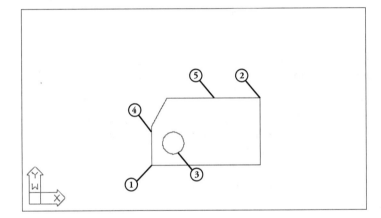

Figure 14.2

Dimensioning the block.

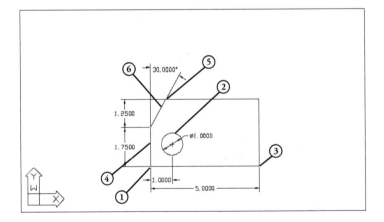

Chapter 7 discussed the importance of drawing accuracy and the importance of using object snaps and coordinate input to create accurate drawings. When dimensioning objects, you see the results of drawing accurately.

The Anatomy of a Dimension

When you place a dimension, AutoCAD creates a dimension object. The dimension object actually consists of a number of objects that act as a single object. Figure 14.3 shows some of the basic parts of a dimension, which are described in the following list:

- **Extension line.** This is the line that extends away from the object being dimensioned. In the case of linear dimensions, there typically are two extension lines for each dimension. The dimension itself is the distance between the two extension lines.

- **Dimension line.** The dimension line typically runs perpendicular to the extension lines and parallel to the object being dimensioned. It has an arrowhead at either end, the type and size of which can be changed. See Chapter 15, "Adding Style to Dimensions," for more on changing the look of dimensions.

- **Dimension text.** The Dimension text indicates the distance between the points picked. AutoCAD automatically creates the dimension text, which you can accept or modify.

- **Center mark.** The center mark is the cross (+) that is placed at the center of a circle or an arc. This is used to identify the point from which the radius or diameter dimension is taken.

- **Leader.** The leader line provides a way in which to annotate the drawing. The line might have multiple segments or might be curved. An arrowhead typically is positioned on the drawing feature referenced by the note.

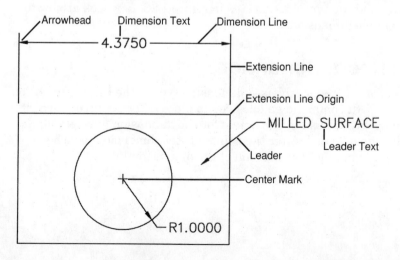

Figure 14.3

The parts of a dimension.

14

Chapter 15, "Adding Style to Dimensions," shows you how to control the appearance of the various parts of a dimension. For now, though, look at how to place some dimensions on your drawing.

Linear Dimensions

The dimensioning commands are fairly easy to recognize—most of them start with DIM and have long names such as DIMLINEAR and DIMCONTINUE. The easiest way to access a dimensioning command is with the dimensioning toolbar shown in figure 14.4. The Dimensioning toolbar contains all the commands you need when creating and editing dimensions.

Figure 14.4

*The Dimension
toolbar.*

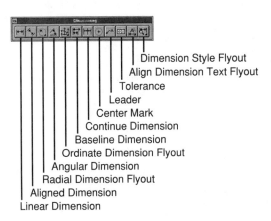

Dimension Style Flyout
Align Dimension Text Flyout
Tolerance
Leader
Center Mark
Continue Dimension
Baseline Dimension
Ordinate Dimension Flyout
Angular Dimension
Radial Dimension Flyout
Aligned Dimension
Linear Dimension

Keeping in mind the terms illustrated in figure 14.3, now look at how to add some simple dimensions.

Adding a Linear Dimension

Probably the most frequently used dimension type is the linear dimension. The DIMLINEAR command enables you to place a horizontal or vertical dimension by either picking two points for the dimension or selecting the object to be dimensioned. After the points for the dimension have been identified, you can place the position of the dimension line.

DIMLINEAR. The DIMLINEAR command creates a linear dimension between any two points. Any two points can be picked to define the linear dimension, or you can press Enter to select the object to be dimensioned.
Toolbar: *Choose Linear Dimension (Dimensioning)*
Screen: *Choose* DRAW DIM, Linear:

After starting the DIMLINEAR command, you are prompted for the following information:

- **First extension line origin or RETURN to select.** You can either select a point from which you want to dimension or press Enter to select a line, arc, circle or polyline segment. If you select a line or arc, AutoCAD dimensions from the endpoints of the object. If you select a circle, AutoCAD dimensions the diameter of the circle between two opposite quadrants of the circle.

- **Second extension line origin.** Select the point to which you want to dimension. This prompt only appears after you have selected a first extension line origin.

- **Dimension line location.** This enables you to dynamically locate the dimension line on the drawing. By default, AutoCAD creates either a horizontal or vertical dimension depending on where you pick. The following options are available to control the placement of the dimension line as well as to modify the dimension text:

  - **Text.** The Text option displays the Edit MText dialog box, which enables you to add to or override the default dimension text. The value of the dimension text is denoted by <>. AutoCAD replaces <> with the value of the dimension.

  - **Angle.** The Angle option enables you to change the rotation angle of the text. You can specify the angle by either typing in a value or picking two points.

  - **Horizontal.** This option forces a horizontal dimension to be created.

  - **Vertical.** This option forces a vertical dimension to be created.

  - **Rotated.** The Rotate option enables you to specify a rotation angle for the dimension line. The value of the dimension is

14

measured between the two points at the specified angle. You can specify the rotation angle by either typing in a value or picking two points.

> When you press Enter to select an object in response to the first dimension prompt, AutoCAD places the first extension line at the end point closest to the point you selected.

When adding dimensions in the Quick Tour exercise, you were instructed to turn on the Endpoint snap each time you picked an endpoint. Dimensioning is the perfect application for running object snaps, because you will frequently be picking points for the dimensions. With the running object snap on, you can complete the dimensioning of your drawing more efficiently.

In the next exercise, you create and add a few dimensions to a drawing for a bracket using the DIMLINEAR command. As you place the dimensions, you take advantage of the object selection capability and simply pick the line segment to be dimensioned. You also turn on the Endpoint running object snap and leave it on through the remainder of this chapter to illustrate the convenience of this feature when adding dimensions.

Creating and Dimensioning a Bracket

Begin a new drawing named DIMBRACK using the default ACAD drawing as the prototype. Then create the layers BRACKET and DIMS. Set the layer colors to your liking and set the BRACKET layer current. Set the snap to .1 and turn it on.

Command: *Choose Polyline (Draw, Polyline)*	Issues the PLINE command
From point: **6,1.5** (Enter)	Begins the polyline
Arc/Close/Halfwidth/Length/Undo/ Width/<Endpoint of line>: **@0,6** (Enter)	Places the next point
<Endpoint of line>: **@6,0** (Enter)	Places the next point
<Endpoint of line>: **@0,-1.5** (Enter)	Places the next point
<Endpoint of line>: **@-4.5,0** (Enter)	Places the next point
<Endpoint of line>: **@0,-4.5** (Enter)	Places the next point

`<Endpoint of line>:` **C** (Enter)	Closes the polyline
Command: *From the* Layer Control *drop-down list, choose* DIMS	Sets the layer DIMS current
Command: *Choose Running Object Snap (Standard Toolbar, Object Snap), choose* **E**ndpoint, *then choose* OK	Sets Endpoint to be the running object snap
Command: *Choose Linear Dimension (Dimensioning)*	Issues the DIMLINEAR command
`First extension line origin or RETURN to select:` (Enter)	Enables you to pick the object to be dimensioned
`Select object to dimension:` *Pick* ① *(see fig. 14.5)*	Places a dynamic dimension on the crosshair for placement
`Dimension line location (Text/ Angle/Horizontal/Vertical/Rotated):` *Pick* ②	Positions the horizontal dimension
Command: (Enter)	Repeats the DIMLINEAR command
`First extension line origin or RETURN to select:` *Pick* ③	Picks the first point for the dimension
`Second extension line origin:` *Pick* ④	Picks the second point to define the dimension, places a dynamic dimension on the crosshair for placement
`Dimension line location (Text/ Angle/Horizontal/Vertical/ Rotated):` *Pick* ⑤	Positions the vertical dimension
Command: *Choose Save (Standard Toolbar)*	Saves the drawing

14

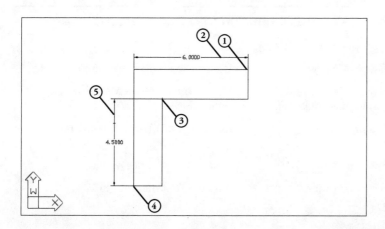

Figure 14.5

Linear dimensions on the bracket.

By using the Linear Dimensioning tool, you are able to create both horizontal and vertical dimensions.

Creating an Aligned Dimension

Of course, not all dimensions are horizontal or vertical. Some are parallel to or aligned with the object at an angle. The DIMLINEAR command enables you to rotate the dimension line, but it involves defining the rotation angle by either typing the angle or picking two points to define the angle. AutoCAD provides a shortcut for creating aligned dimensions with the DIMALIGN command.

DIMALIGN. Similar in capability to the Linear dimension, the DIMALIGN command enables you to create an aligned dimension for a selected object. You can opt to press Enter to select an individual object or pick two points.
Toolbar: *Choose Aligned Dimension (Dimensioning)*
Screen: *Choose DRAW DIM, Aligned:*

In the following exercise, you add a chamfer to the corner of the bracket then dimension the object using the Aligned Dimension tool. To demonstrate the fact that a dimension is recognized as a single object, you erase the existing 6.0000 horizontal dimension, then add a new horizontal dimension. Later in this chapter, you learn how to edit dimensions using grips, which enables you to edit dimensions and avoid erasing an existing dimension.

Adding an Aligned Dimension to a Chamfered Corner

Continue from the previous exercise.

Command: *Choose Erase (Modify)*	Issues the ERASE command
Select objects: *Pick the existing 6.0000 horizontal dimension, then* (Enter)	Erases the all elements of the selected dimension
Command: *Choose Chamfer (Modify, Feature)*	Issues the CHAMFER command
<Select first line>: **D** (Enter)	Issues the Distance option
Enter first chamfer distance <0.0000>: **1** (Enter)	Sets the first distance to 1"

Enter second chamfer distance <1.0000>: (Enter)	Accepts the default of 1" for the second distance
Command: (Enter)	Repeats the CHAMFER command
<Select first line>: *Pick* ① *then* ② *(see fig. 14.6)*	Chamfers the selected corner
Command: *Choose Aligned Dimension (Dimensioning)*	Issues the DIMALIGN command
First extension line origin or RETURN to select: (Enter)	Enables you to select the object to be dimensioned
Select object to dimension: *Pick* ③	Places a dynamic dimension on the crosshair for placement
Dimension line location (Text/ Angle): *Pick* ④	Positions the aligned dimension
Command: (Enter)	Repeats the DIMALIGN command
First extension line origin or RETURN to select: (Enter)	Enables you to select the object to be dimensioned
Select object to dimension: *Pick* ②	Places a dynamic dimension on the crosshair for placement
Dimension line location (Text/ Angle): *Pick* ⑤	Positions the aligned dimension
Command: *Choose Redraw (Standard Toolbar, Redraw)*	Issues the REDRAW command
Command: *Choose Save (Standard Toolbar)*	Saves the drawing

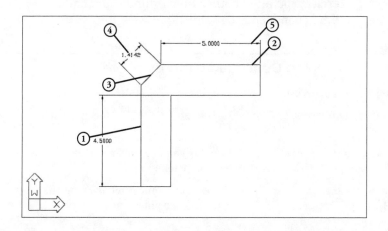

Figure 14.6

The aligned dimension on the chamfer.

14

The DIMALIGN command gives you a quick method for placing horizontal, vertical or aligned dimensions on existing objects.

Continued and Baseline Dimensions

AutoCAD enables you to add to existing linear dimensions by continuing a dimension from either the first or second extension line. AutoCAD automatically places the dimension line to line up with or offset from the existing dimension line. AutoCAD has two commands for continuing dimensions, the DIMCONTINUE and DIMBASELINE commands.

DIMCONTINUE. The DIMCONTINUE command continues a dimension from the last linear dimension placed. By default, the dimension is measured from the second extension line origin of the last linear dimension. You can override this by selecting an extension line from which to continue.
Toolbar: *Choose Continue Dimension (Dimensioning)*
Screen: *Choose* DRAW DIM, Continu:

DIMCONTINUE simply prompts you to select a second extension line origin. AutoCAD automatically creates a dimension measured from the second extension line of the last linear dimension and lines up the dimension lines. If you are not sure where the last linear dimension is, or you want to dimension from another location, you can press Enter and choose an extension line from which to measure.

In the following exercise, you add another linear dimension, and then place a continued dimension along the same dimension line.

Placing a Continued Dimension

Continue from the previous exercise.

Command: *Choose Linear Dimension (Dimensioning)*	Issues the DIMLINEAR command
First extension line origin or RETURN to select: **Enter**	Enables you to pick the object to be dimensioned
Select object to dimension: *Pick* ① *(see fig. 14.7)*	Places a dynamic dimension on the crosshair for placement

Dimension line location (Text/ Angle/Horizontal/Vertical/ Rotated): *Pick* ②	Positions the horizontal dimension
Command: *Choose Continue Dimension (Dimensioning)*	Issues the DIMCONTINUE command
Second extension line origin or RETURN to select: *Pick* ③	Places the continued horizontal dimension
Second extension line origin or RETURN to select: *Press Esc*	Ends DIMCONTINUE command
Command: *Choose Save (Standard Toolbar)*	Saves the drawing

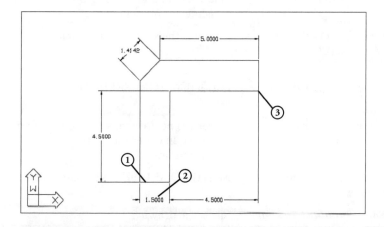

Figure 14.7

Placing a continued dimension.

The DIMBASELINE is similar to the DIMCONTINUE command in that it adds to an existing dimension. The DIMBASELINE command, however, creates a dimension by measuring the distance from the first extension line origin of an existing dimension to a selected point. AutoCAD automatically stacks the dimensions so that each successive dimension is parallel to the first one.

14

DIMBASELINE. The DIMBASELINE command enables you to pick an existing dimension, then pick the next point to be dimensioned. The resulting dimension is parallel to the selected dimension line and shares the first extension line.
Toolbar: *Choose Baseline Dimension (Dimensioning)*
Screen: *Choose DRAW DIM, Baselin:*

In the following exercise, you place another linear dimension and add a baseline dimension to it.

Placing a Baseline Dimension

Continue from the previous exercise.

Command: *Choose Aligned Dimension (Dimensioning)*	Issues the DIMLINEAR command
First extension line origin or RETURN to select: **(Enter)**	Enables you to pick the object to be dimensioned
Select object to dimension: *Pick ① (see fig. 14.8)*	Places a dynamic dimension on the crosshair for placement
Dimension line location (Text/ Angle/Horizontal/Vertical/ Rotated): *Pick ②*	Positions the vertical dimension
Command: *Choose Baseline Dimension (Dimensioning)*	Issues the DIMBASELINE command
Second extension line origin or RETURN to select: *Pick ③*	Places the next dimension from the first extension line, parallel to the first dimension line
Second extension line origin or RETURN to select: *Press Esc*	Ends the DIMBASELINE command
Command: *Choose Save (Standard Toolbar)*	Saves the drawing

Figure 14.8

Placing a baseline dimension.

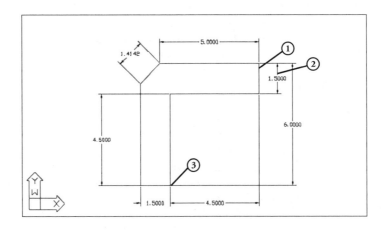

TIP

> Continued and baseline dimensions can be added to any existing
> dimension. If the result is not what you expected, erase the errant
> dimension. Then choose the desired dimensioning command again,
> press Enter, and pick the dimension to be continued from or from
> which the baseline dimension is to be added.

As you can see from the previous few exercises, the process of dimensioning a drawing is relatively simple once you understand what AutoCAD is looking for in the prompts.

So far, you have been placing linear dimensions. Next, you will take a look at some of the other types of dimensions.

Angular and Radial Dimensions

From the linear dimensions, you now move into dimensions for angles, circles, and arcs. Angular dimensions are frequently required for drawings with non-orthogonal line work, such as a piping drawing to indicate the angle for a swivel or adjustable fitting, or in an architectural construction drawing to indicate the angle of a wall. Radial and diameter dimensions indicate the radius or diameter of arcs and circles, such as those found on a shop drawing.

Angular Dimensions

One of the more dynamic dimensioning routines is that of angular dimensioning. As you have seen in the previous exercises while placing linear and aligned dimensions, you see the dimension geometry as you dynamically drag the dimension line to the desired position. When placing an angular dimension, AutoCAD dynamically displays the angle between the lines based upon the current position of the cursor.

14

> **DIMANGULAR.** The DIMANGULAR command enables you to
> dimension the angle between any two lines. Angular dimensioning
> requires the selection of two lines that define the angle to be dimensioned.
> Toolbar: *Choose Dimensioning, Angular Dimension*
> Screen: *Choose DRAW DIM, Angular:*

In the following exercise, you create an angular dimension for the chamfer. At the end of the exercise, you add fillets to all the corners of the polyline object in preparation for learning more about radial dimensioning.

Adding the Angular Dimension and a Fillet

Continue from the previous exercise.

Command: *Choose Angular Dimension (Dimensioning)*	Issues the DIMANGULAR command
Select arc, circle, line, or RETURN: *Pick ① (see fig. 14.9)*	Establishes the first line for the angular dimension
Second line: *Pick ②*	Establishes the second line, which defines the angle and places a dynamic dimension on the cursor

Move the crosshairs away from the two lines to see the dynamic positioning. Continue to move your cursor in a circle around the lines to see how the angular dimension is updated based upon your current cursor location.

Dimension arc line location (Text/Angle): *Pick ③*	Places the angular dimension
Command: *Choose Fillet (Modify, Feature)*	Issues the FILLET command
<Select first object>: **R** (Enter)	Issues the Radius option
Enter fillet radius <0.000>: **.2** (Enter)	Sets the radius to .2"
Command: (Enter)	Repeats the FILLET command
Polyline/Radius/Trim/ <Select first object>: **P** (Enter)	Specifies the Polyline option
Select 2D polyline: *Pick ④*	Applies the fillet to the polyline
Command: (Enter)	Repeats the FILLET command
Polyline/Radius/Trim/ <Select first object>: **R** (Enter)	Issues the Radius option
Enter fillet radius <0.000>: **1.25** (Enter)	Sets the radius to 1.25"

Command: (Enter)	Repeats the FILLET command
Polyline/Radius/Trim/ <Select first object>: *Pick ④ and ⑤*	Applies the fillet to the polyline
Command: *Choose Save (Standard Toolbar)*	Saves the drawing

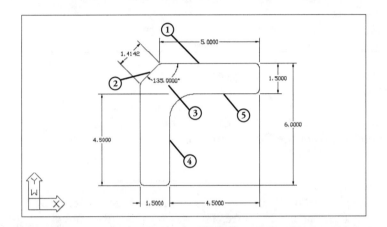

Figure 14.9

*The final position
for the dynamic
angular dimension.*

Dimensioning Diameters and Radii

Objects such as circles, arcs, and fillets are dimensioned using the
DIMRADIUS or DIMDIAMETER commands. Like all of the dimensioning
commands, these two commands enable you to dynamically position the
final dimension.

DIMRADIUS. The DIMRADIUS command returns the radius value
of the selected circle or arc. The arc can be a separate object or part
of a polyline such as a fillet. The radius dimension can be positioned
anywhere about the radius of the defined arc or the perimeter of a
circle.

Toolbar: *Choose Radius Dimension (Dimensioning, Radial
           Dimension)*

Screen: *Choose DRAW DIM, Radius:*

14

DIMDIAMETER. The DIMDIAMETER command returns the diameter value for the circle or arc selected. The length of the diameter dimension line has a default value but can be customized using the dimension style features.

Toolbar: *Choose Diameter Dimension (Dimensioning, Radial Dimension)*

Screen: *Choose* DRAW DIM, Diametr:

A center mark, by default, is simply two lines that cross at the center of the arc or circle selected for a radial or diameter dimension. The dimension line then extends from the center mark to the arrowhead. Center marks can be placed with the DIMCENTER command. The center mark geometry is defined from the Dimension Styles dialog box, which is covered in Chapter 15, "Adding Style to Dimensions."

DIMCENTER. The DIMCENTER command places a center mark at the center of the selected circle or arc. The size of the center mark has a default size but can be changed using the dimension style features.

Toolbar: *Choose Center Mark (Dimensioning)*

Screen: *Choose* DRAW DIM, Center:

In the following exercise, you add several holes to the bracket then dimension them. At the end of the exercise, you add a center mark to the center of the fillet arc.

Dimensioning the Fillet and Holes of the Bracket

Continue from the previous exercise. Before beginning, set the BRACKET layer current.

Command: *Choose Circle Center Radius (Draw, Circle)*

Issues the CIRCLE command

<Center point>: *Using the From and Midpoint object snaps, pick* ① *(see fig. 14.10)*

Establishes the point from which to offset the circle center point

`<Offset>: @1<90` (Enter)	Places the center of the circle
`Diameter/<Radius>: .3` (Enter)	Draws the circle at ②
Command: *Choose Copy Object (Modify, Copy)*	Issues the COPY command
`Select objects: L` (Enter)	Selects the last object
`Select objects:` (Enter)	Ends object selection
`<Base point or displacement>/` `Multiple: M` (Enter)	Specifies the Multiple option
`Base point:` *Pick* ②	Specifies the base point
Copy the circle to the points `@0,2`, `@2.25,4.25`, *and* `@4.25,4.25`	Copies the circles to ③, ④, and ⑤
Set the DIMS layer current	
Command: *Choose Radius Dimension (Dimensioning, Radial Dimension)*	Issues the DIMRADIUS command
`Select arc or circle:` *Pick* ⑥	Places a dynamic radial dimension on the cursor

Slowly move your cursor around the outside of the fillet to see the dynamic dragging of the radius dimension. You will see the same feature in the following diameter dimension.

`Dimension line location` `(Text/Angle):` *Pick* ⑦	Positions the radius dimension
Command: *Choose Diameter Dimension (Dimensioning, Radial Dimension)*	Issues the DIMDIAMETER command
`Select arc or circle:` *Pick* ②	Places a dynamic diameter dimension on the cursor
Place the dimension as shown in figure 14.10	Positions the diameter dimension
Command: *Choose Center Mark (Dimensioning)*	Issues the DIMCENTER command
`Select arc or circle:` *Pick* ⑥	Places a center mark at the center of the arc
Command: *Choose Redraw (Standard Toolbar, Redraw)*	Refreshes the display
Command: *Choose Save (Standard Toolbar)*	Saves the drawing

14

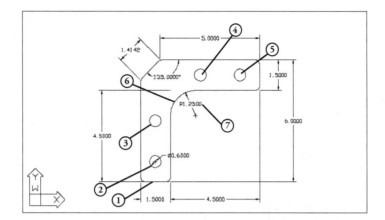

The Dimension Leader Line

In shop drawings or working drawings, there often is a need to add a
callout or note referring to the object being dimensioned. For this,
AutoCAD provides the LEADER command, which enables you to pick the
start of the leader (where the arrowhead is located) and then pick points
for the leader line.

> **LEADER.** The LEADER command enables you to place a leader
> object on the drawing with separate annotation text. The LEADER
> command provides several options for annotation and the type of
> leader line to be created.
> Toolbar: *Choose Leader (Dimensioning)*
> Screen: *Choose DRAW DIM, Leader:*

After you draw the leader line, you press Enter and add the desired
annotation. As you place the leader line points, you are presented with a
few options that define the way the annotation will be added to the
drawing. Those options are explained in the following list:

● **Format.** The Format option refers to the format of the leader line.
You can choose to have straight line segments or have a spline fit to

each point picked for the leader. You also can choose to have an arrowhead at the first point (the default), or you can opt to have no arrowhead.

- **Annotation.** Once the line has been started, the Annotation option provides several additional options with which to annotate the feature. For the leader text, you can place a geometric tolerance symbol, copy an existing object, insert a block, or add multiple lines of text using the Edit MText dialog box. By default, you simply enter the desired annotation when finished picking points for the leader line.

- **Undo.** This common option enables you to undo the last point picked when creating the leader line or spline. The leader can be undone all the way back to where the first point was picked when placing the arrowhead.

In the following exercise, you add a leader to specify the typical radius for the rounded corners.

Single and Multiple Lines of Text for Leaders

Continue from the previous exercise.

Command: *Choose Leader (Dimensioning)*	Issues the LEADER command
From point: *Using the Nearest object, pick* ① *(see fig. 14.11)*	Places the arrowhead of the leader
To point: *Pick* ② (Enter)	Positions the next point of the leader line
Annotation (or RETURN for options): **R 0.2 (TYP.)** (Enter)	Enters the first line of the annotation
Mtext: (Enter)	Places the lines of annotation centered at the end of the leader line
Command: *Choose Save (Standard Toolbar)*	Saves the drawing

14

Figure 14.11

*The dimension
leader line
locations.*

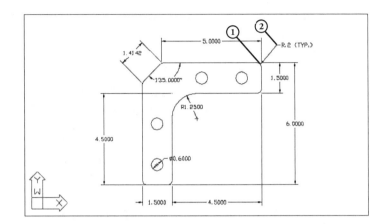

Editing Dimension Locations Using Grips

As you continue to add dimensions to a drawing, there are times when it becomes necessary to relocate a dimension for the purpose of clarity or interference. This is easily done using a dimension's grips. A dimension has grips located at the endpoints of the dimension line, at the insertion point of the dimension text, and at the *defpoints* of the dimension

When you create a dimension, AutoCAD places a point at origins of the extension lines (or the ends of the dimension line for radial dimensions). These points are called the definition points, or *defpoints*, of the dimensions.

TIP

You can use the NODE object snap to snap to a defpoint location.

The defpoints serve a special purpose in dimensions in that they determine the value of the dimension text. AutoCAD measures the distance between the defpoints and returns that value as the dimension text. If you move a defpoint, the dimension text changes. This is commonly referred to as "associativity" and the dimensions placed are called associative dimensions.

NOTE

Using the EXPLODE command on a dimension object separates the dimension into lines, arcs, and text, and all associativity is lost. Leader objects have no associativity with their annotation.

The defpoints have a separate DEFPOINTS layer. The first time you issue a dimensioning command in a drawing, AutoCAD creates a layer called DEFPOINTS and places all the defpoints on it. The DEFPOINTS layer is unique in that it is never plotted. AutoCAD simply ignores all information on the DEFPOINTS layer when plotting.

> Since the DEFPOINTS layer is never plotted, you can use it as a scratch layer. Things such as construction lines, notes, redlining, and floating viewports typically are placed on the DEFPOINTS layer so that they are visible when drawing, but do not plot.

TIP

Each of the grips positions on a dimension serve a unique purpose. Typically, only the STRETCH mode of grip editing is used when editing dimensions because it enables you to move the individual parts of the dimension without affecting the overall dimension. The following list addresses the three different dimension grips and describes how editing these grips changes the dimension:

- **Defpoint grips.** When a defpoint grip is moved using the STRETCH mode, the dimension automatically updates with new dimension text. The new dimension is the distance between the two defpoints.

- **Dimension line grips.** These grips relocate the position of the dimension line. The STRETCH grip mode enables you to reposition the dimension line to a location parallel to the current location, regardless of the current ORTHO setting.

- **Dimension text grip.** When the dimension text is repositioned, the dimension line maintains an axis through the center of the dimension text and moves accordingly.

The exercise that follows takes you through several dimension edits using grips to familiarize you with the relative ease of editing dimensions. You might have noticed that some of dimensions are poorly positioned. You will fix these using grips.

14

Using Grips to Edit Dimension Locations

Continue from the previous exercise.

Command: *Choose Running Object Snap (Standard Toolbar, Object Snap), choose **N**ode, then choose OK*	Sets a running Node object snap

continues

Command: *Select the diameter dimension*	Displays the dimension grips
Command: *Pick the dimension text grip*	Makes the grip hot
<Stretch to point>: *Pick the dimension text grip and move it to the location shown in figure 14.12*	Moves the dimension text and the leader
Command: *Pick the left 4.5 dimension*	Displays the dimension grips
Command: *Pick the top defpoint grip*	Makes the grip hot
<Stretch to point>: *Pick ①* (see fig. 14.12)	Moves the extension line to ① and updates the dimension text
Command: *Pick the bottom defpoint grip*	Makes the grip hot
<Stretch to point>: *Pick ②*	Moves the extension line to ②
Command: *Choose Running Object Snap (Standard Toolbar, Object Snap), choose C**l**ear All, and then choose OK*	Clears the running object snap
Command: *Choose Save (Standard Toolbar)*	Saves the drawing

Figure 14.12

New dimension locations after using grips.

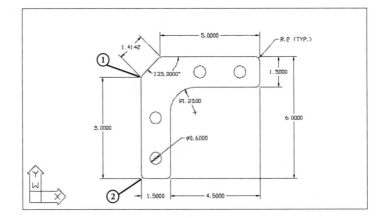

Editing Dimensioned Objects

Another consideration regarding dimensioned drawing, in addition to the issue of moving the dimension, is the dimensioning edits required if the design of the object is modified. Because dimensions are associative, it is important that the defpoints be included when editing the object, just as they are when using grips.

In the following exercise, you use STRETCH to edit the lengths of the legs of the bracket then edit a circle and the diameter dimension.

The Power of Associative Dimensions When Editing the Object

Continue from the previous exercise.

Command: *Choose Stretch (Modify, Resize)*	Issues the STRETCH command
First corner: *Pick* ①, *then* ② *(see fig. 14.13)* (Enter)	Identifies the selection set

Notice that the crossing window encompassed all of the defpoints associated with area to stretch.

Base point: **1.5,0** (Enter)	Specifies a displacement
Second point of displacement: (Enter)	Stretches the objects 1.5" and updates the dimensions
Command: *Choose Redraw (Standard Toolbar, Redraw)*	Refreshes the display
Command: *Choose Save (Standard Toolbar)*	Saves the drawing

Your drawing now should look like figure 14.14.

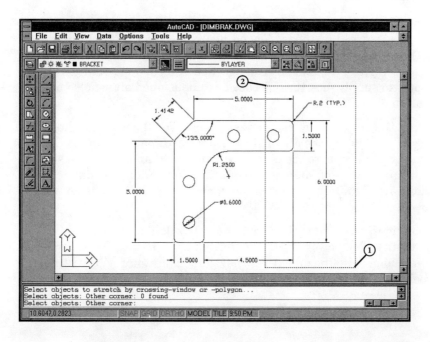

Figure 14.13

Stretching the bracket.

14

Figure 14.14

The completed bracket.

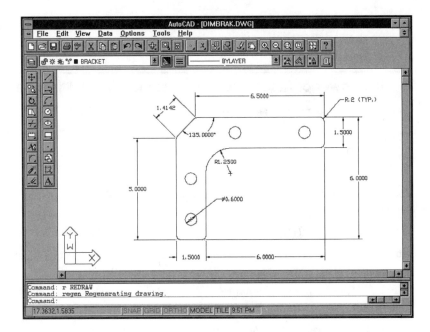

Summary

The AutoCAD dimensioning tools enable you to add dimensions to your drawing using several methods, depending upon the objects to be dimensioned. The DIMLINEAR command takes any two points and returns a horizontal or vertical dimension. You also had several opportunities in this chapter to simply pick the object to be dimensioned after pressing the Enter button or "RETURN to select."

Throughout the entire dimensioning experience, you'll encounter the dynamics of positioning the dimension—from the dimension line for linear and aligned dimensions, to the dynamically updated angular dimension, to the rotating dimension line and text position for radius and diameter dimensions. In virtually every situation, you can see the dimension prior to confirming it's location.

Dimensioning in a vacuum is fine, but changes will always be a part of drawing reality. The power of editing dimensions with grips was displayed as you were able to define an entirely new dimension simply by editing the defpoint grip position. When the drawing gets too cluttered, you can use a grip to position the dimension line and dimension text to a more readable location. You also experienced the way in which an associative dimension automatically updates when the object is edited or stretched.

In Chapter 15, you take your current understanding of dimensioning to the next level as you learn more about dimension styles.

Related Topics

- Drawing a circle—Chapter 5, "The Basic Drawing Commands"
- Editing with grips—Chapter 8, "Editing with Grips"
- Creating chamfers and fillets—Chapter 12, "Constructive Editing"
- Dimension styles—Chapter 15, "Adding Style to Dimensions"

14

Chapter Snapshot

Now that you're familiar with the dimensioning commands, you are ready to learn
about how to control the appearance of
dimensions. This chapter shows how you
can save dimension settings in a dimension
style.

This chapter explores the following:

● How to set up dimension styles

● How to use the Dimension Styles
   dialog box

● How to edit dimension text

15

Adding Style to Dimensions

AutoCAD Release 13 makes dimensioning chores more bearable by letting you easily create dimensions. When you create a dimension, its look is determined by the current dimension settings in the drawing.

In this chapter, you explore how to control the appearance of dimensions by using dimension styles. By using dimension styles, AutoCAD helps you adhere to nearly any dimensioning standard. AutoCAD can contain as many dimension styles you need to adhere to those standards.

Dimension styles, put simply, are named collections of dimension settings. The concept of dimension styles is similar to when you set up text styles in Chapter 11, "Text." Back then, you decided how your text would look, chose the settings for that look, and saved it in a text style. The process of setting up a dimension style is the same—you select the settings for a dimension style, then save those options in a dimension style.

The following Quick Tour exercise introduces you to some of the concepts involved in creating and modifying dimension styles.

The Quick Tour

Start with a new drawing named MECHDIM using the default ACAD.DWG prototype drawing. Create the layers OBJ and DIM and set OBJ as the current layer. Set a snap spacing of 0.25 and set the grid spacing to 1.00.

Command: *Choose Polyline (Draw, Polyline)*	Issues the PLINE command
Draw a polyline from the point **6,1** *to* **@3.5<0**, *to* **@3,1.5** *to* **@3<90** *to* **@-3,1.5** *to* **@3.5<180** *then Close*	Draws the plate outline
Command: *Choose Circle Center Radius (Draw, Circle)*	Issues the CIRCLE command
Draw a circle centered at **11.5,4** *with a radius of* **.5**	Draws a hole in the plate
Command: *Choose* **D**ata, **T**ext Style	Issues STYLE command
Text style name (or ?) <STANDARD>: **ROMANS** (Enter)	Creates a new text style named ROMANS
New style. *In the Select Font File dialog box, select the file* ROMANS.SHX	Assigns the shape file ROMANS.SHX to the text style ROMANS
Height <0.0000>: (Enter)	Accepts the default text height
Width factor <1.0000>: (Enter)	Accepts the default width factor
Obliquing angle <0>: (Enter)	Accepts the default obliquing angle of 0
Backwards? <N> (Enter)	Accepts the text style to left-to-right
Upside-down? <N> (Enter)	Accepts the default
Vertical? <N> (Enter)	Accepts the default

ROMANS is now the current text style.

Command: *Set the layer* DIM *current*	
Command: *Choose* **T**ools, **T**oolbars, **D**imensioning	Displays the Dimensioning toolbar
Command: *Choose Aligned Dimension (Dimensioning)*	Issues DIMALIGNED command
First extension line origin or RETURN to select: (Enter)	Lets you choose a line to dimension

```
Select object to dimension: Pick ①     Selects line to dimension
(see fig. 15.1)
```

```
Dimension line location (Text/Angle):     Places the dimension line
Place the dimension as shown in figure 15.1
```

After using the default dimension settings, you can see how dimension styles can change the appearances of dimensions. The following steps make changes to the STANDARD dimension style.

Command: *Choose Dimension Styles (Dimensioning, Dimension Style)*	Issues the DDIM command
Choose **G**eometry	Displays Geometry dialog box
In the Arrowheads *area, select* OPEN *from the* 1s**t** *drop-down list*	Changes the arrowhead to OPEN
Choose OK	Returns to the Dimension Styles dialog box
Choose **F**ormat	Displays Format dialog box
In the Text *area, remove the* X *from the* **I**nside Horizontal *check box*	Sets the dimension text to align with the dimension line
Choose OK	Returns to the Dimension Styles dialog box
Choose **A**nnotation	Displays the Annotation dialog box
In the Text *area, select* ROMANS *from the* St**y**le *drop-down list*	Sets the STANDARD dimension style to use the text style ROMANS
In the Hei**gh**t *edit box, type* **.125**	
Choose **U**nits	Displays the Units dialog box
In the Dimension *area, select* 0.00 *from the* **P**recision *drop-down list*	Sets dimensions to be displayed to the second decimal place
In the Dimension, Zero Suppression *area, put an* X *in the* **L**eading *and* **T**railing *check boxes*	Sets dimensions to not display leading and trailing zeroes
Choose OK	Returns to Annotation dialog box
Choose OK	Returns to the Dimension Styles dialog box
Choose **S**ave	Saves the changes to the dimension style

continues

15

continued

In the Family *area, click on the* Dia**m**eter *radio button*	Lets you make changes to the Diameter dimension style family member
Choose **F**ormat	Displays the Format dialog box
Place an X *in the* **U**ser Defined *check box*	Sets dimensions to be placed by the user when using the DIMRADIAL command
Choose OK	Returns to Dimension Styles dialog box
Choose **S**ave	Saves changes to the dimension style NORMAL
Choose OK	Returns to the drawing editor
Command: *Choose Diameter Dimension (Dimensioning, Radial Dimension)*	Issues the DIMDIAMETER command
Select arc or circle: *Pick* ① *(see fig. 15.2)*	Selects the circle to dimension its diameter
Dimension line location (Text/Angle): *Place dimension as shown in figure 15.2*	Draws a dimension
Command: *Choose Linear Dimension (Dimensioning)*	Issues DIMLINEAR command
First extension line origin or RETURN to select: *Press* (Enter)	Lets you select a line to dimension
Select object to dimension: *Pick* ②	Selects top line of plate to dimension
Dimension line location (Text/Angle/ Horizontal/Vertical/Rotated): *Place the dimension as shown in figure 15.2*	Places the dimension
Command: *Choose* **S**ave *(Standard Toolbar)*	Saves the drawing

Notice that after you return to the drawing editor, your dimension style changes the dimension to suit what you just changed. Your drawing should now look like figure 15.2.

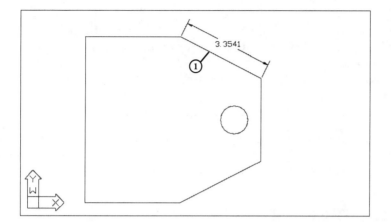

Figure 15.1

Dimensions drawn with the STANDARD style.

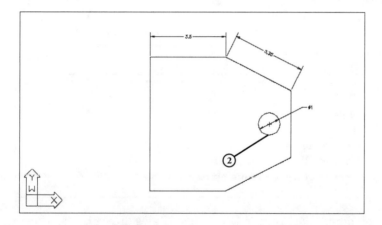

Figure 15.2

Dimensions drawn with the updated STANDARD dimension style.

Dimension Styles

The look of dimensions is controlled by a number of systems variables called the *dimension variables*. There are several dozen dimension variables to control such things as the type and size of the arrowheads, the upper and lower tolerance values, the style of the dimension text, and the orientation of the dimension text.

15

All dimension commands and dimension variables start with the letters DIM. The variable that assigns a color for dimension text is DIMCLRT, for example. For a complete list of the dimension variables and what they control, see Appendix E, "AutoCAD System Variables Table."

Setting each of these variables and keeping track of their values can be a rather tedious task. To help with this, AutoCAD provides dimension styles that enable you to store and update the dimension variable settings.

Creating a Dimension Style

When you create a dimension, the current dimension style is assigned to it. By default, AutoCAD starts you off with the STANDARD dimension style. You can modify STANDARD or create new dimension styles with the DDIM command.

DDIM. The DDIM command displays the Dimension Styles dialog box. You can create and change dimension styles to control the appearance of dimensions.
Toolbar: *Choose Dimension Styles (Dimensioning)*
Screen: *Choose DRAW DIM, DDim:*
Pull-down: *Choose **D**ata, **D**imension Style*

The DDIM command displays the Dimension Styles dialog box as shown in figure 15.3.

Figure 15.3

The Dimension Styles dialog box.

The Dimension Styles dialog box actually is a series of dialog boxes that enable you to easily create and edit dimension styles. The dialog box is divided into the five areas described in the following list:

- **Dimension Style.** This area enables you to create and restore dimension styles. The <u>C</u>urrent drop-down list shows all of the currently defined dimension styles. You set the current style by choosing one of the styles from the list. You can create a new dimension style based on the current dimension style by typing a name in the <u>N</u>ame edit box and choosing the <u>S</u>ave button. Choosing the <u>R</u>ename button renames the current dimension style with the name that appears in the <u>N</u>ame edit box.

- **Family.** This area enables you to set separate dimension settings for various types or *families* of dimensions. See the section "Dimension Style Families" later in this chapter for more on using families.

- **Geometry.** This button displays the Geometry dialog box, which enables you to control the look of the dimension. See the section "Geometry Settings" later in this chapter for more on using this dialog box.

- **Format.** This button displays the Format dialog box, which enables you to control the location and orientation of the dimension text. See the section "Format Settings" later in this chapter for more on using this dialog box.

- **Annotation.** This button displays the Annotation dialog box, which enables you to control such things as the dimension units, tolerances, and dimension text styles. See the section "Annotation Settings" later in this chapter for more on using this dialog box.

When you create a new dimension style, AutoCAD makes a copy of the existing dimension style and gives it a new name. When you make changes to the dimension style and save them, those changes are automatically applied to all the dimensions with that style. If you make changes to a dimension style and do not save the changes, only new dimensions show the changes. Existing dimensions are not updated until the dimension style is saved.

The following exercise instructs you to draw a simple mechanical plate, which you will dimension throughout this chapter. You will set up a dimension style named NORMAL and then save the drawing MECHPLT.DWG.

15

Drawing the MECHPLT Design

Start with a new drawing named MECHPLT using the default ACAD.DWG prototype drawing. Set a snap spacing of 0.25 and set the grid spacing to 1.00. Create the layers OBJECT and DIM. Set the layer OBJECT as the current layer. Assign the color red to the DIM layer.

Command: *Choose Polyline (Draw, Polyline)*	Issues the PLINE command
Draw a polyline from the point **3,3** *to* **@11.5<0**, *to* **@3<100**, *to* **12,7**, *to* **3,7** *then* **C**	Draws the outline of the plate
Command: *Choose Circle Center Radius (Draw, Circle)*	Issues CIRCLE command
Draw a circle with center at **7.5,5** *and a radius of* **1**	Draws a circle
Command: *Choose Line (Draw, Line)*	Issues LINE command
Draw a line from coordinates **4,3** *to coordinates* **4,7**	Draws two lines
Command: *Choose Line (Draw, Line)*	Issues LINE command
Draw another line from coordinates **11,3** *to coordinates* **11,7**	Draws another line segment
Command: *Choose Line (Draw, Line)*	Issues LINE command
Draw a line from coordinates **12,3** *to coordinates* **12,7**	Draws another line segment
Command: *Choose Dimension Styles (Dimensioning, Dimension Style)*	Displays the Dimension Styles dialog box
In the **N**ame *edit box, type* **NORMAL**, *then choose* **S**ave	Creates a new dimension style named NORMAL
Choose OK	Exits the Dimension Styles dialog box
Command: *Choose* **D**ata, **T**ext Style	Issues STYLE command
Text style name (or ?) <STANDARD>: **ROMANS** (Enter)	Creates a new text style named ROMANS
New style. *In the Select Font File dialog box, select the file* ROMANS.SHX	Assigns the shape file ROMANS.SHX to the text style ROMANS

`Height <0.0000>: ⟨Enter⟩`	Accepts the default text height
`Width factor <1.0000>: ⟨Enter⟩`	Accepts the default width factor
`Obliquing angle <0>: ⟨Enter⟩`	Accepts the default obliquing angle of 0
`Backwards? <N> ⟨Enter⟩`	Accepts the text style to left-to-right
`Upside-down? <N> ⟨Enter⟩`	Accepts the default
`Vertical? <N> ⟨Enter⟩`	Accepts the default

ROMANS is now the current text style.

`Command:` *Choose Save (Standard Toolbar)*   Saves the drawing

When you are done, your MECHPLT drawing should resemble figure 15.4.

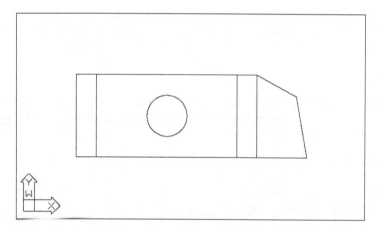

Figure 15.4
The MECHPLT design ready for dimensioning.

The following sections show you how to make changes to the settings to control how your dimensions look.

Geometry Settings

The Geometry dialog box (see fig. 15.5) enables you to control how the physical look of dimensions, the extension lines, dimension lines, center marks, center lines, and arrowheads appear.

15

Figure 15.5

*The Geometry
dialog box.*

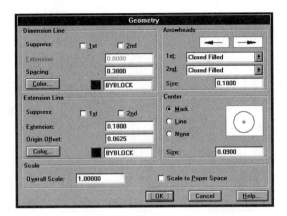

The Geometry dialog box is divided into five areas, Dimension Line, Extension Line, Arrowheads, Center, and Scale. Figure 15.6 gives you some examples of the settings you can control with the Geometry dialog box. The various areas of the Geometry dialog box are described in the following list:

- **Dimension Line.** The Dimension Line area enables you to change the appearance and location of the dimension lines. The Dimension Line area has the following options:

  - **Suppress.** The Suppress option enables you to turn off the first or second half of the dimension line. If you suppress the first half of the dimension line, the dimension line between the first extension line and the dimension text is not shown.

  - **Extension.** The Extension option controls how far an oblique arrowhead (or tick mark) extends past the extension. The distance is measured from the end of the oblique arrowhead perpendicular to the extension line. This option only is available when an oblique arrowhead is chosen in the Arrowheads section.

  - **Spacing.** The Spacing option enables you to control the space between baseline and continued dimensions.

  - **Color.** The Color option displays the Select Color dialog box from which you can assign a color to the dimension line. This is mainly for controlling the line weight of the dimension line when plotting. See Chapter 16, "Composing and Plotting a Drawing," for more on plotting and line weights.

- **Extension Line.** Similar to the Dimension Line area, the Extension Line area controls the look of the extension lines. The Extension Line area has the following options:

  - **Suppress.** The Suppress option enables you to turn off the first or second extension line. This option is useful when the dimension line extends to an existing object such as a wall or interior dimension.

  - **Extension.** The Extension option controls how far the extension line extends past the dimension line.

  - **Origin Offset.** The Origin Offset option enables you to control the small gap between the end of the object you are dimensioning and the start of the extension line.

  - **Color.** The Color option displays the Select Color dialog box from which you can assign a color to the extension line. This is mainly for controlling the line weight of the extension line when plotting. See Chapter 16, "Composing and Plotting a Drawing," for more on plotting and line weights.

- **Arrowheads.** The Arrowhead area enables you to control the type of arrowhead on the dimension. AutoCAD comes with eight predefined arrowheads (see fig. 15.7), or you can specify a block name to use for the arrowhead. See Chapter 13, "Blocks and Overlays," for more on creating blocks. You can set the type of arrowhead either by choosing the option from the drop-down list or by clicking on the arrowhead image tile until the desired arrowhead type is shown.

- **Center.** This area controls the look and size of center marks placed with the DIMCENTER, DIMDIAMETER, and DIMRADIUS commands. The Mark option places a mark with the specified size. The Line option places a mark as well as four lines extending past the edge of the circle or arc. Center marks or lines are not placed when the dimension text is on the inside of the arc or circle. Like the arrowheads, you can change the type of center mark either by selecting one of the options or by clicking on the image tile until the desired setting is shown.

- **Scale.** The Scale area sets the overall scale factor for all parts of a dimension. All of the size-related settings are multiplied by this scale factor. The Scale to Paper Space option enables you to adjust the scale factor for separate floating model space viewports. See Chapter 16, "Composing and Plotting a Drawing," for more on using this option.

15

Figure 15.6

Examples of geometry settings.

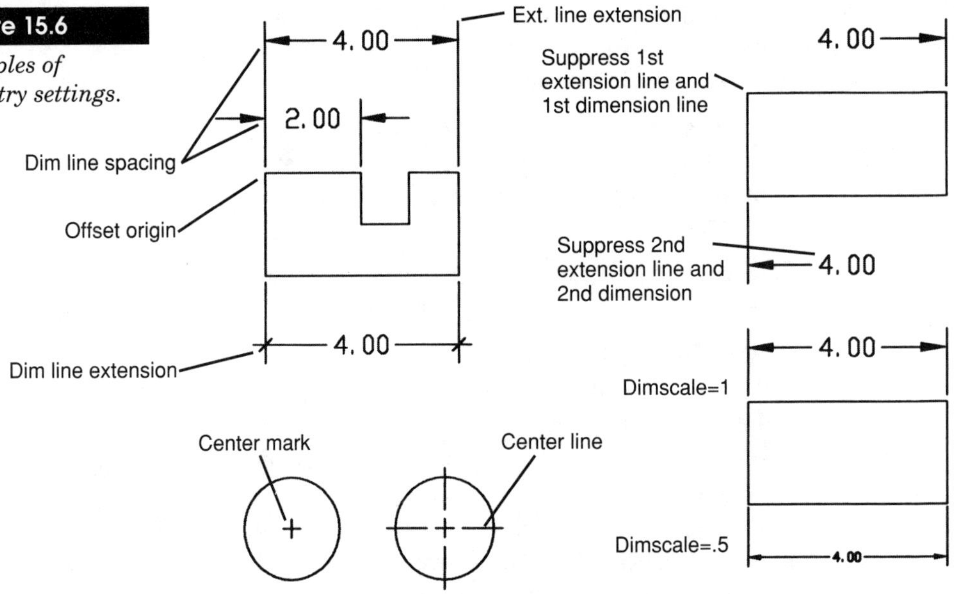

Ext. line extension

4.00

4.00

Suppress 1st extension line and 1st dimension line

2.00

Dim line spacing

Offset origin

Suppress 2nd extension line and 2nd dimension

4.00

Dim line extension

4.00

Center mark

Center line

Dimscale=1

4.00

Dimscale=.5

4.00

Figure 15.7

The predefined arrowheads.

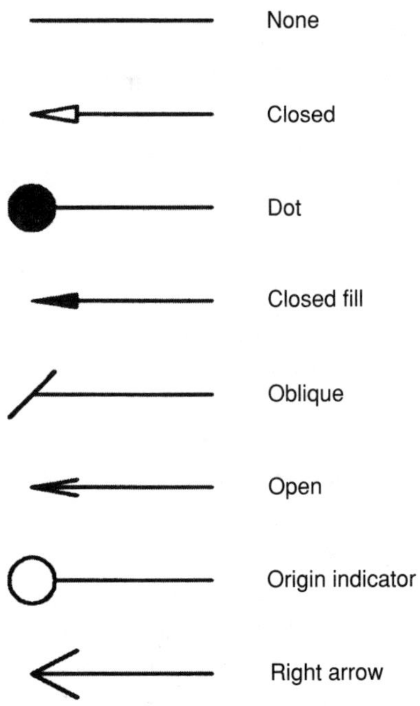

None

Closed

Dot

Closed fill

Oblique

Open

Origin indicator

Right arrow

The Overall Scale factor is stored in the DIMSCALE system variable. It is important because it enables you to adjust the size of your dimensions for plotting. The value of DIMSCALE typically is set to the plot scale factor. If you were plotting a drawing at 1/4"=1', for example, you would set the value of DIMSCALE to 48. See Chapter 4, "Preparing Your Drawing," for more information about determining the plot scale factor.

In the following exercise, you make some changes to the NORMAL dimension style geometry.

Changing the Geometry Settings

Continue from the previous exercise. Change the current layer to the DIM layer. This is the layer where you will place your dimensions.

Command: *Choose Dimension Styles* (*Dimensioning, Dimension Style*)	Issues the DDIM command
Choose **G**eometry	Displays the Geometry dialog box
In the Dimension Line *area, choose* **C**olor, *then select cyan (color 4) and choose* OK	Assigns the color cyan to dimension lines
In the Extension Line *area, choose* Colo**r**, *then select blue (color 5) and choose* OK	Assigns the color blue to extension lines
In the Arrowheads *area, click on the left arrowhead image tile until the* OPEN *arrowhead is current*	Sets the arrowhead to OPEN
In the Center *area, click in the* **L**ine *check box*	Specifies the Center Line option
Choose OK	Returns to Dimension Styles dialog box
Choose **S**ave *then* OK	Saves changes to NORMAL dimension style and ends the DDIM command
Command: *Choose Center Mark* (*Dimensioning, Center Mark*)	Issues DIMCENTER command
Select arc or circle: *Pick* ① (*see fig. 15.8*)	Draws a center mark on the circle
Command: *Choose Linear Dimension* (*Dimensioning*)	Issues DIMLINEAR command

continues

continued

`First extension line origin or` `RETURN to select:` **(Enter)**	Lets you select a line to dimension
`Select object to dimension:` *Pick* ②	Selects the rectangle side to dimension
`Dimension line location (Text/Angle/` `Horizontal/Vertical/Rotated):` *Place* *the dimension line as shown in figure 15.8*	Places the dimension line
`Command:` *Choose Save (Standard Toolbar)*	Saves the drawing

Your drawing should resemble figure 15.8.

Figure 15.8

Using the Geometry Options in the MECHPLT drawing.

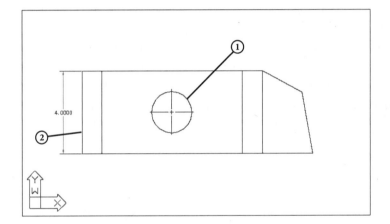

Format Settings

The Format button on the Dimension Styles dialog box displays the Format dialog box (see fig. 15.9). This dialog box enables you to control the placement of the dimension line and the dimension text.

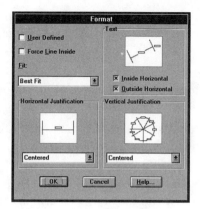

Figure 15.9

The Format dialog box.

The Format dialog box has a number of settings that enable you to control where the dimension lines and text are placed. Figure 15.10 shows examples of some of the settings controlled with this dialog box. The Format dialog box has the following options:

- **User Defined.** This option enables you to control the placement of the dimension text. By default, the dimension text is centered on the dimension line. If **U**ser Defined is turned on, you can adjust the location of the text as you are placing the dimension line.

- **Force Line Inside.** If the dimension text is located outside of the dimension lines, turning on this option causes the dimension line to be placed between the extension lines.

- **Fit.** This option controls where the dimension text and arrows are placed on small dimensions. Examples of the various fit options are shown in figure 15.10. You have the following options from which to choose:

  - **Text and Arrows.** The Text and Arrows option forces both the text and arrowheads outside the extension lines if there is not enough room. Otherwise, it places both the text and arrowheads inside the extension lines.

  - **Text Only.** If space is available, AutoCAD places both the text and the arrowheads between the extension lines. If there is room for the text, the text is placed inside the extension lines and the arrowheads go outside. If there is not enough space for the text, both the text and the arrowheads are placed outside the extension lines.

15

- **Arrows Only.** This is similar to the Text Only option except that, when there is enough space, AutoCAD places the arrowheads inside the extension lines and places the text outside.

- **Best Fit.** By default, AutoCAD uses the Best Fit option. AutoCAD fits whatever it can between the extension lines and puts everything else outside the extension lines

- **Leader.** When there is no space for the text, AutoCAD places the text above the dimension line and creates a leader line from the text to the dimension line.

- **Text.** This area has two options that control the alignment of the text with the dimension line. If the Inside Horizontal is turned on, all dimension text that lies inside the dimension lines will be horizontal, otherwise, it is aligned with the dimension line. The Outside Horizontal option controls dimension text that lies outside the extension line.

- **Horizontal Justification.** This option controls the location of the dimension text between the extension lines. You can choose to have the text centered between the extension lines, justified on the first or second extension line, or placed above the first or second dimension line. If the User Defined setting is turned on, this setting is disabled.

- **Vertical Justification.** This controls the position of the dimension text with regard to the dimension line. You can choose between having the text centered on the dimension line, sit above the extension line, sit outside the dimension line, or conform to the Japanese Industrial Standard (JIS).

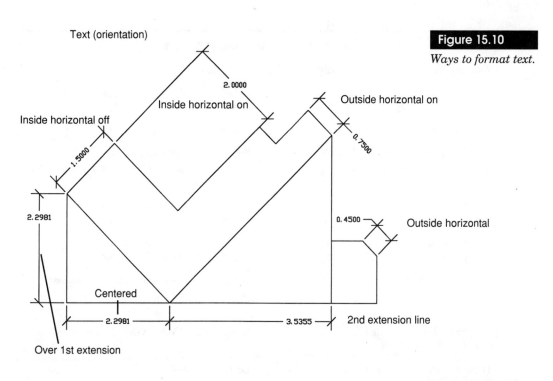

Text (orientation)

Figure 15.10

Ways to format text.

2.0000

Inside horizontal on

Outside horizontal on

Inside horizontal off

0.7500

1.5000

2.2981

0.4500

Outside horizontal

Centered

2.2981

3.5355

2nd extension line

Over 1st extension

Figure 15.11

The Fit options.

.75

.75

.75

Text and Arrows

Text Only

Leader

.75

.75

Arrows Only

Best Fit

In the following exercise, you change some of the format settings and update the dimensions.

15

Using the Format Dialog Box

Continue the MECHPLT drawing from the last exercise.

Command: *Choose Dimension Styles (Dimensioning, Dimension Style)*	Issues the DDIM command
Choose the **F**ormat *button*	Displays Format dialog box
In the Text *area, place an* X *in the* **O**utside Horizontal *check box*	Sets text to be rotated along with dimension line when text is not inside the dimension
In the Text *area, remove the* X *from the* **I**nside Horizontal *check box*	Sets text not to be rotated when text is inside the dimension
Place an X *in the* Force **L**ine Inside *check box and choose* OK	Turns on the option and returns to the Dimension Styles dialog box.
Choose **S**ave, *then* OK	Saves changes to NORMAL dimension style, ends the DDIM command, and updates the dimensions
Command: *Choose Aligned Dimension (Dimensioning)*	Issues the DIMALIGNED command
First extension line origin or RETURN to select: (Enter)	Lets you select an object to dimension
Select object to dimension: *Pick* ① (see *fig. 15.12)*	Picks the line to dimension
Dimension line location (Text/Angle): *Place the dimension line as shown in figure 15.12*	Sets a location for the dimension
Command: *Choose Linear Dimension (Dimensioning)*	Issues the DIMLINEAR command
First extension line origin or RETURN to select: *Using the Endpoint object snap, pick* ②	Selects the first point of the dimension
Second extension line origin: *Using the Endpoint object snap, pick* ③	Selects the other point of dimension
Dimension line location (Text/Angle/ Horizontal/Vertical/Rotated): *Place the dimension as shown in figure 15.12*	Selects the location of the dimension line

Command: *Choose Save (Standard Toolbar)*   Saves the drawing

Notice how the other dimensions have changed to fit the new settings from the Format dialog box.

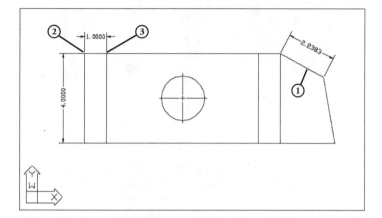

Figure 15.12

Formatting dimensions.

Although placing dimension text is extremely important to your drawing, you might need to change the way the text is shown. So far, for example, all of the dimensions you have placed used decimal units with four units of precision. You might need to show dimensions in feet and inches or convert the units to either inches or millimeters. The next section shows you how to control these settings with the Annotation settings.

Annotation Settings

The Annotation button on the Dimension Styles dialog box displays the Annotation dialog box as shown in figure 15.13. While the Format dialog box enables you to choose *where* the dimension line and text are placed, the Annotation dialog box controls *how* the dimension text is shown. This includes such things as the dimension text style, the type of units used, as well as tolerances and alternate units.

15

Figure 15.13

*The Annotation
dialog box.*

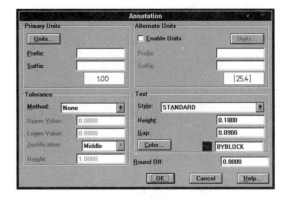

The Annotation dialog box is divided into the following four areas:

- **Primary Units.** This area contains options for controlling how the default dimension text is displayed. The **U**nits button displays the Primary Units dialog box (see fig. 15.14), from which you can set the type of units used for linear and angular dimensions. You also can set the precision of the units as well as the precision of the tolerances. The Primary Units dialog box also enables you to suppress the display of leading and trailing zeros. The **P**refix and **S**uffix options enable you to add text to the start or end of a dimension.

- **Alternate Units.** This area controls the display of alternate units in a dimension. You can, for example, use inches for the primary units but also have the dimensions display the value in millimeters. The U**n**its button displays the Alternate Units dialog box, which has the same options as the Primary Units dialog box. Alternate units are shown in square brackets [].

- **Tolerance.** Enables you to assign and display tolerance values. There are five methods of showing tolerances (see fig. 15.15). The **J**ustification options enable you to control the placement of the dimension text in relation to the tolerances. The He**i**ght option is a scale factor for determining the size of the dimension text. The height of the tolerance text is the height of the dimension text multiplied by the tolerance height scale factor.

- **Text.** This area enables you to control the size and style of the dimension text. The Sty**l**e drop-down list displays all of the currently defined text styles in the drawing. See Chapter 11, "Text," for more on creating text styles. The Heigh**t** option enables you to set the overall height of the dimension text. The **G**ap option controls the size of the break in the dimension line. The gap is the distance between the first break in the dimension line and the start of the dimension text. This value is ignored if the dimension text is placed above the dimension line or outside the extension lines.

● **Round Off.** This area enables you to specify how many decimal places to round dimensions to. If you specified a value of .25, for example, all dimensions would be rounded to the nearest .25 unit.

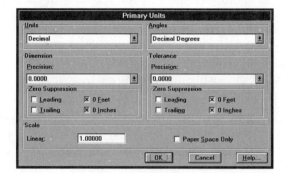

Figure 15.14

The Primary Units dialog box.

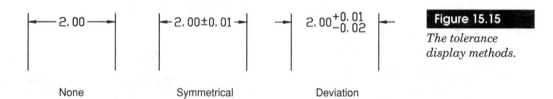

Figure 15.15

The tolerance display methods.

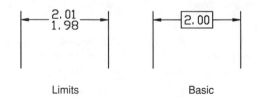

15

> When you set the Primary Units and the Alternate Units with the Annotation dialog box, you do not change the units of the drawing itself. The Annotations dialog box only affects how dimensions display the units.

The Linea**r** option in the Primary Units and Alternate Units dialog box is particularly useful for converting dimensions. If you create a drawing using inches, for example, but later need to dimension it in millimeters, you can change the linear scale factor to 25.4 (1"=25.4mm) and save the change to the dimension. All the dimensions are multiplied by the scale factor and show the metric dimension. You also can use the Paper **S**pace Only option to adjust dimension values when placing dimension in paper space. See Chapter 16, "Composing and Plotting a Drawing," for more information on using this option.

The following exercise walks you through the process of setting some of the annotation options. In the exercise, you assign a new text style to your dimensions and convert the drawing to show millimeters.

Annotating Dimensions

Continue from the previous exercise.

Command : *Choose Dimension Styles (Dimensioning, Dimension Style)*	Displays the Dimension Styles dialog box
Choose the **A**nnotation *button*	Displays Annotation dialog box
In the Text *area, select* ROMANS *from the* Sty**l**e *drop-down list*	Sets dimensions to use the text style ROMANS
In the Text *area, type* **.125** *in the* Heigh**t** *edit box*	Sets the dimension text height to 0.125 units
In the Primary Units area, choose the **U**nits *button*	Displays the Primary Units dialog box
In the Dimension area, select 0.00 *from the* **P**recision *drop-down list and choose* OK	Sets dimensions to display two decimal places and returns to the Annotation dialog box
Choose the OK *button*	Returns you to the Dimension Style dialog box

Choose **S**ave, *then* OK	Saves changes to NORMAL dimension style and ends the DDIM command

Notice how all of the dimensions drawn have changed to fit the new Annotation settings. In the next steps, you convert the dimensions to millimeters.

Command: *Choose Dimension Styles (Dimensioning, Dimension Style)*	Issues DDIM command
Choose the **A**nnotation *button*	Displays the Annotation dialog box
In the Primary Units *area, in the* **S**uffix *edit box, type* **mm**	Sets dimensions to be displayed with the label "mm"
In the Primary Units *area, choose the* **U**nits *button*	Displays the Primary Units dialog box
In the Scale *area, type* **25.4** *in the* Linea**r** *edit box, then choose* OK	Multiplies dimension values by 25.4, converting them into millimeters
Choose OK, *then* **S**ave, *then* OK	Saves changes to the NORMAL dimension style and returns to the drawing editor

Notice that the dimensions have changed to fit the dimension style settings. The dimensions are now labeled as millimeters and the numbers are converted to millimeter units.

Command: *Choose Undo (Standard Toolbar)*	Returns the dimensions to inches
Command: *Choose Save (Standard Toolbar)*	Saves the drawing

Your drawing should look like figure 15.16.

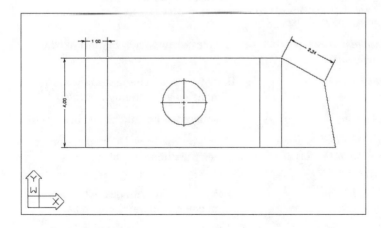

Figure 15.16

Using the Annotation dialog box.

15

Dimension Style Families

As you can see, you have a great deal of flexibility in controlling how dimensions are placed and displayed. So far, all of the changes made to the dimension style have been applied to all of the dimensions. There might be times, however, when you want to have one setting for one type of dimension and another setting for another type of dimension. You might want leader lines, for example, to use a different arrowhead than the other dimensions, or you might want to control the location of dimension text when placing radial dimensions. To address this problem, AutoCAD makes use of *dimension style families*.

Dimension style families, a new feature in AutoCAD Release 13, enable you to define variations on the dimension style for particular types of dimensions. The dimension family includes the base, or *parent*, dimension style and six dimension style family members—Linear, Radial, Angular, Diameter, Ordinate, and Leader. If you make a change to a family member style, only those types of dimensions are affected by the change. If the parent style had closed arrowheads, for example, and you assigned the Leader family to have a dot leader, only leader objects will use the dot arrowhead; the other types of dimensions will have closed arrowheads.

The following exercise shows you how to apply a dimension family override for the DIMDIAMETER command.

Setting and Using the Dimension Family Settings

Continue from the previous exercise.

Command: *Choose Dimension Styles (Dimensioning, Dimension Style)*	Displays Dimension Styles dialog box
Choose the Dia**m**eter *radio button*	Lets you make changes to the Diameter dimension style family member
Choose the **F**ormat *button*	Displays the Format dialog box
Put an X *in the* **U**ser Defined *check box, choose the* OK *button, then the* **S**ave *button*	Turns on the User Defined option and saves the dimension style
Click the L**e**ader *radio button*	Lets you make changes to the Leader dimension style family member
Choose the **G**eometry *button*	Displays the Geometry dialog box

In the Arrowheads *area, click on the left arrowhead image tile until the* DOT *arrowhead is current*	Sets leader dimensions to display the DOT arrowhead
Choose OK, *then* **S**ave, *then* OK	Saves changes to the dimension style NORMAL and returns to the drawing editor

Notice that there are no changes to the existing dimensions made. These dimensions were not created by the DIMDIAMETER and the DIMLEADER commands. The next steps instruct you to use the DIMDIAMETER and the DIMLEADER commands.

Command: *Choose Diameter Dimension (Dimensioning, Radial Dimension)*	Issues the DIMDIAMETER command
Select arc or circle: *Pick* ① *(see fig. 15.17)*	Selects the circle to dimension
Dimension line location (Text/Angle): *Place the dimension as shown in figure 15.17*	Places the dimension
Command: *Choose Leader (Dimensioning)*	Issues DIMLEADER command
From point: *Pick* ②	Selects the starting point of the leader at ②
To point: *Pick* ③	Sets the ending point of the leader at ③
To point (Format/Annotation/Undo) <Annotation>: (Enter)	Selects the Annotation option to enter text
Annotation (or RETURN for options): **Polish** (Enter)	Labels the leader with the text "Polish"
Mtext: (Enter)	Exits the DIMLEADER command
Command: *Choose Save (Standard Toolbar)*	Saves the drawing

Your drawing should now resemble figure 15.17.

Dimension style families give additional power to dimension styles. By automatically switching settings based on what dimensioning command you use, dimensioning becomes more automatic and easier.

15

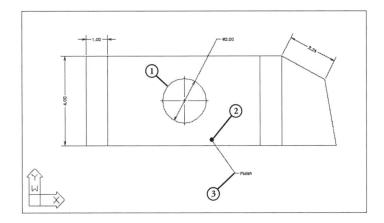

Figure 15.17

Drawing dimensions with dimension families.

Editing Dimension Text

After setting up your dimension styles, you create dimensions in your drawing. Somehow, after all of your effort to adhere to your dimension standards using dimension styles, the dimension still doesn't look quite right. Using the dimension editing commands, you can tweak your dimensions to fit your liking.

One way to edit dimension settings individually is with the DDMODIFY command. The DDMODIFY command enables you to override any setting as well as edit the dimension text. See Chapter 10, "Selecting and Editing Objects," for more on using the DDMODIFY command.

Another command that enables you to edit dimension text is the DIMTEDIT commands.

> **DIMTEDIT.** The DIMTEDIT (Dim Text Edit) command enables you to move, justify, and rotate dimension text.
> Toolbar: *Choose Home (Dimensioning, Align Dimension Text)*
> Screen: *Choose MOD DIM, DimTedit:*

The DIMTEDIT command has the following options:

- **Home.** This option restores dimension text to its original default position. Useful when you have moved dimension text and want it to return to the default position.

- **Angle.** This option enables you to specify a rotation angle for the dimension text.

- **Left.** This option left-justifies dimension text on the dimension line.

- **Right.** This option right-justifies dimension text on the dimension line.

In the following exercise, you use the DIMTEDIT and DDMODIFY commands to make minor changes to your dimensions.

Editing the Existing Dimensions

Continue from the previous exercise.

Command: *Choose Right (Dimensioning, Align Dimension Text)*	Issues DIMTEDIT command with the Right option
Select dimension: *Pick ① (see fig. 15.18)*	Selects a dimension to edit and right-justifies it on the dimension line
Command: *Choose Rotate (Dimensioning, Align Dimension Text)*	Issues DIMTEDIT command with the Right option
Select dimension: *Pick ②*	Selects a dimension to edit and right-justifies it on the dimension line
Enter text angle: **-90** (Enter)	Sets a rotation angle of -90 degrees
Command: *Choose Properties (Object Properties)*	Lets you select an object to change
Select objects: *Pick ③*	Selects a dimension to change
Select objects: (Enter)	Displays the Modify Dimension dialog box
Choose the **E**dit Contents *button*	Displays the Edit Mtext dialog box
In the text area, highlight the word Polish *and press the Delete key*	Deletes the contents of the dimension
In the text area, type **Cadmium Plate**	Labels the leader dimension with "Cadmium Plate"
Choose OK *twice*	Makes changes to the dimension and then returns to the drawing editor
Command: *Choose Save (Standard Toolbar)*	Saves the drawing

15

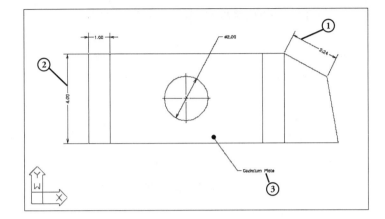

By using these commands and techniques, you can make modifications to your dimensions after they have been created. You also can make modifications by using dimension styles, but in some instances, you only want one dimension to be affected instead of all the dimensions. It's also unreasonable to set up a dimension style for just one dimension. The DIMTEDIT and DDMODIFY commands facilitate the process and save you unnecessary steps.

Summary

One of the best ways to make dimensioning easier is by using the dimension styles and the dimension editing commands. In this chapter, you learned how to set up dimension styles for your drawing standards. As you work with dimensions, you become more proficient with the dimensioning styles and editing commands. The more dimensioning you do, the more critical it becomes to use dimension styles and editing.

In the next chapter, you perform the final stage of your drawing—plotting. You will learn how to set up a drawing to get it ready to plot. You will find how easy it can be to make plotted drawing sheets in AutoCAD Release 13 using paper space and controlling layers.

Related Topics

- Dimension variables—Appendix E, "AutoCAD System Variables Table"

- Using the DDMODIFY command—Chapter 10, "Selecting and Editing Objects"

- Using text styles and editing text—Chapter 11, "Text"

- Dimensioning objects—Chapter 14, "Dimensioning"

15

Chapter Snapshot

This chapter covers two important features of a project, both of which fall under the heading of drawing presentation. Drawing composition and the ability to have the plot accurately reflect the information in the drawing is critical. In this chapter, you will learn about the following issues regarding composition and plotting:

- The relationship of a title block to paper space and what it can contain

- How to have multiple plot scales on the same drawing with floating model space viewports

- Viewport independent layer visibility

- Dimensioning text as it relates to multiple plot scales in the same drawing

- A full review of the Plot Configuration dialog box and some hints on maintaining consistent plot windows

Composing and Plotting a Drawing

N ow that you have been introduced to the essentials of
AutoCAD Release 13, it's time to introduce you to some
tools that enable you to effectively compose your drawing.

Chapter 6, "Controlling What You See," presented some of the
fundamentals of model space and paper space. In the following
Quick Tour exercise, you create a notched block in model space
and use the MVSETUP routine to assist in composing the
drawing in paper space. To complete the exercise you add some
dimensions, then generate a check plot.

The Quick Tour

Begin a new drawing named COMPOSE using the default ACAD drawing as the prototype. Then create the layers TITLE, OBJECT, DIM1, DIM2 and VPORTS. Set the layer colors to your liking and set the OBJECT layer current.

Command: *Choose Polyline (Draw, Polyline)*	Issues the PLINE command
Draw the polyline from **2,2** *to* **@0,3, @2,0, @0,.5, @4,0, @0,-3.5,** *then* **C** *to close the shape.*	Draws the outline of the block

Your drawing should look like figure 16.1.

Command: *Choose* **V**iew, Paper **S**pace	Turns off TILEMODE, switches to paper space
Command: *Choose* **D**ata, Dr**a**wing Limits	Issues the LIMITS command
`<Lower left corner>` `<0.0000,0.0000>` (Enter)	Accepts the default
`Upper right corner` `<12.0000,9.0000>` **17,11** (Enter)	Sets the upper right corner of the drawing limits to 17,11
Command: *Choose Zoom All (Standard Toolbar, Zoom)*	Updates paper space with the drawing limits
Command: *Set the* TITLE *layer current*	
Command: *Choose* **V**iew, Floating Viewports, MV **S**etup	Issues the MVSETUP command
`Align/Create/Scale viewports/` `Options/Title block/Undo:` **T** (Enter)	Issues the Title block option
`Delete objects/Origin/Undo/` `<Insert title block>:` (Enter)	Accepts the default to insert a predefined title block
`Add/Delete/Redisplay/<Number of` `entry to load>:` **8** (Enter)	Chooses the ANSI-B size (in) title block, the title block is inserted into paper space
`Create a drawing named` `ansi-b.dwg? <Y>:` **N** (Enter)	Requests that a drawing not be created from this configuration
`Align/Create/Scale viewports/` `Options/Title block/Undo:` (Enter)	Ends the command
Command: *Set the* VPORTS *layer current*	

Command: *Choose **V**iew, Floating* Viewports, **1** Viewport	Issues the MVIEW command
`ON/OFF/Hideplot/Fit/2/3/4/` `Restore/<First Point>:` *Pick ①,* *then ② as shown in figure 16.2*	Creates a floating viewport in paper space
Command: `Enter`	Repeats the MVIEW command
`ON/OFF/Hideplot/Fit/2/3/4/` `Restore/<First Point>:` *Pick ③,* *then ④*	Creates another floating viewport in paper space
Command: *Choose **V**iew, **F**loating Model* Space	Switches to floating model space, the small viewport created is current
Command: *Choose Zoom Center (Standard Toolbar)*	Issues the ZOOM command with the Center option
`Center point:` *Pick ⑤*	Establishes the new display center
`Magnification or Height <9.0130>:` **2xp** `Enter`	Assigns a viewport display scale factor of 2:1
Command: *Pick in the large viewport*	Sets the large floating viewport to current
Command: *Choose Zoom Center (Standard Toolbar)*	Issues the ZOOM command with the Center option
`Center point:` *Pick the middle of the block for the center point*	Establishes the new display center
`Magnification or Height <9.0130>:` **1xp** `Enter`	Assigns a viewport display scale factor of 1:1
Command: *Choose Dimension Styles (Dimensioning, Dimension Style)*	Opens the Dimension Styles dialog box
*Choose **G**eometry*	Opens the Geometry dialog box
*Place an X in the **S**cale to Paper Space check box*	Turns on Scale to Paper Space
Choose OK	Closes the Geometry dialog box
*Choose **S**ave*	Saves the new conditions to the STANDARD dimension style
Choose OK	Closes the Dimension Styles dialog box
Command: *Choose **T**ools, **T**oolbars,* **D**imensioning	Opens the Dimensioning toolbar

continues

16

continued

Command: *Choose Running Object Snap (Standard Toolbar, Object Snap), choose* **E**ndpoint, *and then choose* OK	Sets a running Endpoint snap
Command: *Set the layer* DIM1 *current*	
Command: *Choose Linear Dimension (Dimensioning)*	Issues the DIMLINEAR command
First extension line origin or RETURN to select: (Enter)	
Select object to dimension: *Pick* ① *as shown in fig. 16.3*	Selects the object
Dimension line location (Text/ Angle/Horizontal/Vertical/ Rotated): *Pick* ②	Places the linear dimension, ends the command
Command: *Pick anywhere in the small viewport*	Sets the small floating viewport current
Command: *From the Layer Control drop-down list, freeze* DIM1 *in the current viewport, then set* DIM2 *current*	Freezes the first dimension in the small viewport, sets DIM2 current
Command: *Choose Linear Dimension (Dimensioning)*	Issues DIMLINEAR command
First extension line origin or RETURN to select: *Pick* ③, *then* ④	Defines the points for the linear dimension
Dimension line location: *Pick* ⑤	Places the dimension, displays the dimension in both viewports
Command: *Pick anywhere in the large viewport, then freeze* DIM2 *in the current viewport*	Freezes the notch dimension in the large viewport
Command: *Double-click the* MODEL *button on the status bar*	Switches to paper space
Command: *Choose Running Object Snap (Standard Toolbar, Object Snap), choose* C**l**ear All, *and then choose* OK	Clears all running object snaps
Command: *Choose Save (Standard Toolbar)*	Saves the drawing
Command: *Choose Print (Standard Toolbar)*	Opens the Plot Configuration dialog box

In the Addition Parameters *area,* *choose the* **L**imits *radio button*	Sets the drawing limits as the area to be plotted
In the Scale, Rotation, and Origin *area* *choose* Rotation and Ori**g**in	Opens the Plot Rotation and Origin dialog box
Set the rotation to **9**0 *and choose* OK	Rotates the plot 90 degrees
Place an X *in the* Scaled **t**o Fit *check box*	Fits the specified plot area onto the paper size selected
Choose F**u**ll, *then* P**r**eview	Displays a full preview of the plot in the Plot Preview dialog box
Choose **E**nd Preview	Closes the Plot Preview dialog box
Choose OK *to plot the drawing*	Plots the drawing to the specified device

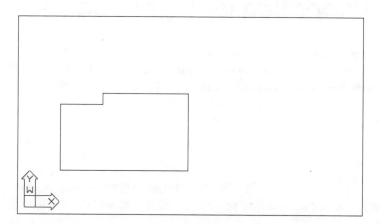

Figure 16.1

The notched block.

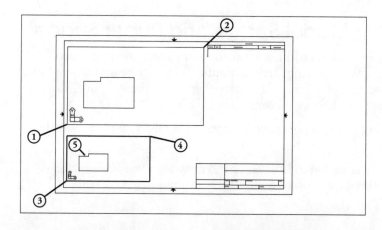

Figure 16.2

Configuring the floating model space viewports.

16

Figure 16.3

*Adding dimensions
to the block.*

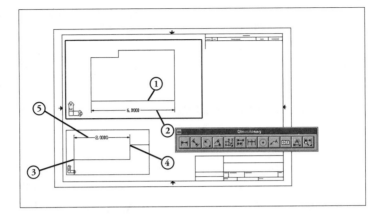

Sheet Composition in Paper Space

After you draw the geometry of your model, you are ready to compose the completed drawing image to get it ready to plot. If your model is 2D and can be plotted full size, you can enter the dimensions, title block, text, and any call-outs for the drawing at full size without regard to the plot scale factor. If, however, the model is smaller or larger than the sheet of paper, or if you need to plot multiple sheets, or multiple views of the model, the task is more complex.

In Chapter 6, you learned the basics of paper space and creating floating viewports. This chapter will expand on the concepts presented in Chapter 6 and show you how to compose a plot sheet by defining, arranging, and properly scaling views and adding properly scaled text and dimensions to the drawing.

Plotting from Model Space and Paper Space

As you've seen referenced in several chapters throughout this book, AutoCAD has two drawing environments: model space and paper space. Although you can plot from either model space or paper space, you must compose your plot sheet differently for each space.

When plotting from model space, composing a plot sheet involves the following:

- The title is scaled to fit around the drawing. The scale factor is determined by the plot scale. If you are plotting at a scale of

1/8"=1'–0", for example, you would insert the title block at a scale factor of 96.

- The model space limits are set to match the paper size at the specified plot scale. To plot a 17×11 sheet at 1/8"=1'-0", for example, you would set the model space limits to 0,0 and 136'×88'.

- In the Plot Configuration dialog box, you specify the specific plot scale. For example, 1/8"=1'-0" is a plot scale or .125=12 or 1=96. The check plot at the end of the Quick Tour exercise was scaled to fit the plot to the selected page. Later in this chapter you review all the features of the Plot Configuration dialog box.

Although plotting from model space works well in some instances, it does have some limitations. For starters, you can only plot a single view at a single plot scale, and if you decide to change the plot scale, you must rescale the title block.

Composing a plot in paper space is a little more flexible but involves a little more setup. The following are some of the advantages of plotting from paper space:

- The title block is inserted full scale, and the paper space limits are set to the size of the title block.

- You can have as many views of your model as you need.

- The plot scale is determined by the zoom scale factor of the viewport, so you can plot at multiple scales on a single plot sheet.

- Paper space is plotted full scale.

Although plotting from model space works well for plotting a single view, plotting from paper space gives you the flexibility to meet all of your plotting needs. Therefore, this chapter will focus on plotting from paper space.

Setting Up Paper Space with MVSETUP

Chapter 4, "Preparing Your Drawing," introduced you to the MVSETUP command to set up model space. When used in paper space, the MVSETUP command automates the process of composing your drawing by using predefined title blocks on a variety of sheets with user-specified floating model space viewports.

16

The following list presents a general overview of the MVSETUP command line options. Each option in the list has several additional options to customize further the configuration of the viewports or a title block. For a more comprehensive review of the extensive MVSETUP features, refer to *Inside AutoCAD Release 13 for Windows and Windows NT*.

- **Align.** The Align option enables you to align objects horizontally and vertically in different viewports. Most often used in 3-view engineering drawings, the Align option automatically pans the selected point in one view to be aligned with a selected point in another view. The Align option also enables you to rotate a viewport about a designated base point. This is similar to using the Z axis option in the UCS command to rotate the current view.

- **Create.** This is the option from which floating model space viewports can be created automatically based on your choice from the Available Mview viewport layout options menu. After you choose a layout option, AutoCAD either automatically creates the viewport configuration or enables you to define the number of viewports, their size, and the spacing between them.

- **Scale viewports.** A drawing that uses floating model space viewports can have a different output scale for each viewport. The Scale viewports option enables you to indicate the units for model space and the units for paper space, thus assigning a ratio or a display scale factor for the selected viewport.

- **Options.** Options presents four drawing configuration choices. You can:

    Choose the desired layer for the title block

    Choose to automatically set the limits for the drawing

    Choose the unit type for the drawing

    Specify if you want to insert a title block or reference it externally

- **Title block.** The Title block option provides a list of 13 predefined title blocks from which to choose. Each selection creates a title block in paper space, after which you have the option to save the created title block as a drawing with a predefined name. Table 16.1 lists the names and sizes for the available choices.

- **Undo.** The Undo option undoes any previously selected and completed option.

Table 16.1
Available MVSETUP Title Block Options

Option Number and Name	Drawing Extents (Width×Height)
1: ISO A4	210mm×297mm
2: ISO A3	420mm×297mm
3: ISO A2	594mm×420mm
4: ISO A1	841mm×594mm
5: ISO A0	1189mm×841mm
6: ANSI-V	8.5"×11"
7: ANSI-A	11"×8.5"
8: ANSI-B	17"×11"
9: ANSI-C	22"×17"
10: ANSI-D	34"×22"
11: ANSI-E	44"×34"
12: Arch/Engineering	36"×24"
13: Generic D Size	36"×24"

Several levels of options are available to assist you in composing the drawing. Although your needs might differ from those available through the matrix of commands, you might want to use the title blocks provided and edit them to suit your specific application.

In the following exercise, you create a new drawing and use MVSETUP to set up paper space with a C-size title block.

Setting Up Paper Space with MVSETUP

Begin a new drawing named PROTO-C using the default ACAD.DWG drawing as the prototype. Set the drawing limits to be 22"×17".

Command: *Double-click on* TILE *in*   Switches to paper space
the status bar

16

continues

continued

Command: *Choose* **V**iew, Floatin**g** Viewports, MV **S**etup	Issues the MVSETUP command
Align/Create/Scale viewports/ Options/Title block/Undo: **O** (Enter)	Issues the Options option
Set Layer/LImits/Units/Xref: **L** (Enter)	Issues the Layer option
Layer name for title block or . for current layer: **TITLE** (Enter)	Requests the title block be placed on a layer named TITLE
Set Layer/LImits/Units/Xref: **LI** (Enter)	Issues the LImits option
Set drawing limits? <N> **Y** (Enter)	Requests that drawing limits be set
Set Layer/LImits/Units/Xref: (Enter)	Ends the Options option
Align/Create/Scale viewports/ Options/Title block/Undo: **T** (Enter)	Issues the Title block option
Delete objects/Origin/Undo/ <Insert title block>: (Enter)	Accepts the default to insert a title block
Add/Delete/Redisplay/<Number of entry to load>: **9** (Enter)	Chooses the ANSI-C size title block, inserts the title block into paper space
Create a drawing named ansi-c.dwg? <Y>: **N** (Enter)	Declines to make ANSI-C.DWG
Align/Create/Scale viewports/ Options/Title block/Undo: **C** (Enter)	Issues the Create option
Delete objects/Undo/<Create viewports>: (Enter)	Accepts the default to create viewports
Redisplay/<Number of entry to load>: **1** (Enter)	Chooses the single viewport layout option
Bounding area for viewports. First point: *Pick* ①, *then* ② *as shown in figure 16.4*	Creates the floating viewport
Align/Create/Scale viewports/ Options/Title block/Undo: **S** (Enter)	Issues the Scale viewports option
Select objects: *Pick* ③, *then press* (Enter)	Selects the viewport, switches to model space
Enter the ratio of paper space units to model space units.	Accepts the default paper space units

Number of paper space units. <1.0>: (Enter)	
Number of model space units. <1.0>: (Enter)	Accepts the default model space units, sets the viewports display scale factor to 1:1, switches back to paper space
Align/Create/Scale viewports/ Options/Title block/Undo: (Enter)	Ends the MVSETUP command
Command: *Choose Save (Standard Toolbar)*	Saves the drawing

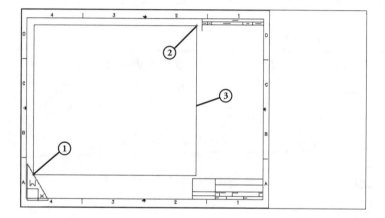

Figure 16.4

The C-size title block with a single viewport.

The Title block option of MVSETUP is a good place to start when creating title blocks. After creating the title block, you can customize it by adding your company logo or changing the layout. You also can use the Title block option to add your own title blocks to the list of predefined title blocks. One of the drawbacks of the predefined MVSETUP title blocks is that they don't take into account your plotter's maximum plot area.

Determining the Plot Area

Most output devices, printers, and plotters cannot print all the way to the edge of the sheet of paper. The area around the edge of the paper is referred to as the *hard clip limits*. An 8.5×11 sheet of paper, for example, may only have a print area of 8×10.5. The hard clip limits vary between each output device. The documentation that comes with your output device should list the maximum plot area for the various sheet sizes.

16

Another way of determining the hard clip limits is to draw and plot a vertical line (length is not important), and then draw and plot a horizontal line. Plot them on the same sheet of paper, using Extents as the area to plot, and Scaled to Fit as the plot scale. Then measure the length of each line to determine the plotter's maximum area for that sheet. See the section, "Choosing Plot Parameters," later in this chapter for more on setting the PLOT command options.

In the following exercise, you open the FURNBLOK drawing created in Chapter 13, "Blocks and Overlays," and set up a border for a title block in paper space. For the purpose of this exercise, you will set up a 36"×24" D-size sheet and subtract 1" from each side to allow for the hard clip limits.

Creating a Simple Title Block and the Viewports

Begin a new drawing named PLOTFURN using the FURNBLOK drawing as the prototype. Then create the layers TITLE, DIMS, and VPORTS. Set the layer colors to your liking and set the TITLE layer current.

Command: *Double-click on* TILE *in the status bar*	Switches to paper space
Command: **LIMITS** (Enter)	Starts the LIMITS command
ON/OFF/<Lower left corner> <0'-0",0'-0">: (Enter)	Accepts the default
Upper right corner <1'-0",0'-9">: **36,24** (Enter)	Sets the upper right corner
Command: *Choose Zoom All (Standard Toolbar, Zoom)*	Updates paper space with the limits
Command: *Choose Rectangle (Draw, Polygon)*	Issues the RECTANG command
First corner: **1,1** (Enter)	Places the first corner
Other corner: **@34,22** (Enter)	Draws the rectangle
Command: *Choose* **V**iew, Floatin**g** viewports, **1** Viewport	Issues the MVIEW command
ON/OFF/Hideplot/Fit/2/3/4/ Restore/First point: *Pick* ①, *then* ② *as shown in figure 16.5*	Creates a floating viewport
Command: *Choose Copy Object (Modify, Copy)*	Issues the COPY command
Select objects: **L** (Enter)	Highlights the viewport

```
Select objects: Enter
```

`<Basepoint or displacement>/` `Multiple: M Enter`	Issues the Multiple option

Place two copies of the upper left viewport as shown in fig. 16.5.

Command: *Choose Save (Standard Toolbar)*	Saves the drawing

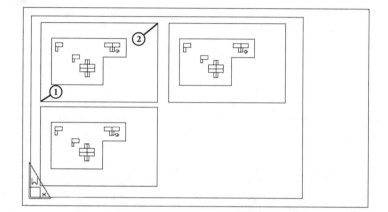

Figure 16.5

The three floating model space viewports for FURNBLOK.

Assigning Display Scale Factors to the Viewports

One of the most powerful features of using paper space to compose a drawing comes into play when you need multiple plot scales on the same sheet. When working with a building floor plan, for example, you might need a floating model space viewport plotted at 1/8"=1' and another viewport plotted at 1/2"=1' for a detailed view of a workstation.

While in model space, the ZOOM command enables you to assign a plot scale to a floating model space viewport. To assign a display scale factor to a floating model space viewport, set the desired viewport to be current, then from the ZOOM command, enter the scale factor followed by the characters XP. The "P" in the XP suffix indicates the factor being entered is specific to the display scale factor for plotting purposes. Table 16.2 is a list of some commonly used display scale factors that can be assigned to floating viewports.

16

Table 16.2

Sample Floating Model Space Viewport Display Scale Factors

Desired Output Scale	*XP Value*
1:1	1XP
1:2	.5XP
1:50	.02XP
1"=10'	1/120XP
1"=20'	1/240XP
1"=30'	1/360XP
3"= 1'	1/4XP
1"= 1'	1/12XP
3/4"=1'	1/16XP
1/2"=1'	1/24XP
3/8"=1'	1/32XP
1/4"=1'	1/48XP
1/8"=1'	1/96XP

The Quick Tour exercise at the beginning of this chapter took you through the process of assigning display scale factors to the floating viewports created in MVSETUP. When a display scale factor is assigned, the display is magnified or reduced from the center of the viewport. For this reason, you should either use the Extents option of ZOOM and then assign the scale factor, or use the Center option with a scale factor.

Now that you've been introduced to the technical issues of assigning display scale factors to viewports, you will assign new display scale factors to two of the viewports in the PLOTFURN drawing.

TIP

In paper space, if a display command such as ZOOM, PAN, or VIEW is current, you cannot switch between floating model space viewports. To switch to a different viewport, you must first cancel the command, switch to the desired viewport, and reissue the display command. When using an editing or drawing command, however, you can switch between viewports with no interruption in the command prompt sequence.

Assigning Different Plot Scales to Two Viewports

Continue from the previous exercise.

Command: *Double-click on* PAPER *on the status bar*	Switches to model space
Command: *Pick anywhere in the lower left viewport*	Sets the lower left viewport current
Command: *Choose Zoom Extents (Standard Toolbar, Zoom)*	Updates the current viewport with the extents of the drawing
Command: (Enter)	Repeats the ZOOM command
<Scale (X/XP)>: **1/48xp** (Enter)	Updates the display with a scale factor for a 1/4"=1'plot
Command: *Pick anywhere in the upper left viewport*	Sets the upper left viewport current
Command: *Choose Zoom Center (Standard Toolbar, Zoom)*	Issues the Center option of ZOOM
Center point: *Pick* ① *as shown in figure 16.6*	Identifies the viewport's new center for the updated display
Magnification or Height <51'6">: **1/24xp** (Enter)	Updates the display with a scale factor for a 1/2"=1' plot
Command: *Pick anywhere in the upper right viewport*	Sets the upper left viewport current
Command: *Choose Zoom Center (Standard Toolbar, Zoom)*	Issues the Center option of ZOOM
Center point: *Pick* ②	Identifies the viewport's new center for the updated display
Magnification or Height <51'6">: **1/16xp** (Enter)	Updates the display with a scale factor for a 3/4"=1' plot
Command: **PS** (Enter)	Switches to paper space

continues

16

continued

Command: *Choose Properties (Object Properties)*	Starts the object selection process
Select objects: *Pick ③, ④, and ⑤, then press* **Enter**	Highlights the 3 viewports, opens the Change Properties dialog box
Choose **L**ayer	Opens the Select Layer dialog box
Choose VPORTS, *then* OK	Selects VPORTS as the new layer property, closes the Select Layer dialog box
Choose OK	Closes the Change Properties dialog box, changes the layer property of the three viewports
Command: *Choose Save (Standard Toolbar)*	Saves the drawing

Figure 16.6

The floating viewports with different display scale factors.

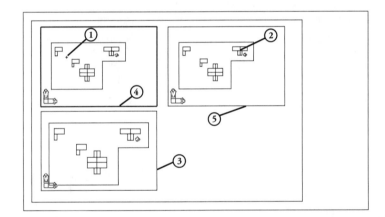

When a display factor is assigned, the display is magnified or reduced from the center of the viewport. It might be necessary to use PAN or ZOOM to see what you want in the viewport. It also might be necessary to change the size of the viewport as you compose the content.

Composing and Aligning Views

After you assign the desired scale to the viewports, you can manipulate the position and size of the viewports as you wish. In the following exercise, you edit the viewports using grips. When a viewport is stretched with a grip, the viewport maintains its rectangular shape. This is contrary to the result of a corner grip being stretched on a rectangle or any other open or closed polygon that would deform or stretch the line segments that had the grip in common.

After you have assigned display scale factors for your viewports (using ZOOM with the XP option), save each viewport's display as a view. That way, if you need to use ZOOM to magnify or reduce the viewport display, you have a saved view that you can restore.

TIP

Editing Viewports with Grips to Compose the Drawing

Continue from the previous exercise.

Command: *Pick the upper right viewport*	Displays the four grips of the viewport
Command: *Press Shift and pick the lower left grip, then the lower right grip, then release Shift*	Displays two hot grips

`** STRETCH **`
`<Stretch to point>/Base point/`
`Copy/Undo/eXit:` *Pick the lower right hot grip, then pick* ① *as shown in fig.16.7*
	Stretches the corner to the new position

Command: `MS` (Enter)	Switches to model space
Command: `VIEW` (Enter)	Starts the VIEW command
`?/Delete/Restore/Save/Window:` `S` (Enter)	Issues the Save option
`View name to save:` `DOUBLE` (Enter)	Saves the current viewport display as a view named "double"
Command: *Pick anywhere in the upper left viewport*	Sets the upper left viewport current
Command: *Choose* **V**iew, Floating Viewports, MV **S**etup	Issues the MVSETUP command
`Align/Create/Scale viewports/` `Options/Title block/Undo:` `A` (Enter)	Issues the Align option

`Angled/Horizontal/Vertical`
`alignment/Rotate view/Undo:`
`V` (Enter)
	Issues the Vertical option

16

continues

continued

`Basepoint:` *Using the Endpoint object snap, pick anywhere in the lower left viewport, then pick* ②	Sets the lower left viewport current, establishes the base point
`Other point:` *Using the Perpendicular object snap, pick anywhere in the upper left viewport, then pick* ③	Sets the upper left viewport current, and aligns the point in the upper left viewport with the point in the lower left viewport
`Angled/Horizontal/Vertical alignment/Rotate view/Undo:` (Enter)	Ends the Align option
`Align/Create/Scale viewports/ Options/Title block/Undo:` (Enter)	Ends the MVSETUP command
`Command:` *Choose Save (Standard Toolbar)*	Saves the drawing

Figure 16.7

The stretched and aligned viewports.

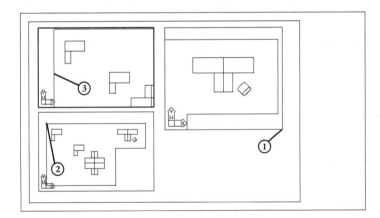

As you noticed in the previous exercise, when a viewport is moved or the size is edited, the display of the viewport remains constant as does the display scale factor. Edits to a viewport frame that happen in paper space do not modify the scale of the viewport's display.

Viewport Independent Layer Visibility

If you have tiled viewports in model space and freeze, or turn off, a layer, the information on that layer is not shown in any of the viewports. This is because layer manipulation in tiled model space is "global" (refers to the entire drawing), viewports not withstanding.

When using floating model space viewports, however, AutoCAD provides several methods by which you can independently freeze layers by viewport.

- **The viewport-specific icon in the layer drop-down list.** The Viewport Freeze/Thaw icon enables you to freeze or thaw specified layer(s) of the current viewport. If you need to freeze or thaw the same layer(s) in another viewport, you must set the other viewport to current, and then make the selection. You can see the result of using this method only when in a floating model space viewport.

- **Viewport-specific buttons in the Layer Control dialog box.** There are four buttons that relate to freezing or thawing layers in floating model space viewports. Similar in functionality to the layer drop-down list viewport icon, the Cur VP: freeze and thaw selections apply only to the layers chosen for the current viewport. If a layer is frozen in a viewport, a "C" will appear in the fourth State column for that layer when DDLMODES is invoked for the viewport. When in paper space, however, any changes to the status of layers from Cur VP: will have no effect on any viewports. After selecting the desired layers from the list, if you freeze or thaw from the New VP: grouping, any new viewports will have those layers frozen or thawed.

- **The VPLAYER command.** This command is designed for layer manipulation specifically in floating viewports. From the command options, you can specify multiple viewports in which to edit the layer status, preconfigure new viewports, or edit the status of layers globally or in selected viewports. For more information on the VPLAYER command, see *Inside AutoCAD 13 for Windows and Windows NT*.

To illustrate the viewport layering functions found in the drop-down list and in the Layer Control dialog box, in the following exercise you copy the chair to several other workstations, and then freeze the CHAIR layer in one viewport. During this exercise, you also learn how to get closer to the drawing using ZOOM without disturbing the plot scale factor assigned to the model space viewport.

When in a floating model space viewport, use the Redraw All tool to redraw all viewports as well as paper space. From the command line, you also can issue the REGENALL command to regenerate all viewports and paper space.

16

Adding Chairs and Freezing Furniture by Viewport

Continue from the previous exercise.

Command: *Pick anywhere in the upper right viewport* — Sets the upper right viewport to current

Command: *Choose Copy Object (Modify, Copy)* — Issues the COPY command

Select objects: *Pick the chair, then press* (Enter) — Highlights the chair

<Base point or displacement>/ Multiple: **M** (Enter) — Issues the multiple option

Base point: *Pick the middle of the chair* — Establishes the base point for the copy

Second point of displacement: *Turn off ortho, then pick* ①,*then* ②, *as shown in figure 16.8, then press* (Enter) — Displays the chair placement in two viewports

Command: *Pick anywhere in the upper right viewport* — Sets the upper right viewport current

Command: *Choose* **O**ptions, **G**rips — Opens the Grips dialog box

Turn off Enable Grips Within **B**locks, *then choose* OK — Disables the display of grips within blocks, closes the dialog box

Command: *Pick the chair, then pick the grip* — Displays the chair grip, displays the hot grip

** STRETCH ** <Stretch to point>/Base point/ Copy/Undo/eXit: **RO** (Enter) — Switches to rotate mode

** ROTATE ** <Rotation angle>/Base point/ Copy/Undo/Reference/eXit: **C** (Enter) — Issues the Copy option

<Rotation angle>/Base point/ Copy/Undo/Reference/eXit: **B** (Enter) — Issues the Base point option

Base point: *Using ENDPoint snap, pick* ③ *as shown in figure 16.8* — Establishes the pivot point for the rotation

<Rotation angle>/Base point/ Copy/Undo/Reference/eXit: *Pick* ④ — Places a copy of the chair

<Rotation angle>/Base point/ Copy/Undo/Reference/eXit: *Press* (Enter)	Clears the hot grip
Command: *From the* Layer Control *drop-down list, choose the viewport* Freeze/Thaw *icon for the layer CHAIRS, then press Enter*	Freezes the layer CHAIRS in the current (upper left) viewport and regenerates the drawing
Command: *Pick anywhere in the lower left viewport*	Sets the lower left viewport to current
Command: *Choose Layers (Object Properties)*	Issues the DDLMODES command, opens the Layer Control dialog box
Choose CHAIRS *and* FURNITURE, *then choose* Fr**z** *from* Cur VP	Sets the layers to be frozen in the current viewport, places a "C" for state of the current viewport
Choose OK	Regenerates the drawing, displaying only the two rectangles created on layer 0 used to make the NEWDESK block
Command: *From the layer drop-down list, choose the viewport Freeze / Thaw icon for the layers CHAIRS and FURNITURE, then press* (Enter)	Thaws the selected layers in the current viewport and regenerates the drawing
Command: *Choose Save (Standard Toolbar)*	Saves the drawing

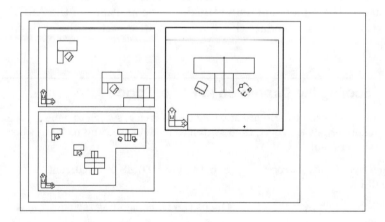

Figure 16.8
Adding chairs to the drawing.

By freezing and thawing layers per viewport, you have a great deal of flexibility in composing a plot sheet.

16

Dimensioning and Paper Space

As you learned in the previous chapter on dimensioning styles, you can assign a scale factor for the dimension geometry. The scale factor enables you to control the desired height of dimensioning annotation as it relates to the plot scale of the drawing. Typically, you set the dimension scale equal to the plot scale factor. If, for example, you were plotting a drawing at 1/2"=1'-0," setting the dimension scale to 24 ensures that dimensions are properly scaled.

When using paper space, however, you can have multiple plot scales. The viewport display scale factor defines the scale for all objects in the viewport. To resolve this conflict of scale assignment for dimensions in floating viewports, the current dimension style's geometry scale factor must be scaled to paper space. The Scale to Paper Space option in the DDIM command enables you to set the dimension scale based on the display scale of the current viewport.

TIP

> You can set the dimension scale by changing the DIMSCALE system variable.

In the following exercise, you add a dimension to the drawing to indicate the distance between the four workstation clusters. In the first part of the exercise, you add the dimension using the default conditions of the ARCH dimension style, and then update the dimension after setting the scale to paper space.

Scaling the Dimension to Paper Space

Continue from the previous exercise. Before starting the exercise, switch to paper space and zoom around the upper left viewport, then switch to model space and pick anywhere in the viewport to set it current.

Command: *From the* Layer Control *drop-down, list choose* DIMS	Sets the layer DIMS to be current
Command: *Choose* **T**ools, **T**oolbars, **D**imensioning	Opens the Dimensioning toolbar
Command: *Choose Running Object Snap (Standard Toolbar, Object Snap), Choose* **E**ndpoint, *Choose* OK	Sets ENDPoint as the running object snap

Command: *Choose Linear Dimension (Dimensioning)*	Issues the DIMLINEAR command
`First extension line origin or RETURN to select:` *Pick* ①, *then* ②, *as shown in figure 16.9*	Identifies the points between which to dimension
`Dimension line location (Text/ Angle/Horizontal/Vertical/ Rotated):` *Pick* ③	Positions the dimension line, ends the command
Command: *Choose Dimension Styles (Dimensioning, Dimension Style)*	Issues the DDIM command, opens the Dimension Styles dialog box
Choose **G**eometry	Opens the Geometry dialog box
Choose Scale to **P**aper space, *then choose* OK	Turns off Overall scale, turns on Scale to Paper Space, closes the dialog box
Choose **S**ave, *then* OK	Saves the new setting to the ARCH dimension style and closes the dialog box

Notice that the dimension text and arrowheads are scaled according to the display scale of the current viewport. The dimensions, however, are not scaled properly for the other viewports. In the following steps, you freeze the DIMS layer in the other viewports.

Command: *Double-click on* MODEL *on the status bar*	Switches to paper space
Command: *Choose Zoom Previous (Standard Toolbar, Zoom)*	Issues the Previous option of ZOOM
Command: *Double-click on* PAPER *on the status bar*	Switches to model space
Command: *Pick anywhere in the lower left viewport*	Sets the lower left viewport to current
Command: *From the* Layer Control *drop-down list, choose the viewport* Freeze/Thaw *icon for DIMS, then choose TITLE*	Sets the layer TITLE to be current, freezes the layer DIMS in the current viewport as the drawing is regenerated
Command: *Choose Save (Standard Toolbar)*	Saves the drawing

When dimensioning in multiple floating viewports, you typically need to create a dimensioning layer for each viewport and freeze and thaw the appropriate layers in each viewport. For a more comprehensive review of using dimensions in viewports, refer to *Inside AutoCAD Release 13 for Windows and Windows NT*.

16

Figure 16.9

*Adding a dimension
to a floating model
space viewport.*

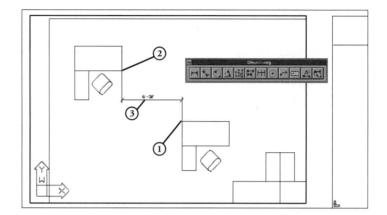

As an alternative to dimensioning in model space, you might want to
consider placing dimensions in paper space. When dimensioning model
space objects in paper space, the dimension scale is always set to 1, and
you can place all of your dimensions on a single layer. But you do have to
adjust the value of the dimension text. If, for example, you drew a line in
model space that was 8' long and set up a floating model space viewport to
display the line at a scale of 1/8"=1'-0" (1/96xp), the line would measure 1"
long in the floating viewport.

AutoCAD enables you to adjust the value of the dimension text by changing the dimension linear scale factor. This can be set with the DDIM
command by specifying the value in the Linea**r** edit box in the Primary
Units dialog box of the DDIM command. See Chapter 15, "Adding Style to
Dimensions," for more information on the DDIM command and its dialog
boxes.

By setting the linear scale factor to the display scale of the viewport,
AutoCAD will adjust the value of the dimension text. In the previous
example, if you set the linear scale factor to 96, AutoCAD multiplies the 1"
dimension by 96 and gets 8', the proper length of the line. The Paper
Space Only option in the Primary Units dialog box tells AutoCAD to
ignore the linear scale factor while in model space.

TIP

You also can set the linear scale factor by changing the system
variable DIMLFAC.

In the following exercise, you set the linear scale factor to match the display scale factor of the upper right viewport and add a dimension in paper space.

Dimensioning from Paper Space

Continue from the previous exercise.

Command: *Choose Dimension Styles (Dimensioning, Dimension Style)*	Opens the Dimension Styles dialog box
Choose **A**nnotation	Opens the Annotation dialog box
Choose **U**nits	Opens the Primary Units dialog box
Double-click in the Linea**r** *edit field*	Highlights the 1.00000
Type **16**, *then press* (Enter)	Changes the Linear scale factor to 16
Choose Paper **S**pace Only	Selects the Paper Space Only option
Choose OK	Closes the Primary Units dialog box
Choose OK	Closes the Annotation dialog box
Choose **S**ave, *and then choose* OK	Saves the settings to the ARCH dimension style
Command: *Double-click on* MODEL *in the status bar*	Switches to paper space
Command: *Choose Linear Dimension (Dimensioning)*	Issues the DIMLINEAR command
First extension line origin or RETURN to select: *Pick* ① *as shown in figure 16.10*	Establishes the first point of the dimension
Second extension line: *Using the Perpendicular object snap, pick* ②	Dynamically displays the dimension line and dimension text
Dimension line location (Text/ Angle/Horizontal/Vertical/ Rotated): *Pick* ③	Places the dimension
Command: *Choose Save (Standard Toolbar)*	Saves the drawing

16

Figure 16.10

Dimensioning from paper space.

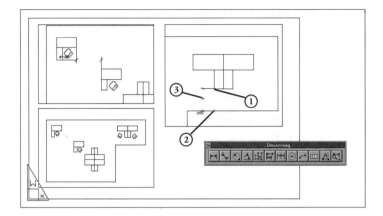

TIP

Previous versions of AutoCAD used a separate prompt known as the Dim: prompt for all dimensioning commands. AutoCAD Release 13 no longer requires the Dim: prompt, but it still is available. When setting DIMLFAC from the Dim: prompt, you can type **V** for viewport and select the floating viewport. AutoCAD automatically sets the DIMLFAC to the display scale of the selected viewport. To access the Dim: prompt, type **DIM** (Enter) at the Command: prompt. The DIMLFAC Viewport option is only available from the Dim: prompt.

NOTE

As of the printing of this book, the features presented in the previous exercise involving dimensioning in paper space contain bugs that prohibit the dimension from updating properly. When dimensioning a drawing composed in paper space that contains floating model space viewports, you should dimension the drawing entirely in model space or entirely in paper space. By doing so, the power of dimension styles then can be utilized to their fullest.

The decision to dimension in paper space or model space is based upon your application. If you have several viewports with multiple display scale factors, it might be more advantageous to set DIMSCALE to 0 and use a different layer for dimensioning each viewport. If, however, you have multiple viewports but all have the same display scale factor, it may be more convenient to set the DIMLFAC using the Viewport option and generate the dimensions in paper space.

Plot Preparation

Plotting a drawing has to be one of the more exciting aspects of using a CAD system, because it is the final realization of the hard work that has gone into the drawing thus far. You end up with something real and tangible.

The Print tool on the Standard Toolbar issues the PLOT command and presents you with the Plot Configuration dialog box. The Plot Configuration dialog box is a bit imposing at the beginning, but as you work through the rest of this chapter, you should feel more comfortable about your ability to generate a plot of your drawing. The Plot Configuration dialog box contains six separate sections of parameters and settings from which you configure the way in which the drawing is to be plotted.

PLOT. The PLOT command is used to plot your drawing. Prior to plotting the drawing, you specify the plot parameters in the Plot Configuration dialog box presented when you issue the PLOT command.

Toolbar: *Choose Print (Standard Toolbar)*
Pull-down: *Choose **F**ile, **P**rint*
Screen: *Choose* File, Print

If you have yet to install a plotter or output device for use with AutoCAD, refer to Appendix A, "Installation and Configuration." Because all printers and plotters have different setting options, the following exercises are presented with regard to the capabilities of the features covered. For more information about your particular configuration, refer to the printer or plotter documents or manuals provided with the hardware. You may want to review the *AutoCAD Installation and Configuration Guide* for detailed information about using your device with AutoCAD. Figure 16.11 displays the Plot Configuration dialog box from which several of the selections in the next several exercises will be made.

16

Figure 16.11

The Plot Configuration dialog box.

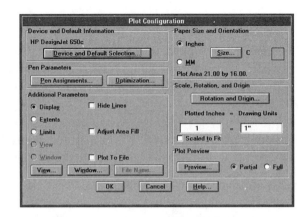

Selecting the Desired Output Device

The **D**evice and Default Selection button displays the Device and Default Selection dialog box, as shown in figure 16.12. This dialog box enables you to choose a previously configured output device. See Appendix A for more information on configuring printers and plotters.

Figure 16.12

The Device and Default Selection dialog box.

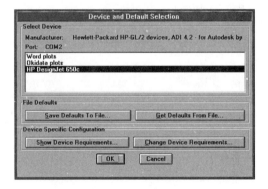

The **S**ave Defaults to File button enables you to save various plot configuration information to a file and is particularly useful if you have multiple plotters with multiple configurations. When the current configuration is saved to a file, a PCP (plotter configuration parameters) file is created. When that configuration is required again, choose the **G**et Defaults From File button, and then choose the desired PCP file.

Every output device has specific requirements or parameters that can only be addressed at the time of configuration. Should you need to change those requirements, you can review the requirements by choosing S**h**ow Device Requirements and make any changes by way of the **C**hange Device Requirements. **C**hange Device Requirements presents you with one or more dialog boxes in which you can make the desired changes.

Modifying the Pen Assignments by Color

One way of getting a wide line on the final drawing is to create the desired line work using a polyline with a width setting. A method more global in nature is to use the **P**en Assignments dialog box to configure line width by color. For plotters that support variable pen width settings, when a color is assigned a pen width, AutoCAD will plot all objects with the specified color with the indicated pen width. If your output device does not support multiple pens or variable pen widths, the **P**en Assignments button will be grayed out. The documentation provided with your output device should indicate your device's capabilities.

If your plotter is capable of multiple linetype output, you can globally set the object linetype from the Plot Configuration dialog box. By default, AutoCAD plots objects based upon the linetype assigned to the object by way of object creation or the Layer Control dialog box Set **L**type selection. At the time of plotting, however, you may assign a global linetype to specific pens of the output device. The **F**eatures button of the **P**en Assignment selection displays the different linetypes available and the number you would enter in the **L**type setting of the **P**en Assignments dialog box.

Choosing Plot Parameters

The Additional Parameters area enables you to specify what portion of the drawing you want to have plotted, as well as some other issues. The following list reviews the Additional Parameters choices:

- **Display.** The Displa**y** option enables you to plot the current model space display or the current display of paper space. The X and Y Plot Origin values discussed later in this section are based upon the lower left corner of the display.

- **Extents.** When plotting the E**x**tents, remember that layers that have been turned off are recognized when AutoCAD considers what is to be plotted. Similar in function to the Extents option of the ZOOM command, the plot is based only on the objects recognized in the drawing extents.

16

- **Limits.** The **L**imits option results in a plot based only on the area defined by the drawing limits. This is contrary to the All option of ZOOM, which displays the drawing extents by default if objects extend beyond the drawing limits.

- **View.** The **V**iew option is only available if the current drawing contains a named view. The corners used to define the named view chosen are used to define the plot area. This option is useful when consistency in plotting the same area is desired.

- **Window.** When the **W**indow parameter is on, the window area picked from the Window Selection dialog box will be the area plotted. The Wi**n**dow button, discussed later in this listing, enables you to window the area for the plot.

- **Hide Lines.** The Hide **L**ines parameter typically is turned on when plotting 3D drawings that contain 3D faces. Hide lines enables you to hide, or not plot, any lines behind a 3D face.

- **Adjust Area Fill.** When the Ad**j**ust Area Fill option is turned on, AutoCAD will maintain dimensional accuracy when plotting with wide pens on all boundaries for polylines or solids. This also is based on the capability of the chosen output device.

- **Plot to File.** By default, a .PLT file using the current drawing name is created when Plot to **F**ile is turned on and you choose OK from the Plot Configuration dialog box.

- **View button.** Choosing the **V**iew button opens the View Name dialog box from which you can choose the named view to be plotted. If a view is chosen, the **V**iew parameter is turned on indicating a named view as the area to be plotted.

- **Window button.** When you choose the Wi**n**dow button, you can either enter absolute coordinates to define the plot area or choose the **P**ick button. The **P**ick button enables you to graphically define the area to be plotted with a window. If the area defined is OK, the **W**indow parameter is turned On.

- **File name button.** Choosing the File n**a**me button enables you to enter a file name other than the default name of the current drawing. The file types that can be plotted are based on the output device. By default, the file extension is .PLT.

If you consistently set your drawing limits, the **L**imits option typically provides an easy way of plotting your drawing. In the following exercise, you begin setting up your paper space environment for plotting.

Choosing the Area to be Plotted

Continue in paper space from the previous exercise.

Command: *Choose Print (Standard Toolbar)*	Issues the PLOT command
In the Additional Parameters *area, choose* Limits	Establishes the drawing limits as the area to be plotted

Selecting a Sheet Size

The Paper Size and Orientation area enables you to choose the plot sheet size. Depending on the capability of your plotter, you may have anywhere from 2 to 16 or more settings for a paper size. The sizes available vary with the type of plotter you have configured. In addition to the predefined sizes, you can add up to 5 different user defined sizes. The user sizes enable you to adjust the plot area to match your plotter's particular hard clip limits.

You also can chose whether you want the paper sizes displayed in inches or millimeters. When you choose MM, the sizes are converted from their inch value to millimeters and the plotted scale is adjusted accordingly.

Orienting the Output

Not all drawings are proportionally composed to fit perfectly on the default orientation of the paper size selected. The Plot Rotation and Origin dialog box enables you to rotate your drawing through the four orthogonal angles, as well as offset the lower left corner of the plot window from the lower left corner of the paper size.

Setting a Plot Scale

The Plotted Inches = Drawing Units area enables you to set the precise scale at which the drawing will be plotted. When plotting from paper space, this setting should be 1=1. AutoCAD will then plot paper space at full scale and the floating model space viewports at their assigned display scale factor.

16

When plotting from model space, however, Plotted Inches = Drawing Units values are based on the desired plot scale. To plot a drawing at 1/8"=1'–0", for example, you set the plot Plotted Inches = Drawing Units to .125=12 or 1=96.

When the Scaled to Fit option is turned on, the area of the drawing to be plotted is scaled to fit in the available plot area of the paper. The Scaled to Fit option is typically used for check plots.

In the following exercise, you set up a user sheet size of 34×22 to plot on. If your plotter does not support this size, you can choose to plot to the maximum sheet size and adjust the plot scale accordingly. You also rotate the drawing 90 degrees (counterclockwise) on the paper and set the plot scale to 1=1.

Setting the Paper Size and Orientation

Continue from the previous exercise.

In the Paper Size and Orientation *area choose* **S**ize	Opens the Paper Size dialog box
Click in the Width *field for* **U**SER	Enables you to enter a user-defined width for the sheet size
Type **36**, *then press Tab*	Sets the USER width to 36"
Type **24**, *then press* (Enter)	Sets the USER height to 24", adds the USER values to the list, as shown in figure 16.13
Choose USER *from the list of available paper sizes, then choose* OK	Sets the paper size to USER, closes the Paper Size dialog box
Choose Rotation and Ori**g**in	Opens the Plot Rotation and Origin dialog box
Choose **9**0 *as the plot rotation*	Sets the output to be rotated 90° when plotted
Turn off Scaled **t**o Fit	Sets plot scale to 1 = 1"

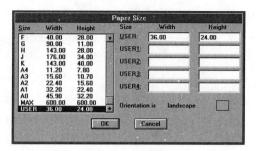

Figure 16.13

The Paper Size dialog box.

Previewing the Output Before Plotting

Prior to the Release 12 feature of the Plot Preview, you basically had to hope for the best after setting the plot parameters and hope that your scale, rotation, pens, viewports, and sheet size were accurate. Then you had to wait for the plotter to do its work.

The best thing since cruise control is the Plot Preview window of the Plot Configuration dialog box. The Part*i*al preview option is somewhat of a misnomer; it simply means that a rectangle representative of the effective plot area at the desired plot scale and rotation is shown on another rectangle representing the paper size.

The F**u**ll preview option displays exactly what you will see on the paper based on the paper size, plot scale, and rotation. The Warnings box warns you about the resulting plot being outside the device's hard clip limits.

In the following exercise, you use the Plot Preview options to preview the plot. You then change the rotation to 0° and take another F**u**ll preview.

Previewing the Named View for Plotting

Continue from the previous exercise.

Turn on Scaled **t**o Fit	Sets the output scale to a plot scale that will fit the defined plot area on the USER paper size
Choose Part**i**al	Sets the plot preview to use rectangle comparisons of paper size to plotted area
Choose P**r**eview	Opens the Preview Effective Plotting Area dialog box

continues

16

continued

Notice that the orientation of the paper which we set to be 90 degrees does not efficiently take advantage of our 36"× 24" paper size.

Choose OK	Closes the dialog box
Choose F**u**ll	Turns on the Full preview option
Choose P**r**eview	Displays a graphic preview of the desired plot area, opens the Plot Preview dialog box
Choose **E**nd Preview	Closes the dialog box
Choose Rotation and Ori**g**in	Opens the Plot Rotation and Origin dialog box
Choose **0**, *then* OK	Sets the rotation of the plot area to 0°, closes the dialog box
Choose P**r**eview	Displays a graphic preview of the desired plot area, opens the Plot Preview dialog box
Choose **E**nd Preview	Closes the dialog box

As you can see from the changing of the plot rotation from 90° to 0°, the drawing will be plotted more efficiently on our sheet. Continue to change the various settings and use preview to see the results. When you are satisfied with the settings, make sure the plotter is ready and choose OK from the Plot Configuration dialog box. If you're prompted to press RETURN, press (Enter) and wait for the plot.

Command: *Choose Save (Standard Toolbar)*	Saves the drawing

If you don't get a plot from your plotter, confirm that you had the right plotter selected and that the connections are secure on the computer and the plotter, then try again. If you still don't get a plot, refer to Appendix B, "Troubleshooting."

Summary

The composition of a final drawing can be streamlined by using the array of features provided by the MVSETUP command and the use of multiple floating model space viewports. You can select from several predefined title blocks, all of which can be edited to your particular application and used as a prototype. Depending on your application, you might want to insert or overlay the title block in model space, but when using multiple plot scales in the floating viewports, the most efficient tool is to have the title block in paper space.

The floating model space viewports are easily edited with grips, positioning, and stretching the viewport to the desired size. You can easily assign a display scale factor to the viewport by way of the XP option of the ZOOM command, which conveniently sets the plot scale factor for that viewport when plotted. You also learned that layer visibility within each viewport can be independently controlled easily from the Layer Control dialog box or the layer drop-down list.

When using paper space, you now know that dimensioning can either be placed in the floating viewports or in paper space. It really depends on the application as to the method that is used, both of which rely upon viewport visibility issues.

And finally, the Plot Configuration dialog box offers a wide range of features that can easily accommodate virtually every output requirement. The primary issue is not so much the capability of the AutoCAD plot routine, as it is the ability of the output device to support the options available. The signature feature of the Plot Configuration dialog box is Preview—something you should always check prior to confirming the final output of your drawing.

Related Topics

- Paper space and model space basics—Chapter 6, "Controlling What You See"

- Editing with grips—Chapter 8, "Editing with Grips"

- External reference overlays—Chapter 13, "Blocks and Overlays"

- Linear dimensioning—Chapter 14, "Dimensioning"

- Dimension styles—Chapter 15, "Adding Style to Dimensions"

16

PART V

Appendices

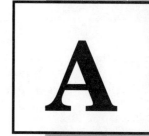

Installation and Configuration

This appendix explains the requirements for the installation of AutoCAD Release 13 for Windows. DOS and Windows configuration issues are important if you want to obtain optimum performance on the Windows platform. This appendix examines the following areas in depth:

- Setting up DOS
- Setting up Windows
- Optimizing the hard drive
- Installing AutoCAD Release 13
- Using AutoCAD's tablet menu

Discussing all possible configurations and variables in detail is not practical for this appendix. The purpose of this appendix is to acquaint you with the most important setup and configuration issues.

This appendix concentrates on DOS, Windows 3.1, and Windows for Workgroups 3.11. The Windows NT version of AutoCAD Release 13 will not be released until early 1995. The Windows version of AutoCAD will run under Windows NT, but will not take full advantage of the multitasking, multithreaded, full 32-bit Windows NT operating system.

Additional information is available in the AutoCAD Release 13 *Installation Guide for Windows* and the README.WRI and README.TXT files available on the installation disks.

The user's guide that ships with DOS provides much useful information on configuration and memory management. You can find valuable information for setting up Windows in the *Microsoft Resource Guides for Windows, Windows for Workgroups, and Windows NT*. The Microsoft Knowledge Base, available on the Internet (ftp.microsoft.com) and on many online services, such as CompuServe and GEnie, also is an invaluable source of information on DOS and Windows.

Installation Requirements

AutoCAD for Windows requires the following minimum hardware and software configuration:

- **An 80386 (minimum requirement), 80486, or Pentium-based computer.** Autodesk recommends a 486 system at least. 486SX systems require a math coprocessor. In 486DX systems, the math coprocessor is designed into the CPU chip.

- **16 MB of RAM minimum.** The more RAM installed in your computer, the faster AutoCAD and Windows operate. Some 386 computers do not support addressing for more than 16 MB RAM. This limitation can be bypassed by using a third-party memory manager, such as QEMM386 from Quarterdeck Office Systems, or by obtaining a BIOS update.

- **A hard disk that has enough free space for 37 MB of AutoCAD files and a 40 MB (minimum) swap file.** The 40 MB swap file must be created from available contiguous disk space. Autodesk recommends a swap file equal to four times the amount of RAM installed in the system. With the minimum recommended 16 MB RAM installed, the optimal size for the swap file is 64 MB. Additional disk space will be required for the storage of drawing (DWG) files.

- **A Windows-supported display adapter.** Your system must be capable of VGA or better resolution, and it must be able to work with

Windows. A coprocessed or an accelerated graphics card is recommended on production AutoCAD systems.

- **A pointing device.** This device can be a mouse or a digitizing tablet with a stylus or puck.

- **Floppy disk drives.** At least one 1.44 or 1.2 MB floppy disk drive is required. Drives for 3.5-inch floppies with 1.44 MB storage remain the most popular floppy drives in PC systems today. 5.25-inch disks with 1.2 MB storage are fast becoming obsolete.

- **IBM-compatible parallel port.** A parallel port is required for the network and international versions of AutoCAD.

- **Hardware lock.** A hardware lock is required for use on networks and for international single-user installations. It attaches to the workstation's parallel port. The hardware lock ships with all versions of AutoCAD that require it.

- **MS-DOS Version 5.0 or later.** MS-DOS Version 6.0 or 6.22 (with DriveSpace disk compression) is strongly recommended.

- **Microsoft Windows 3.1, Windows for Workgroups 3.1, Windows NT 3.1, or later versions.** Your computer must be capable of running Windows in 386-enhanced mode. AutoCAD does not run in standard mode. Microsoft is currently promoting Windows for Workgroups 3.11 as the upgrade path from Microsoft Windows 3.1. Windows NT 3.5 provides significant performance improvement over Windows NT 3.1.

- **Microsoft Win32s version 1.20 or later.** This is supplied with the AutoCAD installation disks.

Optional hardware includes the following:

- **Printer/plotter.** You need one or both of these to be able to produce hard-copy output of your drawings.

- **Digitizing tablet.** You need a digitizing table for tracing hard-copy or tablet menus.

- **Serial port.** You need a serial port to use with digitizers and some plotters.

- **CD-ROM drive.** Software installation from CD-ROM is easier, quicker, and far less painful than installation from floppy disks. Also, large data files and software libraries often are distributed on CD-ROM.

Update your DOS operating system to version 6.0 or 6.22. DOS version 6.*x* offers valuable features for optimizing DOS and Windows performance.

Use SCANDISK regularly to check the condition of the directories and files on your hard drive. Use DEFRAG regularly to defragment files and optimize the performance of your hard drive. Use MEM to determine how your computer utilizes its memory, and use MEMMAKER to optimize memory usage.

Configuring Your DOS Startup Files

When you boot your system, DOS reads two initialization files that configure your hardware, reserve space in memory, set device characteristics, customize the information that DOS displays, and launch memory-resident programs (TSRs) and other applications. These two files are CONFIG.SYS and AUTOEXEC.BAT.

You can use any ASCII text editor to view and edit these files. In fact, you can use any word processor to edit these files, as long as you save them as ASCII text files after you edit them. The Notepad application included with Windows is an ASCII text editor.

You can find the SYSEDIT.EXE file in the Windows/System directory. Running SYSEDIT launches Notepad and loads your AUTOEXEC.BAT, CONFIG.SYS, WIN.INI, and SYSTEM.INI files. If you run Windows for Workgroups, the PROTOCOL.INI, MAIL.INI, and SCHDPLUS.INI files are loaded as well. Figure A.1 shows SYSEDIT.EXE with AUTOEXEC.BAT and CONFIG.SYS visible.

CONFIG.SYS

This section discusses the settings and device drivers typically found in a CONFIG.SYS file. Be aware that the contents of CONFIG.SYS files on different systems vary according to the hardware and software used on the given system.

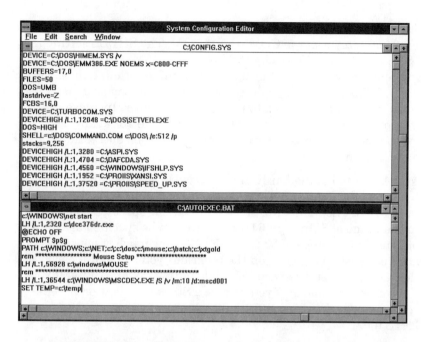

Figure A.1

*Typical
AUTOEXEC.BAT
and CONFIG.SYS
files.*

HIMEM.SYS and EMM386.EXE are discussed later in this appendix, in
the section "Memory Management."

Buffers reserve memory to hold hard disk data during read and write
operations. Each buffer uses approximately 532 bytes of memory. Your
system setup determines the number of buffers that should be allocated. If
your system uses SMARTDrive and disk compression (for example,
DoubleSpace or DriveSpace) and DOS is loaded high, you should set
BUFFERS=10. If you use SMARTDrive or other disk-caching software
without disk compression, you should set BUFFERS=1. Use BUFF-
ERS=20 or higher if you do not use SMARTDrive or some other form of
disk caching.

FILES specifies the number of files that DOS can access at any one time.
Autodesk recommends that you use FILES=50 or greater when you run
AutoCAD for Windows. FILES does not use much memory; a large value
helps when you use Windows AutoCAD and AutoLISP.

DOS=HIGH,UMB loads part of DOS into upper memory and provides
support for loading device drivers and TSRs into the upper memory area
to free conventional memory. The DEVICEHIGH command in
CONFIG.SYS and the LOADHI command in AUTOEXEC.BAT load
various device drivers into high memory.

SHELL defines the command interpreter that DOS is to use. By default, the system command interpreter is COMMAND.COM. The SHELL setting in CONFIG.SYS enables you to specify the amount of RAM available to use to store environment variable settings and other information. Use /E:256 or more for DOS 5.0 or later. If you receive the error message Out of environment space, you might need to try a higher number. Increase the number, reboot, and try the operation that caused the error again. You might need to repeat the process several times before you successfully eliminate the error message.

DOS uses STACKS to handle hardware interrupts. The first number in STACKS=9,256 is the quantity of stacks; the second number is the size of each stack in bytes. The number of stacks that can be specified as 0 is a number in the range of 8 through 64. Stack size can be specified as 0 or a number of bytes in the range of 32 through 512. How much stack space you need on your system depends on the programs you run and if each program leaves enough stack space to handle hardware interrupts. If your computer becomes unstable or if you receive a Stack Overflow or Exception Error 12 message, increase the number or size of stacks in your CONFIG.SYS file.

AUTOEXEC.BAT

See figure A.2 for a listing of an AUTOEXEC.BAT file.

Figure A.2

A typical AUTOEXEC.BAT file as seen in the Windows Notepad text editor.

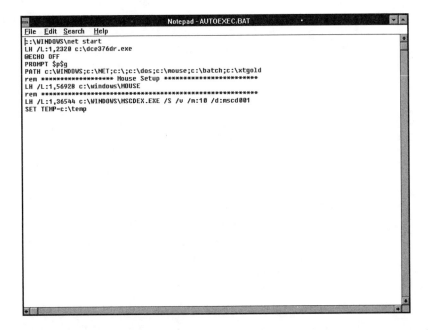

A

PROMPT changes the appearance of the command prompt in DOS. The $p adds the current drive and path to the command prompt. $g adds > (the greater-than sign) to the command prompt. Other possibilities include $t to add the time, $d to add the date, and $v to add the DOS version number to the display of the command prompt.

DOS 6 has made the > sign and the display of the current drive and path the default command prompt display. There is no need to have the PROMPT command in your AUTOEXEC.BAT file if you are running DOS 6 and that is the appearance you want for your command prompt.

Entering PROMPT without any text following will clear the default and the command prompt will display as c> without any indication of path. If you then enter PROMPT $g, the command prompt will display as >.

DOS versions 5.0 and 6.*x* now have extensive online help systems. To get information about a DOS command at the DOS command prompt, enter **HELP**, followed by the name of the command (**HELP COMMAND**).

TIP

The PATH command enables you to specify the directories DOS should search for executable files. MS-DOS recognizes up to 127 characters in the PATH command, including drive letters, colons, and backslashes. During initial installation, many programs add their directory to the PATH statement in the AUTOEXEC.BAT file. Because the PATH command uses conventional memory according to its length, you might want to examine your AUTOEXEC.BAT and remove unnecessary entries from your PATH statement.

Keep your AUTOEXEC.BAT and CONFIG.SYS files as uncluttered as possible. Keep your PATH down to the absolute minimum to save conventional memory and avoid possible conflicts.

TIP

The SET statement enables you to display, set, or remove DOS environment variables. SET commonly is included in the AUTOEXEC.BAT file to set a directory for the storage of temporary files. A program creates temporary files to hold data while a program runs. The program itself should delete temporary files after you close it. When an application or system crashes, the temporary files (TMP) often remain in the directory established by the SET TEMP statement.

Do not use the APPEND command in DOS if you also are running Windows. APPEND enables programs to open data files in specified directories as if they were in the current directory. Use the PATH command rather than the APPEND command.

When you use DOS 5.0 or later, while the computer is booting and after Starting MS-DOS... appears on-screen, you can press F5 to bypass the CONFIG.SYS and AUTOEXEC.BAT files. Or, you can press F8 to step through your AUTOEXEC.BAT and CONFIG.SYS files one command at a time. By using F8, you can choose whether to run each line in both the AUTOEXEC and CONFIG files.

SMARTDRV.SYS is a disk-caching utility that speeds up hard disk access. You can install another disk-caching utility instead, such as PC-CACHE from Central Point Software.

While disk caching is an important tool for speeding up access to program and data files, write caching can be dangerous. If your computer crashes or freezes while data is in the cache, not only do you lose that data, but it can corrupt the associated files. If you use DOS SMARTDRV, use the /X switch to disable write caching.

If you edit your CONFIG.SYS and AUTOEXEC.BAT files, your changes do not take effect until after you reboot your computer. To perform a warm reboot, press Ctrl+Alt+Del after you exit Windows.

Try to avoid using TSR programs. Because of the way they use memory, they often cause problems with other programs running under DOS and Windows. Screen savers are notorious for causing problems with DOS and Windows applications. If you have difficulties with your system, see if disabling your screen saver helps solve your problem.

A

Memory Management

Conventional memory is the 640 KB of memory located in the 0000 to
A000 address range. Applications programs and DOS typically use this
memory. A `low resources` or `out of resources` message often indicates that
a system has limited conventional memory available.

The memory between 640 KB and 1 MB is the *upper memory area* (UMA).
You load device drivers and buffers (required by a variety of hardware,
such as video display boards and network interface cards) and the ROM
BIOS into the UMA. Most systems that use expanded memory load the
expanded memory page frame into UMA.

Extended memory (XMS) is memory beyond 1 MB. You must have an
extended memory manager, such as HIMEM.SYS, before you can access
extended memory. You need extended memory for Windows and all
Windows-based applications.

The first 64 KB of extended memory is called the *high memory area*
(HMA). The setup for MS-DOS 6.*x* automatically installs a portion of DOS
to run in the HMA.

The extended memory area can be used only to store data, not to store
executable code.

Expanded memory (EMS) is used to page 16 or 64 KB portions of memory
into the expanded memory page frame, located in the UMA.

HIMEM.SYS and EMM386.EXE

MS-DOS provides two memory managers—HIMEM.SYS and
EMM386.EXE—to manage extended and expanded memory.

HIMEM.SYS manages extended memory according to the XMS specification so that no two programs use the same area of extended memory. It
also provides access to the first 64 KB of the extended memory area (the
HMA).

EMM386.EXE performs two functions. It provides access to the upper
memory area, and can make extended memory emulate expanded
memory.

Many programs originally designed to run under DOS require expanded memory. To provide expanded memory for those programs, EMM386 can take a defined amount of extended memory and use it as expanded memory. The amount of extended memory used as expanded memory is determined by the switches used with EMM386 in the CONFIG.SYS file. Following are examples of different ways to set up extended memory usage:

```
DEVICE=C:\DOS\EMM386.EXE NOEMS
```

The NOEMS switch tells EMM386 not to allocate any extended memory as expanded memory.

```
DEVICE=C:\DOS\EMM386.EXE NOEMS X=C800-CFFF
```

The X=C800-CFFF switch instructs EMM386 to exclude a region of the upper memory area from use. Sometimes you must reserve a region of upper memory for a device, such as a network interface card or a graphics adapter.

```
DEVICE=C:\DOS\EMM386.EXE RAM=2048
```

The RAM=2048 switch instructs EMM386 to allocate 2 MB of extended memory as expanded memory. The quantity could be 512, 1024 (1 MB), or some other quantity.

```
DEVICE=C:\DOS\EMM386.EXE MIN=0
```

With the MIN=0 switch, no extended memory is reserved as expanded memory, but EMM386 dynamically allocates expanded memory as applications require it.

Third-party software providers, such as Quarterdeck Systems, offer software that has the same functionality as HIMEM.SYS and EMM386.EXE. Some users believe Quarterdeck's QEMM as a memory manager is superior to the memory managers included with MS-DOS.

Understanding Windows Resources

One of the most frustrating problems that users experience when they use Windows is running out of resources. If you run out of resources, the amount of memory you have and the size of your swap file no longer matter. Running out of resources can prevent you from launching applications—worse, your programs and Windows itself can crash.

In the Windows Program Manager, you can choose **H**elp, **A**bout Program Manager to see the amount of Windows resources in terms of percentage available (see fig. A.3). Many shareware programs, such as Metz FreeMem, provide a status bar that enables you to monitor system resources.

Figure A.3

The status of Windows resources, as seen in the About Program Manager dialog box.

The heart of the Windows environment consists of USER.EXE, GDI.EXE, and KRNL386.EXE. Both USER.EXE and GDI.EXE are limited in size to 64 KB data segments, known as *heaps*. The 64 KB limitation owes to the baggage that DOS carries as an operating system for the 8086/80286 architecture.

Windows derives the percentage of resources available shown in the About Program Manager dialog box from the free heap space in USER.EXE and GDI.EXE, and shows the smaller of the two percentages. If GDI.EXE has 35 percent free heap space and USER.EXE has 60 percent free heap space, for example, 35 percent resources available (System Resources, at the bottom of the screen) is displayed.

The USER.EXE heap stores information about active windows as data structures, including application windows, dialog boxes, radio buttons, check boxes, and minimized windows. The GDI.EXE heap stores information about graphical objects, including pens, brushes, cursors, fonts, and icons.

In Windows 3.1 and higher, most resource problems result from low resources in the GDI.EXE (GDI stands for Graphics Device Interface). If the GDI.EXE heap fills up with graphical objects, Windows reports a low system resources error.

Resources for certain GDI.EXE objects are not always released when some graphical applications are closed. Sometimes, you have to restart Windows to release all objects in the GDI.EXE heap.

To keep system resources at an acceptable level, you might try the following:

- Keep as few applications open as possible.

- Minimize little-used groups in Program Manager.

- Do not use wallpaper. If you must use wallpaper, use a small bitmap and tile the wallpaper.

- If you run an application that eats system resources every time you execute it, leave it open instead of closing and reopening it.

- Do not load fonts you do not need.

- Make sure that your screen savers are not causing resources to leak away.

- Close and restart Windows from time to time.

Configuring Windows

Two INI files—WIN.INI and SYSTEM.INI—form the basis for most Windows configuration. INI stands for initialization, and these files initialize Windows. Similarly, application programs generally have INI files located in the \WINDOWS directory or in the application's own directory. By default, AutoCAD Release 13 installs an ACAD.INI file in the \ACADR13\WIN directory. Almost all INI files are text files that you can view and edit by using a text editor.

Some information on the WIN.INI and SYSTEM.INI files is available in two files that you can find in the \WINDOWS directory—WININI.WRI and SYSINI.WRI. Full details on the INI files are available in the Windows Resource Kit and in the Windows for Workgroups Resource Kit.

TIP

To view and edit INI files, you should associate the extension INI with the Notepad text editor. After you associate an INI file, you can launch it in Notepad by double-clicking on the document file in File Manager.

To associate INI files with Notepad, open File Manager and choose **F**ile, **A**ssociate. In the **F**iles with Extension text box, type **INI**. In the **A**ssociate With text box, select Text File (NOTEPAD.EXE), then choose OK. You can use these instructions to associate any file extension with any program application.

WIN.INI

WIN.INI contains settings that Windows uses to customize the Windows environment according to your preferences. The following lists some of the areas that are configured in the WIN.INI file:

- Mouse
- Keyboard
- Desktop
- Colors
- Extensions
- Serial and parallel ports
- Fonts
- Printers

The following example line is from a WIN.INI file that associates the AutoCAD program file with the DWG extension.

```
dwg=C:\ACADR13\WIN\acad.exe ^.dwg
```

When you use File Manager to associate an extension with an application, an according line of text using the preceding format is written into the WIN.INI file.

SYSTEM.INI

The SYSTEM.INI file contains settings that customize Windows for use with your system's hardware. The following lines from a SYSTEM.INI boot section define drivers used in Windows.

```
[Boot]
shell=progman.exe
```

```
network.drv=wfwnet.drv
mouse.drv=mouse.drv
language.dll=
sound.drv=mmsound.drv
comm.drv=comm.drv
```

The following are lines from the 386-Enhanced section of SYSTEM.INI:

```
[386Enh]
device=C:\WINDOWS\SYSTEM\WIN32S\W32S.386
device=*vpd
mouse=*vmd
device=lpt.386
device=serial.386
```

The reference to WIN32S.386 refers to the Win32s virtual device driver that is installed with AutoCAD Release 13.

If you move programs and files from one drive to another in a system that has partitioned or multiple disk drives, be careful. You must manually edit the appropriate INI files to correct the path. In fact, if programs do not run or cannot find necessary files, you might find that a line in an INI file points to an incorrect path.

Swap File

Windows uses a swap file to free up real memory for needed operations. *Swap files* reserve space on the hard drive for Windows to store information from memory to this file. The minimum requirement for AutoCAD Release 13 is a 40 MB permanent swap file.

Before you change or create a swap file, run SCANDISK to verify the integrity of the files and directories on your hard disk. Then, run DEFRAG to defragment and consolidate the files on your hard disk. A permanent swap file requires contiguous disk space.

The following exercise shows you how to create a permanent swap file or increase the size of your current swap file.

Increasing the Size of a Swap File

In Windows, open the Main program group, then launch Control Panel

Opens Control Panel from the Main group in Program Manager

Double-click on the Enhanced icon, choose **V**irtual Memory *and then* **C**hange

Accesses the New Swapfile Settings section of the Virtual Memory dialog box (see fig. A.4)

In the New **S**ize *box, type the size you want for your swap file, then choose* OK

Indicates the size of your new swap file (you do not have to use the recommended size)

Windows asks you to confirm the change; answer Yes *if the settings are correct*

Changes the Swap File settings

Windows will restart to activate the swap file change

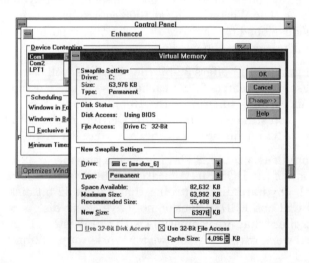

Figure A.4

Increasing the Windows swap file size.

Maximizing Windows Virtual Memory and the Swap File

AutoCAD benefits from a huge Windows swap file. You can increase the usable size of the Windows swap file with the Windows Virtual Memory multiplier PageOverCommit switch in the [386Enh] section of the

Windows SYSTEM.INI file. The default value of 4 tells Windows to use 4×
physical memory. Autodesk recommends up to 128 KB for the swap file for
large or complex drawings, particularly when using solids. If you set a 128
MB permanent swap file and you have 16 MB of RAM, Windows will use
only 64 MB unless you put the following line in the [386Enh] section of
the SYSTEM.INI file:

```
PageOverCommit=8
```

With this setting, Windows will use 16 MB × 8 = 128 MB of Virtual Swap
space.

32-Bit Access and Other Issues

Windows 3.1 provides you with the option of using 32-bit disk access to
speed up data transfers between the hard disk and the system. You must
have a Western Digital 1003–compatible disk controller before you can
use 32-bit disk access. The Western Digital 1003 controller interface is the
standard that was developed for the IBM PC AT and is reportedly used by
90 percent of the disk drives in the market.

Windows for Workgroups 3.11 offers 32-bit file access as well. When you
use 32-bit file access, you create a 32-bit cache to use with your files on
your hard disk. This cache is superior to the 16-bit cache that
SMARTDrive uses. You still can set up SMARTDrive to cache data from
floppy drives because 32-bit file access is only a hard drive cache.

Along with functioning as a cache, 32-bit file access provides a 32-bit path
for the manipulation of the DOS File Allocation Table (FAT). The result is
faster disk I/O with any hard disk controller that have a 32-bit disk access
driver. Typically SCSI and ESDI drives do not have 32-bit disk access
drivers. Disk controllers that are compatible with the Western Digital
1003 controller will work with the Windows for Workgroups 32-bit file
access.

The virtual device drives that implement 32-bit file access in Windows for
Workgroups are VFAT.386 and VCACHE.386

Win32s

Applications developed under Microsoft's 32-bit Applications Program-
ming Interface (API) are called *Win32 applications*. Win32 applications
are designed to run under the Windows NT and Windows 95 32-bit
operating systems. Win32s is a set of dynamic data links and virtual

device drivers that enable 32-bit applications to run under the 16-bit Windows and Windows for Workgroups environments.

The Win32s API provides binary compatibility for Win32 applications running on Windows 3.1 and Windows NT. 32-bit applications run differently under Windows 3.1 than under Windows NT. Windows 3.1 runs Win32 applications non-preemptively in a single, shared address space. Windows NT runs Win32 applications preemptively in a separate address space.

Windows NT

Windows NT uses a virtual DOS machine called WOW (for Win16 On Win32) to run 16-bit Windows applications. All 16-bit Windows applications run in WOW. In WOW, only one Win16 application can run at a time; others are blocked. With respect to other Windows NT processes, WOW is preemptively multitasked (can run concurrently with other Windows NT applications).

AutoCAD Release 13 for Windows runs as a 16-bit Windows application under Windows NT. It uses 32-bit code through the Win32s API. AutoCAD Release 13 for Windows NT takes full advantage of the Windows NT non-preemptive, 32-bit, multitasking operating system. When released in early 1995, Release 13 for Windows NT should offer superior performance over both Release 13 for DOS and Release 13 for Windows.

Windows NT uses a registry database for the storage and maintenance of configuration information. Analogous to the INI files in Windows 3.1, the Registry is a centralized database that stores application configuration data, hardware configuration data, device driver configuration data, and network protocol and adapter card settings. Windows NT supports the use of INI files for those applications designed to run under Windows 3.1. Windows 95 also uses a registry for storage of configuration information.

Installing AutoCAD

For proper installation of AutoCAD Release 13 for Windows, make sure that your system meets the minimum requirements itemized at the beginning of this appendix. If you install from floppy disks, back up your disks before you begin. If you install from CD-ROM, you should back up the single floppy disk, known as the *installation disk,* that starts the installation process.

TIP

To set up applications under Windows, launch File Manager and choose **F**ile, **R**un. Then enter the path and **SETUP** in the **C**ommand Line box:

`X:\SETUP`

Replace the `X:\` with the correct disk drive for your system.

Similarly, you can choose **F**ile, **R**un from Program Manager. Another method you can use to launch SETUP is to use File Manager to view the directory that contains the SETUP.EXE file, then double-click on that file. Some applications use a file named INSTALL.EXE rather than SETUP for installations.

Installation of Win32s

If Win32 is not installed on your system, you should install it before you install AutoCAD. The Win32s files are on the CD-ROM or on floppy disks, depending on the media you ordered. You must install Win32s from Windows. Run the SETUP program from the Win32s disk or the Win32s directory on the CD-ROM. After you install Win32s, reboot Windows. A 32-bit game called FreeCell is included with Win32s (see fig. A.5). Microsoft recommends that you run FreeCell to verify that Win32s has installed properly.

Figure A.5

FreeCell, a 32-bit game that runs under 16-bit Windows through the Win32s API.

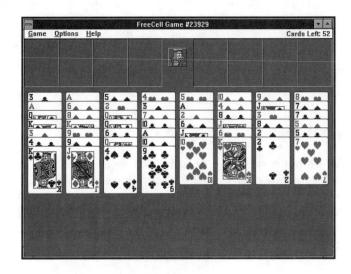

Installation Options

After you finish playing FreeCell, insert the AutoCAD installation disk in the floppy drive and run the setup program from within Windows. AutoCAD prompts you to enter your name, your company name, your dealer's name, and your dealer's telephone number. Enter the information as appropriate. AutoCAD next prompts you to choose between installing AutoCAD for Windows only, DOS only, or for Windows and DOS.

Next, AutoCAD gives you three installation options: Typical Installation, Custom Installation, and Minimum Installation. Choose the installation that is appropriate for your system. If you choose Custom Installation, a dialog box appears that enables you to choose the following:

- Executables and Support

- Learning Tools

- Application Development Tools

- External Database Access

- Examples and Samples

- Fonts

    - **T**rueType

    - **P**ostScript

    - **S**HX Source Files

- Speller Dictionaries

    - **E**nglish

- Electronic Documentation Viewer

As you select or deselect each component, AutoCAD displays how much disk space is required for the custom installation. Following the selection of components, AutoCAD prompts for the directories in which to install Release 13. It suggests two directories, ACADR13\WIN and ACADR13\COMMON.

AutoCAD explains in the dialog box that "the AutoCAD directory structure is split into separate file trees for containing files specific to Windows and files shared by both DOS and Windows platforms." AutoCAD displays the required disk space for each of the file trees. To complete the installation, choose **C**ontinue and insert disks as instructed or indicate the correct CD-ROM drive. The installation program does the remainder of the work.

Configuring AutoCAD

The first time you launch AutoCAD, you must configure AutoCAD for your system's hardware, network, and other configuration parameters. You need to know what type of graphics controller, plotter, and pointing device you have.

If you want to create more than one AutoCAD configuration, create a separate startup icon for each configuration. Each different configuration can specify different ACAD.CFG and ACAD.INI files to support a different set of devices—such as digitizers or plotters, different setups for the same devices, or a different set of support directories for different types of projects.

File Locking

During the configuration process AutoCAD asks if you want to enable file locking. *File locking* controls access to open files in network environments and prevents multiple users from altering active drawings. With file locking enabled, AutoCAD places a write lock on any open file. The only user who can modify the file is the one who opened the file.

It is possible to open a file and place a read lock on the file. A *read lock* tells others on the network that someone has opened a file for viewing. You can place a read lock on a file by choosing **F**ile, **O**pen, **R**ead Only when opening a file from the menu bar.

AutoCAD creates a lock file that uses the original file name with an extension related to the original file. When working in a drawing file or externally referencing a drawing, the lock file has a DWK extension. When saving, exiting, or inserting a block in an externally referenced drawing, the lock file has a DWL extension. See table A.1 for examples of a few different lock file extensions.

Table A.1
Examples of Extensions for Locked Files

File Type	File Extension	Locked File Extension
Drawing	DWG	DWK
Drawing	DWG	DWL
DXF	DXF	DFK
Shape	SHX	SXK

File Type	File Extension	Locked File Extension
Plot	PLT	PLK
Menu	MNS	MSK
Menu	MNX	MXK

A lock file can contain one write lock but many read locks. AutoCAD does not create a lock file for an unnamed drawing. Upon closing a locked file, AutoCAD unlocks the original file and deletes the associated lock file.

TIP

If you install AutoCAD for a single user, do not enable file-locking. File-locking is necessary in a network environment, but does not serve a useful purpose in a single-user environment.

If you need to reconfigure AutoCAD for a different hardware device, the AutoCAD configuration menu enables you to identify and change parameters for the graphics display, digitizer, and plotter that make up your workstation configuration.

Reconfiguring AutoCAD

After you install and configure AutoCAD for Windows, you can examine or change your configuration setup.

The following exercise starts the configuration menu to make changes in your AutoCAD configuration. If you change your digitizer, video board, plotter or want to change the setup of these devices, you can do so using configure.

Reconfiguring AutoCAD for Windows

Choose **O**ptions, **C**onfigure   Displays AutoCAD Text Window

Command line: **CONFIG**

Current AutoCAD configuration

Video display: *Your current display*

Digitizer: *Your current input device*

continues

continued

```
Plotter (#): Your current plotters

Speller dialect: Language chosen
(American English is an option)

Press RETURN to continue: (Enter)        Displays the configuration menu

Configuration menu
 0. Exit to Main Menu
 1. Show current configuration
 2. Allow detailed configuration
 3. Configure video display
 4. Configure digitizer
 5. Configure plotter
 6. Configure system console
 7. Configure operating parameters
```

To configure or change a device driver, select the item you want to change from the configuration menu. AutoCAD asks you questions about your hardware setup, and you respond with answers or a number selection from a list of choices. Configuration depends on your specific hardware. AutoCAD prompts you to supply values for each device. If you need more information, consult your AutoCAD *Installation Guide for Windows* or the device driver manufacturer's documentation.

When you choose to configure a particular device in AutoCAD's configuration menu, AutoCAD looks in the subdirectory specified in the Drivers text box of the **E**nvironment settings in the Preferences dialog box for the appropriate driver files.

If you move the driver files, edit the ACAD.INI file to indicate the new driver directory before you launch AutoCAD. Change the ACADDRV= setting to reflect the new driver directory. This enables you to reconfigure AutoCAD when you start it the next time.

If you need to reconfigure a device or restore its default settings, select that device type from the configuration menu, answer Yes at the Do you want to select a different one <N> prompt, then select the same device from the available device list.

ADI Drivers

The *Autodesk Device Interface* (ADI) is a standard interface developed by Autodesk that gives all hardware developers specifications for writing device drivers that work with AutoCAD. 4.2 ADI drivers written for AutoCAD Release 12 work with Release 13.

> Drivers designed to run on 16-bit platforms will not work with Release 13.

Autodesk recommends that you use appropriate ADI 4.2 drivers for pen plotters but use the Windows system printer for raster output devices, such as laser printers. For Windows, AutoCAD's ADI drivers take the form of dynamic link library files. Each type of driver uses a specific nomenclature, as shown in table A.2.

Table A.2
ADI 4.2 Driver Nomenclature

Type of Driver	ADI Name
Display	DS*.DLL
Combined rendering and display	RC*.DLL
Plotter	PL*.DLL
Digitizer	DG*.DLL

All drivers included with AutoCAD for Windows, other than null drivers, are ADI drivers. AutoCAD for Windows ADI drivers work only with AutoCAD for Windows; real-mode and protected-mode ADI drivers that you use with AutoCAD for DOS do not work with AutoCAD for Windows. If your printer or plotter requires an ADI driver for AutoCAD that Autodesk did not supply, see the manufacturer's instructions. Be sure to add any required commands to your CONFIG.SYS or AUTOEXEC.BAT files.

Calibrating a Digitizing Tablet

A digitizing tablet can be used for tracing and digitizing drawings into AutoCAD. The tablet first must be calibrated in order to digitize points on a drawing and then map those points to the drawing coordinate system. The tablet can be calibrated in either model space or paper space; the tablet will be calibrated in which ever space you are in at the time of calibration. If you switch from one space to another, tablet mode will be turned off.

To calibrate, attach the paper you want to trace to the digitizing tablet. The paper must be flat and attached securely to the tablet; it can be placed at any angle. Choose **O**ptions, **T**ablet, Ca**l**ibrate or enter **TABLET** followed by **CALIBRATE** at the command line to calibrate the tablet. The menu will prompt you to enter digitizing points and coordinates for each point.

The accuracy of the drawing is directly related to the amount of points entered. Once calibrated you have a choice of three transformations:

- **Orthogonal.** Use for dimensionally accurate drawings and for drawings with most points along single lines. Translation, uniform scaling, and rotation are specified with two translation points.

- **Affine.** Use when horizontal dimensions are stretched in relation to vertical dimensions. Translation, independent X and Y scaling, and skewing are specified with three calibration points.

- **Projective.** This is similar to perspective projection of one plane onto another plane. With projective transformation, straight lines map into straight lines but parallel lines do not always stay parallel. Parallel lines that appear to converge are corrected with projective transformation.

With only two points entered, AutoCAD automatically performs an orthogonal transformation. With three or more points entered, AutoCAD determines which of the three transformations best suits the calibration. See figure A.6 for an example of the results of the computation for the three types of transformations. The table provides you with the information you need to select the best transformation for your application.

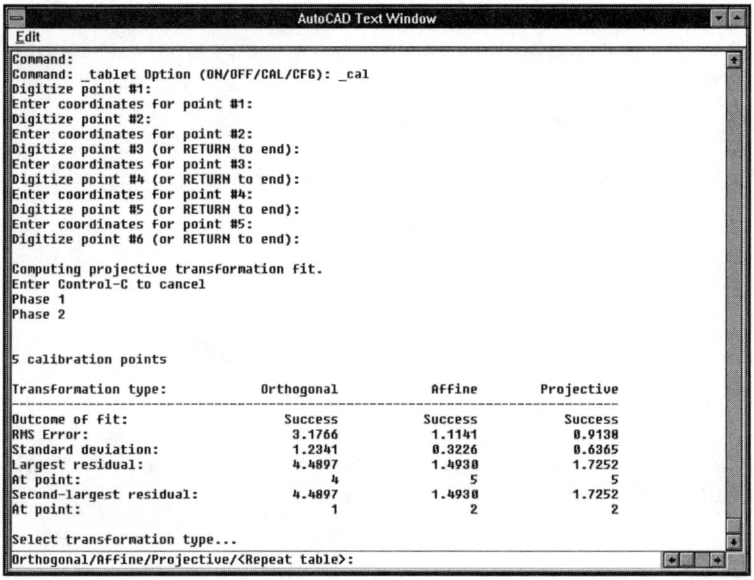

Figure A.6

The transformation table from the Tablet calibration procedure.

```
                                    AutoCAD Text Window
 Edit
Command:
Command: _tablet Option (ON/OFF/CAL/CFG): _cal
Digitize point #1:
Enter coordinates for point #1:
Digitize point #2:
Enter coordinates for point #2:
Digitize point #3 (or RETURN to end):
Enter coordinates for point #3:
Digitize point #4 (or RETURN to end):
Enter coordinates for point #4:
Digitize point #5 (or RETURN to end):
Enter coordinates for point #5:
Digitize point #6 (or RETURN to end):

Computing projective transformation fit.
Enter Control-C to cancel
Phase 1
Phase 2


5 calibration points

Transformation type:        Orthogonal        Affine        Projective
---------------------------------------------------------------------------
Outcome of fit:             Success           Success       Success
RMS Error:                  3.1766            1.1141        0.9138
Standard deviation:         1.2341            0.3226        0.6365
Largest residual:           4.4897            1.4930        1.7252
At point:                   4                 5             5
Second-largest residual:    4.4897            1.4930        1.7252
At point:                   1                 2             2

Select transformation type...
Orthogonal/Affine/Projective/<Repeat table>:
```

The following list explains the results reported in the table:

- **Outcome of fit.**

  - **Exact.** Correct number of points for a transformation.

  - **Success.** More than enough points for a transformation.

  - **Impossible.** Not enough points for a transformation.

  - **Failure.** Sufficient points but transformation failed. This typically is due to collinear or coincident points.

  - **Canceled.** The computational process was canceled. This happens only with projective transformation. Projective will show canceled when three points are entered. You still can choose projective transformation, however. AutoCAD will use the results computed for the transformation.

- **RMS Error.** RMS stands for root-mean-square; it measures how close the transformation is to a perfect fit. The smaller the number the better.

- **Standard Deviation.** This indicates the consistency of error over all the points.

- **Largest residual.** The largest error between where the point was mapped by the transformation and where the point would be mapped if the fit were perfect.

- **At point.** The point with the largest error.

- **Second largest residual.** The size of the error of the second least accurate point

- **At point.** The point with the second largest error.

Using AutoCAD's Standard Tablet Menu

AutoCAD provides a standard tablet menu and includes a plastic template for an 11-by-11-inch digitizer tablet. To use the standard AutoCAD tablet menu, affix the AutoCAD standard plastic template to the digitizing tablet and use the AutoCAD TABLET command to configure the tablet (see fig. A.7).

Figure A.7

The standard AutoCAD tablet menu.

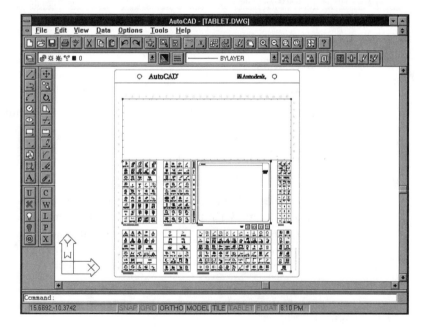

The TABLET.DWG Drawing

AutoCAD also comes with a drawing file, TABLET.DWG, which reproduces the plastic template menu. You can use this drawing to create a custom template drawing for your digitizer.

If you know how to edit drawings and customize the tablet menu, you can make your own tablet drawing, supporting the menu with your own tablet menu programs. If you customize your tablet menu, make a backup copy of TABLET.DWG, call it MYTABLET.DWG, and make your changes to the copy, not to the original.

Configuring Your Tablet Menu

This section assumes that you use an 11-by-11-inch or larger digitizer configured according to the *AutoCAD Installation Guide.*

If you use the AutoCAD template, place it on your digitizer. If you use the plotted TABLET drawing, trim the drawing, leaving about a 1/2-inch border, and tape it to your digitizer. Because every tablet is different, and because every user trims and tapes differently, you must configure the tablet so that AutoCAD can know exactly where the tablet commands are located on the surface of the tablet.

Use the TABLET command from inside the drawing editor to configure the tablet. A series of donuts—tablet pick points on the drawing (or template)—are used as guides when defining each of the four menu areas on the standard AutoCAD TABLET.

The standard menu is divided into four menu areas by columns and rows. In figure A.6, for example, the columns are numbered 1 to 25 across the top and the rows are lettered A to Y on the left. Menu area 1 is the top rectangular area. The first donut pick point is near A and 1 in the upper left corner. Menu area 1 has 25 columns and 9 rows of menu boxes.

When you configure the tablet, AutoCAD prompts you to pick three points for each menu area and to enter the number of columns and rows. For AutoCAD's standard TABLET, use the default selections for columns and rows.

In Release 13, AutoCAD uses the concept of screen pointing areas. Within a screen pointing area, a digitizer behaves like a system mouse. AutoCAD permits the configuration of two screen pointing areas for a digitizer—a fixed screen pointing area and a floating screen pointing area.

Autodesk recommends using a small area of the tablet that maps to the entire monitor display for the screen pointing area. To digitize points into AutoCAD with tablet mode on, you cannot use a fixed screen pointing area. You must use a floating screen area because of the one-to-one relationship that exists between the digitizer and the drawing when tablet mode is on. When you use a floating screen pointing area, you can access menus from anywhere on the tablet surface. You can use the F12 key or a defined button on the tablet pointing device to switch between fixed and floating screens.

The following exercise takes you through the configuration of the AutoCAD tablet menu. If you have not used a tablet menu it is wise to use the supplied AutoCAD menu and template before customizing your own tablet menu.

Configuring the AutoCAD Tablet Menu

Choose **O**ptions, **T**ablet, **C**onfigure	Configures your digitizing tablet
Enter the number of tablet menus desired (0-4) <0>: **4** (Enter)	Selects four menu areas on your tablet menu template
Do you want to align tablet menu areas? <N>: **Y** (Enter)	Specifies size and location of each tablet menu area
Digitize upper left corner of menu area 1: *Pick point* Menu 1 - UL	Selects appropriate donut
Digitize lower left corner of menu area 1: *Pick point* Menu 1 - LL	Selects appropriate donut
Digitize lower right corner of menu area 1: *Pick point* Menu 1 - LR	Selects appropriate donut
Enter the number of columns for menu area 1: (1-5015) <25> (Enter)	Selects the default
Enter the number of rows for menu area 1: (1-1795) <9> (Enter)	Selects the default
Digitize upper left corner of menu area 2: *Pick point* Menu 2 - UL	Selects the appropriate donut
Digitize lower left corner of menu area 2: *Pick point* Menu 2 - LL	Selects the appropriate donut
Digitize lower right corner of menu area 2: *Pick point* Menu 2 - LR	Selects the appropriate donut

A

Enter the number of columns for menu area 2: (1-2208) <11> **Enter**	Selects the default
Enter the number of rows for menu area 2: (1-1814) <9> **Enter**	Selects the default
Digitize upper left corner of menu area 3: *Pick point* Menu 3 - UL	Selects the appropriate donut
Digitize lower left corner of menu area 3: *Pick point* Menu 3 - LL	Selects the appropriate donut
Digitize lower right corner of menu area 3: *Pick point* Menu 3 - LR	Selects the appropriate donut
Enter the number of columns for menu area 3: (1-608) <9> **Enter**	Selects the default
Enter the number of rows for menu area 3: (1-1812) <13> **Enter**	Selects the default
Digitize upper left corner of menu area 4: *Pick point* Menu 4 - UL	Selects the appropriate donut
Digitize lower left corner of menu area 4: *Pick point* Menu 4 - LL	Selects the appropriate donut
Digitize lower right corner of menu area 4: *Pick point* Menu 4 - LR	Selects the appropriate donut
Enter the number of columns for menu area 4: (1-1505) <25> **Enter**	Selects the default
Enter the number of rows for menu area 4: (1-1392) <7> **Enter**	Selects the default
Do you want to respecify the Fixed Screen Pointing area (N) **Y** **Enter**	
Digitize lower left corner of screen pointing area: *Pick point* Screen Menu - LL	Selects the appropriate donut
Digitize upper right corner of screen pointing area: *Pick point* Screen Menu - UR	Selects the appropriate donut
Do you want to specify the Floating Screen Pointing area (N) **Y** **Enter**	
Do you want the Floating Screen Pointing Area to be the same size as the Fixed Screen Pointing Area? <Y> **Enter**	

continues

continued

```
Would you also like to specify a button toggle
the Floating Screen Area? <N> (Enter)
```

Enter **Yes** if you want to select a non-pick button to toggle the floating screen area ON and OFF.

After configuration is complete, choose a few commands from the tablet and draw in the screen pointing area to test the configuration. The standard AutoCAD tablet menu is configured for your digitizer, and the configuration parameters are stored on your disk in a file.

Raster File Format

AutoCAD supplies an ADI 4.2 driver that plots drawings to a raster-format file. With a raster-format file, AutoCAD drawings can be used in illustrations, publishing, and multimedia presentations. The raster-format driver emulates a plotter and represents width and height in pixels. Among the raster formats supported by the AutoCAD ADI driver are GIF, TIFF, PCX, BMP, TGA, and Group 3 Fax.

Realizing the full power of AutoCAD while using it in the Windows environment requires paying close attention to the configuration of your computer. It is necessary to optimize DOS and Windows to the fullest extent possible with memory management, swap files, and disk utilities to fully realize the power of AutoCAD. As 32-bit operating systems such as Windows NT proliferate, many of the configuration issues and limitation of DOS and the 16-bit environment will disappear. Until that time comes it is well worth spending the time necessary to understand what is required to optimize your system and then to bring that system up to its full potential.

B

Troubleshooting

This appendix contains tips, hints, and solutions to the most common problems found when using AutoCAD under the Windows or Windows NT environments.

When it comes to solving problems in AutoCAD, you might have to become something of a detective. There are good ways and bad ways to approach problem solving; the following list presents some general guidelines to solving problems:

1. Isolate the problem. If you can make the problem show up repetitively, it is easier to troubleshoot. Write down exactly you were doing when the problem occurred. It may just be operator error; it may not.

2. Determine which part of the system is being affected by the problem (such as memory, Windows, disk, and so forth). Most error messages give a clue as to which part of the system the problem is with.

3. Analyze the problem to determine the best course of action. Take, for example, a problem that you have determined to be a memory problem. Is the problem a result of a Windows memory conflict or a DOS memory conflict? Once you have determined whether the problem is a DOS or Windows memory problem, you have eliminated quite a few possible causes of the problem.

4. Remove as many unknowns from the equation as possible. For example, a heap error is a Windows memory management problem; therefore, do not look at DOS memory management issues to solve this problem. (This becomes easier with experience.)

5. Come up with a solution and try it. Then start with step 1 again.

6. Repeat until the problem is solved.

Most problems can be solved in an hour or two at the most. If you have not solved the problem by that time, ask someone else. Utilize resources such as your AutoCAD dealer or CompuServe. Many answers to common problems can be found through these two resources.

Many of the errors or problems that occur in AutoCAD can be attributed to the setup of the machine. This includes, but is not limited to, the DOS environment, the Windows environment, and the AutoCAD environment. Each of these environments must be set up correctly for AutoCAD to run.

Also, none of the environments can be changed—either by the user or another program—while AutoCAD is running. This will result in a variety of errors. The rest of this appendix discusses a few common errors and their solutions.

Common Problems in the DOS Environment

The two most common problems in the DOS environment are an insufficient number of files, and conflicts with TSRs.

Insufficient Files

AutoCAD cannot open a file or issue a command when a FILES error occurs. This error is a result of the DOS environment. The DOS CONFIG.SYS file has a statement called FILES=. For a standard AutoCAD installation, FILES should be set to 50. This setting enables AutoCAD and Windows to have as many as 50 files open at the same time, though running other programs concurrently with AutoCAD might require a higher number. Fifty is usually more than enough for a standard AutoCAD session. Use any text editor that creates pure ASCII text files and perform the following steps:

1. Modify the FILES= line of the CONFIG.SYS file to equal 50.

2. Save the file.

3. Reboot your machine to put the changes into affect.

Conflicts

DOS TSRs also can be a problem. A TSR (terminate-and-stay resident program) loads itself into memory and waits for a key event to occur before the TSR carries out its function. A key event may be something simple like the passage of time. A screen saver TSR waits for a predetermined amount of time of inactivity before trying to take more memory to run its program. This key is highly dependent upon the nature of the TSR. Most TSRs are well behaved and use only the memory they occupied when they were loaded. If a TSR takes over other memory when it is activated, memory corruption can occur if AutoCAD is running. The question is, how can you tell if it is a misbehaved TSR? A badly behaved TSR can cause AutoCAD to lock up when it appears nothing is wrong. If this happens repeatedly, go through yopur AUTOEXEC.BAT and CONFIG.SYS files and remove any unnecessary programs or drivers. (Refer to your DOS and Windows documentation, as well as Appendix A, "Installation and Configuration," of this book to find the minimum configuration needed to run AutoCAD). If the problem still occurs, then it is not caused by a TSR and you need to look elsewhere to solve the problem.

Common Windows Errors

Some of the problems that can occur in AutoCAD are a result of the Windows or Windows NT operating systems and not the AutoCAD program itself. These problems include user error when multi-tasking and Windows general protection faults (GPF). This section deals with how to solve or avoid these types of problems.

User Errors

Windows also can cause major problems. Because Windows is a multitasking environment, you can switch to other programs while running AutoCAD. Many times, it is necessary to switch to the Windows File Manager and do some basic file management. When you do so, do not delete some of the AutoCAD temporary files just because they look like junk. If you are running AutoCAD and you want to do some file management in File Manager, be careful not to delete any unknown files.

> If you delete an AutoCAD temporary file while in Windows file manager, upon switching back to the AutoCAD session, AutoCAD will crash and you will be forced to restart Windows.

Sometimes Windows drivers can cause a crash in AutoCAD. If you get any of the errors mentioned in this appendix and nothing seems to correct them, try reconfiguring your Windows video drivers to run as a straight VGA setup. Some video drivers might not be stable enough to work with AutoCAD. If this is the case, contact your display adapter manufacturer to acquire the latest drivers. Do the following to change the Windows setup to a basic VGA video setup:

1. Open the Main program group by double-clicking on it.

2. Double-click on the Windows Setup icon. Your current setup will be displayed in the Windows Setup dialog box.

3. Choose **C**hange System Settings from the **O**ptions pull-down menu.

4. Change your video display setting by selecting VGA from the **D**isplay list.

5. When you choose OK, you will be prompted to restart Windows for the changes to take effect. Make sure you have exited all Windows programs and closed any DOS sessions before restarting.

When Windows restarts, it will run at the new resolution. You now can try to re-create the problem. If the problem is gone, it was a result of your video driver.

B

General Protection Faults

Another common Windows problem is the dreaded general protection fault (GPF). Reasons for its occurrence are numerous, but usually the problem stems from a section of the computer's memory being corrupted. If you get a GPF in AutoCAD or any other program while running AutoCAD, perform the following steps:

1. Save all your work, and exit all programs and Windows.

2. Reboot the system.

3. Start where you left off.

Because Windows runs more than one program at a time, those programs are forced to share memory. (This problem does not show up as much on Windows NT because Windows programs can be run in their own protected memory spaces. See your Windows NT documentation on how to run a program this way.) Because the programs share memory space, if one program corrupts part of that memory space, it inevitably will cause problems in other programs, and eventually the entire system. The best solution is to restart the Windows environment before any more corruption takes place.

Understanding AutoCAD Error Messages

AutoCAD keeps an error log of all errors that occur on the system in a file called ACAD.ERR. This file usually is located in the \ACADR13\WIN directory, but may end up in your current drawing directory. When AutoCAD detects an error, it displays the message on-screen and records it to this file. Sometimes errors are bad enough that AutoCAD cannot display the error problem on the screen. If this is the case, check the ACAD.ERR file to see if the error was recorded there. The following is an example error from an ACAD.ERR file:

```
FATAL ERROR:  Heap error
12/11/1994 at 22:30:04.720 Drawing: C:\ACADR13\COMMON\SAMPLES\SEXTANT
_ _ _ _ _
```

Each successive error is appended to this file. Some common errors that AutoCAD will notify you of are heap errors, segmentation faults, entity read errors, entity regen errors, and internal errors.

Heap Error

A fairly common error in AutoCAD Release 13 for Windows, heap errors occur when Windows runs out of virtual memory. Autodesk recommends a minimum swap file size of 40 MB for AutoCAD. If you get this error, AutoCAD will tell you that it cannot continue, but that it can save the changes in the drawing (which is good compared to some errors). To solve the error, change the size of your permanent Windows swap file as described in Appendix A.

See your Windows documentation on how to change your virtual memory settings. The process is different for Windows NT, so be sure to note the appropriate documentation. Windows will give you recommended and maximum virtual memory settings.

> If you have enough disk space but Windows will only let you create a small permanent swap file, you might need to defragment your hard drive and then try creating the swap file again. (DOS 6.*x* has a utility called DEFRAG that will accomplish this.)

Segmentation Fault

This error is similar to the heap error, and generally is the result of a swap file that is too small. Refer to the heap error to solve this problem as well. If changing the swap file does not correct the error, start removing TSRs and drivers as mentioned previously.

EREAD: Entity Read Error

Entity read errors occur when AutoCAD is reading a file from disk or from memory and it finds a corrupted entity or a sequence of bytes that makes no sense. File corruption can be caused by hardware errors (fairly rare), power surges, and abnormal program termination (crash) of an AutoCAD session. A file that displays this error might be recovered through AutoCAD's AUDIT and drawing RECOVER commands. Audit and drawing recovery both search the AutoCAD database for any errors and try to fix any errors that are found. If an error cannot be fixed, AutoCAD skips that section of the file and moves on to the next. This way, you might not recover all of the file, but you will recover at least some of it. Audit works from within files that are already open. To issue an Audit, complete the following steps:

1. Load the drawing into AutoCAD (if it is not already loaded).

2. Issue the AUDIT command.

3. When prompted by AutoCAD to fix any errors detected, enter **YES**. Now AutoCAD will fix any errors as it detects them.

4. Watch the text screen because AutoCAD will display errors as it finds them.

Drawing recovery is used when AutoCAD cannot completely load a drawing without an error. This process runs an AUDIT as AutoCAD loads the file. If the file cannot be recovered by this method, it might not be recoverable. Another method of cleaning up a drawing is to issue the WBLOCK command to remove unnecessary information from the drawing file. (Note that the WBLOCK command removes all unnecessary information). See Chapter 16, "Composing and Plotting a Drawing," for more information on the WBLOCK command.

Frequently back up your files and use AutoCAD's autosave feature to avoid losing your valuable work.

TIP

EREGEN: Entity Regen

This error is similar to the EREAD error, but occurs when AutoCAD is trying to regenerate an object on the screen and finds an error in the translation process. AutoCAD crashes if this error occurs. As with EREAD errors, use the AUDIT or RECOVER commands to retrieve the file.

Internal Error

Internal errors are accompanied by a description of the error. The description looks rather cryptic and probably contains a minute section of the program code. If the error has the word write anywhere in it, it is probable that AutoCAD was performing a write operation to disk. This message probably is indicative of the fact that AutoCAD is running out of disk space. If you get an internal error, AutoCAD will ask you if you want to save the file. The internal error problem is solved by freeing up disk space, or purchasing a larger hard drive. AutoCAD creates its own temporary files outside of the Windows swap file. This creation of extra temorary files means AutoCAD will use more disk space than that allocated by a Windows swap file. Do not be surprised if you exit AutoCAD and Windows, and find you have a lot of disk space left. When you leave AutoCAD and Windows, the temporary files are deleted and you will have the resulting space left over.

SCANDR

This error message occurs when AutoCAD cannot update its temporary files due to an error of its own. Because AutoCAD crashes, you must go through the drawing recovery process described previously and hope to get the files back. Otherwise, revert to your backup files, which AutoCAD saves with BAK extensions.

Exploring Other Problems in AutoCAD

Problems other than DOS, Windows and AutoCAD-specific problems can occur on your machine. These include the following:

- File locking
- Cleaning up a crashed system
- Solving Windows plotting problems
- 80386 and Pentium problems
- DSVIEWER problems
- Opening multiple drawings
- Plotting ACIS solids
- Restoring default configurations
- Memory manager problems

File Locking

If you try to load a locked file intoAutoCAD, you system should respond by telling you that the file was locked by *name* user on *mm/dd/yy* date. If you are on a single-user system, make sure file locking is turned off (see Appendix A, "Installation and Configuration"). If the file is locked, perform the following steps while in AutoCAD:

1. Choose **F**ile, **M**anagement, **U**nlock File to display the File Utilities dialog box. Then click on **U**nlock File to be able to unlock the file.

2. Click on the file from the File(s) to Unlock dialog box and choose OK when AutoCAD asks if you want to unlock the file.

This error usually occurs when the system crashes. When AutoCAD opens a file and file locking is turned on, a lock file with a DWK extension is created. If the system crashes, this file is not erased and the file still appears to be locked. The other way to solve this problem is to delete the lock file from DOS or File Manager.

Cleaning Up a Crashed System

If AutoCAD crashes, a clean-up process is inevitable. Basically, two or three things need to be done. A *crash* is defined as a system shutdown without proper exit from AutoCAD (that is, a power outage, pressing your system's reset button, pressing Ctrl+Alt+Del, or system lockup with reboot). If this occurs, several files will be left in your current drawing directory. These files are the temporary files AutoCAD was using when it crashed. Some of these files might also be hidden. Perform the following steps to recover from a crashed system:

1. Run CHKDSK /F or, if you have DOS 6.0 or later, run SCANDISK. Both programs scan the hard drive for lost chains and clusters.

2. If the programs find lost chains, do not convert the chains into files; they are useless. SCANDISK might ask if you want to save the files; reply no.

3. Delete all files with an AC$ extension in all of your directories. These are crashed AutoCAD files.

4. There might also be some junk files that are laying around. These files might have a filename similar to BBCDLFJL. Delete these as well.

5. If file locking was turned on, you might have locked files to deal with. If that is the case, refer to the previous section.

Solving Windows Plotting Problems

Under the Windows version of AutoCAD, plot configuration is a little different than the DOS version. You have two choices for configuration of the plotters: use the default Windows system printer, or choose a plotter directly supported by AutoCAD. Since AutoCAD can support multiple plotter configurations, using a system printer presents a small problem. If you have more than one type of printer hooked up to the system or network, and you are using the system printer option for each different printer, you have to change the Control Panel default printer to match the configured plotter in AutoCAD. Unfortunately, Windows does not provide a way to automate switching between configured system printers. Your best option here is to try to use the native AutoCAD plotter driver instead of the system printer. This provides direct printing to the plotter, but does not provide the normal background spooling Windows applications can provide.

80386 and Pentium Problems

Some early 80386 chips are not compatible with AutoCAD. These chips (sometimes referred to as *B-Step chips*) will lock into an infinite loop when executing certain math coprocessor instructions. The error is in the 80386 chip itself and not AutoCAD or the math coprocessor. These errors are known as the Intel 80386 Erratum #17 and Erratum #21. The chips with the following markings exhibit these problems:

16 MHz chips	20 MHz chips	25 MHz chips
A80386-16	A80386-20	A80386-25
S40343	S40362	SX050
A80386-16		
S40344		

Errata #17 and #21 also can be detected by using the CHKBSTEP.COM program that shipss with the DOS version of AutoCAD. This program is located in the ACADR13\DOS directory. You run the program by typing the command CHKBSTEP at the command prompt. The program will detect whether or not you have a B-Step chip. If you do, first try to determine if it is an Erratum #17 chip by changing the DOS memory extender. Use the command cfig386 -errata17 acad.exe to accomplish this. Next, try to run AutoCAD again. If the problem occurs again, you have an Erratum #21 error and you must replace the 80386 chipset. (Contact your manufacturer to get a bug-free chipset).

Most Pentium chips from Intel exhibit an FDIV error. This error occurs in double-precision floating-point divide operations. The Pentium chip truncates all numbers past the fourth decimal place; this error occurs once every 2 or 3 billion operations.

Because the error occurs rather infrequently, it does not pose a problem for most users. However, scientific, mechancal, or any precise type of drawing might show errors due to these chips. There are many programs available on CompuServe and most BBSs that will test your Pentium chip for the error. If you decide you need to replace the chip, contact your manufacturer or Intel directly. They will replace the chip at no cost.

DSVIEWER Does Not Work

The DSVIEWER (Serial View) under AutoCAD will not work correctly under certain configurations of the display driver for Windows. The problem can exhibit itself as incorrect screen redraws or incorrect zoom windows. The Windows display driver must be configured as the accelerated driver with the display list turned on. If your Aerial display does not work correctly, check your video configuration by using the CONFIG command. (See your AutoCAD documentation for more information on the CONFIG command).

Opening Multiple Drawings

AutoCAD Release 13 does not support opening multiple drawings. This is a result of the Win32s that enable AutoCAD to run under 16-bit Windows.

Release 13 can, however, open multiple drawings under Windows NT. In Windows NT, AutoCAD runs in native mode and does not have to translate 32-bit instructions to 16-bit.

Plotting ACIS Solids

Plotting solids can sometimes be difficult because of the way AutoCAD interprets the geometry. When AutoCAD plots or hides complex solids, the geometry is converted to triangles and will be rendered with a faceted look instead of a smooth surface. Change the system variable DISPSILH to 1 to remove the triangles. This problem also occurs when using the HIDE command.

Restoring Default Toolbar Configurations

Although AutoCAD enables you to customize its toolbars and create your own palettes, you sometimes will want to restore the factory defaults for those palettes. The process is fairly simple to accomplish. Complete the following steps:

1. Exit AutoCAD.

2. Edit your ACAD.INI file using a text editor, such as Notepad or EDIT. The default location for ACAD.INI is \ACADR13\WIN. Find the section titled Toolbars. Each toolbar is listed with its group name first, such as ACAD.MODIFY. Each toolbar you have created will have its own name. Delete any lines in this section of the file that refer to any toolbars you have created.

3. Save the ACAD.INI file.

4. Delete the ACAD.MNR, ACAD.MNC, and ACAD.MNS files from your ACADR13\WIN\SUPPORT directory. Each of these files will be re-created from the original ACAD.MNU file when you restart AutoCAD.

5. Restart AutoCAD to restore the original AutoCAD toolbars.

AutoCAD Patches

Because AutoCAD is such a large program, bugs are bound to pop up in the software. Many of these bugs are corrected by Autodesk as soon as possible. Even so, every once in a while, Autodesk releases patches for AutoCAD, in the form of patch files. The patches generally are available from CompuServe, in Autodesk's FTP site: ftp.autodesk.com (for those with Internet access), or directly from your dealer.

Some problems that you might not be able to solve are indeed the result of bugs, and the solution lies in applying the appropriate patches to AutoCAD. When the patches are applied, the AutoCAD version number changes; for example, Release 13 is the first release, whereas 13a is the first patched version. If the patch is considered a substantial upgrade, it will be given a revision number such as c1 or c2.

B

> As of this writing, Autodesk has released the 13_c1 patch to both CompuServe and the FTP site.

The patches come with instructions for application—follow them explicitly. Before making any modifications, make sure you back up the ACAD.EXE file. Also, write down your current AutoCAD configuration, because some patches make enough changes to require you to reconfigure after they run.

Looking At Memory Manager Problems

Both DOS and Windows include memory managers. (See Appendix A "Installation and Configuration" for a description.) If you use a third party memory manager such as QEMM386 or 386MAX, be aware that some of the features may cause problems wen running AutoCAD. These programs load many TSRs and drivers above the DOS 640 KB barrier. (See DOS documentation about the 640 KB limitation.)

QEMM386 has a feature called Stealth that rearranges the memory between 640 KB and 1 MB on systems; this enables QEMM to load a large amount of drivers above 640 KB. Unfortunately, many programs are not compatible with the Stealth feature. Because this directly affects the mapping of parts of the video memory, high resolution applications such as Windows and or AutoCAD might not run correctly. To be safe, do not use QEMM386's Stealth feature.

Also, be aware of which memory regions QEMM or any other memory manager is including or excluding for use in its optimizing process. You may or may not want certain regions of memory optimized, especially if you are using a network card in your system.

Optimizing AutoCAD for Windows Performance

A utoCAD Release 13 for Windows expands greatly on the use of the Windows Graphical User Interface (GUI). With toolbars and tabbed folders, such as the Object Snap toolbar and the Environment tabbed folder, the look and feel of the Windows version of AutoCAD is indistinguishable from the most advanced of Windows applications.

This appendix provides an in-depth explanation of toolbars and their management and customization. This appendix also discusses setting AutoCAD preferences from the **O**ptions, **P**references dialog boxes.

Toolbars are defined in the menu file, such as ACAD.MNU. Additions or modifications to toolbars are stored in MNS, MNR, and MNC files in the same directory of the menu. For example, changes to ACAD.MNU are stored in the ACAD.MNS, ACAD.MNR, and ACAD.MNC files, which are by default in the ACADR13\WIN\ Support directory. You can restore the factory defaults by deleting these MNS, MNR, and MNC files. AutoCAD will re-create them with defaults. Toolbar settings also are stored in the ACAD.INI file; you can delete the lines referencing specific toolbars from the ACAD.INI file. To restore factory defaults, you might need to delete lines from the ACAD.INI file as well as delete MNS, MNR, and MNC files. The default ACAD.INI file is in the ACADR13\WIN directory and the ACAD.MNU file is in the ACADR13\WIN\Support directory. Changes to toolbars and preferences affect the files in these directories unless you set up different configuration (for ACAD.INI) or support (for menus) directories. You also must copy the menu file to the support directory. If you delete the ACAD.INI directory, AutoCAD will re-create it with its factory defaults.

Understanding Toolbars

Release 13 of AutoCAD for Windows adds numerous toolbars to the graphical user interface. Release 13 also allows for customization and creation of these toolbars. Figure C.1 shows some of the many toolbars provided with Release 13. See the map showing all of Release 13's toolbars in Appendix F.

Toolbar Examples

Figure C.2 shows the Tool Windows and Dimensioning toolbars. The Tool Windows toolbar opens other toolbars; in this case, the Dimensioning toolbar is opened by clicking on the fourth tool from the left in the Tool Windows toolbar.

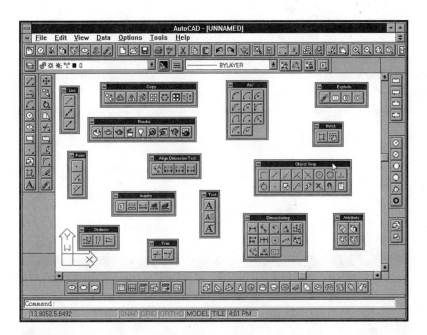

Figure C.1

Many—but far from all—of the toolbars packaged with AutoCAD Release 13.

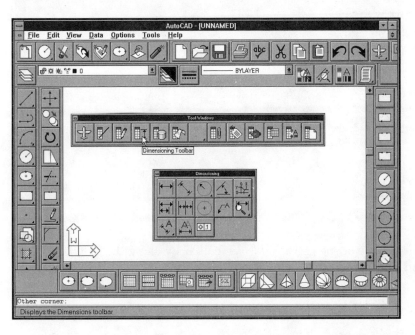

Figure C.2

The Dimensioning toolbar is launched from the Tool Windows toolbar.

Toolbars can be set to two sizes, large or small. All toolbars are affected by the choice; one toolbar cannot be set for large and another for small. Toolbars set for small are shown in figure C.1 and toolbars set for large are shown in figures C.2 and C.3.

Flyouts

The triangle at the lower right of a tool icon indicates that a tool has a flyout. A *flyout* is a child toolbar that is opened by the tool on the parent toolbar; the Bind flyout is shown in figure C.3. Whichever tool on the flyout is selected last becomes the current default on the parent toolbar.

Figure C.3

The Bind flyout on the External References toolbar.

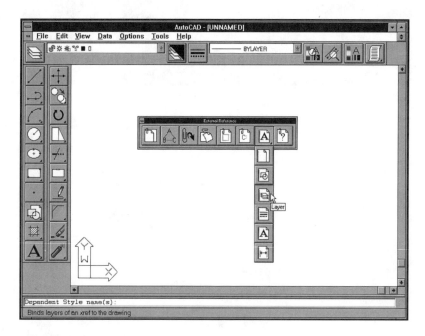

Any flyout can be opened as a separate toolbar by using the TOOLBAR command (the Show Toolbar dialog box).

Docking and Floating Toolbars

Toolbars can be docked along the edges of the AutoCAD screen, or they can be floated anywhere on-screen. In figure C.4, the Dimension toolbar is docked on the right side of the screen, the Object Properties toolbar is docked along the top, the Modify toolbar is docked on the left side, and the Solids toolbar is docked on the bottom. The Tool Windows toolbar is floating in the middle of the drawing window.

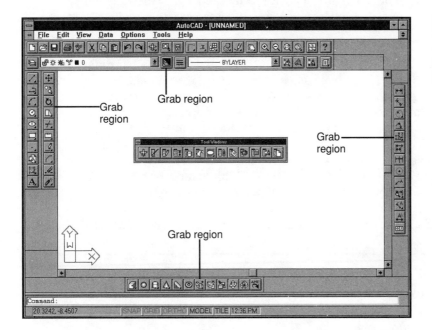

Figure C.4

Four docked toolbars and one floating toolbar.

To dock a floating toolbar, position the cursor on the toolbar's title bar, press the pick button, and drag the toolbar to the desired edge of the screen. As the toolbar approaches the docking area it changes shape to illustrate how it will look in that location. After the toolbar is placed, release the pick button.

To float a docked toolbar, position the pointing device over the gray area that surrounds the tool icons in a toolbar. This gray area is referred to as the *grab region*. Press the pick button and drag the toolbar away from its docked location. When in the desired location, release the pick button.

Customizing Toolbars

A powerful feature of Release 13 is its capability to create and customize toolbars and tools. You can create new tools and toolbars, or modify and delete existing tools from existing toolbars.

Creating a Toolbar

The Toolbars dialog box is the gateway to creating and modifying toolbars. You access the Toolbars dialog box by clicking on a tool icon with the Enter button of the pointing device or by choosing **T**ools, Customize Tool**b**ars. The following exercise shows how to create a toolbar.

TBCONFIG. The TBCONFIG command opens the Toolbar dialog box. From this dialog box you can create, delete, and modify your toolbars. AutoCAD requires the Toolbar dialog box to be open for the creation and modification of Tool Button and Flyouts. This is true even though you do not directly access the Button Properties and Flyout Properties dialog boxes from the Toolbar dialog box. In fact, the Toolbar dialog box can remain open while you perform a variety of actions to customize your toolbars. Unlike many Windows applications, you do not need to close and reopen the dialog box each time you complete an action.

TIP

The easiest way to activate the Toolbars dialog box is to click on any tool in any toolbar with the Enter button of the pointing device.

Creating a New Toolbar

Command: *Choose* **T**ool, Customize Tool**b**ars	Issues the TBCONFIG command and opens the Toolbar dialog box (see fig. C.5)
Choose **N**ew	Opens the New Toolbar dialog box (see fig. C.5)
Type **Optimize** *in the* **T**oolbar Name *box*	Enters a name for the toolbar
Leave ACAD *as the menu group*	Specifies the menu group for the toolbar configuration
Choose OK	Closes the New Toolbar dialog box and displays new toolbar entry (ACAD.Optimize) in the **T**oolbars list
Choose **C**lose	Creates an empty toolbar named Optimize (see fig. C.6)

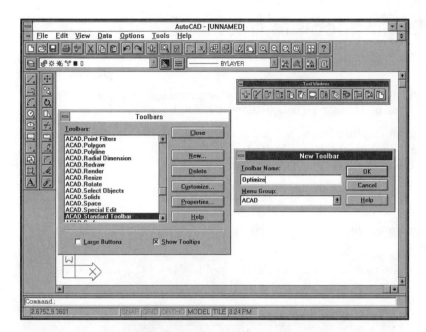

Figure C.5

The Toolbars and New Toolbar dialog boxes.

C

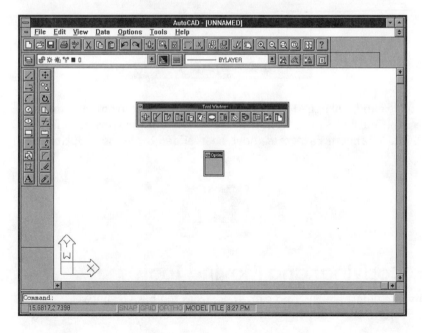

Figure C.6

The new and empty Optimize toolbar.

Adding Existing Tools to a Toolbar

You easily can add existing tools to any toolbar by performing the following steps:

1. Open the Toolbars dialog box by clicking on a tool with the Enter button or by choosing **T**ools, Customize Tool**b**ars.

2. Select the toolbar from the **T**oolbars list. (The list defaults to the tool clicked on with the Enter button, or the first tool if opened by the pull-down menu or TBCONFIG command.)

3. Choose C**u**stomize to open the Customize Toolbars dialog box (see fig. C.7).

4. From C**a**tegories, select the appropriate category for the tool you want.

5. Using the pick button, drag the desired tool from the icon box below the C**a**tegories box and drop it on the toolbar.

Figure C.7

The Customize Toolbars dialog box.

Multiple tools can be dragged and dropped onto a toolbar from multiple categories. In figure C.8 tools from the Draw, Attribute, External Reference, and Miscellaneous categories have been added to the new Optimize toolbar.

Figure C.8

Tools added to the Optimize toolbar.

Deleting, Copying, and Moving Tools

You easily can delete, move, and copy tools from toolbars or between toolbars. Perform the following steps to delete a tool from a toolbar:

1. Open the Toolbars dialog box by clicking on a tool with the Enter button or by choosing **T**ools, Customize Tool**b**ars.

2. Choose C**u**stomize to open the Customize Toolbars dialog box.

3. Using the pick button, drag the tool off the toolbar. Upon releasing the pick button the tool will be deleted.

Perform the following steps to move a tool from one toolbar to another:

1. Open the Toolbars dialog box.

2. Choose C**u**stomize to open the Customize Toolbars dialog box.

3. Using the pick button, drag the tool to the new toolbar.

Perform the following steps to copy a tool:

1. Open the Toolbars dialog box.

2. Choose C**u**stomize to open the Customize Toolbars dialog box.

3. Press Ctrl on the keyboard while dragging the tool from one toolbar to the other.

Tools also can be repositioned within the toolbars. To do so, perform the following steps:

1. Open the Toolbars dialog box.

2. Choose C**u**stomize to open the Customize Toolbars dialog box.

3. Drag and drop a tool to wherever you want it positioned in that toolbar.

> Space can be inserted between tools in a toolbar by using the Customize Toolbars dialog box. Choose **C**ustomize from the Toolbars dialog box and drag a tool less than halfway across the adjacent tool to create space between tools. This process can be reversed to remove a space between tools.
>
> You can change the shape (aspect ratio) of a floating toolbar by dragging the bottom or side borders of that toolbar.

All toolbar dialog boxes can be opened from the Command: prompt. The command to open the Toolbar dialog box is TBCONFIG. The TOOLBAR command can be used to hide or show all toolbars, launch individual toolbars, and position toolbars as docked or floating.

Setting Toolbar Properties

You can use the Toolbar Properties dialog box to display or hide toolbars, change their names, assign the help string for the status bar, and verify their alias names. To open the Toolbar Properties dialog box, choose **T**ools, Customize Tool**b**ars or click on a tool icon with the Enter button to open the Toolbars dialog box, then choose **P**roperties. The Toolbar Properties dialog box appears as shown in figure C.9.

Figure C.9

The Toolbar Properties dialog box.

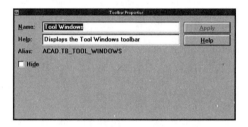

The following exercise illustrates how to show and hide toolbars.

Showing and Hiding a Toolbar

Click on a tool in a toolbar with the Enter button	Opens the Toolbar dialog box
Select ACAD.Tool Windows, *then choose* **P**roperties	Opens the Toolbar Properties dialog box for Tool Windows
Clear the **Hi**d**e** *check box, then choose* **A**pply	Displays the Tool Windows toolbar
Choose **C**lose *in the Toolbars dialog box*	Closes both dialog boxes
Click on a tool in a toolbar with the Enter button	Opens the Toolbar dialog box
Select ACAD.Tool Windows, *then choose* **P**roperties	Opens the Toolbar Properties dialog box for Tool Windows

You can select another toolbar name in the Toolbars dialog box without closing the Toolbar Properties dialog box.

Put a check in the **Hi**d**e** *check box, then choose* **A**pply	Closes the Tool Windows toolbar
Choose **C**lose *in the Toolbar dialog box*	Closes both dialog boxes

> If you can remember the names of your toolbars it is easier to show
> and hide toolbars by using the command line. Enter **toolbar**, then
> the name of the toolbar you want to show or hide, and enter **S** for
> SHOW or **H** for HIDE.

TIP

Alias in Toolbar Properties

AutoCAD's Alias feature serves as a link to AutoCAD's menus. A toolbar's
alias includes a prefix that refers to the toolbar menu group and a name
as it appears in the menu file. You must use the toolbar alias when using
the TOOLBAR command to display and position a toolbar.

Help in Toolbar Properties

The text entered in the Help box is displayed in the status bar at the
bottom left of the main AutoCAD window whenever the cursor is positioned in the grab area of a toolbar.

Creating and Customizing Tools

AutoCAD provides the user with the capability to create and customize
tools as well as toolbars.

Creating a Tool

You can create a tool by using the Toolbars dialog box. Open the Toolbars
dialog box, then click on any non-flyout tool in the toolbar with the Enter
button of the pointing device to open the Button Properties dialog box (see
fig. C.10).

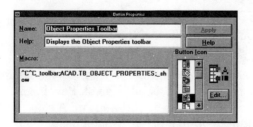

Figure C.10

*The Button Proper-
ties dialog box.*

To create a new tool, perform the following steps:

1. Enter a name for that tool in the **N**ame box of the Button Properties dialog box.

2. In the He**l**p box, type the text you want displayed in the status line.

3. In the box under **M**acro, enter the commands that the tool will perform. Preface transparent commands with an apostrophe and preface other commands with ^C^C to cancel pending commands.

4. Select an icon for the tool from the Button **I**con list. To change a command that is performed by an existing tool, edit the commands in the **M**acro box.

Editing an Icon

Button icons are bitmapped images, saved as BMP files. To edit a button icon, select an icon from the Button Properties dialog box and choose **E**dit, which opens the Button Editor dialog box. The editing tools are limited, but similar to those found in a Paintbrush-type application.

To edit a button's icon, perform the following steps:

1. Open the Toolbar dialog box by clicking on a tool in a toolbar with the Enter button of your pointing device. Alternatively, at the command line enter **TBCONFIG**.

2. Click on the tool whose icon you want to edit with the Enter button of your pointing device. This opens the Button Properties dialog box (refer to fig. C.10).

NOTE

> If the icon you want to edit is on a flyout or is the child of a flyout button, you must click on the appropriate flyout tool on the parent toolbar; then click on the appropriate button on the child toolbar.

3. Choose **E**dit in Button Icon area of the Button Properties dialog box to edit the icon (see fig. C.11).

4. Select your tool of choice for editing the icon. Tools include a grid with a single box representing a single pixel. Pencil, Line, Circle, and Erase drawing tools can create or edit an icon. A color palette is available for adding color on a pixel-by-pixel basis.

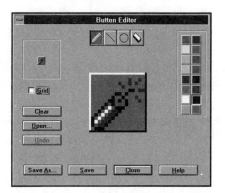

Figure C.11

The Button Editor dialog box for editing and creating button icons.

Creating and Modifying a Flyout

To create a flyout, perform the following steps:

1. Open the Toolbars dialog box.

2. Choose C**u**stomize to open the Customize Toolbars dialog box.

3. From the bottom of the C**a**tegories list, select Custom (see fig. C.12), which displays a blank tool icon and a blank flyout tool icon.

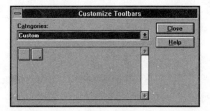

Figure C.12

A step in the creation of a flyout.

4. To add a flyout to an existing toolbar, drag the flyout icon (the button with the triangle in the lower left corner) to a toolbar and drop it. To create a flyout in a new toolbar, drag the flyout icon to any place on the screen and drop it.

5. Click on the new flyout tool with the Enter button to display the Flyout Properties dialog box.

6. In the A**s**sociated Toolbar list, select the toolbar you want associated with the flyout.

7. Select an icon from the Button **I**con list to specify an icon for the flyout.

You also can use the Flyout Properties dialog box to modify existing flyouts by clicking on the existing flyout tool with the Enter button.

Setting Preferences

User preferences can be set for the graphics window, digitizer input, fonts, colors, directories, and more in the Preferences dialog box (see fig. C.13). The Preferences dialog box is opened by the PREFERENCES command, which is issued by choosing **O**ptions, **P**references.

Figure C.13

The Preferences dialog box with the System tab folder open.

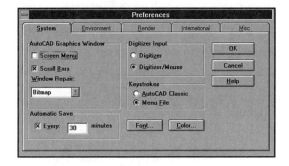

System

With the **S**ystem tab folder open, the Screen Men**u** and the Scroll Bar**s** can be turned on or off in the AutoCAD graphics window. The mode in which a graphics image is rebuilt when an overlying window is removed is selected by **W**indow Repair. The default AutoCAD display driver is set for Bitmap. Automatic Save determines how frequently (in minutes) AutoCAD automatically saves the active drawing.

The Digitizer Input box presents a choice between Digiti**z**er or Di**g**itizer/ Mouse. With Digiti**z**er chosen, AutoCAD accepts input from the selected configured digitizing device. If a mouse is on the system and there is not a digitizer, AutoCAD will accept the mouse input. With Di**g**itizer/Mouse selected, AutoCAD accepts input from the last-moved pointing device.

The Keystrokes section provides the capability to choose whether you want to use accelerated keystrokes to access pull-down menu items. The choice is between **A**utoCAD Classic or Menu **F**ile.

The Fo**n**t button enables the user to specify the font used in the graphics and text windows. Changing the font in the text window affects the fonts used on the command line and the font used in the AutoCAD Text Window. Changing the font in the graphics window affects the font used in the screen menu. To see the screen menu it must be selected in the AutoCAD Graphics Window area.

The **C**olor button allows you to change the appearance of the AutoCAD applications window. With this option you can change the background colors of your Graphics and Text Windows Backgrounds, the color of the text itself, and the color of the crosshairs of your AutoCAD pointing device.

Environment

The **E**nvironment tab folder (see fig. C.14) enables you to set paths for

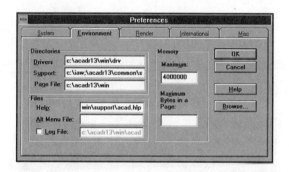

Figure C.14

The Preferences dialog box with the Environment tab folder open.

AutoCAD variables, configuration files, menus, and driver files.

In the Directories section, **D**rivers sets the ACADDRV variable by specifying the search path for ADI drivers. S**u**pport sets the ACAD environment variable by telling AutoCAD which directories contain text fonts, hatch patterns, menus, and AutoLISP files. Pa**g**e File sets the ACADPAGEDIR variable; it also specifies the directory for the first page file.

The Files section sets the ACADHELP environment variable. Hel**p** tells AutoCAD the name and location of the help file. The **A**lt Menu File text box is used to indicate the path and name of an alternate menu for the AutoCAD tablet by setting the ACADALTMENU environment variable. With **L**og File, the name of and path for the log file is determined. The contents of the text box will be written to the log file if the **L**og File check box is selected.

The AutoCAD memory pager is set up in the Memory section. The memory pager divides the current drawing between pages of memory. Data is written to disk when the memory becomes full. Maximum specifies the quantity of memory in bytes that the memory pager can receive from Windows. Autodesk recommends using this option only if it is necessary to reduce the allocation of physical memory for coexistence with another application. Maximum sets the ACADMAXMEM variable. Maximum Bytes in a Page determines the maximum amount of bytes available for the first page file. It also sets the ACADMAXPAGE variable.

Render

The **R**ender tab folder of the Preferences dialog box (see fig. C.15) specifies directories and sets the following variables:

- **Config File Dir.** Rendering configuration file; sets the AVECFG variable.

- **F**ace File Dir. Temporary storage for the faces of meshes; sets the AVEFACEDIR variable.

- **P**age File Dir. First page file; sets the AVEPAGEDIR variable.

- **Map File Pa**th. Map file; sets the AVERDFILE variable.

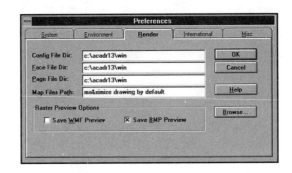

Figure C.15

The Preferences dialog box with the Render tab folder open.

International

The **I**nternational tab folder (see fig. C.16) enables the user to specify either En**g**lish or Me**t**ric measurements, and provides a choice between standard or metric prototype drawings.

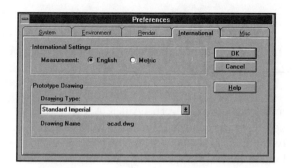

Figure C.16

*The Preferences
dialog box with the
International tab
folder open.*

Miscellaneous

The final tab folder under Preferences is **M**isc, shown in figure C.17. In
the Options section, the **T**ext Editor box specifies the text editor used with
MTEXT. Typing internal in the **T**ext Editor box specifies the AutoCAD
MText Editor. Any ASCII text can be used by the MText command and
you specify which text editor in this dialog box.

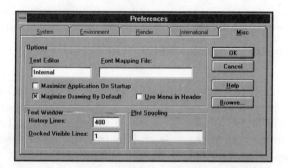

Figure C.17

*The Preferences
dialog box with the
Misc tab folder
open.*

The **F**ont Mapping File is an ASCII text file that allows you to substitute
one font file for another. This option is valuable if you want a drawing to
only use specific fonts. You also might want to use faster drawing SHX
fonts for drawing, and higher quality, slower moving PostScript fonts for
final plotting. Additionally, if a drawing contains a font that you do not
have, you can use the **F**ont Mapping File to specify which of your fonts
will substitute for that font.

The font mapping file is an ASCII text file that can be created or edited
with any ASCII text editor. It has an extension of FMP.

The text editor must be in the directory specified in S**u**pport in the Directories area of the **E**nvironment tab folder (refer to figure C.14).

Also in the Options section are settings for maximizing an application window on startup and for maximizing the AutoCAD drawing window. The checkbox for **U**se Menu in Header tells AutoCAD whether to use the menu file in the drawing header. If **U**se Menu in Header is not selected, AutoCAD uses the loaded menu file for every drawing regardless of any other menu file specified in a drawing's header.

The Text Window section enables the user to specify the number of lines visible in the command-line and text windows. History **L**ines specifies how many lines appear at any time above the current command line and in the text window. **D**ocked Visible Lines specifies how many lines appear when the command-line window is docked.

The **P**lot Spooling option sets the ACADPLCMD environment variable and specifies conditions for using a plot spooler. A *plot spooler* buffers plot output from the computer so that the computer can become available quickly for further work while plotting is handled in the background.

The **B**rowse button searches for files for the **T**ext Editor, **F**ont Mapping File, and **P**lot Spooling boxes.

In this appendix, you learned that AutoCAD Release 13 for Windows provides a plethora of tools for customizing its user interface. By taking advantage of the standard Windows GUI, an AutoCAD user can tailor his work environment to best suit his needs and desires. Using and working with AutoCAD's customization tools is without question the most effective way to learn how to customize your AutoCAD environment.

AutoCAD Command Equivalency Table

This appendix contains a table of AutoCAD commands with their dialog box names, and the aliases, pull-down menu items, and tools that issue them.

You will also find useful annotated maps of pull-down menus and toolbars in Appendix F.

In the Command Name and Options column, names and options shown in bold are new in Release 13. Many menu items and tools issue specific options along with commands. For example, the **V**iew, **Z**oom, **A**ll menu item and the Zoom All tool both issue the ZOOM command with the All option. These options are indicated in the Command Name and Options column for those menu items and tools, indented under the command name. In many cases, multiple options are issued; these are shown separated by commas. Often, menu items and tools issue a command, pause for input, then issue specific options; this pause for input is indicated with a backslash—for example, \,Center for the Arc Start Center End tool under the ARC command indicates that tool issues the ARC command, pauses for the user to input a start point, and then issues the Center option.

In the Dialog Box column, the names shown are those that appear in the dialog box title bar.

Aliases are abbreviations that can be entered at the Command: prompt to issue commands. In the Alias column, the alias names shown are in the standard ACAD.PGP file in the ACADR13\COMMON\SUPPORT directory. Aliases for dimensioning commands are prefaced with D, and commands that open dialog boxes are prefaced with DD.

In the Pull-Down Menu, Item column, items are shown in the form *Menuname, childmenuname, menuitemname,* and hot keys are indicated with bold and underline; for example, **V**iew, **Z**oom, **A**ll translates to "Choose **V**iew to open the **V**iew pull-down menu, then choose **Z**oom to open the **Z**oom child menu, then choose **A**ll to issue the ZOOM command with the All option." A few commands, such as OPEN, have keyboard shortcuts, such as Ctrl+O; these are shown in their pull-down menu item labels—such as **F**ile, **O**pen Ctrl+O—and are therefore shown in the Pull-Down Menu, Item column.

Tools are listed in the form *Toolname (Toolbarname, Flyoutname)*; for example, *3 Points (Draw, Arc)* translates to "From the Arc flyout of the Draw toolbar, choose 3 Points to issue the ARC command." The tool names are those that appear in the ToolTips, and the toolbar names and flyout names are those that appear in their title bars when open as floating toolbars. Of course, if the 3 Points tool is the current default (last-used) tool from the Arc flyout, it will appear on the Draw toolbar and can be directly chosen, and if the Arc flyout is currently open as an individual toolbar, you can choose 3 Points directly from it. Tool names shown in bold are the default tools of their flyouts. These tools are the ones that initially appear (each time you start AutoCAD) on the parent toolbar and in the ToolTip of the tool that opens the flyout; however, during an AutoCAD session after you have used another tool from the flyout, it becomes the current default tool.

The — in any column indicates that an entry for the column is not applicable in that row of the table.

NOTE

The Dim: prompt is obsolete in Release 13. All of the R13 dimensioning commands now can be entered at the Command: prompt. Although the Dim: prompt still is present for compatibility purposes, the following commands, which were available at the Dim: prompt in earlier releases of AutoCAD, are obsolete and have been intentionally omitted from this table:

HOMETEXT, HORIZONTAL, NEWTEXT, OBLIQUE, ROTATED, SAVE, STATUS, TROTATE, UPDATE, VARIABLES, VERTICAL

D

Table D.1
Command, Dialog Box, Alias, Menu, Tool Equivalents

Command Name and Option	Dialog Box	Alias	Pull-Down Menu, Item	Toolname (Toolbar, Flyout)
.X	—	—	—	.X (Standard, .X)
.XY	—	—	—	XY (Standard, .X)
.XZ	—	—	—	XZ (Standard, .X)
.Y	—	—	—	Y (Standard, .X)
.YZ	—	—	—	YZ (Standard, .X)
.Z	—	—	—	Z (Standard, .X)
3D	—	—	—	—
3DARRAY	—	—	—	—
R,\,\	—	—	—	3D Rectangular Array (Modify, Copy Object)
P,\,\	—	—	—	3D Polar Array (Modify, Copy Object)
3DFACE	—	—	—	3D Face (Surfaces, 3D Face)
3DMESH	—	—	—	3D Mesh (Surfaces, 3D Mesh)
3DPOLY	—	—	—	3DPolyline (Draw, Polyline)
3DSIN	3D Studio Import File	—	—	—
3DSOUT	3D Studio Output File	—	—	—

Command Name and Option	Dialog Box	Alias	Pull-Down Menu, Item	Toolname (Toolbar, Flyout)
ABOUT	AUTOCAD(R)	—	**Help, About Autocad**	—
ACISIN	Select Acis File	—	—	—
ACISOUT	Create Acis File	—	—	—
AI_BOX	—	—	—	**Box** (Surfaces, Box)
AI_DISH	—	—	—	**Dish** (Surfaces, Dish)
AI_DOME	—	—	—	**Dome** (Surfaces, Dome)
AI_MESH	—	—	—	**Mesh** (Miscellaneous, Mesh)
(AI_PROPCHK)	Modify	—	—	—
AI_PYRAMID	—	—	—	**Pyramid** (Surfaces, Pyramid)
AI_SPHERE	—	—	—	**Sphere** (Surfaces, Sphere)
AI_TORUS	—	—	—	**Torus** (Surfaces, Torus)
AI_WEDGE	—	—	—	**Wedge** (Surfaces, Wedge)
ALIGN	—	—	—	Align (Modify, Rotate)
AMECONVERT	—	—	—	**AME Convert** (Solids, AME Convert)
APPLOAD	Load AutoLISP, ADS, ARX	—	**Tools, Applications**	—
APERTURE	—	—	—	—

continues

D

Table D.1, Continued
Command, Dialog Box, Alias, Menu, Tool Equivalents

Command Name and Option	Dialog Box	Alias	Pull-Down Menu, Item	Toolname (Toolbar, Flyout)
ARC	—	A	—	**3 Points** (Draw, Arc)
\,C,\	—	—	—	Arc Start Center End (Draw, Arc)
\,C,A	—	—	—	Arc Start Center Angle (Draw, Arc)
\,E,A	—	—	—	Arc Start End Angle (Draw, Arc)
\,E,D	—	—	—	Arc Start End Direction (Draw, Arc)
\,E,R	—	—	—	Arc Start End Radius (Draw, Arc)
\,C,\,\	—	—	—	Arc Center Start End (Draw, Arc)
C,\,A	—	—	—	Arc Center Start Angle (Draw, Arc)
C,\,L	—	—	—	Arc Center Start Length (Draw, Arc)
\	—	—	—	Arc Continue (Draw, Arc)
AREA	—	—	—	Area (Object Properties, List)
ARRAY	—	—	—	—

Command Name and Option	Dialog Box	Alias	Pull-Down Menu, Item	Toolname (Toolbar, Flyout)
R,\,\	—	—	—	Rectangular Array (Modify, Copy Object)
P,\,\	—	—	—	Polar Array (Modify, Copy Object)
ASEADMIN	—	—	—	**Administration** (External Database, Administration)
ASEEXPORT	—	—	—	**Export Links** (External Database, Export Links)
ASELINKS	—	—	—	**Links** (External Database, Links)
ASEROWS	—	—	—	**Rows** (External Database, Rows)
ASERUNREP	—	—	—	—
ASESELECT	—	—	—	**Select Objects** (External Database, Select Objects)
ASESQLED	—	—	—	**SQL Editor** (External Database, SQL Editor)
ATTEDIT	—	—	—	**Edit Attribute Globally** (Attribute, Edit Attribute Globally)
ATTEXT	Select Template File	—	—	—

continues

D

Table D.1, Continued
Command, Dialog Box, Alias, Menu, Tool Equivalents

Command Name and Option	Dialog Box	Alias	Pull-Down Menu, Item	Toolname (Toolbar, Flyout)
ATTREDEF	—	—	—	**Redefine Attribute** (Attribute, Redefine Attribute)
BHATCH	Boundary Hatch	—	—	**Hatch** (Draw, Hatch)
BLIPMODE	—	—	—	—
BLOCK	—	—	—	Block (Draw, Insert)
BMPOUT	Create BMP FIle	—	—	—
BOUNDARY	Boundary	—	—	Boundary (Draw, Rectangle)
BOX	—	—	—	Corner (Solids, Center)
CE, \	—	—	—	**Center** (Solids, Center)
BREAK	—	—	—	**1 Point** (Modify, 1 Point)
\,F,@	—	—	—	1 Point Select (Modify, 1 Point)
\,\	—	—	—	2 Points (Modify, 1 Point)
\,F,@	—	—	—	2 Points Select (Modify, 1 Point)
CAL	—	—	—	Calculator (Standard, Snap From)

D

Command Name and Option	Dialog Box	Alias	Pull-Down Menu, Item	Toolname (Toolbar, Flyout)
CHAMFER	—	—	—	**Chamfer** (Modify, Chamfer)
CHANGE	—	—	—	—
CHPROP	—	—	—	—
CIRCLE	—	C	—	Circle (Draw, Circle)
\,r	—	—	—	**Circle Center Radius** (Draw, Circle)
\,D	—	—	—	Circle Center Diameter (Draw, Circle)
2P,\	—	—	—	Circle 2 Point (Draw, Circle)
3P,\	—	—	—	Circle 3 Point (Draw, Circle)
TTR,\	—	—	—	Circle Tan Tan Radius (Draw, Circle)
COLOR	—	—	—	—
COMPILE	Select Shape, Font File	—	**T**ools, Compi**l**e	—
CONE	—	—	—	Center (Solids, Elliptical)
E,\	—	—	—	Elliptical (Solids, Elliptical)
CONFIG	—	—	**O**ptions, **C**onfigure	—

continues

Table D.1, Continued
Command, Dialog Box, Alias, Menu, Tool Equivalents

Command Name and Option	Dialog Box	Alias	Pull-Down Menu, Item	Toolname (Toolbar, Flyout)
COPY	—	**CP**	—	**Copy Object** (Modify, Copy Object)
COPYCLIP	—	—	**E**dit, **C**opy Ctrl+C	**Copy** (Standard)
COPYEMBED	—	—	—	—
COPYHIST	—	—	—	—
COPYLINK	—	—	**E**dit, Copy **V**iew	—
CUT	—	—	—	—
CUTCLIP	—	—	**E**dit, Cu**t** Ctrl+X	**Cut** (Standard)
CYLINDER	—	—	—	Center (Solids, Elliptical)
E, \	—	—	—	**Elliptical** (Solids, Elliptical)
DBLIST	—	—	—	—
DDATTDEF	Attribute Definition	—	—	**Define Attribute** (Attribute, Define Attribute)
DDATTE	Attribute Edit	—	—	**Attribute Edit** (Attribute, Attribute Edit)
DDATTEXT	Attribute Extraction	—	—	—
DDCHPROP	Change Properties	—	—	—

D

Command Name and Option	Dialog Box	Alias	Pull-Down Menu, Item	Toolname (Toolbar, Flyout)
DDCOLOR	Select Color	—	**D**ata, **C**olor	**Color Control** (Object Properties)
DDEDIT	Edit Text	—	—	Text Edit (Modify, Edit Polyline)
DDEMODES	Object Creation Modes	—	**D**ata, **O**bject Creation	**Object Creation** (Object Properties)
DDGRIPS	Grips	—	**O**ptions, **G**rips	—
DDIM	Dimension Styles	—	**D**ata, **D**imension Styles	**Dimension Styles** (Dimensioning, Dimension Styles)
DDINSERT	Insert	—	—	**Insert Block** (Draw, Insert Block)
DDLMODES	Layer Control	—	**D**ata, **L**ayers	**Layers** (Object Properties)
DDLTYPE	Select Linetype	—	**D**ata, Linetype	**Linetype** (Object Properties)
DDMODIFY	Modify (Varies)	—	**E**dit, P**r**operties	Properties (Object Properties)
DDOSNAP	Running Object Snap	—	—	Running Object Snap (Standard, Snap From)
DDPSTYLE	Point Style	—	—	—
DDRENAME	Rename	—	**D**ata, Rename	—
DDRMODES	Drawing Aids	—	**O**ptions, **D**rawing Aids	—

continues

Table D.1, Continued
Command, Dialog Box, Alias, Menu, Tool Equivalents

Command Name and Option	Dialog Box	Alias	Pull-Down Menu, Item	Toolname (Toolbar, Flyout)
DDSELECT	Object Selection Settings	—	Options, Selection	—
DDSTYLE	—	—	—	—
DDUCS	UCS Control	—	View, Named UCS	Named UCS (Standard, Preset UCS)
DDUCSP	UCS Orientation	—	View, Preset UCS	Preset UCS (Standard, Preset UCS)
DDUNITS	Units Control	—	Data, Units	—
DDVIEW	View Control	—	View, Named Views	Named Views (Standard, Named Views)
DDVPOINT	Viewpoint Presets	—	—	—
DELAY	—	—	—	—
DIM	—	—	—	—
DIMALIGNED	—	—	—	Aligned Dimension (Dimensioning, Aligned Dimension)
DIMANGULAR	—	—	—	Angular Dimension (Dimensioning, Angular Dimension)

Command Name and Option	Dialog Box	Alias	Pull-Down Menu, Item	Toolname (Toolbar, Flyout)
DIMBASELINE	—	—	—	**Baseline Dimension** (Dimensioning, Baseline Dimension)
DIMCENTER	—	—	—	**Center Mark** (Dimensioning, Center Mark)
DIMCONTINUE	—	—	—	**Continue Dimension** (Dimensioning, Continue Dimension)
DIMDIAMETER	—	—	—	Diameter Dimension (Dimensioning, Radius Dimension)
DIMEDIT	—	DIMED	—	—
O,\	—	—	—	Oblique Dimension (Dimensioning, Dimension Styles)
DIMLINEAR	—	—	—	**Linear Dimension** (Dimensioning, Linear Dimension)
DIMORDINATE	—	—	—	**Automatic** (Dimensioning, Automatic)
\,X	—	—	—	X-Datum (Dimensioning, Automatic)
\,Y	—	—	—	Y-Datum (Dimensioning, Automatic)

continues

D

Table D.1, Continued
Command, Dialog Box, Alias, Menu, Tool Equivalents

Command Name and Option	Dialog Box	Alias	Pull-Down Menu, Item	Toolname (Toolbar, Flyout)
DIMRADIUS	—	—	—	**Radius Dimension** (Dimensioning, Radius Dimension)
DIMTEDIT	—	**DTED**	—	—
\,**H**	—	—	—	**Home** (Dimensioning, Home)
\,**A**	—	—	—	Rotate (Dimensioning, Home)
\,**L**	—	—	—	Left (Dimensioning, Home)
\,**C**	—	—	—	Center (Dimensioning, Home)
\,**R**	—	—	—	Right (Dimensioning, Home)
DIMSTYLE	—	—	—	—
DIST	—	—	—	Distance (Object|Properties, List)
DIVIDE	—	—	—	Divide (Draw, Point)
DONUT	—	—	—	Donut (Draw, Circle)
DRAGMODE	—	—	—	—
DSVIEWER	—	**AV**	—	**Aerial View** (Standard, Aerial View)

Command Name and Option	Dialog Box	Alias	Pull-Down Menu, Item	Toolname (Toolbar, Flyout)
DTEXT	—	—	—	Dtext (Draw, Mtext)
DVIEW	—	**DV**	View, 3D Dynamic View	—
DWGINFO	—	—	—	—
DXBIN	Select DXB File	—	—	—
DXFIN	Select DXF File	—	—	—
DXFOUT	Create DXF File	—	—	—
EDGE	—	—	—	**Edge** (Surfaces, Edge)
EDGESURF	—	—	—	**Edge Surface** (Surfaces, Edge Surface)
ELEV	—	—	—	—
ELLIPSE	—	—	—	**Ellipse Center** (Draw, Ellipse)
\,\	—	—	—	Ellipse Axis End (Draw, Ellipse)
A,\,\	—	—	—	Ellipse Arc (Draw, Ellipse)
END	—	—	—	—
ERASE	—	**E**	—	**Erase** (Modify, Erase)
EXPLODE	—	—	—	**Explode** (Modify, Explode)
EXPORT	Export Data	—	File, Export	—
EXTEND	—	—	—	Extend (Modify, Trim)

continues

D

Table D.1, Continued
Command, Dialog Box, Alias, Menu, Tool Equivalents

Command Name and Option	Dialog Box	Alias	Pull-Down Menu, Item	Toolname (Toolbar, Flyout)
EXTRUDE	—	—	—	**Extrude** (Solids, Extrude)
FILES	File Utilities	—	—	—
FILL	—	—	—	—
FILLET	—	—	—	Fillet (Modify, Chamfer)
FILTER	Object Selection Filter	—	—	Selection Filters (Standard, Select Window)
GIFIN	—	—	—	—
GRAPHSCR	—	—	—	—
GRID	—	—	—	—
GROUP	Object Grouping	—	—	**Object Group** (Standard, Object Group)
HATCH	—	—	—	—
HATCHEDIT	Hatchedit	—	—	Hatchedit (Modify, Polyline Edit)
HELP	—	—	**H**elp	**Help** (Standard)
HIDE	—	—	—	**Hide** (Render, Hide)
ID	—	—	—	Locate Point (Object Properties, List)
IMPORT	Import File	—	**F**ile, **I**mport	—

Command Name and Option	Dialog Box	Alias	Pull-Down Menu, Item	Toolname (Toolbar, Flyout)
INSERT	—	—	—	—
INSERTOBJ	Insert New Object	—	**E**dit, **I**nsert Object	—
INTERFERE	—	—	—	**Interfere** (Solids, Interfere)
INTERSECT	—	—	—	Intersection (Modify, Explode)
ISOPLANE	—	—	—	—
LAYER	—	**LA**	—	—
LEADER	—	**LEAD**	—	**Leader** (Dimensioning, Leader)
LENGTHEN	—	—	—	Lengthen (Modify, Stretch)
LIGHT	Lights	—	—	**Lights** (Render, Lights)
LIMITS	—	—	**D**ata,	Drawing Limits
LINE	—	**L**	—	**Line** (Draw, Line)
LINETYPE	—	**LT**	—	—
LTSCALE	—	—	—	—
LIST	—	—	—	**List** (Object Properties, List)
LOAD	Select Shape File	—	**D**ata, **S**hape File	—

continues

D

Table D.1, Continued
Command, Dialog Box, Alias, Menu, Tool Equivalents

Command Name and Option	Dialog Box	Alias	Pull-Down Menu, Item	Toolname (Toolbar, Flyout)
LOGFILEON	—	—	—	—
LOGFILEOFF	—	—	—	—
MASSPROP	—	—	—	Mass Properties (Object Properties, List)
MATLIB	Materials Library	—	—	**Materials Library** (Render, Materials Library)
MEASURE	—	—	—	Measure (Draw, Point)
MENU	Select Menu File	—	—	—
MENULOAD	Menu Customization	—	<u>T</u>ools, Customize <u>M</u>enus	—
MENUUNLOAD	Menu Customization	—	—	—
MINSERT	—	—	—	**Insert Multiple Blocks** (Miscellaneous, Insert Multiple Blocks)
MIRROR	—	—	—	Mirror (Modify, Copy Object)
MIRROR3D	—	—	—	3D Mirror (Modify, Copy Object)

continues

Command Name and Option	Dialog Box	Alias	Pull-Down Menu, Item	Toolname (Toolbar, Flyout)
MLEDIT	—	—	—	Multiline Edit (Modify, Polyline Edit)
MLINE	—	—	—	Multiline (Draw, Polyline)
MLSTYLE	Multiline Styles	—	Data, Multiline Style	**Multiline Styles** (Object Properties)
MOVE	—	**M**	—	Move (Modify)
MSLIDE	Create Slide File	—	Tools, Slide, Save	—
MSPACE	—	**MS**	View,	Floating Model Space
MTEXT	—	**T**	—	**Mtext** (Draw, Mtext)
MULTIPLE	—	—	—	—
MVIEW	—	—	View, Floating Model Space	Floating Model Space (Standard, Model Space)
MVSETUP	—	—	—	—
NEW	Create New Drawing	—	File, New	**New** (Standard)
OFFSET	—	—	—	Offset (Modify, Copy Object)
OLELINKS	—	—	Edit, Links	—

D

Table D.1, Continued
Command, Dialog Box, Alias, Menu, Tool Equivalents

Command Name and Option	Dialog Box	Alias	Pull-Down Menu, Item	Toolname (Toolbar, Flyout)
OOPS	—	—	—	**Oops!** (Miscellaneous, Oops!)
OPEN	Open Drawing	—	**F**ile, **O**pen Ctrl+O	**Open** (Standard)
OSNAP	—	—	—	—
FROM	—	—	—	**Snap From** (Standard, Snap From)
ENDP	—	—	—	Snap to Endpoint (Standard, Snap From)
MIDP	—	—	—	Snap to Midpoint (Standard, Snap From)
INT	—	—	—	Snap to Intersection (Standard, Snap From)
APPINT	—	—	—	Snap to Apparent Intersection (Standard, Snap From)
CEN	—	—	—	Snap to Center (Standard, Snap From)
QUAD	—	—	—	Snap to Quadrant (Standard, Snap From)
PER	—	—	—	Snap to Perpendicular (Standard, Snap From)

continues

D

Command Name and Option	Dialog Box	Alias	Pull-Down Menu, Item	Toolname (Toolbar, Flyout)
TAN	—	—	—	Snap to Tangent (Standard, Snap From)
NODE	—	—	—	Snap to Node (Standard, Snap From)
INS	—	—	—	Snap to Insertion (Standard, Snap From)
NEA	—	—	—	Snap to Nearest (Standard, Snap From)
QUICK	—	—	—	Snap to Quick (Standard, Snap From)
NONE	—	—	—	Snap to None (Standard, Snap From)
PAN	—	**P**	**V**iew, **P**an, **P**oint	**Pan Point** (Standard, Pan Point)
\, \	—	—	**V**iew, **P**an, **L**eft	Pan Left (Standard, Pan Point)
\, \	—	—	**V**iew, **P**an, **R**ight	Pan Right (Standard, Pan Point)
\, \	—	—	**V**iew, **P**an, **U**p	Pan Up (Standard, Pan Point)
\, \	—	—	**V**iew, **P**an, **D**own	Pan Down (Standard, Pan Point)

Table D.1, Continued
Command, Dialog Box, Alias, Menu, Tool Equivalents

Command Name and Option	Dialog Box	Alias	Pull-Down Menu, Item	Toolname (Toolbar, Flyout)
\,\	—	—	**V**iew, **P**an, Up **L**eft	Pan Up Left (Standard, Pan Point)
\,\	—	—	**V**iew, **P**an, Up **R**ight	Pan Up Right (Standard, Pan Point)
\,\	—	—	**V**iew, **P**an, dard, Down **L**eft	Pan Down Left (Stan-Pan Point)
\,\	—	—	**V**iew, **P**an, Down **R**ight	Pan Down Right (Standard, Pan Point)
PASTECLIP	—	—	**E**dit, **P**aste Ctrl+V	**Paste** (Standard)
PASTESPEC	Paste Special	—	**E**dit, Paste **S**pecial	—
PCXIN	—	—		—
PEDIT	—	—		**Polyline Edit** (Modify, Polyline Edit)
PFACE	—	—		—
PLAN	—	—		—
PLINE	—	**PL**		**Polyline** (Draw, Polyline)
PLOT	Plot	—	**F**ile, **P**rint Ctrl+P	**Print** (Standard)
POINT	—	—		**Point** (Draw, Point)
POLYGON	—	—		Polygon (Draw, Rectangle)

Command Name and Option	Dialog Box	Alias	Pull-Down Menu, Item	Toolname (Toolbar, Flyout)
PREFERENCES	Preferences	—	Options, Preferences	—
PSDRAG		—		—
PSFILL		—		PostScript Fill (Draw, Hatch)
PSIN		—		—
PSLTSCALE		—		—
PSOUT		—		—
PSPACE		PS	View, Paper Space	—
PURGE		—	Data, Purge	—
QSAVE		—	File, Save Ctrl+S	Save (Standard)
QTEXT		—		—
QUIT		—	File, Exit	—
RAY		—		Ray (Draw, Line)
RCONFIG		—	Options, Render Configure	—
RECOVER		—		—
RECTANG		—		Rectangle (Draw, Rectangle)
REDEFINE		—		—
REDO		—	Edit, Redo	Redo (Standard)
REDRAW		R	View, Redraw View	Redraw View (Standard, Redraw View)

continues

D

Table D.1, Continued
Command, Dialog Box, Alias, Menu, Tool Equivalents

Command Name and Option	Dialog Box	Alias	Pull-Down Menu, Item	Toolname (Toolbar, Flyout)
REDRAWALL	—	—	View, Redraw All	Redraw All (Standard, Redraw View)
REGEN	—	—	—	—
REGENALL	—	—	—	—
REGENAUTO	—	—	—	—
REGION	—	—	—	Region (Draw, Rectangle)
REINIT	Re-Initialization	—	Tools, Reinitialize	—
RENAME	—	—	—	—
RENDER	Render	—	—	Render (Render, Render)
RENDSCR	—	—	—	—
REPLAY	Replay	—	Tools, Image, View	—
RESUME	—	—	—	—
REVOLVE	—	—	—	Revolve (Solids, Revolve)
REVSURF	—	—	—	Revolved Surface (Surfaces, Revolved Surface)
RMAT	Materials	—	—	Materials (Render, Materials)
ROTATE	—	—	—	Rotate (Modify, Rotate)

continues

D

Command Name and Option	Dialog Box	Alias	Pull-Down Menu, Item	Toolname (Toolbar, Flyout)
ROTATE3D	—	—	—	3D Rotate (Modify, Rotate)
RPREF	Rendering Preferences	—	—	**Rendering Preferences** (Render, Rendering Preferences)
RSCRIPT	—	—	—	—
RULESURF	—	—	—	**Ruled Surface** (Surfaces, Ruled Surface)
SAVE	—	—	—	—
SAVEAS	Save Drawing As	—	File, Save As	—
SAVEASR12	Save Release 12 Drawing As	—	—	—
SAVEIMG	Save Image	—	Tools, Image, **S**ave	—
SCALE	—	—	—	Scale (Modify, Stretch)
SCENE	Scenes	—	—	**Scenes** (Render, Scenes)
SCRIPT	Select Script File	—	Tools, **R**un Script	—
SECTION	—	—	—	**Section** (Solids, Section)
SELECT	—	—	—	—
W	—	—	—	**Select Window** (Standard, Select Window)
C	—	—	—	Select Crossing (Standard, Select Window)

Table D.1, Continued
Command, Dialog Box, Alias, Menu, Tool Equivalents

Command Name and Option	Dialog Box	Alias	Pull-Down Menu, Item	Toolname (Toolbar, Flyout)
G	—	—	—	Select Group (Standard, Select Window)
P	—	—	—	Select Previous (Standard, Select Window)
L	—	—	—	Select Last (Standard, Select Window)
ALL	—	—	—	Select All (Standard, Select Window)
WP	—	—	—	Select Window Polygon (Standard, Select Window)
CP	—	—	—	Select Crossing Polygon (Standard, Select Window)
F	—	—	—	Select Fence (Standard, Select Window)
A	—	—	—	Select Add (Standard, Select Window)
R	—	—	—	Select Remove (Standard, Select Window)
SETVAR	—	—	—	—
SHADE	—	—	—	**Shade** (Render, Shade)
SHAPE	—	—	—	**Shape** (Miscellaneous, Shape)

D

Command Name and Option	Dialog Box	Alias	Pull-Down Menu, Item	Toolname (Toolbar, Flyout)
SHELL	—	—	—	—
SKETCH	—	—	—	**Sketch** (Miscellaneous, Sketch)
SLICE	—	—	—	**Slice** (Solids, Slice)
SNAP	—	—	—	—
SOLID	—	—	—	2D Solid (Draw, Rectangle)
SPELL	Check Spelling	—	T__ools, S__pelling	**Spelling** (Standard)
SPHERE	—	—	—	**Sphere** (Solids, Sphere)
SPLINE	—	—	—	Spline (Draw, Polyline)
SPLINEDIT	—	—	—	Splinedit (Modify, Polyline Edit)
STATS	Statistics	—	D__ata, Stat__us	**Statistics** (Render, Statistics)
STATUS	—	—	D__ata, Status	—
STLOUT	Create STL File	—	—	—
STRETCH	—	—	—	**Stretch** (Modify, Stretch)
STYLE	—	—	D__ata, T__ext Style	—
SUBTRACT	—	—	—	Subtract (Modify, Explode)
SYSWINDOWS	—	—	—	—

continues

Table D.1, Continued
Command, Dialog Box, Alias, Menu, Tool Equivalents

Command Name and Option	Dialog Box	Alias	Pull-Down Menu, Item	Toolname (Toolbar, Flyout)
TABLET	—	—	Options, Tablet	—
TABSURF	—	—	—	**Extruded Surface** (Surfaces, Extruded Surface)
TBCONFIG	Toolbars	—	Tools, Customize Toolbars	—
TEXT	—	—	—	Single Line Text (Draw, Mtext)
TEXTSCR	AutoCAD Text Window	—	Tools, Text Window	—
TIFFIN	—	—	—	—
TILEMODE	—	—	View, Tiled Model Space	**Tiled Model Space** (Standard, Model)
(System variable) 0	—	—	View, Paper Space	Paper Space (Standard, Model Space)
TIME	—	—	Data, Time	—
TOLERANCE	Symbol	—	—	**Tolerance** (Dimensioning, Tolerance)
TOOLBAR	—	—	Tools, Toolbar	—
ACAD.TB_DRAW	—	—	Tools, Toolbar, Draw	Draw Toolbar (Standard, Aerial View)
ACAD.TB_MODIFY	—	—	Tools, Toolbar, Modify	Modify Toolbar (Standard, Aerial View)

Command Name and Option	Dialog Box	Alias	Pull-Down Menu, Item	Toolname (Toolbar, Flyout)
ACAD.TB_DIMENSIONING	—		Tools, Toolbar, Dimensioning	Dimensioning Toolbar (Standard, Aerial View)
ACAD.TB_SOLIDS	—		Tools, Toolbar, Solids	Solids Toolbar (Standard, Aerial View)
ACAD.TB_SURFACES	—		Tools, Toolbar, Surfaces	Surfaces Toolbar (Standard, Aerial View)
ACAD.TB_ETERNAL REFRENCES	—		Tools, Toolbar, External	External References Toolbar References (Standard, Aerial View)
ACAD.TB_ATTRIBUTE	—		Tools, Toolbar, Attribute	Attribute Toolbar (Standard, Aerial View)
ACAD.TB_RENDER	—		Tools, Toolbar, Render	Render Toolbar (Standard, Aerial View)
ACAD.TB_EXTERNAL DATABASE	—		Tools, Toolbar, External	External Database Toolbar Database (Standard, Aerial View)
ACAD.TB_MISCELLANEOUS	—		Tools, Toolbar, Miscellaneous	Miscellaneous Toolbar
ACAD.TB_SELECT_OBJECTS	—	—	Tools, Toolbar, Select Objects	Select Objects Toolbar

continues

D

Table D.1, Continued
Command, Dialog Box, Alias, Menu, Tool Equivalents

Command Name and Option	Dialog Box	Alias	Pull-Down Menu, Item	Toolname (Toolbar, Flyout)
ACAD.TB_OBJECT _SNAP	—	—	**T**ools, **T**oolbar, **O**bject Snap	Object Snap Toolbar
ACAD.TB_POINT _FILTERS	—	—	**T**ools, **T**oolbar, **P**oint Filters	Point Filters Toolbar
ACAD.TB_USC UCS	—	—	**T**ools, **T**oolbar,	UCS Toolbar
ACAD.TB_VIEW **V**iew	—	—	**T**ools, **T**oolbar,	View Toolbar
ACAD.TB_OBJECT _PROPERTIES	—	—	**T**ools, **T**oolbar, Objects	Object Properties Toolbar P**r**operties
ACAD.TB_TOOLBAR	—	—	**T**ools, **T**oolbar, Standard Tool**b**ar	Standard Toolbar
TORUS	—	—	—	**Torus** (Solids, Torus)
TRACE	—	—	—	**Trace** (Miscellaneous, Trace)
TREESTAT	—	—	—	—
TRIM	—	—	—	**Trim** (Modify, Trim)
UCS	—	—	—	—
W	—	—	**V**iew, **S**et UCS, **W**orld	World UCS (Standard, Preset UCS)

Command Name and Option	Dialog Box	Alias	Pull-Down Menu, Item	Toolname (Toolbar, Flyout)
O	—	—	View, Set UCS, Origin	Origin UCS (Standard, Preset UCS)
ZA	—	—	View, Set UCS, ZAxis Vector	Z Axis Vector (Standard, Preset UCS)
3	—	—	View, Set UCS, 3 Point	3 Point (Standard, Preset UCS)
OB	—	—	View, Set UCS, Object	Object UCS (Standard, Preset UCS)
V	—	—	View, Set UCS, View	View UCS (Standard, Preset UCS)
X	—	—	View, Set UCS, Xaxis Rotate	X Axis Rotate (Standard, Preset UCS)
Y	—	—	View, Set UCS, Yaxis Rotate	Y Axis Rotate (Standard, Preset UCS)
Z	—	—	View, Set UCS, Zaxis Rotate	Z Axis Rotate (Standard, Preset UCS)
P	—	—	View, Set UCS, Previous	Previous (Standard, Preset UCS)

continues

D

Table D.1, Continued
Command, Dialog Box, Alias, Menu, Tool Equivalents

Command Name and Option	Dialog Box	Alias	Pull-Down Menu, Item	Toolname (Toolbar, Flyout)
R	—	—	**V**iew, **S**et UCS, **R**estore	Restore (Standard, Preset UCS)
S	—	—	**V**iew, **S**et UCS, **S**ave	Save (Standard, Preset UCS)
UCSICON	—	—	—	—
UNDEFINE	—	—	—	—
UNDO	—	—	**E**dit, **U**ndo Ctrl+Z	**Undo** (Standard)
UNION	—	—	—	Union (Modify, Explode)
UNLOCK	—	—	—	—
VIEWRES	—	—	—	—
VLCONV	Visual Link Data Converter	—	—	—
VPLAYER	—	—	—	—
UNITS	—	—	—	—
VPOINT	—	—	**V**iew, 3D **V**iewpoint, **T**ripod	—
NON,0,0,1	—	—	**V**iew, 3D **V**iewpoint Presets, **T**op	Top View (Standard, Named Views)

continues

D

Command Name and Option	Dialog Box	Alias	Pull-Down Menu, Item	Toolname (Toolbar, Flyout)
NON,0,0,-1	—	—	**V**iew, 3D V**i**ewpoint Presets, **B**ottom	Bottom View (Standard, Named Views)
NON,-1,0,0	—	—	**V**iew, 3D V**i**ewpoint Presets, **L**eft	Left View (Standard, Named Views)
NON,1,0,0	—	—	**V**iew, 3D V**i**ewpoint Presets, **R**ight	Right View (Standard, Named Views)
NON,0,-1,0	—	—	**V**iew, 3D V**i**ewpoint Presets, **F**ront	Front View (Standard, Named Views)
NON,0,1,0	—	—	**V**iew, 3D V**i**ewpoint Presets, **B**ack	Back View (Standard, Named Views)
NON,-1,-1,1	—	—	**V**iew, 3D V**i**ewpoint Presets, **S**W Isometric)	SW Isometric View (Standard, Named Views)
NON,1,-1,1	—	—	**V**iew, 3D V**i**ewpoint Presets, **S**E Isometric	SE Isometric View (Standard, Named Views)
NON,1,1,1	—	—	**V**iew, 3D V**i**ewpoint Presets, **N**E Isometric)	NE Isometric View (Standard, Named Views)
NON,-1,1,1	—	—	**V**iew, 3D V**i**ewpoint Presets, **N**W Isometric	NW Isometric View (Standard, Named Views)

Table D.1, Continued
Command, Dialog Box, Alias, Menu, Tool Equivalents

Command Name and Option	Dialog Box	Alias	Pull-Down Menu, Item	Toolname (Toolbar, Flyout)
VPORTS	—	—	—	—
VSLIDE	Select Slide File	—	Tools, Slide, View	—
WBLOCK	—	—	—	—
WEDGE	—	—	—	Corner (Solids, Center)
CE, \	—	—	—	**Center** (Solids, Center)
WMFIN	Import WMF	—	—	—
WMFOPTS	WMF Import Options	—	—	—
WMFOUT	Create WMF File	—	—	—
XBIND	—	—	—	—
B, \	—	—	—	Block (External Reference, All)
LA, \	—	—	—	Layer (External Reference, All)
LT, \	—	—	—	Linetype (External Reference, All)
S, \	—	—	—	Style (External Reference, All)

Command Name and Option	Dialog Box	Alias	Pull-Down Menu, Item	Toolname (Toolbar, Flyout)
D,\	—	—	—	Dimension Style (External Reference, Clip)
XLINE	—	—	—	Construction Line (Draw, Line)
XPLODE	—	—	—	—
XREF	—	—	—	—
A,\	—	—	—	**Attach** (External Reference, Attach)
O,\	—	—	—	**Overlay** (External Reference, Overlay)
R,\	—	—	—	**Reload** (External Reference, Reload)
D,\	—	—	—	**Detach** (External Reference, Detach)
P,\	—	—	—	**Path** (External References, Path)
?,\	—	—	—	**List** (External Reference, List)
B,\	—	—	—	**All** (External Reference, All)

continues

D

Table D.1, Continued
Command. Dialog Box. Alias. Menu. Tool Equivalents

Command Name and Option	Dialog Box	Alias	Pull-Down Menu, Item	Toolname (Toolbar, Flyout)
XREFCLIP	—	—	—	**Clip** (External Reference, Clip)
ZOOM	—	**Z**	—	—
2X	—	—	View, Zoom, In	**Zoom In** (Standard)
.5X	—	—	View, Zoom, Out	**Zoom Out** (Standard)
W	—	—	View, Zoom, Window	**Zoom Window** (Standard)
All	—	—	View, Zoom, All	**Zoom All** (Standard, Zoom)
P	—	—	View, Zoom, Previous	Zoom Previous (Standard, Zoom)
X	—	—	View, Zoom, Scale	Zoom Scale (Standard, Zoom)
D	—	—	View, Zoom, Dynamic	Zoom Dynamic (Standard, Zoom)
C	—	—	View, Zoom, Center	Zoom Center (Standard, Zoom)
Left	—	—	View, Zoom, Left	Zoom Left (Standard, Zoom)
Limits	—	—	View, Zoom, Limits	Zoom Limits (Standard, Zoom)

Command Name and Option	Dialog Box	Alias	Pull-Down Menu, Item	Toolname (Toolbar, Flyout)
E	—	—	**V**iew, **Z**oom, **E**xtents	Zoom Extents (Standard, Zoom)
Vmax	—	—	**V**iew, **Z**oom, **V**max	Zoom Vmax (Standard, Zoom)

D

E

System Variables Table

This appendix contains a table of AutoCAD system variables. You can use this table to find AutoCAD's environment settings and their values. Table E.1 represents all the variables available through AutoCAD, AutoLISP, and the AutoCAD Development System. The system variable name and the default AutoCAD prototype drawing (ACAD.DWG) settings are shown. A brief description is given for each variable, and the meaning is given for each code. Most variables are set by various dialog boxes or commands. These variables also can be set or checked by the SETVAR command, and most can be entered directly at the Command: prompt. However, those names shown italicized can only be directly accessed by the SETVAR command because AutoCAD has a command with the same name as the variable. All values are saved with the drawing unless noted with (CFG) for ConFiGuration file or (NS) for Not Saved. The Command Name column lists the commands that set the system variables. Variables marked (RO) are read-only, which means you cannot change them.

Variable names and features shown in bold are new in Release 13.

Table E.1
System Variables Table

Variable Name	Default Setting	Command Name	Variable Description
ACADPREFIX	"C:\ACADR13\COMMON\ SUPPORT\;C:\ACADR13..."	—	(NS)(RO) Directory search path set by the DOS ACAD environment variable.
ACADVER	"13"	—	(NS)(RO) Release number of your copy of AutoCAD.
AFLAGS	0	DDATTDEF, ATTDEF	(NS) Current state of ATTDEF modes. The value is the sum of the following: 0 = No attribute mode selected 1 = Invisible 2 = Constant 4 = Verify 8 = Preset
ANGBASE	0.0000	DDUNITS, UNITS	The direction of angle 0 in the current UCS.
ANGDIR	0	DDUNITS, UNITS	The direction of angle measure from 0: 0 = Counterclockwise 1 = Clockwise
APERTURE	10	DDOSNAP, APERTURE	(CFG) OSNAP target size in pixels.

Variable Name	Default Setting	Command Name	Variable Description
AREA	0.0000	AREA, LIST, DBLIST	(NS)(RO) Stores the last computed area.
ATTDIA	0	INSERT	Controls the attribute-entry method: 0 = Attribute prompts 1 = DDATTE dialog box
ATTMODE	1	ATTDISP	Controls attribute display: 0 = OFF 1 = Normal 2 = ON
ATTREQ	1	INSERT	Attribute values used by insert: 0 = Uses default 1 = Prompts for values
AUDITCTL	0	—	(CFG) Controls whether AutoCAD creates an ADT file (Audit Report): 0 = No File 1 = ADT File
AUNITS	0	DDUNITS, UNITS	Sets Angular Units mode: 0 = Decimal Degrees 1 = Degrees/minutes/seconds 2 = Gradians 3 = Radians 4 = Surveyor's Units
AUPREC	0	DDUNITS, UNITS	Sets number of decimal places for angular units.

continues

E

Table E.1, Continued
System Variables Table

Variable Name	Default Setting	Command Name	Variable Description
BACKZ	0.0000	DVIEW	(RO) The DVIEW back clipping plane offset in drawing units. (See VIEWMODE.)
BLIPMODE	1	—	Controls display of marker blips: 1 = Blips 0 = No Blips
CDATE	19941211.22041537	TIME	(RO)(NS) Current date and time in YYYYMMDD.HHMMSS format.
CECOLOR	"BYLAYER"	DDEMODES,COLOR	The color for new objects
CELTSCALE	1.0000	LTSCALE, PSLTSCALE	Sets global linetype scale for new objects.
CELTYPE	"BYLAYER"	DDEMODES, LINETYPE	Sets the linetype for new objects.
CHAMFERA	0.0000	CHAMFER	The first chamfer distance.
CHAMFERB	0.0000	CHAMFER	The second chamfer distance.
CHAMFERC	0.0000	CHAMFER	The chamfer length.
CHAMFERD	0.0000	CHAMFER	The chamfer angle.

Variable Name	Default Setting	Command Name	Variable Description
CHAMMODE	0	CHAMFER	(NS) Determines method AutoCAD uses to create chamfers: 0 = Requires two chamfer distances 1 = Requires chamfer length and angle
CIRCLERAD	0.0000	CIRCLE	(NS) Default radius value for new circles: 0 = None
CLAYER	"0"	DDLMODES, LAYER	The current layer.
CMDACTIVE	0	CMDACTIVE	(NS)(RO) (Used primarily by ADS) Indicates that an AutoCAD command is active: 0 = None 1 = Ordinary command 2 = Ordinary and transparent 4 = Script 8 = Dialog box
CMDDIA	1	—	(CFG) Controls whether the PLOT command uses a dialog box or command prompts: 0 = prompts 1 = Dialog box

continues

E

Table E.1, Continued
System Variables Table

Variable Name	Default Setting	Command Name	Variable Description
CMDECHO	1	—	(NS) Controls the echoing of prompts and input during AutoLISP functions: 0 = Disables echoing 1 = Enables echoing
CMDNAMES	""	—	(NS)(RO) Names of any active commands.
CMLJUST	0	DTEXT, TEXT	(CFG) Sets Multi-Line text justification: 0 = Top 1 = Middle 2 = Bottom
CMLSCALE	1.0000	DTEXT, TEXT	(CFG) Sets overall width of Multi-Line text: Scale factor 2 = Twice width of style def. Scale Factor 0 = Collapses multiline into single line Negative Scale Factor = Flips order of offset lines
CMLSTYLE	"STANDARD"	MTEXT, DTEXT, TEXT	(CFG) Sets the style for Multi-Lines.

Variable Name	Default Setting	Command Name	Variable Description
COORDS	1	[^D][F6]	Controls updating of coordinate display: 0 = Updated on pick points only 1 = Absolute continuously updated 2 = Relative only during prompts
CVPORT	2	VPORTS	The current viewport's number.
DATE	2449698.91977245	TIME	(NS)(RO) The current date and time in Julian format.
DBMOD	0	Most	(NS)(RO) Drawing modification status. Sum of the following: 0 = None 1 = Object database modified 2 = Symbol table modified 4 = Database variable modified 8 = Window modified 16 = View modified
DCTCUST	""	**SPELL**	(CFG) Current custom spelling dictionary and path.
DCTMAIN	"enu"	**SPELL**	(CFG) Current main spelling dictionary file:

continues

E

Table E.1, Continued
System Variables Table

Variable Name	Default Setting	Command Name	Variable Description
			enu = American English
			ena = Australian English
			ens = British English (ise)
			enz = British English (ize)
			ca = Catalan
			cs = Czech
			da = Danish
			nl = Dutch (Primary)
			nls = Dutch (Secondary)
			fi = Finnish
			fr = French (unaccented capitals)
			fra = French (accented capitals)
			de = German (Scharfes s)
			ded = German (Dopple s)
			it = Italian
			no = Norwegian (Bokmal)
			non = Norwegian (Nynorsk)
			pt = Portuguese (Iberian)
			ptb = Portuguese (Brazilian)
			ru = Russian (infrequent io)
			ru I = Russian (frequent io)
			es = Spanish (unaccented capitals)
			esa = Spanish (accented capitals)
			sv = Swedish

Variable Name	Default Setting	Command Name	Variable Description
DELOBJ	1	—	Controls whether objects used to create other objects are deleted from the database: 0 = Objects are deleted 1 = Objects are retained
DIASTAT	1	DD?????	(NS)(RO) Last dialog box exit code: 0 = Cancel 1 = OK
DISPSILH	0	—	Controls display of silhouette curves of body objects in wireframe mode: 0 = Off 1 = On
DISTANCE	0.0000	DIST	(NS)(RO) Stores the distance computed by the DIST command.
DONUTID	0.5000	DONUT	(NS) Sets the default inner diameter for new donut objects.
DONUTOD	1.0000	DONUT	(NS) Sets the default outer diameter for new donut objects.
DRAGMODE	2	DRAGMODE	Controls object dragging during editing commands: 0 = No dragging 1 = On (if requested) 2 = Auto

continues

E

Table E.1, Continued
System Variables Table

Variable Name	Default Setting	Command Name	Variable Description
DRAGP1	10	—	(CFG) Sets regen-drag input sampling rate.
DRAGP2	25	—	(CFG) Sets fast-drag input sampling rate.
DWGCODEPAGE	"ansi_1252"	—	(RO) The code page used for the drawing.
DWGNAME	"UNNAMED"	—	(RO) The drawing name as entered by the user.
DWGPREFIX	"C:\ACADR13\WIN\"	—	(NS)(RO) The current drawing's drive and directory path.
DWGTITLED	0	NEW	(NS)(RO) Indicates whether the current drawing has been named or not: 0 = No 1 = Yes
DWGWRITE	1	OPEN	(NS) Indicates whether the current drawing is opened as read only:

Variable Name	Default Setting	Command Name	Variable Description
			0 = Read-only 1 = Read/write
EDGEMODE	0	TRIM, EXTEND	Controls determination of cutting and boundary edges: 0 = Use selected edge without extension 1 = Extends selected edge to imaginary extension of cutting or boundary object
ELEVATION	0.0000	ELEV	The current elevation in the current UCS for the current space.
ERRNO	0	—	(NS) An error number generated by AutoLISP and ADS Applications. (See the *AutoLISP Release 13 Programmer's Reference* or the *AutoCAD Development System Programmer's Reference Manual*.) Not listed by SETVAR.
EXPERT	0	—	(NS) Suppresses successive level of Are you sure? warnings: 0 = None 1 = REGEN/LAYER

continues

E

Table E.1, Continued
System Variables Table

Variable Name	Default Setting	Command Name	Variable Description
			2 = BLOCK/WBLOCK/SAVE 3 = LINETYPE 4 = UCS/VPORT 5 = DIM
EXPLMODE	1	EXPLODE	Controls whether the EX-PLODE command supports nonuniformly scaled (NUS) blocks: 0 = Does not explode NUS blocks 1 = Explodes NUS blocks
EXTMAX	-1.0000E+20,-1.0000E+20,-1.0000E+20		(RO) The X,Y coordinates of the drawing's upper right extents in the WCS.
EXTMIN	1.0000E+20,1.0000E+20,1.0000E+20		(RO) The X,Y coordinates of the drawing's lower left extents in the WCS.
FACETRES	0.5000	HIDE, SHADE, RENDER	Adjusts smoothness of shaded and hidden-line removed objects. Valid from 0.01 to 10.0.
FFLIMIT	0	—	(CFG) Limits number of PostScript and TrueType fonts in memory. From 0 to 100. 0 is no limit.

Variable Name	Default Setting	Command Name	Variable Description
FILEDIA	1	—	(CFG) Controls display of file dialog boxes: 0 = Only when a tilde (~) is entered 1 = On
FILLETRAD	0.0000	FILLET	Stores the current fillet radius.
FILLMODE	1	SOLID, FILL	Turns on the display of fill traces, solids, and wide polylines: 0 = Off 1 = On
FONTALT	"txt"	—	(CFG) Specifies alternative font when AutoCAD cannot locate requested font.
FONTMAP	""	—	(CFG) Specifies a mapped font file to use when AutoCAD cannot locate the font file.
FRONTZ	0.0000	DVIEW	(RO) The DVIEW front clipping plane's offset in drawing units. (See VIEWMODE.)
GRIDMODE	0	DDRMODES, GRID	Controls display of the grid in the current viewport: 0 = Off 1 = On

E

continues

Table E.1, Continued
System Variables Table

Variable Name	Default Setting	Command Name	Variable Description
GRIDUNIT	0.0000,0.0000	DDRMODES, GRID	The X,Y grid spacing for the current viewport.
GRIPBLOCK	0	DDGRIPS	(CFG) Controls the display of grips for objects in blocks: 0 = Off 1 = On
GRIPCOLOR	5	DDGRIPS	(CFG) The current color of unselected grips. Can be any AutoCAD color from 1 to 255.
GRIPHOT	1	DDGRIPS	(CFG) The current color of selected grips. Can be any AutoCAD color from 1 to 255.
GRIPS	1	DDSELECT	(CFG) Controls the display of entity grips and grip editing: 0 = Off 1 = On
GRIPSIZE	3	DDGRIPS	(CFG) The size of grip box in pixels; 0 = PICKBOX

Variable Name	Default Setting	Command Name	Variable Description
HANDLES	1	HANDLES	Controls the creation of entity handles for the current drawing: 1 = On
HIGHLIGHT	1	DDRMODES	(NS) Controls object selection highlighting: 0 = Off 1 = On
HPANG	0	BHATCH, HATCH	(NS) The current hatch angle.
HPBOUND	1	BHATCH, BOUNDARY	Type of object created by the BHATCH and BOUNDARY commands: 0 = Polyline 1 = Region
HPDOUBLE	0	BHATCH, HATCH	(NS) Controls user-defined hatch pattern doubling: 0 = Off 1 = On
HPNAME	"ANSI31"	BHATCH, HATCH	(NS) The default hatch pattern for new hatches.
HPSCALE	1.0000	BHATCH, HATCH	(NS) The default hatch pattern scale. Must be nonzero.

continues

E

Table E.1, Continued
System Variables Table

Variable Name	Default Setting	Command Name	Variable Description
HPSPACE	1.0000	BHATCH, HATCH	(NS) The default spacing for user-defined hatch patterns.
INSBASE	0.0000,0.0000,0.0000	BASE	Insertion base point X,Y,Z coordinate of current drawing in current space and current UCS.
INSNAME	""	DDINSERT,INSERT	(NS) Default block name for IN-SERT or DDINSERT.
ISOLINES	4	—	Controls number of isolines per surface on objects.
LASTANGLE	0.0000	ARC	(NS)(RO) The angle of the last arc entered in the current UCS for the current space.
LASTPOINT	0.0000,0.0000,0.0000	—	The last point entered in the current UCS and current space.
LENSLENGTH	50.0000	DVIEW	(RO) The lens length of the current viewport perspective.
LIMCHECK	0	LIMITS	Controls object creation outside the drawing limits:

Variable Name	Default Setting	Command Name	Variable Description
			0 = Enables object creation 1 = Disables object creation
LIMMAX	12.0000,9.0000	LIMITS	The upper right limit of the WCS in current space.
LIMMIN	0.0000,0.0000	LIMITS	The lower left limit of the WCS in current space.
LOCALE	"en"	—	(RO)(NS) The ISO language code of the AutoCAD version being used.
LOGINNAME	""	CONFIG	(CFG)(RO) User name created by the CONFIG command or input when AutoCAD is loaded.
LTSCALE	1.0000	LTSCALE	Global linetype scale factor.
LUNITS	2	DDUNITS, UNITS	The Linear units mode: 1 = Scientific 2 = Decimal 3 = Engineering 4 = Architectural 5 = Fractional
LUPREC	4	DDUNITS, UNITS	Precision of decimal or fractional units.
MACROTRACE	0	—	(NS) Controls the Diesel, macro-debugging display. Not listed

continues

E

Table E.1, Continued
System Variables Table

Variable Name	Default Setting	Command Name	Variable Description
			by SETVAR. 0 = On 1 = Off
MAXACTVP	16	—	(NS) Maximum number of viewports to regenerate at one time.
MAXSORT	200	—	(CFG) The maximum number of symbols and file names to be sorted in lists.
MENUCTL	1	—	(CFG) Controls page switching of the screen menu: 0 = Does not switch with keyboard command entry 1 = Does switch with keyboard command entry
MENUECHO	0	—	(NS) Controls the display of menu actions on the command line; the value is the sum of the following: 1 = Suppresses menu input 2 = Suppresses system prompts 4 = Disables ^P toggle of menu echoing

Variable Name	Default Setting	Command Name	Variable Description
			8 = Displays DIESEL input/output strings
MENUNAME	"C:\ACADR13\WIN\SUPPORT\ACAD.mnc"	MENU	(NS)(RO) Name and path of currently loaded menu.
MIRRTEXT	1	MIRROR	Controls how MIRROR reflects text: 0 = Retains text direction 1 = Mirrors text
MODEMACRO	""	—	(NS) A DIESEL language expression to control status-line display.
MTEXTED	"Internal"	DDEDIT	(CFG) Name of program to use for editing mtext objects.
OFFSETDIST	-1.0000	OFFSET	(NS) Default distance for the OFFSET command. Negative value enables the THROUGH option.
ORTHOMODE	0	[^O][F8]	Sets the current Ortho mode: 0 = Off 1 = On
OSMODE	0	DDOSNAP, OSNAP	Sets the current object snap mode; value is the sum of the following:

continues

E

Table E.1, Continued
System Variables Table

Variable Name	Default Setting	Command Name	Variable Description
			0 = NONe
			1 = ENDpoint
			2 = MIDpoint
			4 = CENter
			8 = NODe
			16 = QUAdrant
			32 = INTersection
			64 = INSertion
			128 = PERpendicular
			256 = TANgent
			512 = NEArest
			1024 = QUIck
			2048 = APPint
PDMODE	0	POINT	Controls the graphic display of POINT objects.
PDSIZE	0.0000	POINT	Controls the size of POINT objects: Negative = Percentage of viewport size Positive = Absolute size 0 = 5% of graphics area height
PELLIPSE	0	ELLIPSE	The ellipse type created with ELLIPSE command: 0 = True ellipse 1 = Polyline representation of an ellipse

Variable Name	Default Setting	Command Name	Variable Description
PERIMETER	0.0000	AREA, LIST, DBLIST	(NS)(RO) Last perimeter value calculated by AREA, LIST, DBLIST.
PFACEVMAX	4		(NS)(RO) Maximum number of vertices per face.
PICKADD	1	DDSELECT	(CFG) Controls whether selected objects are added to, or are replaced (added with Shift + select), the current selection set: 0 = Replace (Shift to add only) 1 = Added (Shift to remove only)
PICKAUTO	1	DDSELECT	(CFG) Controls the implied (AUTO) windowing for object selection: 0 = Off 1 = On
PICKBOX	3	DDSELECT	(CFG) Object selection pick box size, in pixels.
PICKDRAG	0	DDSELECT	(CFG) Determines whether the pick button must be depressed

continues

E

Table E.1, Continued

System Variables Table

Variable Name	Default Setting	Command Name	Variable Description
			during window corner picking in set selections: 0 = Off 1 = On
PICKFIRST	1	DDSELECT	(CFG) Enables entity selection before command selection (noun/verb paradigm): 0 = Off 1 = On
PICKSTYLE	1	—	(CFG) Controls group selection and associative hatch selection: 0 = No group or associative hatch selection 1 = Group selection 2 = Associative hatch selection 3 = Group and associative hatch selection
PLATFORM	"Microsoft Windows (Intel) Version 3.10"	—	(NS)(RO) Indicates the operating system in use. String value.
PLINEGEN	0	—	Sets the linetype pattern generation around the vertices of a 2D polyline. Does not apply

Variable Name	Default Setting	Command Name	Variable Description
			to polylines with tapered segments. 0 = Polylines are generated to start and end with a dash at each vertex. 1 = Generates the linetype in a continuous pattern around the vertices of the polyline
PLINEWID	0.0000	PLINE	Default width for new polyline objects.
PLOTID	""	—	(CFG) Current plotter configuration description.
PLOTROTMODE	1	PLOT	Controls plot orientation: 0 = Rotation icon aligns at lower left for 0, top left for 90, top right for 180, lower right for 270 1 = Aligns lower left corner of plotting area with lower left corner of paper
PLOTTER	0	PLOT	(CFG) Current plotter configuration number.
POLYSIDES	4	POLYGON	(NS) Default number of sides for POLYGON objects (3-1024).

continues

E

Table E.1, Continued
System Variables Table

Variable Name	Default Setting	Command Name	Variable Description
POPUPS	1	—	(NS)(RO) Status of the currently configured display driver: 0 = Does not support dialog boxes, menu bar, pull-down menus, and icon menus 1 = Supports these features
PROJMODE	1	TRIM, EXTEND	(CGF) Current projection mode for TRIM or EXTEND operations: 0 = True 3D (no projection) 1 = Project to the XY plane of the current UCS 2 = Project to the current view plane
PSLTSCALE	1	—	Paper space scaling of model space linetypes: 0 = Off 1 = On
PSPROLOG	""	—	(CFG) The name of the PostScript post-processing section of the ACAD.PSF to be appended to the PSOUT command's output.

Variable Name	*Default Setting*	*Command Name*	*Variable Description*
PSQUALITY	75	PSQUALITY	(CFG) The default quality setting for rendering of images by the PSIN command.
QTEXTMODE	0	QTEXT	Sets the current state of quick text mode: 0 = Off 1 = On
RASTERPREVIEW	0	SAVE, SAVEAS	Controls whether a preview image is saved and in which format the image is saved: 0 = BMP only 1 = BMP and WMF 2 = WMF only 3 = No preview image created
REGENMODE	1	REGENAUTO	Indicates the current state of REGENAUTO: 0 = Off 1 = On
RIASPECT	0.0000	GIFIN, TIFFIN	(NS) Controls the aspect ratio of imported raster images.
RIBACK	0	GIFIN, TIFFIN, PCXIN	(NS) The background color of imported raster images. Based on AutoCAD colors.

continues

Table E.1, Continued
System Variables Table

Variable Name	Default Setting	Command Name	Variable Description
RIEDGE	0	GIFIN, TIFFIN, PCXIN	(NS) Controls the edge detection feature: 0 = Disables edge detection 1-255 = Threshold for edge detection
RIGAMUT	256	GIFIN, TIFFIN, PCXIN	(NS) Number of colors used when color images are imported.
RIGREY	0	GIFIN, TIFFIN. PCXIN	(NS) Imports images as grayscale: 0 = Disables grayscale image importing >0 = Converts each pixel to grayscale.
RITHRESH	0	GIFIN, TIFFIN, PCXIN	(NS) Controls brightness of imported images: 0 = Disables brightness control >0 = Only pixels brighter than value are imported
RE-INIT	0	REINIT	(NS) A code that specifies the type(s) of reinitializations to perform. The sum of:

Variable Name	Default Setting	Command Name	Variable Description
			1 = Digitizer port 2 = Plotter port 4 = Digitizer device 8 = Display device 16 = Reload ACAD.PGP
SAVEFILE	"AUTO.SV$"	CONFIG, PREFERENCES	(CFG)(RO) The default directory and file name for automatic file saves.
SAVENAME	""	SAVEAS	(RO)(NS) Stores the file name you save the drawing to.
SAVETIME	120	CONFIG	(CFG) The default interval between automatic file saves, in minutes: 0 = Disable automatic saves
SCREENBOXES	0	CONFIG	(CFG)(RO) The number of available screen menu boxes in the current graphics screen area.
SCREENMODE	3	[F1]	(CFG)(RO) Indicates the active AutoCAD screen mode or window: 0 = Text 1 = Graphics 2 = Dual Screen

continues

E

Table E.1, Continued
System Variables Table

Variable Name	Default Setting	Command Name	Variable Description
SCREENSIZE	1008.0000,578.0000		(RO) Size of the current viewport in pixels.
SHADEDGE	3	SHADE	Controls the display of edges and faces by the SHADE command: 0 = Faces shaded, edges not highlighted 1 = Faces shaded, edges in background color. 2 = Faces not filled, edges in object color. 3 = Faces in object color, edges in background color
SHADEDIF	70	SHADE	Sets the ratio of diffuse reflective light to ambient light, expressed as a percentage of diffuse reflective light.
SHPNAME	""	SHAPE	(NS) The default shape name.
SKETCHINC	0.1000	SKETCH	The recording increment for SKETCH segments.
SKPOLY	0	SKETCH	Determines whether sketch uses lines or polylines: 0 = Generate lines 1 = Generate polylines

Variable Name	Default Setting	Command Name	Variable Description
SNAPANG	0	DDRMODES, SNAP	The angle of SNAP/GRID rotation in the current viewport and UCS.
SNAPBASE	0.0000,0.0000	DDRMODES, SNAP	SNAP/GRID base point in the current viewport and UCS.
SNAPISOPAIR	0	DDRMODES, SNAP, [^E], [F5]	The current isoplane for the current viewport: 0 = Left 1 = Top 2 = Right
SNAPMODE	0	DDRMODES, SNAP, [^B], [F9]	Indicates the state of SNAP for the current viewport: 0 = Off 1 = On
SNAPSTYL	0	DDRMODES, SNAP	The snap style for the current viewport: 0 = Standard 1 = Isometric
SNAPUNIT	1.0000,1.0000	DDRMODES, SNAP	The snap X,Y increment for the current viewport.
SORTENTS	96	DDSELECT	(CFG) Controls the display of object sort order: 0 = Disable SORTENTS 1 = Sorts for object selection 2 = Sorts for object snap

continues

E

Table E.1, Continued
System Variables Table

Variable Name	Default Setting	Command Name	Variable Description
			4 = Sorts for redraws
			8 = Sorts for MSLIDE creation
			16 = Sorts for REGENs
			32 = Sorts for plotting
			64 = Sorts for PostScript output
			Sum numbers to select more than one.
SPLFRAME	0	—	Controls display of control polygons for spline-fit polygons, defining meshes of surface-fit polygons, and invisible 3D face edges:
			0 = Off
			1 = On
SPLINESEGS	8	—	The number of line segments in each spline curve.
SPLINETYPE	6	—	Controls the type of curve generated by PEDIT spline:
			5 = Quadratic B-spline
			6 = Cubic B-spline
SURFTAB1	6	—	Sets the density of a mesh in the M direction.
SURFTAB2	6	—	Sets the density of a mesh in the N direction.

Variable Name	Default Setting	Command Name	Variable Description
SURFTYPE	6	—	Controls the type of surface generated by PEDIT Smooth: 5 = Quadratic B-spline surface 6 = Cubic B-spline surface 8 = Bezier surface
SURFU	6	—	Surface density in the M direction of 3D polygonal meshes.
SURFV	6	—	Surface density in the N direction of 3D polygonal meshes.
SYSCODEPAGE	ASCII	—	(RO) Code page used by the system.
TABMODE	0	TABLET	(NS) Controls the use of Tablet mode: 0 = Disables tablet mode 1 = Enables tablet mode
TARGET	0.0000,0.0000,0.0000	DVIEW	(RO) The UCS coordinates of the target point in the current viewport.
TDCREATE	2449698.91946285	TIME	(RO) Time of the creation of the current drawing in Julian format.
TDINDWG	0.00048947	TIME	(RO) Total amount of editing time

continues

E

Table E.1, Continued

System Variables Table

Variable Name	Default Setting	Command Name	Variable Description
			elapsed on the current drawing in Julian format.
TDUPDATE	2449698.91946285	TIME	(RO) The date and time when the drawing was last saved, in Julian format.
TDUSRTIMER	0.00049144	TIME	(RO) User-controlled elapsed time in Julian format.
TEMPPREFIX	""	CONFIG	(NS)(RO) The directory for placement of AutoCAD's temporary files. Defaults to current drawing directory.
TEXTEVAL	0	—	(NS) Controls the checking of text input (except by DTEXT) for AutoLISP expressions: 0 = No 1 = Yes
TEXTFILL	0	TEXT	Controls the filling of Bitstream, TrueType, and Adobe Type1 fonts: 0 = Display as outlines 1 = Display as filled images

Variable Name	Command Name	Default Setting	Variable Description
TEXTQLTY	TEXT	50	Controls the resolution of Bitstream, TrueType, and Adobe Type1 fonts: 0–100 (higher is better resolution)
TEXTSIZE	TEXT	0.2000	Default height for new text objects.
TEXTSTYLE	TEXT, STYLE	"STANDARD"	Default text style for new text objects.
THICKNESS	ELEV	0.0000	Current 3D thickness.
TILEMODE	TILEMODE	1	Enables and disables paper space and viewport objects: 0 = Off 1 = On
TOOLTIPS	—	1	(CFG) Controls the display of ToolTips: 0 = Off 1 = On
TRACEWID	TRACE	0.0500	The current width of traces.
TREEDEPTH	—	3020	A code number (4 digits) representing the maximum number of division for spatial database index for model space (first two digits) and paper space (last two digits).

continues

Table E.1, Continued
System Variables Table

Variable Name	Default Setting	Command Name	Variable Description
TREEMAX	10000000	—	(CFG) The maximum number of nodes for spatial database organization for the current memory configuration.
TRIMMODE	1	FILLET, CHAMFER	(NS) Controls whether AutoCAD trims selected edges for fillets and chamfers: 0 = Leave edges intact 1 = Trim edges back
UCSFOLLOW	0		Controls automatic display of the plan view in the current viewport when switching to a new UCS: 0 = Off 1 = On
UCSICON	1	UCSICON	Controls the UCS icon's display. Value is the sum of the following: 0 = Off 1 = On 2 = At origin
UCSNAME	""	DDUCS, UCS	(RO) The name of the current UCS

Variable Name	Default Setting	Command Name	Variable Description
			for the current space: "" = unnamed
UCSORG	0.0000,0.0000,0.0000	DDUCS, UCS	(RO) The WCS origin of the current UCS for the current space.
UCSXDIR	1.0000,0.0000,0.0000	DDUCS, UCS	(RO) The X direction of the current UCS.
UCSYDIR	0.0000,1.0000,0.0000	DDUCS, UCS	(RO) The Y direction of the current UCS.
UNDOCTL	5	UNDO	(NS)(RO) The current state of UNDO. Value is the sum of the following: 1 = Enabled 2 = Single command 4 = Auto mode 8 = Group active
UNDOMARKS	0	UNDO	(NS)(RO) The current number of marks in the UNDO command's history.
UNITMODE	0	—	Controls the display of user input of fractions, feet and inches, and surveyor's angles: 0 = per LUNITS 1 = As input

continues

E

Table E.1, Continued
System Variables Table

Variable Name	Default Setting	Command Name	Variable Description
USERI1-5	0	—	User integer variables. USERI1 to USERI5. Not listed by SETVAR.
USERR1-5	0.0000	—	User real-number variables USERR1 to USERR5. Not listed by SETVAR.
USERS1-5	""	—	User string variables (up to 460 characters long) USERS1 to USERS5. Not listed by SETVAR.
VIEWCTR	7.9248,4.5408,0.0000	ZOOM, PAN, VIEW	(RO) The X,Y,Z center point coordinates of the current viewport in the current view.
VIEWDIR	0.0000,0.0000,1.0000	DVIEW	(RO) The camera point offset from the target in the WCS.
VIEWMODE	0	DVIEW, UCS	(RO) The current viewport's viewing mode. Value is sum of following: 0 = Disabled 1 = Perspective 2 = Front clipping on

E

Variable Name	Default Setting	Command Name	Variable Description
			4 = Back clipping on 8 = UCSFOLLOW On 16 = FRONTZ offset in use
VIEWSIZE	9.0816	ZOOM, VIEW	(RO) The current view's height in drawing units.
VIEWTWIST	0	DVIEW	(RO) The current viewport's view-twist angle.
VISRETAIN	0	VISRETAIN	Controls retention of xref file layer setting in the current drawing. 0 = Off 1 = On
VSMAX	47.5487,27.2449,0.0000	ZOOM, PAN, VIEW	(RO) The upper right X,Y,Z coordinates of the current viewport's virtual screen for the current UCS.
VSMIN	-31.6991,-18.1632,0.00	ZOOM, PAN, VIEW	(RO) The lower left X,Y,Z coordinates of the current viewport's virtual screen for the current UCS.
WORLDUCS	1	UCS	(NS)(RO) Indicates if the current UCS = WCS: 0 = False

continues

Table E.1, Continued
System Variables Table

Variable Name	Default Setting	Command Name	Variable Description
			1 = True
WORLDVIEW	1	DVIEW,UCS	Controls the automatic changing of a UCS to the WCS during the DVIEW and VPOINT commands: 0 = Off 1 = On
XREFCTL	0	—	(CFG) Controls the creation of an XLG log file that contains xref results: 0 = No file 1 = XLG file

F

Menu Maps and Toolbars

The figures in this appendix provide a guide to the pull-down menus and toolbars in AutoCAD Release 13.

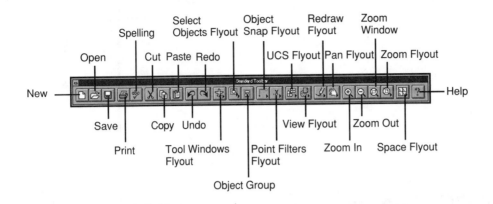

New
Open
Spelling
Cut Paste Redo
Select Objects Flyout
Object Snap Flyout
Redraw Flyout
Zoom Window
UCS Flyout
Pan Flyout
Zoom Flyout
Help

Save
Print
Copy Undo
Tool Windows Flyout
Point Filters Flyout
View Flyout
Zoom In
Zoom Out
Space Flyout

Object Group

Aerial View — Draw Toolbar
Modify Toolbar — Dimensioning Toolbar
Solids Toolbar — Surface Toolbar
External Reference Toolbar — Attribute Toolbar
— External Database Toolbar
Render Toolbar
Object Properties Toolbar · Standard Toolbar

Select Window — Select Crossing
Select Group — Select Previous
Select Last — Select All
Select Window Polygon — Select Crossing Polygon
Select Fence — Select Add
Select Remove · Selection Filter

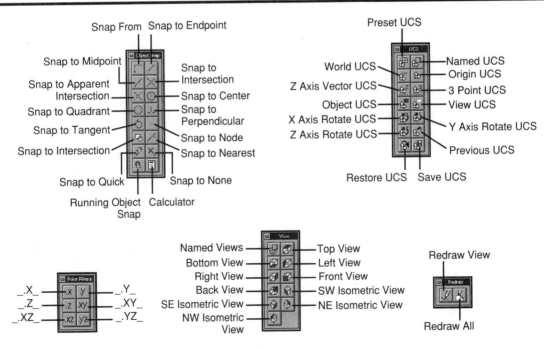

Snap From · Snap to Endpoint
Snap to Midpoint
Snap to Apparent Intersection
Snap to Quadrant
Snap to Tangent
Snap to Intersection
Snap to Quick
Running Object Snap · Calculator
Snap to Intersection
Snap to Center
Snap to Perpendicular
Snap to Node
Snap to Nearest
Snap to None

Preset UCS
World UCS — Named UCS
Z Axis Vector UCS — Origin UCS
Object UCS — 3 Point UCS
X Axis Rotate UCS — View UCS
Z Axis Rotate UCS — Y Axis Rotate UCS
Restore UCS · Save UCS — Previous UCS

Named Views — Top View
Bottom View — Left View
Right View — Front View
Back View — SW Isometric View
SE Isometric View — NE Isometric View
NW Isometric View

_.X_ _.Y_
_.Z_ _.XY_
_.XZ_ _.YZ_

Redraw View
Redraw All

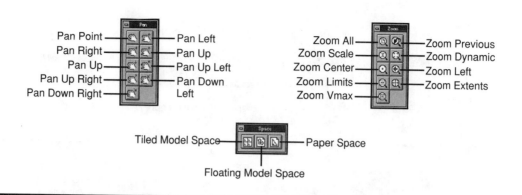

Pan Point — Pan Left
Pan Right — Pan Up
Pan Up — Pan Up Left
Pan Up Right — Pan Down Right — Pan Down Left

Zoom All — Zoom Previous
Zoom Scale — Zoom Dynamic
Zoom Center — Zoom Left
Zoom Limits — Zoom Extents
Zoom Vmax

Tiled Model Space — Paper Space
Floating Model Space

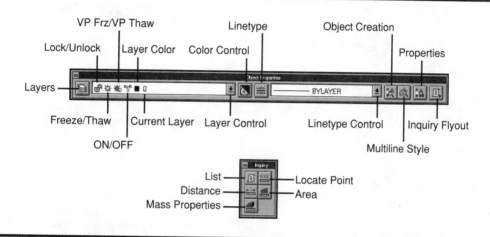

VP Frz/VP Thaw
Lock/Unlock   Layer Color   Color Control   Linetype   Object Creation   Properties
Layers
Freeze/Thaw   Current Layer   Layer Control   Linetype Control   Inquiry Flyout
ON/OFF   Multiline Style

BYLAYER

List — Locate Point
Distance — Area
Mass Properties

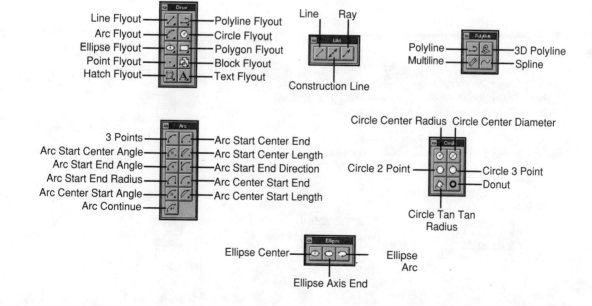

Line Flyout — Polyline Flyout
Arc Flyout — Circle Flyout
Ellipse Flyout — Polygon Flyout
Point Flyout — Block Flyout
Hatch Flyout — Text Flyout

Line   Ray
Construction Line

Polyline — 3D Polyline
Multiline — Spline

3 Points — Arc Start Center End
Arc Start Center Angle — Arc Start Center Length
Arc Start End Angle — Arc Start End Direction
Arc Start End Radius — Arc Center Start End
Arc Center Start Angle — Arc Center Start Length
Arc Continue

Circle Center Radius   Circle Center Diameter
Circle 2 Point — Circle 3 Point
Donut
Circle Tan Tan Radius

Ellipse Center — Ellipse Arc
Ellipse Axis End

F

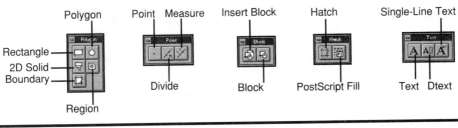

Polygon

Rectangle
2D Solid
Boundary

Region

Point   Measure

Divide

Insert Block

Block

Hatch

PostScript Fill

Single-Line Text

Text   Dtext

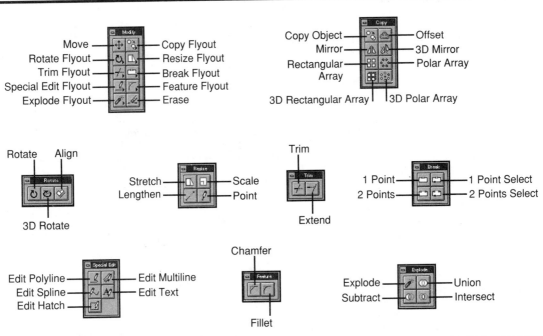

Move — Copy Flyout
Rotate Flyout — Resize Flyout
Trim Flyout — Break Flyout
Special Edit Flyout — Feature Flyout
Explode Flyout — Erase

Copy Object — Offset
Mirror — 3D Mirror
Rectangular Array — Polar Array

3D Rectangular Array   3D Polar Array

Rotate   Align

3D Rotate

Stretch — Scale
Lengthen — Point

Trim

Extend

1 Point — 1 Point Select
2 Points — 2 Points Select

Edit Polyline — Edit Multiline
Edit Spline — Edit Text
Edit Hatch

Chamfer

Fillet

Explode — Union
Subtract — Intersect

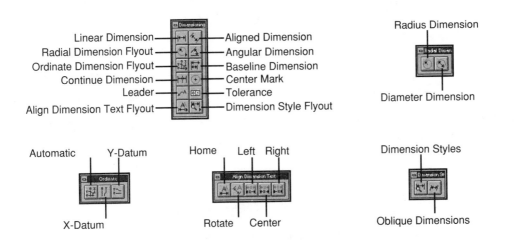

Linear Dimension — Aligned Dimension
Radial Dimension Flyout — Angular Dimension
Ordinate Dimension Flyout — Baseline Dimension
Continue Dimension — Center Mark
Leader — Tolerance
Align Dimension Text Flyout — Dimension Style Flyout

Radius Dimension

Diameter Dimension

Automatic   Y-Datum

X-Datum

Home   Left   Right

Rotate   Center

Dimension Styles

Oblique Dimensions

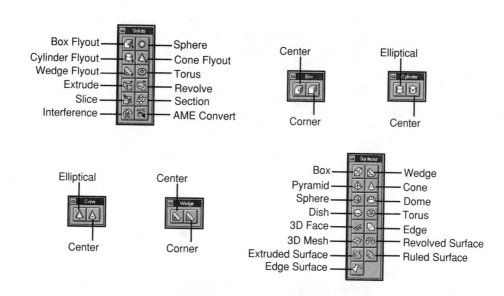

Box Flyout — Sphere
Cylinder Flyout — Cone Flyout
Wedge Flyout — Torus
Extrude — Revolve
Slice — Section
Interference — AME Convert

Center — Box — Corner

Elliptical — Cylinder — Center

Elliptical — Cone — Center

Center — Wedge — Corner

Box — Surfaces — Wedge
Pyramid — Cone
Sphere — Dome
Dish — Torus
3D Face — Edge
3D Mesh — Revolved Surface
Extruded Surface — Ruled Surface
Edge Surface

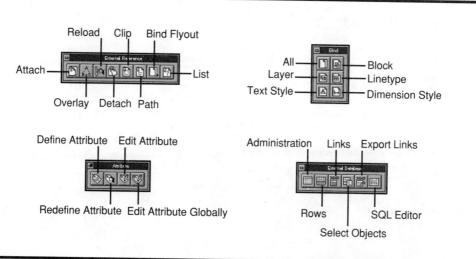

Reload   Clip   Bind Flyout

Attach — External Reference — List
Overlay   Detach   Path

All — Bind — Block
Layer — Linetype
Text Style — Dimension Style

Define Attribute   Edit Attribute

Administration   Links   Export Links

Redefine Attribute   Edit Attribute Globally

Rows   SQL Editor
Select Objects

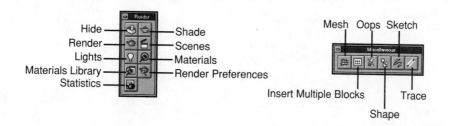

Hide — Shade
Render — Scenes
Lights — Materials
Materials Library — Render Preferences
Statistics

Mesh   Oops   Sketch

Insert Multiple Blocks   Trace
Shape

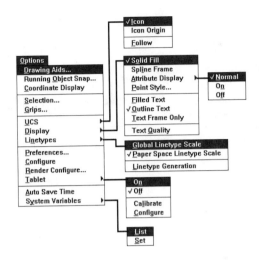

Options
- Drawing Aids...
- Running Object Snap...
- Coordinate Display
- Selection...
- Grips...
- UCS ▶
- Display ▶
- Linetypes ▶
- Preferences...
- Configure
- Render Configure...
- Tablet ▶
- Auto Save Time
- System Variables ▶

- √ Icon
- Icon Origin
- Follow

- √ Solid Fill
- Spline Frame
- Attribute Display
- Point Style...
- Filled Text
- √ Outline Text
- Text Frame Only
- Text Quality

- √ Normal
- On
- Off

- Global Linetype Scale
- √ Paper Space Linetype Scale
- Linetype Generation

- On
- √ Off
- Calibrate
- Configure

- List
- Set

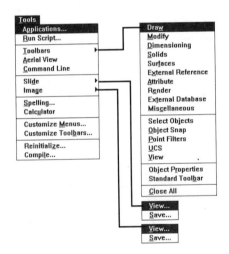

Tools
- Applications...
- Run Script...
- Toolbars ▶
- Aerial View
- Command Line
- Slide ▶
- Image ▶
- Spelling...
- Calculator
- Customize Menus...
- Customize Toolbars...
- Reinitialize...
- Compile...

Draw
- Modify
- Dimensioning
- Solids
- Surfaces
- External Reference
- Attribute
- Render
- External Database
- Miscellaneous
- Select Objects
- Object Snap
- Point Filters
- UCS
- View
- Object Properties
- Standard Toolbar
- Close All

- View...
- Save...

- View...
- Save...

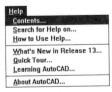

Help
- Contents...
- Search for Help on...
- How to Use Help...
- What's New in Release 13...
- Quick Tour...
- Learning AutoCAD...
- About AutoCAD...

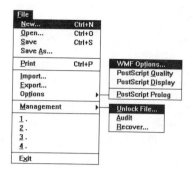

File
New...	Ctrl+N
Open...	Ctrl+O
Save	Ctrl+S
Save As...	
Print	Ctrl+P
Import...	
Export...	
Options	▶
Management	▶
1 .	
2 .	
3 .	
4 .	
Exit	

WMF Options...
- PostScript Quality
- PostScript Display
- PostScript Prolog

Unlock File...
- Audit
- Recover...

Edit
Undo	Ctrl+Z
Redo	
Cut	Ctrl+X
Copy	Ctrl+C
Copy View	
Paste	Ctrl+V
Paste Special...	
Properties...	
Links...	
Insert Object...	

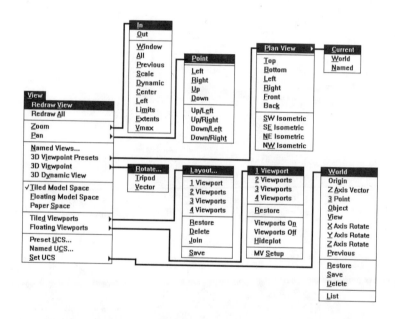

View
- **Redraw View**
- Redraw All
- Zoom ▶
- Pan ▶
- Named Views...
- 3D Viewpoint Presets ▶
- 3D Viewpoint ▶
- 3D Dynamic View
- ✓ Tiled Model Space
- Floating Model Space
- Paper Space
- Tiled Viewports ▶
- Floating Viewports ▶
- Preset UCS...
- Named UCS...
- Set UCS ▶

In
- Out
- Window
- All
- Previous
- Scale
- Dynamic
- Center
- Left
- Limits
- Extents
- Vmax

Point
- Left
- Right
- Up
- Down
- Up/Left
- Up/Right
- Down/Left
- Down/Right

Plan View ▶
- Top
- Bottom
- Left
- Right
- Front
- Back
- SW Isometric
- SE Isometric
- NE Isometric
- NW Isometric

Current
- World
- Named

Rotate...
- Tripod
- Vector

Layout...
- 1 Viewport
- 2 Viewports
- 3 Viewports
- 4 Viewports
- Restore
- Delete
- Join
- Save

1 Viewport
- 2 Viewports
- 3 Viewports
- 4 Viewports
- Restore
- Viewports On
- Viewports Off
- Hideplot
- MV Setup

World
- Origin
- Z Axis Vector
- 3 Point
- Object
- View
- X Axis Rotate
- Y Axis Rotate
- Z Axis Rotate
- Previous
- Restore
- Save
- Delete
- List

F

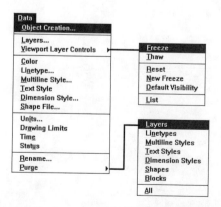

Data
- **Object Creation...**
- Layers...
- Viewport Layer Controls ▶
- Color
- Linetype...
- Multiline Style...
- Text Style
- Dimension Style...
- Shape File...
- Units...
- Drawing Limits
- Time
- Status
- Rename...
- Purge ▶

Freeze
- Thaw
- Reset
- New Freeze
- Default Visibility
- List

Layers
- Linetypes
- Multiline Styles
- Text Styles
- Dimension Styles
- Shapes
- Blocks
- All

Index

Symbols

A

WANT MORE INFORMATION?

CHECK OUT THESE RELATED TOPICS OR SEE YOUR LOCAL BOOKSTORE

CAD and 3D Studio

As the number one CAD publisher in the world, and as a Registered Publisher of Autodesk, New Riders Publishing provides unequaled content on this complex topic. Industry-leading products include AutoCAD and 3D Studio.

Networking

As the leading Novell NetWare publisher, New Riders Publishing delivers cutting-edge products for network professionals. We publish books for all levels of users, from those wanting to gain NetWare Certification, to those administering or installing a network. Leading books in this category include *Inside NetWare 3.12*, *CNE Training Guide: Managing NetWare Systems*, *Inside TCP/IP*, and *NetWare: The Professional Reference*.

Graphics

New Riders provides readers with the most comprehensive product tutorials and references available for the graphics market. Best-sellers include *Inside CorelDRAW! 5*, *Inside Photoshop 3*, and *Adobe Photoshop NOW!*

Internet and Communications

As one of the fastest growing publishers in the communications market, New Riders provides unparalleled information and detail on this ever-changing topic area. We publish international best-sellers such as *New Riders' Official Internet Yellow Pages, 2nd Edition*, a directory of over 10,000 listings of Internet sites and resources from around the world, and *Riding the Internet Highway, Deluxe Edition*.

Operating Systems

Expanding off our expertise in technical markets, and driven by the needs of the computing and business professional, New Riders offers comprehensive references for experienced and advanced users of today's most popular operating systems, including *Understanding Windows 95*, *Inside Unix*, *Inside Windows 3.11 Platinum Edition*, *Inside OS/2 Warp Version 3*, and *Inside MS-DOS 6.22*.

Other Markets

Professionals looking to increase productivity and maxmize the potential of their software and hardware should spend time discovering our line of products for Word, Excel, and Lotus 1-2-3. These titles include *Inside Word 6 for Windows*, *Inside Excel 5 for Windows*, *Inside 1-2-3 Release 5*, and *Inside WordPerfect for Windows*.

Orders/Customer Service **1-800-653-6156**   Source Code **NRP95**

New Riders Publishing   201 West 103rd Street ◆ Indianapolis, Indiana 46290 USA

REGISTRATION CARD

AutoCAD Release 13 for Beginners

Name _____ Title _____

Company _____ Type of business _____

Address _____

City/State/ZIP _____

Have you used these types of books before? ☐ yes ☐ no

If yes, which ones? _____
_____

How many computer books do you purchase each year? ☐ 1–5 ☐ 6 or more

How did you learn about this book? _____

Where did you purchase this book? _____

Which applications do you currently use? _____
_____

Which computer magazines do you subscribe to? _____
_____

What trade shows do you attend? _____
_____

Comments: _____
_____
_____

Would you like to be placed on our preferred mailing list? ☐ yes ☐ no

☐ **I would like to see my name in print!** You may use my name and quote me in future New Riders products and promotions. My daytime phone number is: _____

New Riders Publishing 201 West 103rd Street ◆ Indianapolis, Indiana 46290 USA

Fax to 317-581-4670 Orders/Customer Service 1-800-653-6156 Source Code NRP95

Fold Here

- -

BUSINESS REPLY MAIL
FIRST-CLASS MAIL PERMIT NO. 9918 INDIANAPOLIS IN

POSTAGE WILL BE PAID BY THE ADDRESSEE

**NEW RIDERS PUBLISHING
201 W 103RD ST
INDIANAPOLIS IN 46290-9058**